Everyday Life in Medieval England

Christopher Dyer

Hambledon and London
London and New York

Hambledon and London

102 Gloucester Avenue
London, NW1 8HX

838 Broadway
New York
NY 10003-4812

First Published 1994
This Edition 2000

1 85285 201 1 (paper)
1 85285 112 0 (cased)

A description of this book is available from the
British Library and from the Library of Congress.

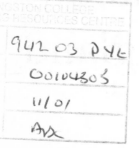
Printed on acid-free paper and bound in
Great Britain by Cambridge University Press

Everyday Life in
Medieval England

Contents

Acknowledgements

The following essays first appeared in the following publications and are reprinted by the kind permission of the publishers.

1   D. Hooke (ed.), *Medieval Villages*, Oxford University Committee for Archaeology (monograph no. 5, 1985), pp. 27–32.

2   M. Aston, D. Austin and C. Dyer (eds), *The Rural Settlements of Medieval England* (Oxford, Basil Blackwell, 1989), pp. 45–57.

3   *Economic History Review*, 2nd series, 35 (1982), pp. 19–34.

4   *Medieval Archaeology*, 34 (1990), pp. 97–121.

5   *Agricultural History Review*, 36 (1988), pp. 21–37.

6   M. Aston (ed.), *Medieval Fish, Fisheries and Fish Ponds in England*, Oxford, British Archaeological Reports, British Series, 182 (1989), pp. 27–38.

7   *Jardins et vergers en l'Europe occidentale (VIIe–XVIIIe siècles)*, Centre Culturel de l'Abbaye de Flaran, 9e journées internationales d'histoire (1989), pp. 115–32.

8   *Medieval Archaeology*, 30 (1986), pp. 18–45.

9   *Economic History Review*, 2nd series, 43 (1990), pp. 356–76.

10   T.H. Aston and R.H. Hilton (eds), *The English Rising of 1381* (Cambridge University Press, 1984), pp. 9–24.

11   *Proceedings of the Suffolk Institute of Archaeology and History*, 36 (1988), pp. 274–87.

12   H. Mayr-Harting and R.I. Moore (eds), *Studies in Medieval History Presented to R.H.C. Davis* (The Hambledon Press, London, 1985), pp. 91–106.

13   *Economic History Review*, 2nd series, 42 (1989), pp. 305–26.

14   *Journal of Historical Geography*, 18 (1992), pp. 141–57.

15   J.Kermode (ed.), *Enterprise and Individuals in Fifteenth-Century England* (Alan Sutton, Stroud, 1991), pp. 1–24.

Illustrations

Tables

Preface

This book aims to recapture the way of life of ordinary people in the middle ages. The subjects covered include settlement, food, houses, gardens, wages and trade. The essays also consider the relations between aristocrats and peasants, artisans and wage-earners, and the ways in which society changed. The essays fall into four groups: settlement (chapters 1-4); standards of living (chapters 5-8); social relations (chapters 9-11); and the market (chapters 12-15). They are written by a historian relying mainly on documents, but they also use archaeological evidence, and employ some of the methods of archaeology and geography. They are designed to reveal new aspects of the past by asking questions which have not been asked before, and by exploring old problems using different sources and approaches. A number of the essays are focussed on the west midland region (mainly the historic counties of Gloucestershire, Warwickshire and Worcestershire), but three are concerned mainly with the south-east and East Anglia. All of them view the regional examples within a national or continental frame.

Christopher Dyer

Birmingham
22 July 2000

Introduction

This book is about the lives of ordinary medieval people. It deals with their material conditions, their social relationships, and their ideas. But its theme is also change and development over the medieval period – some of the essays go back to the early Middle Ages, or even into earlier periods, but the main focus of attention is on the thirteenth, fourteenth and fifteenth centuries.

The history of 'everyday life' seemed to be the most appropriate way to describe the subject matter of these essays, although the phrase, much used among German social historians, is not so well known in the English-speaking world. The history of 'everyday life' suggests a descriptive type of writing, in which all aspects of past existence – villages and towns, houses, work, clothes, food, customs – are recorded in detail. It is important to reconstruct as much as we can of material culture; if we aspire to 'total history', then standards of living and ways of life deserve our close attention. But while we begin with material culture, we find that it provides a point of entry into the whole field of social and economic history.

If we examine houses, for example, we may begin with an assessment of their quality, and conclude that we have been misled by the often repeated assertion that medieval peasants lived in flimsy hovels. The new insight that peasant houses were substantially built, using professional labour, leads us to reassess the resources available to peasants, their contacts with the market, their ability to obtain credit, and the social distance between them and their superiors. Pursuing the theme of the relationship between material goods and the social hierarchy, investigation of foodstuffs such as garden produce or fish shows that they helped to define status, in which some items of food acted as symbols of wealth while others were associated with poverty and penance. Insights into the changes in diet of the lower classes can be gained from the study of food allowances given to harvest workers. A remarkable transformation in food consumption from the mid-thirteenth to the mid-fifteenth century has implications for agricultural production, which had to adapt from supplying a predominantly cereal diet to one with a high meat content. Research into such subjects as housing and diet shows the value of viewing the economy from the position of the consumer, rather than giving excessive prominence to producers. And finally investigation of rural settlement patterns involves us in identifying those areas where large villages predominated, and others with hamlets and scattered farmsteads. But to explain the differences we need to know about rural landscapes, agricultural techniques, power of lords, the extent of community organisation, and environmental influences such as soils and climate. If we can detect the reasons for the different settlement patterns, we would be much nearer to understanding the vital formative period – between the ninth and the twelfth century – when nucleated villages were created.

One of the themes that run through these essays is the re-examination of social relationships, and particularly the predominance of aristocratic power. There were many ways in which the medieval aristocracy (which includes the higher secular nobility, the gentry, and the higher clergy) imposed themselves on the rest of society. They ruled over estates and manors which provided a flow of money and labour from tenants. They wielded extensive powers of jurisdiction by holding courts, and they exercised much control over unfree slaves and serfs. At their behest the landscape was reorganised for more efficient production in compact demesnes, granges, mills and reclaimed wastes, or mainly for pleasure in the case of parks, pools and gardens. They channeled trade through the boroughs and markets that they founded and protected. And by their own spending power, they were able to mould the trading system, encouraging the concentration of rich merchants in large towns to supply their specialist needs. Just as the political theorists can talk of a descending principle by which authority was derived from above, so it is often presumed that society also was organised on a descending principle.

While recognising that the aristocracy were able to arrange the world to suit themselves in many ways, their ability to command was hedged about by many limitations. They were inhibited by the superior authority of the state, with which they were often allied, but sometimes found themselves in rivalry. Their internal divisions, leading them into competition, put another restriction on their power. But we must also take into account an _ascending_ tendency in medieval society – the lower orders, peasants, artisans, even wage earners, had their own interests, which often diverged from those of the ruling élite, and while they laboured under many disadvantages, they were able to check and restrain, sometimes even reverse the actions of the aristocracy. The lower classes derived some strength from their own resources. The system worked by allowing them possession of land, workshops and equipment, from which the lords drew some profit through rents. Lords cultivated their demesnes in the thirteenth and fourteenth centuries, but even then the bulk of land was managed by peasants, and lords gained most of their income from rents. They found that rather than reducing their tenants to mindless subordination, it was best to leave them to organise themselves. The problem for the lords was that if left to take their own initiatives, peasants and artisans could act against them – like peasants who used their accumulated savings to pay a lawyer to bring an action against their lord. More important than cash or possessions was the confidence and ability to conceive of a better life that flowed from even modest resources. That sense of self reliance was encouraged by the official positions in the government of the manor, village and town filled by ordinary people. Again, lords preferred to leave the time-consuming and troublesome tasks of running courts and collecting rents to their tenants, but there was a price to pay in terms of the authority and knowledge of law and government that these petty officials acquired. The lower orders of society remained weak and poor as individuals, but found strength by forming lateral associations with neighbours and workmates, and we find that the village community, so often utilised by the lords and state to assist in government, could also serve as the organisation for peasant opposition. Wage earners also found that by forming work gangs or by making illicit alliances they could increase their bargaining power.

Peasants demonstrated their confidence and bargaining strengths by resisting the demands of their lords for rents and services. The rising of 1381, it might be objected, hardly counts as 'everyday', but the point of the arguments presented below is that, while it was indeed a unique event, it was rooted in the mundane life of rural society. The people who participated were a cross section of the villagers of south-east England; the rebellion was based on the normal units of self government, the village communities; and the demands and actions of the rebels were related to agitations and frictions that had been continuing for decades before the rising itself.

Most people resisted authority, not by violent disturbances but by quietly ignoring the regulations and conducting their lives in the way that suited them. Serfs moved about a great deal, in contradiction of the supposed restrictions on the unfree, and in the case of wage earners who were required to obey the new laws on labour introduced after the Black Death of 1349, they migrated, left one job for another, changed their occupations, and broke employment contracts. People learned how to manipulate the system, by exploiting their influence as officials, concealing acts that infringed the rules, or bending customs and laws in their own favour.

It would be wrong, however, to see the everyday lives of ordinary people simply in terms of their contacts with, and sometimes resistance to, the power of the lords and the state. We might be drawn into making this supposition because so much of the evidence, created by an official bureaucracy, was naturally concerned with enforcing the rules, and highlighted those who failed to comply. Ordinary people in town and country built up their own economic and social relationships, not in opposition to lords, but in response to their own needs. Buying and selling, for example, often bypassed the official institutions set up by lords and the state, leading to the growth of centres of trade which lacked market charters. Many towns did not acquire formal institutions, like borough privileges, which might be thought to have been essential in a legalistic world.

Landscapes and settlements were formed in response to the decisions of ordinary people, acting on their own initiative rather than in response to orders from above. Some of the suburbs that developed on the edge of towns as early as the eleventh century, and on a larger scale in the later Middle Ages, may sometimes have been encouraged by lords, but their essential origin lay in the flow of relatively poor immigrants anxious to gain an income from the employment and commercial opportunities provided by the town. Lords no doubt planned many towns and some rural settlements; but peasants certainly provided the immigrants who lived in these places, and peasant initiatives are likely to lie behind much land clearance, and the organisation and reorganisation of settlements. The debate about the origin of villages has to be conducted in terms of probabilities, because of the lack of detailed written evidence in the period of village formation between the ninth and the twelfth centuries. In dealing with the opposite process, the shrinkage and desertion of settlements after 1300, the abundant documentation shows conclusively that both lords and villagers had a part to play. Lords often sought to prevent migration and preserve the village; but sometimes removed the remaining inhabitants from a decayed place. The peasants, however, by taking over the holdings of their neighbours, or neglecting the discipline that governed the husbandry of the field system, but above all by their emigration and immigration, were often the decisive force behind the decline, continuation or desertion of a settlement.

The general lesson that can be learnt from these studies is that medieval people were not caught in a totally constricting web of custom and law. They habitually made choices and arrived at decisions, and while the lords and the state had their own way on many occasions, the rest of society had an important say in such crucial matters as where they lived, the methods of production that they employed, and where and how they bought and sold. There is some truth in the old adage that the people make their own history, though it must also be added that they did not do so in conditions of their own choosing. Modern historians have long argued about the means by which a capitalist economy emerged from the supposed straitjacket of medieval feudalism. Part of the answer lies in the relative freedom of feudal society, particularly in its later stages. Also in seeking the first capitalists we should not look for outsiders – acquisitive gentry, converted to a new profit-making attitude, or great merchants, or innovative geniuses such as the early explorers – but instead we should recognise the contribution of modestly wealthy countrymen responding to economic and social circumstances, like the Heritage family who are the focus of the last essay in this book.

The definition and explanation of historical change is another theme running through these essays. In the 1970s a rather deterministic view prevailed that the expansion of the early Middle Ages and the contraction of the fourteenth and fifteenth centuries resulted from changes in population and ecology. In the thirteenth century, it was said, excessive numbers of people overburdened the land and reduced its fertility, so precipitating a crisis of famine and disease in the period 1290-1370. The crisis was not resolved by the demographic catastrophe, because high mortality from a succession of epidemics kept the population low until after 1500. These essays reflect the movement of historical thinking away from this emphasis on soils and biology. The discussion of 'marginal land' attempts to show the difficulties in accepting an ecological explanation of economic expansion and contraction. Some of the essays lend some support to the view that social factors lay at the root of change, not just in the sense of the conflict between lords and peasants, but also the less easily researched though still important shifts within peasant communities and between rural and urban society. A group of essays on trade reflect the recent general tendency among economic historians to give greater attention to medieval urban growth and commercial development. Towns seem larger and more numerous than once thought. The proportion of the population that lived in towns is estimated in these essays on a number of occasions, probably with excessive caution. I now suspect that they are all too low, and that from a town-dwelling proportion of 10 per cent in the eleventh century the figure grew to 20 per cent by 1300 and remained at that level for the rest of the Middle Ages. Such figures lead us to assess highly the influence of towns on the rest of society. If we investigate the contacts between towns and different social groups, we find that the aristocracy bought relatively few goods and services from small towns, and it follows that this substantial proportion of the urban sector depended on lower class consumers. Everyone, in other words, had by the late thirteenth century been drawn into the commercial economy. This could have helped to stimulate the growth of population in the twelfth and thirteenth centuries.

These essays involve no innovation in historical methods. If we explore aspects of medieval life that are poorly documented – informal trading centres, gardens, the internal government of the village community – we depend on gathering as much information as possible, not just from documents but also from unwritten sources such as archaeology, architecture and topography. As in any historical enquiry in this period, much depends also on reading between the lines, and adopting a critical attitude toward the 'official' version. Historians of the later Middle Ages have benefited enormously from the systematic use of manorial court rolls in the last twenty years. These have made possible a prosopographical technique, shown here in the essays on the 1381 rising, by which a great deal is learned from the accumulation of a mass of biographical details. The techniques of landscape history have been used to reconstruct the development over the millennia of a single village (Pendock in Worcestershire), which involves the co-ordination of every available type of evidence about places as well as people.

Methods of analysis and the interpretation of evidence are merely the nuts and bolts of historical research. The motive force comes from the definition of problems and posing of questions, and in this historians are shameless borrowers from other disciplines – the social sciences, geography and archaeology in my case. I hope that readers of these essays find the questions interesting, and gain some satisfaction from the inevitably incomplete solutions that are offered.

1

Power and Conflict in the Medieval English Village

The purpose of this essay is to define the village as it is seen and understood by historians; this will lead to an emphasis on the village as a social entity. As the bulk of the written evidence comes from the later Middle Ages, the development of the village in that period will be the main theme, with a brief and more speculative venture into the early medieval history of the village at the end. The new archaeological and topographical evidence will not be covered here in any detail.

Those who study the village must clear from their minds a good deal of sentimental lumber that has surrounded the subject for more than a hundred years. The word 'village' inevitably conjures up pictorial images deriving from artistic and commercial representations of thatched cottages grouped round church towers, and from fictional accounts of village life from Thomas Hardy to the 'Archers'. The idealisation of village life in recent times is a reflection of a real historical experience, the urbanisation and industrialisation that led people to look back to a way of life that seemed, in retrospect, to represent simple, innocent and communal values.

More recently historians have been concerned, with varying degrees of enthusiasm, with stripping away the layers of myth and sentiment that have formed around the pre-industrial village. This is an entirely proper exercise, but the revisionism has now reached the point where the very existence of the village as a community is being denied. Nineteenth-century scepticism on the subject[1] has been revived by those who claim that the interests and actions of individuals were more important than those of any grouping of people.[2] Another line of attack has been to see the landlord rather than the village as the motive force behind the creation of field systems.[3] Such arguments are an understandable reaction to the woolliness of some previous thinking, but in reviewing our state of knowledge here the reality of the village community will be reasserted.

[1] F.W. Maitland, *Domesday Book and Beyond: Three Essays in the Early History of England* (Cambridge, 1897), pp. 184–8.
[2] A. Macfarlane, *The Origins of English Individualism: The Family, Property and Social Transition* (Oxford, 1979).
[3] B.M.S. Campbell, 'The regional uniqueness of English field systems? Some evidence from eastern Norfolk', *Agricultural History Review*, 29 (1981), pp. 16–28.

There is a good deal of room for debate on this issue because the village has left us virtually no records. The institutions that did produce documents, the manor, the central government, and the church, give us information about villages, but when we read these documents we see the village through the eyes of the landlords, royal officials, or the higher clergy, people whose lives and experience lay outside the village. There are those who find this a minor problem, and believe that the records of the manor reflect closely the life of the village.[4] This is wishful thinking, and if we are to overcome the problem of the bias of the records, and to glimpse the village from the point of view of the inhabitants, we need to work hard at our sources, and to treat them critically.

Firstly, the power of the landlord must be put into perspective. Lords lived a life of comparative leisure and comfort because they drew their income from the work of the rest of society. Their main interest in the peasants lay in gaining rents and services from them; this meant that they had some influence over many aspects of peasant life – farming, buying and selling, marriage and children. This influence stopped a long way short of a total dictatorial control of daily life. It is now even argued that the lives of serfs were not weighed down with particularly heavy burdens;[5] this is not very convincing in view of the obvious resentment of many serfs to their condition, which they clearly regarded as disadvantageous;[6] but most historians would agree that lords exercised an intermittent and imperfect control over their subordinates. The main inhibition on their power lay in the inefficiency of medieval government at all levels. The existence of many tiers of overlapping and competing jurisdictions effectively prevented any single authority exercising absolute control.

The aristocratic mentality also prevented landlords from taking too much interest in their subordinate villagers. The nobility, both lay and clerical, saw their proper occupations as war, prayer, hunting and courtly entertainment. Estate management was a tedious chore, delegated to inferiors wherever possible. The preferred method of running a landed estate was to lease out manors to farmers for fixed rents. The system broke down under the pressure of inflation round about 1200, and for two centuries the detailed administration of agricultural production became the concern of most landlords. Even then a cadre of professional managers took over the bulk of the necessary supervisory work. Many great lords, though they wandered from manor to manor, owned so much land that

---

[4] J.A. Raftis, 'Social structures in five East Midland villages', *Economic History Review*, 2nd series, 18 (1965), pp. 83–100.

[5] M.J. Hatcher, 'English serfdom and villeinage: towards a reassessment', *Past and Present*, 90 (1981), pp. 3–39.

[6] R.H. Hilton, *Bond Men Made Free: Medieval Peasant Movements and the English Rising of 1381* (London, 1973), pp. 85–90.

they never saw some of their properties. The lesser lords, the gentry, who often held land in only one or two places, were necessarily closer to the soil than the great magnates. Often the farmers of manors and the administrators of the large estates were recruited from their ranks. However, even these smaller landowners might be absentees from their own estates because they were pursuing military or administrative activities elsewhere. And the gentry who did live on their own lands were still limited in their powers over the peasantry because, in comparison with the magnates, they tended to have small numbers of servile and customary tenants.[7] So at all levels the aristocracy lacked either the inclination or the opportunity to exercise a complete domination over the lives of the peasantry.

The main limitation on the power of the landlords lay in the underdevelopment of society that prevented the employment of full-time officials and police. Without these resources, the obvious method of governing a village was to enlist the help of the peasants themselves. The election of such officials as reeves and rent-collectors became an obligation on tenants; service for individuals elected was often a compulsory condition of customary tenure. The manorial courts, the principal tribunals of seigneurial justice, were each presided over by the lord's steward, a member of the gentry, but the other court officials, the jurors, chief pledges, ale-tasters and affeerers, were all tenants. The advantage of involving the peasantry in such duties lay in the cheapness and ease of recruiting petty officials; the lord's rule was helped by their intimate local knowledge; above all, orders were more likely to meet with some compliance because they came from a locally respected neighbour. The lord was in effect enlisting the local hierarchy to carry out his administration. The disadvantage from the lord's point of view was that in gaining the co-operation of the local élite he had to share a little power and profit with them, and allow them to use their position to advance their own interests. Their involvement was bound to have a softening effect on the harshness of the lord's rule – indeed, that was part of their function, to make social exploitation more acceptable and therefore workable. It is out of this complicated relationship that we can learn from the archives of the manor about the life of the village. Through the leading men acting as jurors, reeves, haywards and the like, manor and village became closely associated.

Let us turn to the village in its own right. The word was scarcely used in the Middle Ages. In Latin documents we read of the *villa* or *villata*, which is commonly translated as 'vill', though in Middle English the equivalent word was 'town' – still preserving its original meaning of a small settlement in modern North American speech. The use of this word tells us nothing

[7]   E.A. Kosminsky, *Studies in the Agrarian History of England in the Thirteenth Century* (Oxford, 1956), pp. 274–8.

about the form of settlement, as both compact, nucleated villages and groupings of scattered hamlets and farms were called 'vills'. The terms 'hamlet', 'berewick', 'member' and so on were used to indicate the constituent elements of a single 'vill'. The term 'vill' then did not necessarily refer to a concrete grouping of homes and fields, but to a unit of government.

The vill often appears in the records of central government. It was the smallest unit of administration, and was expected in the later Middle Ages to provide representatives to attend various royal courts, to pay collective fines, to undertake public works, to be responsible for maintaining law and order (by setting a watch and electing a constable), to contribute foot soldiers to royal armies, and to pay taxes, even to the point after 1334 of assessing and collecting a quota of taxation.

Although the evidence for the obligations is abundant, we know very little about how they were carried out within the villages. Occasionally complaints about the non-payment of taxes by one villager to another came to the notice of the courts. Irregularities in the discharge of military obligations are also known, like the case at Halesowen, Worcestershire, in 1295, of Thomas Hill, who collected money from the men elected to serve by offering to go as a substitute and then absconded with the cash.[8]

The normal routine of deliberation, assessment and election of representatives was conducted verbally and is consequently not recorded. Yet the effectiveness of the internal governing machinery of the vill cannot be dismissed. No doubt the tasks were carried out slowly and reluctantly, but in the long run taxes were paid, armies levied and bridges repaired.

We are better informed about the self-governing role of the vill in organising its own fields. Here the business of the vill sometimes overlapped with the jurisdiction of the lord's court, so that court rolls surviving from the mid-thirteenth century onwards record by-laws and the punishment of offenders against these rules.[9] The earlier by-laws tend to be preoccupied with the problems of the harvest, such as the prevention of sheaf-stealing and the regulation of gleaning. After 1400 the majority of by-laws deal with the control of animals and grazing. Here lay the heart of the matter for the village community, the protection and maintenance of the means of livelihood of the inhabitants.

Now we are more fully informed about those rules and regulations that were made and enforced through the lord's court, and it is possible to see the lord rather than the villagers as the guiding force behind the by-laws and the management of the fields. However, a good deal of this local legislation was of little interest to the lord, such as the by-laws dealing with the arrangements for the hiring of a common herdsman. Also there are

---

[8]　G.C. Homans, *English Villagers of the Thirteenth Century* (Cambridge, Massachusetts, 1941), p. 330.

[9]　W.O. Ault, *Open-Field Farming in Medieval England* (London and New York, 1972).

occasional references to villagers acting on their own initiative, significantly from vills with many lords, like Wymeswold, Leicestershire, where a village meeting in *c*.1425 made decisions about the organisation of the fields.[10] Places like Wymeswold in which the villages did not coincide with a single manor were in a majority, so it is likely that such meetings were not uncommon. In the rare case of a manor containing more than one village, such as the huge manor at Wakefield, Yorkshire, the constituent vills held their own meetings, for which the lord's clerk used the term 'plebiscite'.[11]

Although the regulation of the fields was the most important function of the villages' internal governing machinery, the vill was responsible for much else: for example, for the assessment and collection of lump sums paid to the lord, such as tallages, common fines and recognitions. The villagers could act as collective tenants, as in agreeing to pay a rent for a pasture so as to preserve it as a common,[12] or by becoming group lessees of the lord's demesne. The ultimate development of this was at Kingsthorpe, Northamptonshire, where in the early thirteenth century the vill leased the whole manor, including the court, and it came nearer than any other English village to the privileged self-government of the continental rural communes.[13]

The villagers played a major part in the maintenance of law and order, and the reinforcement of prevailing norms and values. This was partly through co-operation with the view of frankpledge, the petty court of royal justice held by many lords, and the church courts. There were also more informal, ritualistic methods of dealing with those who failed to conform, such as the humiliation of 'rough music', which is well known from post-medieval incidents, and is also recorded in late medieval France.[14] The existence of rough music in the English medieval village is indicated by the semi-official institution of the 'hue and cry', raised against malefactors, which may well represent the origin of the custom.

The involvement of the vill with the church grew in the later Middle Ages, with the development of the responsibilities of the churchwardens as guardians of the cemetery, church building and furnishings.[15] They in turn

[10] A.E. Bland, P.A. Brown and R.H. Tawney, *English Economic History: Select Documents* (London, 1914), pp. 76–9.

[11] Ault, *Open-Field Farming*, p. 66.

[12] R.A. Wilson, ed., *Court Rolls of the Manor of Hales, iii* (Worcestershire Historical Society, 1933), pp. 158–9.

[13] W.O. Ault, 'Village assemblies in medieval England', in *Album Helen Maud Cam: Studies Presented to the International Commission for the History of Representative and Parliamentary Institutions* (Louvain and Paris, 1960).

[14] E.P. Thompson, 'Rough Music: le charivari anglais', *Annales: Economies, Sociétés, Civilisations*, 27 (1972), pp. 285–312; C. Gauvard and A. Gokalp, 'Les conduites de bruit et leur signification à la fin du Moyen Age: le charivari', *Annales: Economies, Sociétés, Civilisations*, 29 (1974), pp. 693–704.

[15] E. Mason, 'The role of the English parishioner, 1100–1500', *Journal of Ecclesiastical History*, 27 (1976), pp 17–29.

reinforced the social ties that bound the villagers by organising church ales, mass drinking sessions to raise funds. Normally money for the church was levied by the informal constraints of social pressure and neighbourly disapproval, but occasionally, as at Ingatestone, Essex, in 1359, the churchwardens used the lord's court to extract money for a new church tower from a reluctant parishioner.[16]

As is well known, the church extended its influence over the ceremonies of the village which were not necessarily Christian in origin or meaning. So the Rogation processions, or the celebration of Plough Monday, clearly had a secular, even magical purpose. We know very little about rural folklore practices in the Middle Ages, because they are often not documented until comparatively recent times, so we have to assume that the popular festivals and celebrations existed in the medieval village.[17] We are only rarely helped by specific references in our records; for example, at Polstead, Suffolk, in 1363 John atte Forth was fined 3s. 4d. because 'with others', 'he entered the close of the lord and ... played in the lord's hall a game called a summer game'.[18] This is likely to have been a traditional 'role reversal' ceremony in which social tensions were released through a temporary adoption of the lord's authority by a peasant, which in this case was greeted intolerantly by the lord, who, like many of his class in the generation after the Black Death, was not in the mood for jocular banter with his subordinates.

So the village had a real existence as an organisation, a unit of government controlling its own fields and inhabitants, partly in the interests of the 'community', partly in the interests of external authorities, such as the state, the landlord, or the church. In addition to these formal, obligatory functions, it is also possible to glimpse activities, like 'rough music', church ales, or 'summer games', that in some cases originated out of the government of the village, which show the villagers joining in collective groups in pursuit of commonly agreed objectives. The problem for the social historian is understanding the nature of this collective action. In the past, as has already been mentioned, there was a tendency to idealise the sense of community, and to assume neighbourly co-operation and the identification of individuals with the village which has no real justification in the evidence. In investigating the processes of decision making which every vill carried out we must distrust the preambles to the by-laws which state that they were drawn up with the consent of all. By analogy with other examples of medieval government, it is likely that some opinions counted for more than

[16] Essex Record Office, D/DP M19.
[17] C. Phythian-Adams, *Local History and Folklore* (London, Standing Conference for Local History, 1975).
[18] British Library, Add. Roll 27685.

others, and that the views of the 'wiser and better part', or the 'sad and discrete' men, prevailed at village meetings or court sessions. These were the men who filled the positions of reeves, jurors, churchwardens and constables. They were not a small clique, but there was an element of oligarchy in their selection. The same people often held more than one office, simultaneously or successively. Sons often followed their fathers as office-holders. There was a tendency for the wealthier peasants to occupy a high proportion of the offices. However, this should not be exaggerated; there were so many jobs that the oligarchy was necessarily broad. The better-off sections of village society were not divided from their poorer neighbours by an enormous gulf: in many villages in *c*. 1300 the best-endowed tenants had only a 15- or 20-acre holding. It therefore seems unlikely that the élite of the village ran things entirely for their own benefit, as they did not form an interest group separate from the other villagers.

This point can be examined by looking at the lines of conflicts in rural society. A classic form of dispute pitted the vill against the landlord; in the thirteenth and fourteenth centuries this involved the villagers bringing law suits in the royal courts to prove their freedom and their exemption from certain services and dues.[19] They needed to organise financial resources and to brief lawyers to do this, and this was often done under the leadership of the élite. In other words, the government of the vill, so often employed in the service of outside authority, was turned against the lord.

Conflict between lords and peasants was not always as clear-cut as in the cases mentioned above. While some villagers might express their opposition to the lord by acts of insubordination, like failing to do labour services or pay dues, there would be others willing to take the easy course of co-operating with authority and therefore helping to punish their rebellious neighbours. Some peasants identified so strongly with their lords that we find them, in the civil wars of the mid-fifteenth century for example, joining the aristocratic armies in large numbers.[20]

Was there a serious tension between rich and poor villagers? We know that such hostilities exist now. Williams' well-known study of Gosforth in Cumberland in the 1950s revealed some embittered relationships between the different strata in a village that would have appeared socially harmonious to a casual observer.[21] In the medieval village there was a potential division of interest between the employing tenants and the employed smallholder; almost every settlement contained holdings too small to provide for the needs of a family without supplementation of income by earnings in

[19] R.H. Hilton, 'Peasant movements in England before 1381', *Economic History Review*, 2nd series, 2 (1949), pp. 119–36.

[20] A.E Goodman, *The Wars of the Roses, Military Activity and English Society, 1452–97* (London, 1981), pp. 205–9.

[21] W.M. Williams, *The Sociology of an English Village: Gosforth* (London, 1956), pp. 86–120.

agriculture or industry, and a substantial minority of peasants needed to employ workers, at least in seasonal peaks of effort, or in the old age of the tenant. By-laws sometimes sought to maintain a supply of wage labour in the harvest by forbidding the able-bodied to glean, or to leave the village in search of higher wages, indicating that the employing interest was influencing the deliberations of the vill. Also some by-laws imply a division of interest between the 'respectable' villagers and a potentially criminal group of gamblers, gossips, thieves and prostitutes. Yet it would be difficult to sustain the argument that there was a conflict between two entrenched groups within each village. Many employees were 'life-cycle servants', that is, young people beginning working life as servants in a neighbour's household, saving up money and gaining experience in preparation for life as a peasant or peasant's wife in later years. When a wealthier peasant died, his eldest son would inherit the holding, but the daughters or younger brothers were likely to have been provided with a smallholding. So wage-earning servants and smallholders might be the relatives of the substantial tenants, and therefore unlikely to be bitterly opposed to one another. Although we no longer believe that every village was organised into an elaborate system of co-aration, whereby every household contributed oxen to make up plough teams, there is no doubt that a good deal of borrowing went on, not just of draught animals, but also of a wide range of goods and services in what has been called a 'blurring of the distinction' between the economies of the different peasant households.[22]

'Social interactions', acts of co-operation and conflict between villagers, have been investigated by various researchers using the mass of information in series of court rolls. These studies indicate considerable differences in behaviour between social groups, so that in his work on late thirteenth-century Redgrave, Suffolk, Smith has shown that the poorest people had a very limited range of contacts with other villagers, in contrast with the number and variety of interactions of their wealthier neighbours.[23] Pimsler, in a study of Elton, Huntingdonshire, has again highlighted the frequency with which wealthier villagers appear as pledges, that is guarantors and sureties for those coming before the lords' courts, and argues that the pledging system was not a cosy manifestation of neighbourly co-operation.[24] In analysing violent conflict among villagers at Broughton, Huntingdonshire, Britton found that while a number of fights were between rich

---

[22] R.H. Hilton, *The English Peasantry in the Later Middle Ages: The Ford Lectures for 1973, and Related Studies* (Oxford, 1975), pp. 48–53.

[23] R.M. Smith, 'Kin and neighbours in a thirteenth-century Suffolk community', *Journal of Family History*, 4 (1979), pp. 285–312.

[24] M. Pimsler, 'Solidarity in the medieval village? The evidence of personal pledging at Elton, Huntingdonshire', *Journal of British Studies*, 17 (1977), pp. 1–11.

and relatively poor individuals, there was a great deal of quarrelling also among the élite families.[25] Other researchers have also noted the lack of a clear social pattern in acts of violence.[26] All of these pieces of research suggest that indeed there were important social differences between villagers, but it is unlikely that these were sufficiently divisive to lead to a polarisation of village society between rich and poor, employers and employees, substantial tenants and cottagers.

Such an interpretation is a long way from saying that villages were socially harmonious. Any glance at a set of court rolls reveals constant disagreements and conflicts. There was clearly a casual and easy resort to violence, not just the minor fist fights and assaults with sticks, pitch-forks and knives recorded in manorial court rolls, but also murder, leading to a homicide rate well in excess of that of modern urban U.S A.[27] Can we make any sense of this quarrelsome behaviour? The best-documented fourteenth-century village in continental Europe, Montaillou in the Pyrenees, was split by a feud between a leading family, the Clergues, and others. Many villagers belonged to the clientage of the Clergues and their opponents, and similar links of patronage have been detected in English villages.[28]

Certainly we are sometimes conscious of alignments of villagers, who involved themselves in struggles, but were also capable of settling them. For example, at Chaddesley Corbett, Worcestershire, in 1398 two inhabitants of the hamlet of Hillpool were at odds with one another. Richard Trowbrug was accused of trespass against John Eylof, and also beat him. John Eylof also had a reputation for violence, having made a very serious attack on Richard Ermyte. Evidently Trowbrug had friends in Hillpool, because the vill, which was supposed to report his wrong-doing, concealed the cases. But after this act of favouritism had been exposed, the machinery of law enforcement was invoked. Trowbrug was fined, and both he and Eylof were bound by four pledges each to be of good behaviour. If either broke the peace, their pledges would be liable to pay the enormous sum of £10.[29] The point to notice in this case is that the two neighbours quarrelled over a real issue, trespass by animals in a crop of beans. Such incidents often originated in this way. The community of villagers became involved in two roles – initially as parties to the dispute, but then agreeing to settle the affair in the

[25] E. Britton, *The Community of the Vill, a Study in the History of the Family and Village Life in Fourteenth-century England* (Toronto, 1977), pp. 115–23.

[26] C.C. Dyer, *Lords and Peasants in a Changing Society: The Estates of the Bishopric of Worcester, 680–1540* (Cambridge, 1980), pp. 370–2.

[27] B.A. Hanawalt, *Crime and Conflict in English Communities 1300–1348* (London and Cambridge, Massachusetts, 1979), pp. 261–73.

[28] E. Le Roy Ladurie, *Montaillou, village occitan de 1294 à 1324* (Paris, 1975), pp. 88–107; Smith, 'Kin and neighbours'.

[29] Shakespeare Birthplace Trust Record Office, Stratford-upon-Avon, DR5/2743.

interests of good order. Later in the medieval period one is conscious of a growing number of conflicts between individuals and the community in which the differences of interest were so great that the problem could not be readily solved. A major source of such deep disputes was the use of grazing land in an increasingly pastoral age, when individuals sought to maximise their agricultural activities by over-stocking common pastures and enclosing land for their exclusive use. A striking example of such an individual was Thomas Baldwyn of Lower Shuckburgh, Warwickshire, who refused to accept the rulings of his vill from 1387 until his death in 1400.[30] Such problems multiplied in the fifteenth and early sixteenth centuries, with the growth of yeoman farmers the scale of whose agricultural operations made co-operation within an open-field system increasingly difficult to achieve.

To sum up, the late medieval village had a separate existence, influenced by, and overlapping with, the administration of the landlord, but retaining some independence from higher authorities. The internal life of the village was dominated by the élite, who occupied positions of authority and made important decisions. Village society was fractious, but the leaders sought to control violence, and the conflicts arose out of feuds and friction between neighbours rather than divisions rooted in differences in wealth and economic functions.

We are aware of important changes in the village in the relatively short period, less than three centuries, when we can observe it closely. The organisation of the community was still developing in the thirteenth century. It was then that the institution of churchwardens developed, adding new administrative and social dimensions to the life of the vill, and the full growth of the hierarchy of officials in the manorial courts did not come until the end of the thirteenth century.[31] Reports of the death of the village in the late fourteenth and fifteenth centuries have been shown to be much exaggerated.[32] Even in the early sixteenth century villages were alive and well, and the formal community organisation still had a long history ahead of it. Stresses and strains are visible in the fifteenth century, in the anti-social behaviour of the yeoman graziers, and in the most extreme cases the collapse of a minority of villages in the adverse circumstances of population decline.

If so many developments are discernible in two or three centuries, we are justified in looking for other changes before 1200. We now believe that the

[30] C.C. Dyer, *Warwickshire Farming, 1349–c.1520: Preparations for Agricultural Revolution* (Dugdale Society Occasional Paper, 27, 1981), p. 32.

[31] J.S. Beckerman, *Customary Law in English Manorial Courts in the Thirteenth and Fourteenth Centuries* (unpublished Ph.D. thesis, University of London, 1972).

[32] Z. Razi, 'Family, land and the village community in later medieval England', *Past and Present*, 93 (1981), pp. 3–36.

village as a distinctive nucleated settlement originated in an evolutionary process, probably in the seventh to eleventh centuries, in association with the growth of regular field systems. The development of the vill as a unit of government and social organisation is more problematical. As we have seen, its physical shape could take the form of dispersed settlements and hamlets, linked by invisible bonds of administration and common action. A plausible hypothesis, in view of the crucial importance of the regulation and defence of common pastures in the life of the village, would be to link the emergence of the vill as an organisation with a growing scarcity of agricultural resources. We would expect this to appear very early in the feldon districts, and there is indeed evidence from tenth-century charters of the existence of distinct village territories that were available for alienation from larger land units to create new small estates. In woodlands and uplands we might expect the evolution of well-defined vills to be more protracted, and we find in the wooded north of Worcestershire, for example, that the precise boundaries between one vill and the next were still being defined in the thirteenth century.

Finally a note of caution is needed on the question of village planning. It is very tempting to see in the symmetry of some villages, in the use of units of measurements in their layout and in the regularity of field systems, the hand of the landlord as the single authority capable of such systematic organisation. The bulk of planned villages probably date back to before the period of full documentation, to the eleventh or twelfth centuries, so there can be no certainty in the matter. However, we do know that field systems were rearranged by a combination of lords and village communities in the later Middle Ages; cases involving lords were more likely to be recorded, and in view of the obvious capabilities of the village in self-government, we can assume that the lords need not have been involved directly in such tasks. Because of the remoteness of many lords from the concerns of the village, and the underdevelopment of administrative machinery in the period before 1200, we should surely open our minds to the possibility, indeed the likelihood, that villagers rather than lords were responsible for the planning of villages and field systems.

2

'The Retreat from Marginal Land':
The Growth and Decline of Medieval Rural Settlements

Everyone who studies rural settlement needs to combine general ideas with detailed local studies. This essay examines a grand generalisation that has long shaped our approach to settlement studies, in the light of recent research into agriculture, villages, hamlets and fields.

The theory to be tested is that there was a 'retreat from marginal land' in the later Middle Ages, which is widely believed to explain the contraction in cultivated land and in rural settlements.[1] Behind this idea lies the reasonable proposition that fluctuations in the population provided the impetus for changes in settlements. Numbers of people in England grew rapidly between 1086 and 1300, perhaps from about 2 to 5 or 6 million. Before 1086 demographic history is very uncertain, though the total for Roman Britain at its height is believed to have been nearer to the estimate for 1300 than that for 1086, so there must have been a great decline at some time between c. 300 and 1000. Most historians, in view of the collapse of the commercial, industrial and urban economy of the Roman province, combined with the sixth-century plague epidemic, would be inclined to locate the population nadir, as on the continent, in about 600, and assume that recovery was going on from the seventh century. Many continental scholars believe that after a set-back in the ninth century a new wave of economic and demographic expansion was in full swing in the tenth and eleventh centuries, and it might be thought that England followed the same pattern, as it did after 1086. Everyone agrees that the population expansion ended at some time around 1300, but some advocate as early a date as c. 1280, others a date after 1349, and the majority opt for some intermediate period, such as the time of the Great Famine of 1315–17. Numbers declined to about $2\frac{1}{2}$ million in the late fourteenth century and did not begin to recover until 1520 or later.[2]

---

[1] M.M. Postan, *The Medieval Economy and Society* (London, 1972), pp. 15–26.

[2] J. Hatcher, *Plague, Population and the English Economy 1348–1530* (London, 1977), pp. 68–73; P. Salway, *Roman Britain* (Oxford, 1981), pp. 542–52; R. Hodges and D. Whitehouse, *Mohammed, Charlemagne and the Origins of Europe* (London, 1983), pp. 52–3; R. Fossier, *Enfance de l'Europe* (Paris, 1982).

Evidence for the Retreat

The history of settlement before 1086 is especially controversial. Two historians considering evidence from Kent have arrived at very different conclusions, one stressing that settlements had been extensive for centuries before Domesday, while another argues for a long-term expansion of cultivation over the downs and the weald in the pre-Conquest period.[3] However, there is a general consensus for the whole country that Domesday depicts a well-settled countryside with as large an area as 7 or 8 million acres under the plough.[4] It is assumed that people for whom the cultivation of cereals provided the main source of foodstuffs would have selected the most fertile land by a process of trial and error. Therefore the further expansion of population led to the more intense exploitation of existing arable land, and the extension of cultivation over inferior 'marginal' lands. The frontier of cultivation was extended up the slopes of hills, into drained marshes and fens, and over former woodland. By about 1300 many of these newly acquired lands were producing poor cereal yields, and they were abandoned as not being worth further effort. This had repercussions on a society bearing a heavy weight of numbers, and therefore starvation and misery followed. The contraction of society continued through the fourteenth and much of the fifteenth century, hastened by the Black Death of 1348-9 and a series of subsequent epidemics. In this view of the sequence of events, the 'retreat from marginal land' was more than a signal of troubles ahead – it was the trigger for a chain reaction that transformed the historical process.

Both archaeological and documentary evidence support this view of the retreat from the margins. It seems to fit into a long-term sequence of the ebb and flow of settlement going back to the neolithic, indicated by the changing use of such upland areas as the chalk downs of southern England, which were once thought to be the centres of prehistoric cultures, and can now be regarded as fringe lands, utilised with varying intensity depending on the level of population in the more hospitable valleys. In the early medieval period abundant evidence for settlement and exploited resources is provided by the distribution of pagan cemeteries and the estates mentioned in pre-850 charters. Both are often concentrated in districts with high quality agricultural land, such as north-east Kent or the valley of the Warwickshire Avon. The choice of the best land in prehistory and the early Middle Ages is suggested by the excavation of gravel sites which show that these easily-worked soils have attracted settlement over thousands of

[3]   P.H. Sawyer, *From Roman Britain to Norman England* (London, 1978), pp. 136–49; A. Everitt, *Continuity and Colonization. The Evolution of Kentish Settlement* (Leicester, 1986).
[4]   H.C. Darby, *Domesday England* (Cambridge, 1977), pp. 129–32.

years.[5] According to one interpretation of the Scandinavian invasion of the ninth century, any new settlements at that date had to be founded on inferior sites because the best land had already been taken into cultivation.[6] On Dartmoor arable farming arrived late and was abandoned after a short time. In the case of Holne Moor a large extension of cultivated fields in the thirteenth century reverted to grazing land in the fourteenth. Recent re-interpretations of the deserted hamlet of Houndtor based on pollen analysis suggest that the settlement was associated with an expansion of cereal cultivation in the early thirteenth century, and both settlement and arable farming retreated to lower slopes a century later.[7] Documents recording grain tithes in the Derbyshire Peak district, supported by archaeological evidence of relict medieval fields, show that in the early fourteenth century oats were being grown as high as 300m above sea level, and that production began to decline in the 1340s.[8] Hamlet settlements at about 250m have been located by a combination of documentary and archaeological research in Bilsdale in north Yorkshire. They seem to have grown up in the thirteenth century, and in the next century were either completely abandoned or reduced drastically in size.[9] The poor returns from recently settled lands are apparent from the documents. Much of the arable land in areas of colonisation in the northern part of the West Midlands is found to have been under oats, for example 62 per cent of the crops on the manor of Knowle (Warwickshire) in the 1290s, when land there was still being brought into cultivation.[10] Oats were the least valuable of all grains, their low price reflecting the fact that every eight bushels of grain yielded only two or three bushels of meal, whereas other grains lost only 20 per cent or less of their volume in the milling process. On the demesne lands of the bishopric of Winchester, which produced a wide variety of crops, the dozen manors with some of the worst records of deteriorating yields in the late thirteenth and early fourteenth century were those which had seen the largest extension of cultivation by the assarting of woodland and the ploughing up of hill pastures.[11]

[5] D. Powlesland, 'Excavations at Heslerton, North Yorkshire 1978–82', *Archaeological Journal*, 143 (1986), pp. 53–173.

[6] The arguments are summarised in C.D. Morris, 'Aspects of Scandinavian settlement in northern England', *Northern History*, 20 (1984), pp. 1–22, esp. p.13.

[7] A. Fleming and N. Ralph, 'Medieval settlement and land use on Holne Moor, Dartmoor: the landscape evidence', *Medieval Archaeology*, 26 (1982), pp. 101–37; D. Austin and M.J.C. Walker, 'A new landscape context for Houndtor, Devon', *Medieval Archaeology*, 29 (1985), pp. 147–52.

[8] I.S.W. Blanchard, 'Economic change in Derbyshire in the late Middle Ages' (unpublished Ph.D. thesis, University of London, 1967), pp. 50–1, 58, 64; W.E Wightman, 'Open-field agriculture in the Peak District', *Derbyshire Archaeological Journal*, 81 (1961), pp. 111–25.

[9] J. McDonnell, 'Medieval assarting hamlets in Bilsdale, north-east Yorkshire', *Northern History*, 22 (1986), pp. 269–79.

[10] Westminster Abbey Muniments, 27694.

[11] J.Z. Titow, *Winchester Yields* (Cambridge, 1972), pp. 32–3.

Contemporaries were only too aware of the problems, and at the end of the thirteenth century and especially in the first half of the fourteenth the documents contain a growing number of references to the stoney, sandy or infertile nature of land. Juries who supplied the information for the extents of Inquisitions Post Mortem, or assessors collecting taxes like the levy of the ninth lamb, fleece and sheaf of 1341, repeated these complaints. Estate managers commented on the sterile nature of demesne lands preparatory to the drastic step of leasing them out to tenants, leaving the peasants with the headache of obtaining a return from inferior soils.[12] When we observe the agrarian scene in about 1300 we can appreciate the logic of the pattern of settlement and cultivation. The remaining areas of dense woodland were often in places with steep slopes and thin soils, such as the Forest of Dean in Gloucestershire or parts of the Sussex weald. In some cases colonisation had been pushed to its limits, like the drainage schemes in eastern England or the Sussex levels, where already in the early fourteenth century the battle against flooding was being lost. Further strides in reclamation would not come until new techniques were introduced after 1500.[13]

Doubts and Objections to the 'Retreat' Idea

However, not all of our evidence supports the idea of a 'retreat from marginal land'. Firstly, there is the difficulty of defining which areas were 'marginal' and which were not. Most land in lowland England is capable of producing some crops, and judgements as to its quality depend on complex questions of chemistry, texture, environment, technology and economics. The views of modern soil scientists and farmers may not help us to decide the quality of a soil under medieval conditions. For example, lias clays in the West Midlands have been described in a soil survey as 'marginal' for spring barley, yet we know that on this land barley yielded as well in the Middle Ages as on other soils.[14] The modern view is partly based on the difficulties of using heavy tractors on sticky clay, and in this respect at least the medieval ox-plough enjoyed an advantage. The character of a soil may have changed over the centuries. The modern moorlands, for example, have apparently deteriorated to their present unproductive state through mismanagement. Chalk downland may similarly have once been much more suited to cultivation.[15] Changes in climate, even a small shift in

[12] A.R.H. Baker, 'Evidence in the *Nonarum Inquisitiones* of contracting arable lands in England during the early fourteenth century', *Economic History Review*, 2nd ser., 19 (1966), pp. 518–32; C. Dyer, *Lords and Peasants in a Changing Society* (Cambridge, 1980), pp. 79–82.

[13] For example, P. Brandon, *The Sussex Landscape* (London, 1974), pp. 111–18.

[14] J. M. Ragg, *Soils and their Use in Midland and Western England* (Soil Survey of England and Wales, Bulletin no. 12, Harpenden, 1984), pp. 372–4.

[15] M. Aston, *Interpreting the Landscape* (London, 1985), pp. 24–5.

average temperatures, as has been shown in a study of the Lammermuir Hills in southern Scotland, could have made extensive corn growing risky and unprofitable, and led to the conversion of the land into rough pasture.[16] We must also remember that a medieval peasant producing grain mainly for his own use would have had a perception of land values that differed from that of a medieval demesne manager, or a modern capitalist farmer, both of whom would have been more aware of labour costs and market returns. 'Marginal' is a relative, not an absolute, term, and it is best applied comparatively.

Secondly, there seems to be no close correlation between the chronology of settlement and soil types. We find that settlements practising arable farming were being established at an early date in places where by any imaginable standard, either medieval or modern, extreme conditions made cultivation difficult and precarious. The houses excavated at Simy Folds in upper Teesdale at a height of 351m have been dated to the eighth century, and a similar site at Gauber High Fell near Ribblehead is thought to belong to the ninth.[17] In East Anglia the fifth-century settlement of West Stow was established on the sandy soils of the Breckland, only to be abandoned after 200 years.[18] It surely cannot be thought that at the early dates of these settlements, no better land was available than these bleak uplands or sandy heaths?

In the woodland areas of the Midlands one notes puzzling differences in the settlement history of land of apparently similar quality. For example, in north Worcestershire, land at Cofton Hackett appears in a charter of 780 as a 5-hide estate, presumably supporting a peasant population. It contained a good deal of agriculture and settlement at the time of the writing of a charter boundary clause in 849, yet much comparable arable land in adjoining Alvechurch was not taken into cultivation until the thirteenth century.[19] In general, close examination of settlements in Feckenham Forest in Worcestershire or Wychwood in Oxfordshire shows that the soils that were subject to assarting from wood or pasture in the thirteenth century were not much different from those that had been used as arable over a much longer period.[20] Some of the woodlands that were being

[16] M.L. Parry, *Climatic Change, Agriculture and Settlement* (Folkestone, 1978), pp. 73–94.

[17] D. Coggins, K.J. Fairless and C.E. Batey, 'Simy Folds: an early medieval settlement site in upper Teesdale', *Medieval Archaeology*, 27 (1983), pp. 1–26; A. King, 'Gauber high pasture, Ribblehead – an interim report', in *Viking Age York and the North*, ed. R.A. Hall (CBA Research Report no. 27, 1978), pp. 21–5.

[18] S.E. West, 'The Anglo-Saxon village of West Stow: an interim report of the excavation, 1965–8', *Medieval Archaeology*, 13 (1969), pp. 1–20, esp. p. 3.

[19] Dyer, *Lords and Peasants*, pp. 22–3, 90–5.

[20] The Feckenham observation is based on the author's fieldwork. For Wychwood, B. Schumer, *The Evolution of Wychwood to 1400: Pioneers, Frontiers and Forests* (Leicester University Dept of English Local History, Occasional Papers, 3rd ser., 6, 1984).

cleared in the thirteenth century were not fragments of primeval forest, but former Romano-British cornfields, which had undergone a process of woodland regeneration in the early Middle Ages.[21]

It has become customary to divide lowland England into champion and woodland landscapes, that is between the areas of extensive arable cultivation in open fields attached to nucleated villages, and those with a mixture of arable, pasture and wood, organised in enclosed fields and characterised by dispersed settlements. The usual explanation of the difference was that the champion areas were 'old-settled' and the woodlands the product of colonisation, largely in the twelfth and thirteenth centuries. Revisionism has now gone so far that one writer has suggested as alternative terms 'planned' and 'ancient' countrysides.[22] He means that the champion landscape is planned in the sense that it has gone through two radical reorganisations in the last 1200 years, firstly with the laying out of the furlongs and strips of the open fields in the early Middle Ages, the second with the enclosure movement of the eighteenth century. By contrast the hedge lines and sunken tracks of the woodlands often preserve remnants of pre-Conquest, Roman or late prehistoric boundaries and roads. This idea presents us forcefully with the stark truth that many woodlands have a much older settlement history than was once believed, but it takes the paradox too far because some at least of the woodland landscapes can be shown to have been the result of colonising new land after 1100.

The third criticism of the 'retreat from marginal land' concerns the retreat itself. If the theory was to hold good, the deserted settlements should be found on the poor quality soils of late colonisation, on the principle that the last settlement to be founded should be the first to be abandoned. In some parts of Europe, especially in eastern Germany, this seems often to have been the case. But the bulk of English deserted villages were in the champion districts. This means that the actual nucleated settlement may have been created as late as the eleventh or twelfth century, and no earlier than the ninth, but the land from which the inhabitants obtained their living had been under cultivation long before, and often its use extended back into prehistory. In the first phase of desertion before the Black Death, in the classic period of 'retreat', villages in areas such as north-east Gloucestershire and north Oxfordshire were declining and even disappearing. For example, Tusmore, reported as deserted after the first epidemic, was in severe difficulties in 1341, and the Black Death evidently gave it a final blow.[23] These places were far from colonising settlements; the

---

[21] P.T.H. Unwin, 'The changing identity of the frontier in medieval Nottinghamshire and Derbyshire', in *Villages, Fields and Frontiers*, ed. B.K. Roberts and R.E. Glasscock (BAR International ser., 185, 1983), pp. 339–51.

[22] O. Rackham, *The History of the Countryside* (London, 1986).

[23] See below, Chapter 3, p. 31.

majority were sited on lands which had supported populations in the Iron Age and in the Roman period.

Settlements were abandoned in the fourteenth and fifteenth centuries in woodlands and uplands also, some of them relatively new, some of them occupying old-cultivated land. The desertion of these hamlets and farmsteads has not attracted the same attention as desertions of whole villages. With a village went a complete field system, which was changed radically with conversion to pasture. The loss of a third or a half of the hamlets and farms in an area of dispersed settlement produced a patchwork effect on the landscape, which did not have the same impact either on contemporary observers or on modern historians. Without more research we cannot be sure of the scale of desertion of small settlements, but it is likely on the basis of present samples that the numbers of households affected by late medieval desertion were rather greater in the champion villages than in the woodland hamlets. Even if the numbers were approximately equal, only a proportion of the dispersed settlements can be regarded as the products of late colonisation. At Hanbury (Worcestershire), for example, at least a dozen deserted farms lay near to land that had been cultivated before the Conquest and in Roman times, quite probably without any interruptions. Many settlements of twelfth- and thirteenth-century colonisation survived until modern times, both in the woodlands of the Midlands and the hills of west Yorkshire.[24] In other words, the retreat of settlement affected people living on old-cultivated lands rather more than those on recent assarts. Occasionally new settlements were founded in the fifteenth century in the woodland districts, mainly cottages on waste land, a process which emphasises again that the champion landscapes bore the brunt of desertions.[25]

Alternative Approaches

We have to take a number of varied influences into account in explaining the formation and decay of settlements. These were matters of choice by the people of the time, who were acting in response to a number of motives, not all of them based on economic rationality. Cistercian monks, for example, deliberately sought out 'deserts' in pursuit of an ascetic ideal, though they sometimes changed their initial site if it proved inhospitable.[26] The

[24] M.L. Faull and S.A. Moorhouse, *West Yorkshire: An Archaeological Survey to A.D. 1500* (Wakefield, 1981), pp. 585–613.
[25] New houses were being built on the waste in *c.* 1470 at Ombersley, Worcestershire, and Sedgley, Staffordshire: Hereford and Worcester CRO, ref. 705:56, B.A. 3910/24; Staffordshire RO, D 593/0/3/3.
[26] R.A. Donkin, *The Cistercians: Studies in the Geography of Medieval England and Wales* (Pontifical Institute of Mediaeval Studies, Studies and Texts, 38, Toronto, 1978), pp. 31–6.

enforcement of forest law is another example of a non-economic influence on settlement. Royal officials collected fines in the forest from those who poached the deer or assarted the woods; their activities annoyed the inhabitants, but did not prevent the clearance of new land. However, the preservation of woods near royal hunting lodges, like those that survived into the seventeenth century around Feckenham in Worcestershire, suggests that royal interest in hunting had some inhibiting effect on assarting. The aristocratic parks that proliferated in the thirteenth and fourteenth centuries had irrational functions as pleasure grounds and status symbols. The modest profits from the venison and the use of the park for grazing cattle did not justify the loss of money deriving from the land's use as arable. Parks often contained land of cultivable quality, as is shown both by the inclusion within them of former arable, and the occasional record of lords ploughing up part of the land after the park had been enclosed.[27] The park could become a focus for settlement itself, as at Walsall (Staffordshire) in the early thirteenth century when the lord moved his manor house from the developing town to a site in the park which had previously been under cultivation.[28] In short, whether for reasons of ideology, status or pleasure, lords established settlements on poor land, or prevented the cultivation of potential arable.

Peasants could exercise some choices also, though within limits imposed on them by their lords, their village communities and their own lack of resources. There was no exact correlation between the legal status of peasants and the settlement pattern, but assarts and new lands of the twelfth and thirteenth centuries were often held by free tenure, and the highest proportion of customary or servile tenants is found in the nucleated villages of the champion. The free tenants were more tenacious in keeping their holdings in adverse circumstances, and they had good economic reasons to do so. A smallholding in customary tenure could pay rents and dues totalling 10d. to 12d. per acre, while a rent for an assart was often 2d. to 4d. per acre. The customary tenant was liable to extra dues, such as entry fines, while the freeholder owed only a modest relief. These burdens made the free land a more attractive asset, and its tenant may have been encouraged to continue cultivation even with poor yields. The market could exercise a considerable influence on settlement, in combination with other circumstances. Take, for example the Essex manor of Havering atte Bower, occupying a large area of poor land, London clay in the north and glacial gravels in the south, the one type difficult to work, the other easy, but neither especially fertile. Yields of wheat and oats from the demesne of

---

[27] For example, at Beoley, Worcestershire, and Berkeley, Gloucestershire: BL, Egerton Rolls 8661; J. Smyth, *The Lives of the Berkeleys* (Gloucester, 1883), pp. 14–16.

[28] S. and S. Wrathmell, 'Excavations at the moat site, Walsall, Staffordshire', *Transactions of the South Staffordshire Archaeological and Historical Society*, 16 (1974–5), pp. 19–53; 18 (1976–7), pp. 30–45.

Hornchurch (an enclave within Havering) were among the lowest recorded in medieval England. Yet the tenants of Havering enjoyed the privilege of free tenure on a royal demesne manor, which gave them the benefits both of low rents and free disposal of their land. Havering lay near to the large London market, to which the tenants had easy access by road. The manor was extensively assarted in the thirteenth century, providing a classic example of land hunger pushing the frontier of colonisation onto unrewarding soils. However, when the great contraction came, the settlements of Havering showed obstinate longevity. The numbers of tenants declined less than on many manors on more fertile soils, and they exhibited every sign of prosperity through the recession of the fourteenth and fifteenth centuries.[29] Closer to London a ring of villages occupying much land that was by no means of the highest quality, such as Stepney, Fulham and Lambeth, were stimulated by the closeness of the urban market to adopt horticulture as well as more conventional farming. Their records show few signs of the ruinous buildings and vacant holdings that appear so prominently in those of Midland villages around 1400.[30]

Social circumstances could therefore improve the value of poor land, but human factors could also ruin potentially good land. The Gloucestershire Cotswold villages that were in evident decline by 1341 have already been mentioned. Their land had supported a rich Romano-British civilisation, and arable cultivation was extensive by the tenth and eleventh centuries. Modern Cotswold farmers now grow abundant crops of cereals and vegetables. In the early fourteenth century hundreds of acres of arable lay uncultivated, and tenants were giving up their holdings and leaving their villages, complaining of poverty. The fertility of the soil in a two-course rotation depended on the combination of sheep and corn, the sheep being folded on the arable after feeding on the hill pastures, and treading their dung into the stoney soils. Any disturbance of the system could have had a disastrous effect on cereal yields, as can be shown from accounts of the demesne of Temple Guiting in 1327, where the temporary absence of the sheep reduced the grain yields to the point that the lord of the manor was making a loss on arable cultivation. We do not know the sequence of events that gave the peasants similar agricultural problems. Was it the slow drain on their resources of rent and tax demands? Or the shock of the sheep scab epidemics in the late thirteenth century? Or perhaps a combination of such setbacks reduced the size of the village flocks and 'marginalised' the land that had supported peasant populations for centuries?[31]

[29] M.K. McIntosh, *Autonomy and Community: The Royal Manor of Havering, 1200–1500* (Cambridge, 1986), esp. pp. 137–52.

[30] PRO, SC 2/188/65; 191/62; 205/12; 205/15.

[31] C. Dyer, 'The rise and fall of a medieval village: Little Aston (in Aston Blank), Gloucestershire', *Transactions of the Bristol and Gloucestershire Archaeological Society*, 105 (1987), pp. 165–81.

The English landscape is too complicated to allow us to think of a moving frontier of settlement, like that of North America in the last century. This analogy is bound to give us a conception of assarting as taking place on the edge of a vast expanse of trees, through which a progressive wave of human conquerors reduced woodland to arable by vigorous use of axe and fire. It is often stated that this process was organised and directed by landlords, who either issued charters to the colonists and collected the profits in rents from the new land, or added land to their demesnes. Our documents tell a complex story. Assarting as a concept and an institution was an innovation of the twelfth century. Before that date new lands were incorporated into the field system and tenures of the village without being given a special status.[32] Twelfth- and thirteenth-century assarting was a piecemeal process, often initiated by local peasants, not by colonists from a distance, and lords tended to play a relatively passive role. The tenants of larger holdings were often prominent in the movement, intending either to add to their existing land, or to provide a holding for their younger son or daughter, who could not, under the rules of primogeniture, inherit any part of the main holding.[33] Assarting seems to have been a gradual process, as individual tenants took over and eventually brought under the plough parcels of former common land. It was sometimes a movement that created whole new settlements, but more often it involved shifts within a partially developed and settled agrarian landscape.

Long-term expansion and decline of settlements took place within distinctive agrarian systems of each region and district, which would be affected by changes in demography and the economy in different ways. It was once thought that each regional type reflected the ethnic composition of the population, but this is easily disproved because the agrarian regions do not coincide with the areas of supposed British, German or Scandinavian settlement. In its dying moments one protagonist of this approach had to invent a hitherto unknown ethnic group, the Friso-Jutes, to explain the peculiarities of eastern England.[34] Nor can we accept that regional differences represent different phases in an evolutionary development, with East Anglia having advanced through a champion system of nucleated villages and open fields, while in the west woodlands were changing into champion villages. Such evolutionary movements can rarely be traced in our evidence. For example, it was once believed that in the thirteenth century, influenced by population pressure, many villages working a two-field system changed over to three fields in order to increase the area under corn. In fact this

[32] P.D.A. Harvey (ed.), *The Peasant Land Market in Medieval England* (Oxford, 1984), pp. 13–14.

[33] M. Stinson, 'Assarting and poverty in early fourteenth-century western Yorkshire', *Landscape History*, 5 (1983), pp. 53–67.

[34] G.C Homans, 'The rural sociology of medieval England', *Past and Present*, 4 (1953), pp. 32–43.

happened infrequently. The peasants were evidently reluctant to risk more intensive cultivation which would have endangered the delicate balance between arable and pasture, and might have led to a reduction in manuring and to a decline in grain yields.[35]

A Regional Example

The effects of the periods of growth and decline on agrarian systems can best be appreciated by taking two concrete examples, both from the West Midlands. One is the champion (Feldon) district of south Warwickshire and south-east Worcestershire, the other the wood/pasture district to the south of the modern city of Birmingham, in the Middle Ages in the Arden of Warwickshire and Feckenham Forest in Worcestershire.

The Feldon settlements at their peak of development in the thirteenth century were predominantly nucleated villages practising a two-course rotation in open fields.[36] They had limited resources of pasture and wood, and relied on long-distance contacts through estate links or the market for firewood and timber. The soils were mainly lias clay, with some alluvial gravels in the Avon valley. They maintained fertility by practising sheep and corn husbandry, and achieved the normal medieval grain yields of about three to four times the seed sown. A high proportion of the peasants held by customary tenure, for which their primary obligation was the payment of an annual cash 'rent of assize' which normally varied from 7s. to 21s. per yardland. Their ability to pay in cash indicates that they sold a good deal of their produce. The majority of holdings were assessed in terms of the standard yardland unit, mostly in halves and quarters; the yardland varied in size between 20 and 40 acres of arable land.

The area supported a large pre-medieval population, and was well settled in the pre-Conquest period. As the villages were already large by the time of Domesday, the expanding population of the subsequent two centuries put the inhabitants under considerable pressure. To some extent they intensified the use of land by subdividing holdings (if the lord

[35] H.S.A. Fox, 'The alleged transformation from two-field to three-field systems in medieval England', *Economic History Review*, 2nd ser., 39 (1986), pp. 526–48.

[36] This last section is informed by such published works as R.H. Hilton, *A Medieval Society*, 2nd edn (Cambridge, 1983); idem, *The English Peasantry in the Later Middle Ages* (Oxford, 1975); J.B. Harley, 'Population trends and agricultural developments from the Warwickshire Hundred Rolls of 1279', *Economic History Review*, 2nd ser., 11 (1958–9), pp. 8–18; B.K. Roberts, 'A study of medieval colonisation in the Forest of Arden, Warwickshire', *Agricultural History Review*, 16 (1968), pp. 101–13; A.R.H. Baker and R.A. Butlin (eds), *Studies of Field Systems in the British Isles* (Cambridge, 1973), pp. 221–30, 345–63; C. Dyer, *Warwickshire Farming, 1349–c. 1520* (Dugdale Society Occasional Paper, 27, 1981); Z. Razi, *Life, Marriage and Death in a Medieval Parish* (Cambridge, 1980); T.R. Slater and P.J. Jarvis (eds), *Field and Forest: An Historical Geography of Warwickshire and Worcestershire* (Norwich, 1982).

consented), so that the numbers of complete yardland tenements diminished. They also used their fields more intensively by 'inhoking' or 'hiching', that is by taking part of the fallow field and planting it, thereby cultivating rather more than half of the arable each year. But there were limits beyond which they could not go. Excessive fragmentation of holdings would have impoverished them all: impartible inheritance ensured that one heir would receive a viable holding. Younger sons might be able to marry a widow and then acquire her land, or buy a smallholding in the village, but as most holdings could support no more than a nuclear family, there was much emigration.

The system was therefore operating at high pressure in the thirteenth century, with each village developing a delicate balance in land holding and cultivation, having always to consider not just the needs of the villagers but also the surplus that had to be produced for the lords' rents and the state's taxes. The equilibrium was evidently upset in the early fourteenth century, probably by a combination of external demands and internal malfunctions of the agrarian system. After 1349, under the influence of both disease and migration, the villages had to adjust to new circumstances. The balance between tenants of holdings of different sizes was disturbed by the reduction in the numbers of smallholders and the rise of a few kulaks. The field systems had to be changed drastically so that labour-intensive cultivation could give way to an extension of grazing land. Villages which had grown up to serve a specific purpose – feeding large communities by extensive cereal cultivation – were neither large nor in need of so much grain. Some of them faced catastrophe by the early fifteenth century, when a rump of peasants picked their way through weedy derelict fields to cultivate the remaining strips, and defended their crops from the expanding flocks of the village kulaks and intrusive neighbours. Landlords were faced with either restoring the village by combating migration and rebuilding derelict houses, or rationalising their decaying assets by removing the remaining villagers and transforming the field system into an enclosed pasture. Some lords carried out this latter policy vigorously and speedily, but many delayed until the whole village had gone. So by the early sixteenth century a fifth of the villages had been deserted, and the remainder were much reduced in size. With varying degrees of success, the survivors adopted a system of mixed husbandry, with a reduced arable area cultivated on a four-field system.

In the woodlands the dispersed settlements in the thirteenth century cultivated some open fields of a complicated kind, and often held lands in severalty (enclosures). They relied a good deal on pasture, both in their closes and on large heaths and commons. The soil is predominantly red Triassic marl, which is not necessarily inferior to the lias of the Feldon, but which because of the higher ground of the Birmingham plateau suffers more from coldness and wetness. The peasants practised a combination of cereal cultivation (with some emphasis on oats) with a good deal of pastoral husbandry, especially cattle herding. The power of lords in the district was weaker than in the south: the Benedictine monasteries exercised less influence and there were more gentry landlords. Rents and obligations were correspondingly lower, and a high proportion of the tenants held by free tenure. There were more smallholders (measured in terms of arable land) than in the Feldon, but they were not necessarily poorer because they had access to extensive common pastures, and they were involved in crafts and industries, such as charcoal-burning and wood- and metal-working.

There is evidence of settlements in the woodlands of Arden and Feckenham from the Bronze Age onwards. Judging from the Domesday account of the area settlements were relatively thin. Charters of the ninth and tenth centuries suggest an agrarian landscape not unlike that of the thirteenth century, in which areas of woodland, pasture and marsh were interspersed with enclosures, patches of cultivation and isolated settlements. In the twelfth and thirteenth centuries the settlements became more numerous, and assarting extended the areas of cultivation and enclosure. A marked increase in the numbers of markets and small boroughs provided commercial outlets for pastoralists to sell their surplus of animals and animal products, and for the rural craftsmen. Their grain consumption was partially met by trade from the Feldon district. Extra people could be accommodated by adjusting but not transforming the system. There were signs of stress in the thirteenth century, when some communities resisted the enclosure of common pastures with violence. But although the peasants of Halesowen, the best documented manor in the district, suffered grievously in the famine of 1315-17, they were able to make up their numbers in the succeeding generation. The drop in population in the late fourteenth and fifteenth centuries was naturally accompanied by the abandonment of many settlements and a reversion of much arable to pasture. There may have been some small-scale regeneration of woodland, and areas were turned over entirely to grass. Enterprising lords specialised in large-scale meat production for the market, without destroying peasant communities, who were themselves profiting from small-scale pastoralism. The changes were not traumatic. They could be absorbed within the system, and indeed the profits of farming and industry meant that in 1524-5 the inhabitants of the 'underdeveloped' Arden of Warwickshire paid a larger share of their county's taxes than they had done two centuries earlier.

These case studies suggest three general conclusions. Firstly, that the retreat of the later Middle Ages affected settlement on all types of land, and that its most dramatic consequences were felt in the old-settled villages, not on the newly-colonised 'marginal soils'. Secondly, that the negative term 'retreat' derives from a deep-rooted prejudice that arable cultivation represents an advance towards civilisation – yet the highly commercial wood/pasture economy brought many of the inhabitants of such districts considerable prosperity, and gave their settlements a vigorous and extended life. Thirdly, that we should not abandon such concepts as long-term growth and decline in the Middle Ages. To understand them more fully, and to know why and how they occurred, we must explore them in the context of local agrarian and social systems.

3

Deserted Medieval Villages in the West Midlands

The fact that thousands of settlements throughout Europe were abandoned in the later Middle Ages is well known, but the causes of the phenomenon are still uncertain.[1] There are important divergencies between the explanations in favour on the continent and in England. While European deserted villages are seen in the context of population decline or falling grain prices – both trends beginning in the fourteenth century – English desertions are commonly associated with enclosing landlords seeking profits from pastoral farming in the period after 1450. Professor Le Roy Ladurie has highlighted the contrast between the continental and English pictures: the fate of the English villages was 'exceptional in Europe'; continental villages were not 'killed by sheep "who eat up men"', and 'they died earlier'.[2] These marked differences are surprising, as England experienced similar economic trends to those affecting the rest of Europe. Professor Postan has also pointed out the difficulty of reconciling the orthodox English view with our overall interpretation of medieval social and economic history: the German *Wüstungen* have been 'rightly interpreted . . . as evidence of retreating cultivation in the later Middle Ages', while in England deserted villages 'appear to date from the enclosures for sheepfarming'.[3]

The argument presented here will be that the causes and chronology of English desertions have some similarities with those on the continent, and that English villages, as well as falling victims to acquisitive landowners, were abandoned because they were adversely affected by long-term changes in land-use, population and social structure that were widespread in the medieval countryside.

The sources available for the investigation of villages in the later Middle Ages are scattered and fragmentary. The absence of long series of high-quality fiscal records in the period after 1334 makes it difficult to draw a comprehensive picture of the changing fortunes of all villages. Instead, the

---

[1] This essay was greatly assisted by reading C.J. Bond, 'Deserted medieval villages in Warwickshire and Worcestershire', in P.J. Jarvis and T.R. Slater, eds., *Field and Forest: an Historical Geography* of *Warwickshire and Worcestershire* (Norwich, 1982), pp. 147–71.

[2] École Pratique des Hautes Études, VIe section, *Villages désertés et histoire économique* (Paris, 1965), p. 184.

[3] M.M. Postan, *Medieval Economy and Society* (London, 1972), p. 115.

method of enquiry used here has been to assemble as many individual case studies as possible from a single region, the West Midlands. Most of the examples come from the counties of Gloucester, Warwick and Worcester, and some will also be drawn from Derbyshire, Oxfordshire and Staffordshire. As in England as a whole, the distribution of known deserted village sites within the region is very uneven, with the main concentrations in low-lying river valleys and clay plains (such as those of central Worcestershire, south and east Warwickshire, north and central Oxfordshire, and south-east Staffordshire), and also on the Cotswold hills. There is relatively little evidence of deserted villages in the woodland districts of the region.[4]

Regional studies have their limitations, and this investigation may reveal no more than a pattern of depopulation peculiar to the West Midlands. However, the region has some importance in its own right because of its large number of known deserted village sites, some 240 in the three central counties alone, which is almost a tenth of the national total. Some districts within the region have high densities of deserted villages, up to a quarter or a fifth of the places known to have existed, and in one locality, near Southam in south-east Warwickshire, seven contiguous settlements have been lost, leaving an area of 30 sq. km. villageless.[5] Nor can the region be regarded as entirely atypical, as its terrain and social structure have many similarities with the wide belt of Midland and central southern England in which desertions were particularly numerous.

The number of totally abandoned village sites is in itself impressive, but there is further evidence for widespread settlement contraction. The shrinkage of villages has left abundant traces in the form of earthworks and scatters of building débris and medieval pottery, such as the 12 ha site at Long Itchington (Warwickshire), where traces of about thirty houses have been identified.[6] Similarly, the sites of about eighty deserted houses have been discovered at Hanbury (Worcestershire), a woodland parish, showing that depopulation also affected areas of dispersed settlement.[7] However, neither shrunken villages nor deserted hamlets have been systematically listed in the region, and a full assessment of their importance awaits further research.

[4]   M.W. Beresford and J.G. Hurst, eds., *Deserted Medieval Villages* (London, 1971), p. 66; for a more up-to-date map of Worcestershire sites, see C.J. Bond, 'Deserted villages in Worcestershire', in B.H. Adlam, ed., *Worcester and its Region* (Worcester, 1974), p. 40.

[5]   M.W. Beresford, *Lost Villages of England* (London, 1954), p. 234; Beresford and Hurst, *Deserted Medieval Villages*, p. 36.

[6]   P.R. Wilson, 'Depopulation in Long Itchington Parish', *Warwickshire History*, 4 (1979-80), pp. 120–32.

[7]   *Medieval Village Research Group Annual Report*, 29 (1981), p. 13.

Early Desertions

Late medieval desertions will be the main subject of this essay, but these should be put into the context of a much longer period of settlement growth and contraction. Archaeological research has now revealed the sites of dozens of Anglo-Saxon settlements throughout England, including the West Midlands, where occupation ceased at various times between the sixth and tenth centuries.[8] Pre-Conquest charters also refer to places of which the names are not traceable in later documents, for example *Haeccaham* (Worcestershire) and *Timbinctun* (Gloucestershire).[9] Perhaps such places changed their names and survive as modern villages, but there is also a possibility that deserted settlements lie behind the lost place-names. The most likely explanation of these early medieval desertions is that they represent the casualties of a process of nucleation or 'balling', in which a scattered and fluent pattern of settlement gradually shifted and coalesced to form the larger nuclear settlements that were to dominate much of the Midland countryside in the later Middle Ages.[10] These early desertions remind us that depopulation, as in recent times, can be a feature of an economy experiencing overall growth, and indeed could be a by-product of the expansion process, as the most favoured places developed at the expense of those lower down in the settlement hierarchy.

By the late eleventh century greater stability had emerged, so that a high proportion of the places named in Domesday have continued to be inhabited until modern times. Still, some Domesday names either do not reappear in twelfth- and thirteenth-century documents, or were perpetuated into the later Middle Ages as field names rather than as settlement sites, suggesting that the nucleation process was still continuing in the two centuries after 1086.[11] In an age of considerable seigneurial power some settlements might be moved in order to make way for expanding demesnes or parks. An example is Osmerley in Worcestershire, which appeared in Domesday as a manor with ten bordars and four slaves and bondwomen. In *c.* 1140 the Cistercian monastery of Bordesley was founded nearby, and in the late twelfth century the abbey acquired land in the area from lay landowners and consolidated its control over Osmerley. By 1243, Osmerley's

---

[8]   P.A. Rahtz, 'Buildings and rural settlement', in D.M. Wilson, ed., *The Archaeology of Anglo-Saxon England* (London, 1976), pp. 49–98.

[9]   P.H. Sawyer, *Anglo-Saxon Charters: An Annotated List and Bibliography* (London, 1968), nos. 141, 190.

[10]   On nucleation see C.C. Taylor, 'The Anglo-Saxon countryside', in T. Rowley, ed., *Anglo-Saxon Settlement and Landscape* (British Archaeological Reports, 6, 1974), pp. 5–15.

[11]   E.g. four places named in Warwickshire and ten in Worcestershire in 1086 cannot now be identified, see H.C. Darby and G.R. Versey, *Domesday Gazetteer* (Cambridge, 1975), pp. 435–44, 458–66. On late nucleation see C.C. Taylor, 'Polyfocal settlement and the English village', *Medieval Archaeology*, 21 (1977), pp. 189–93.

territory was partly occupied by the abbey's park, and a monastic grange was also established there in the thirteenth century. No trace of a village of Osmerley appears in later records, and it must be assumed that the tenants had been expelled or bought out in the late twelfth or early thirteenth century.[12] Lay landlords might also take over tenant holdings, like Roger Parvus, who in the mid-twelfth century 'expelled the rustics' from six yardlands (*c.* 180 acres) at Stanley Pontlarge in Gloucestershire, and 'retained and cultivated it'.[13] No total desertions can be attributed to expansions of lay demesnes, but such actions may lie behind the disappearance of some places from the post-Domesday records. Most lords in the thirteenth century preferred to keep their tenants and maximise their income from rents and seigneurial dues, and most tenants would have been anxious to remain on their holdings because of the scarcity of land. Seigneurial reorganisation of settlement, a major cause of desertions in Italy,[14] seems to have had only minor effects in England.

The Chronology of Late Medieval Desertion

The early fourteenth century marks the beginning of the main phase of village desertion which continued into the fifteenth century. The decades around 1300, as is now generally recognised, were a turning-point in the history of the rural economy. Internal colonisation petered out, and the cultivated area began to contract, so that the records of West Midland manors after *c.* 1320 contain an increasing number of references to land lying 'frisc' (uncultivated) or being infertile, arable strips put down to pasture, vacant tenant holdings, and holdings being surrendered because of the poverty and incapacity of the tenants.

The *Nonarum Inquisitiones* for Gloucestershire and Oxfordshire show that these changes were hitting some villages acutely by 1341. In these two counties there were specific and circumstantial complaints, mainly in the central Cotswolds and north-east Oxfordshire, that in twenty-two places land was uncultivated, sometimes amounting to two or three ploughlands (about 200-300 acres) in a single village, and nine villages were said to have tenants who were 'poor' or 'impotent', or it was reported that tenants had migrated.[15] Eight of these places were later to be deserted, such as Harford

[12] *Domesday Book* (Record Commission, 1783), fo. 177v.; T. Madox, *Formulare Anglicanum* (1702), pp. 2–3, 49, 56–7; *Taxatio Ecclesiastica* (Record Commission, 1802), p. 229; Worcestershire County Record Office (hereafter WCRO), ref. 821 BA 3814, fos. 68, 83.

[13] D. Royce, ed., *Landboc sive Registrum Monasterii . . . de Winchelcumba* (Exeter, 1892), i, p. 224.

[14] *Medieval Village Research Group Annual Report*, 23 (1975), p. 47, summarising an essay by C. Klapisch-Zuber.

[15] *Nonarum Inquisitiones* (Record Commission, 1807), pp. 132–41; on this document in general, see A.R.H. Baker, 'Evidence in the *Nonarum Inquisitiones* of contracting arable lands in England in the early fourteenth century', *Econ. Hist. Rev.*, 2nd ser., 19 (1966), pp. 518–32.

and Ailworth (Gloucestershire), where 'many tenants left their holdings and left them vacant and uncultivated' or at Little Aston in Aston Blank (Gloucestershire) 'seven parishioners of the hamlet of Little Aston . . . abandoned their holdings and left the parish'. The villages of Radcot and Grafton (Oxfordshire) were assessed at £4 'and no more because the fields are infertile and because of the mortality of sheep'. The troubles of these districts seem to have begun earlier. In the records of the tax collected in 1316, during the great famine, in the north-eastern corner of Oxfordshire that seemed to be facing such problems in 1341, Shelswell was reported to be 'small and poor', and Langley, on the Cotswolds, had only four tenants.[16]

The significance of the places apparently experiencing the beginnings of depopulation before the Black Death is that they lay in districts where later desertions were also concentrated, as if we are witnessing a phase of a long-term process. The districts affected were not those which had been recently colonised or which contained poor soils. There is evidence in the 1320s of the abandonment of land and dwellings in areas where there had been much assarting in Derbyshire and Staffordshire, which could be seen as marking a withdrawal from marginal lands, but this retreat does not seem to have resulted in the desertion of villages.[17] The parts of Gloucestershire and Oxfordshire reported as having difficulties in 1341 had well-established settlements and soils of average quality. A possible explanation of their troubles lies in an over-extension of arable cultivation and a shortage of livestock, especially difficult problems on the Cotswolds, where sheep-folding was needed to maintain fertility. Nor should we discount the 'impotence' and 'poverty' of tenants mentioned both in the 1341 inquisitions and in contemporary Cotswold court rolls, to which rent demands and frequent taxes would have been contributory factors.[18]

The evidence for desertions becomes abundant in the century after 1349. The plague itself is unlikely to have killed off whole village populations, but it could have weakened settlements and created opportunities for migration. A case of desertion caused directly by the plague is apparently provided by Tusmore (Oxfordshire), the tax of which was remitted in 1354, and it was reported to be void of inhabitants in 1357. However, two carucates of Tusmore's arable were said to be lying uncultivated in 1341, and it would seem that the plague merely hastened the end of a settlement already in decline.[19]

[16] K.J. Allison, M.W. Beresford, and J.G. Hurst, *The Deserted Villages of Oxfordshire* (University of Leicester English Local History Department Occasional Papers, 17, 1965), pp. 5–6.

[17] J.R. Birrell, 'The Honour of Tutbury in the fourteenth and fifteenth centuries' (unpublished M.A. thesis, University of Birmingham, 1962), pp. 53–6.

[18] An example of a set of court rolls containing a number of such references is that of the Winchcomb Abbey estate, Gloucestershire County Records Office (hereafter GRO), D 678/96.

[19] D. Miles and T. Rowley, 'Tusmore deserted village', *Oxoniensia*, 41 (1976), pp. 309–15, on the post-1349 evidence.

There are a number of examples of desertions recorded in tax lists and manorial documents in the 1370s and 1380s in the Gloucestershire Cotswolds at Wontley (by 1372), Bidfield, Hilcot, Lasborough, Ledgemore (1381) and Upton in Blockley (1383). In the Avon valley, at Hatton-on-Avon, most of the tenants had gone by 1385.[20]

Other villages suffered the first stage of desertion in the late fourteenth century, like Weston-juxta-Cherington (Warwickshire), where eleven holdings out of twenty-six were lying 'in the lord's hands' in 1355. By this time in many villages the vacancies created by the plague had largely been filled, but at Weston the use of vacant holdings as demesne pasture suggests that the lord had accepted the long-term nature of the loss of his tenants.[21] Similarly at Preston (Gloucestershire) in 1351, twelve holdings lay vacant and the eventual re-occupation of land by resident tenants was made more difficult because tenancies were taken by people who lived at nearby Kempley.[22] Half of the tenant land at Fulbrook (Warwickshire), four yardlands out of eight, was lying in the lord's hands in 1392. By 1428 there were only four households there, and in 1461 a substantial part of Fulbrook's land was being leased as an enclosed pasture.[23] Many villages that were to survive shrank in size in the late fourteenth century, but rarely as drastically as at Weston or Fulbrook. At Todenham (Gloucestershire), the shrinkage was permanent, and has left its mark on the modern landscape. A group of eleven cottage holdings at Homestall End in Todenham had been abandoned by 1384, and as early as 1368 five of them had been enclosed in a croft as a demesne pasture for lambs. The earthworks probably marking the site of these cottages are still visible in a pasture field on the edge of the modern village.[24]

Villages that were eventually to be deserted often went into a long process of decline that continued into the fifteenth century. As Professor Beresford has shown, most villages still retained a tax-paying population when the poll taxes were levied in 1377-81.[25] Some examples of a slow but cumulative decline have already been the subject of detailed studies, such as Brookend (Oxfordshire), which had sixteen tenants in 1279, still retained fifteen in 1363, but was reduced to three by 1441. At Woollashill (Worcestershire),

[20] C. Dyer, *Lords and Peasants in a Changing Society: The Estates of the Bishopric of Worcester, 680-1540* (Cambridge, 1980), pp. 245–6; *Victoria County History of Gloucestershire* (hereafter *VCH*), ix, pp. 10, 176, 284; R.H. Hilton and P.A. Rahtz, 'Upton, Gloucestershire, 1959–64', *Transactions of the Bristol and Glos. Archaeological Society*, 85 (1966), pp. 70–146.

[21] Shakespeare's Birthplace Trust Record Office (hereafter SBT), DR 98/865–6.

[22] GRO, D 936a/M2.

[23] PRO, DL 43 14/3 fo. 61; *Feudal Aids*, v, p. 187; D. Styles, ed., *Ministers' Accounts of the Collegiate Church of St Mary, Warwick* (Dugdale Society, 26, 1969), pp. 68, 74, 76.

[24] B.F. Harvey, *Westminster Abbey and its Estates in the Middle Ages* (Oxford, 1977), p. 262; GRO, D 1099 M30/17.

[25] Beresford and Hurst, *Deserted Medieval Villages*, pp. 9–10.

the twenty or so original tenant holdings were occupied by thirteen tenants in 1424, and nine in 1442. By the mid-sixteenth century only two tenants remained. At Kingston (Warwickshire) seventeen tenants are recorded in 1394, thirteen in 1430 (of whom at least three were absentees) and the whole village may have gone by 1437 and certainly by 1461.[26] The farm of the tithe-corn of Upper Ditchford (Gloucestershire) was halved in value between 1384 and 1419, and ceased completely, signalling the end of arable farming, in about 1475, when the site was leased as a sheep pasture. At Craycombe (Worcestershire) the decline cannot be followed, but the village is known to have disappeared by 1438.[27]

New cases of serious decline in the late fourteenth or early fifteenth century can be added to these, such as Hill (Worcestershire) where eleven tenants were listed in 1388, but only five in 1447, or Thornton in Ettington (Warwickshire), with the twenty-one holdings of 1279 concentrated into the hands of five tenants, together with the divided demesne, by 1447.[28] Three of the land-holders recorded in the 1447 Thornton rental were apparently relatives, Richard, Thomas and William Phypps, and we may doubt if their lands were in reality occupied as separate holdings. Radbourne (Warwickshire) was probably in decline in 1379, when only fourteen people contributed to the poll tax, though valors of 1385/6 imply that there was still a considerable tenant population paying rents totalling £5 8s. 10$\frac{1}{2}$d. per annum to John Catesby, the lord of the manor. In 1411 John's son, another John Catesby, was leasing land in the village from two ecclesiastical lords, Combe Abbey and Coventry Priory, including four messuages that had previously been in the hands of separate tenants. By 1443 the village had disappeared completely, and its site was occupied by a great pasture.[29] At Westcote in Tysoe (Warwickshire) fifteen tenants were listed in 1279, and in spite of the plague one of the three manors could still muster thirteen tenants in 1352. This total was reduced to eleven in 1389, and there seem to have been very few left when the place was leased as a pasture in 1444.[30] Goldicote (Warwickshire) had thirteen tax-payers in 1327, implying a considerably larger number of householders, but a rental in 1460 shows

[26] T.H. Lloyd, 'Some documentary sidelights on the deserted Oxfordshire village of Brookend', *Oxoniensia*, 29–30 (1964–5), pp. 116–28; C.C. Dyer, 'The deserted medieval village of Woollashill, Worcestershire', *Transactions of the Worcestershire Archaeological Society*, 3rd. ser., 1 (1965–7), pp. 55–61; R.H. Hilton, *The English Peasantry in the Later Middle Ages* (Oxford, 1975), p. 165; SBT, DR 98/438, 463a.

[27] Dyer, *Lords and Peasants*, pp. 247–51.

[28] WCRO, ref. 009:1 BA 2636/193; PRO SC 11/819.

[29] PRO, E179/192/23; J.R. Birrell, ed., 'The *Status maneriorum* of John Catesby 1385 and 1386', in R. Bearman, ed., *Miscellany*, i (Dugdale Society, 31, 1977), p. 23; PRO, E 164/21, fo. 251; PRO, SC 6 1041/19.

[30] Magdalen College, Oxford, Muniment Room (hereafter Magd. Coll.), Westcote 2, 18, 113, 116.

only three tenants with very large land-holdings.[31] Littleton in Dumbleton (Gloucestershire) must have been in a very decayed state when '200 acres of land or more' in its fields were included in the leasehold of the demesne farmer of Dumbleton in 1433.[32] In 1444/5 the tithe-corn of Cestersover (Warwickshire) was in theory being rented out for £4, but three-quarters of this sum was allowed to the farmer because 'the land lies frisc'. When Sir Henry Waver, citizen of London, emparked the lands of Cestersover in 1466 the village must have been in an advanced stage of decay.[33]

The picture of declining villages losing their tenants over a century or more after 1349 is supported by archaeological evidence from the most extensively excavated village site in the region, Barton Blount (Derbyshire), where the occupation of houses ceased at various times between the late fourteenth and late fifteenth centuries.[34]

It has been necessary to emphasise the evidence for a piecemeal reduction in the number of tenants and in the cultivated land of villages in the period up to the middle of the fifteenth century because this phase of rural depopulation has not received sufficient attention in the past. It must be said that the mid- or late fifteenth-century manorial documents of some villages that we know to have been deserted later – Bickley (Worcestershire), Idlicote (Warwickshire) and Netherton (Worcestershire) – give no strong impression of settlements in advanced deterioration;[35] but these are out-numbered by the examples already given.

The Role of the Landlord

The final phase of desertion in the late fifteenth century is more fully recorded because it attracted comment from contemporaries and consequently has received more attention from modern historians. The interest of contemporaries may have been a response to a growing problem, but also reflects the newly articulated concern among educated people about social and economic problems that was to flourish among the 'commonwealth men' in the sixteenth century. The earliest expression of disquiet was John Rous's petition to the Coventry parliament in 1459, the text of which has unfortunately not survived. Rous went on in the 1480s to

[31] F.J. Eld, ed., *Lay Subsidy Roll for the County of Worcester 1 Edward III* (Worcestershire Hist. Soc., 1895), p. 59; PRO, SC2 210/4.

[32] R.E.G. Kirk, ed., *Accounts of the Obedientars of Abingdon Abbey* (Camden Soc., new ser., 51, 1892), pp. 153–5.

[33] PRO, SC6 1039/18; *Calendar of Patent Rolls, 1461–7*, p. 542.

[34] G. Beresford, *The Medieval Clay-Land Village: Excavations at Goltho and Barton Blount* (Soc. for Medieval Archaeology Monographs, 6, 1975), pp. 53–4.

[35] Worcester Cathedral Library, C670; SBT, DR18/30/15; E.K. Vose, 'Estates of Worcester Cathedral Priory' (unpublished typescript, School of History, University of Birmingham), p. 29.

compile his famous list of sixty Warwickshire deserted villages. He thought that all the villages that he observed in ruins were the victims of the greed of 'destroyers and mutilators' who had enclosed fields, made parks and expelled peasants. He was sometimes mistaken, for example when he linked the expulsion of the villeins of Fulbrook with the enclosure of a park there by the duke of Bedford in 1421.[36] As we have seen, Fulbrook's holdings were half-empty in 1392. At least ten other villages listed by Rous can be shown to have been in a serious state of decay at various dates between 1385 and 1444, and we may doubt whether he had much first-hand knowledge of the circumstances that led to the desertion of these places.[37]

Rous was a more reliable witness for his own day, and his evident anger at the destruction of villages must have been provoked by a real problem. Independent sources seem to confirm his version of events in some cases. At Chesterton in 1484, at about the same time that Rous included it in his list, there was a dispute between two tenants and John Peyto, the lord of the manor, over his conversion of arable into pasture.[38] The tithe records of Middle Ditchford (Gloucestershire) show that, although the area under crops had been considerably reduced by 1383, arable cultivation ceased abruptly in the 1480s, as if there had been some sudden enclosure or eviction.[39] The clergy of St Mary's Warwick recorded in their accounts that the tenants of Compton Verney rectory had been 'expelled' by Richard Verney, probably in about 1447. The court rolls of Compton Verney show that the village was declining in the early fifteenth century, so the removal of the rectory tenants may have come at a late stage of the village's decay.[40] Calcutt (in Grandborough) also figures in Rous's chronicle. A list of tenants paying rents from Calcutt to Coventry Priory in 1411 shows that there were then eight, two of them each responsible for four holdings. A single court roll of 1474 lists four Calcutt tenants of customary holdings. One had recently died, and no new tenant came to take his holding. Of the others one had a single tenement, another held two, and a third held three. Each was said to have been 'dismissed from the aforesaid holding' (*et dimissus est de tenemento predicto*). A rental compiled a little later lists eight tenants in Calcutt, but they appear to be holding very small amounts of land, as the sum of the rents comes to only 14s. $4\frac{1}{2}$d. Just one of the customary tenements mentioned in 1474 owed a rent of 20s. 0d. per annum. It seems that the customary tenants of Calcutt had been evicted, leaving a few free

---

[36] J. Rous, *Historia Regum Angliae* (Oxford, 1745), pp. 122–4.
[37] The villages are Billesley Trussell, Chapel Ascote, Cestersover, Compton Verney, Hatton-on-Avon, Hodnell, Kingston, Radbourne, Thornton and Westcote.
[38] Hilton, *English Peasantry*, pp. 171–2.
[39] Dyer, *Lords and Peasants*, pp. 251, 260.
[40] Styles, *Ministers' Accounts*, p. 77; Hilton, *English Peasantry*, pp. 161–73.

tenants with smallholdings as the last vestige of the village. One of the eight was an absentee gentleman, Thomas Catesby.[41]

While these more objective sources support Rous in attributing some late fifteenth-century depopulations to acts of seigneurial policy, the evidence from Compton Verney, Middle Ditchford and Calcutt also points to some shrinkage before any expulsion or enclosure. The same conclusion emerges from a close examination of the presentments made to the Enclosure Commissions of 1517. Here are reports in plenty of houses ruined, tenants expelled and ploughs displaced. But they record relatively few large-scale depopulations, so that in Warwickshire only five presentments involved more than ten households. One of these was at Wormleighton, where in 1499 the occupants of fifteen messuages and cottages had been forced to depart 'tearfully', and 240 acres of arable were enclosed; shortly afterwards another six messuages were destroyed. This act of deliberate removal of tenants took place in a shrunken village, as two centuries before there had been forty-five tenants and 800 acres of arable.[42] Another case of depopulation, at Weston-juxta-Cherington, involved eight dwellings and 200 acres of land, but the village had clearly been reduced in size 150 years earlier.[43] Similarly at Walton Deyville the number of messuages and cottages recorded as decayed in 1497 and 1509 (thirteen) is very much less than the thirty-three listed in 1279.[44]

The Walton presentment, like many made in 1517, chooses its words carefully; it says that the houses were 'allowed to fall into ruin' and that the tenants 'withdrew'. The enclosure commissions, as Dr Blanchard has shown, were often recording, not deliberate acts of destruction, but the last phase of a decline in the rural population that had been going on for at least a century and a half.[45]

Dr Kerridge has reminded us that the 1517 commissions recorded presentments, that is accusations rather than proven cases. In his defence, Sir Edward Belknap, accused of enclosure at Burton Dassett (Warwickshire), argued that the decay of the village had taken place over a long period going back to the reign of Edward IV. This had not been the result of any deliberate policy on the part of previous landlords, who had rather neglected the place, but was caused by declining demand for arable land – 'for at that time was great scarcity of pasture in that part, and arable land was in such abundance that men could not get tenants to occupy their

---

[41] PRO, E 164/21, fo. 249; Staffordshire County Record Office, D 641/1/4v/2.

[42] I.S. Leadam, ed., *The Domesday of Inclosures* (Royal Hist. Soc., 1897), ii, pp. 389–453, 647–93; H. Thorpe, 'The lord and the landscape', in *Volume jubilaire M.A. Lefèvre* (Louvain, 1964), pp. 82–96.

[43] Leadam, *Domesday*, pp. 415–16; see above for vacant holdings at Weston in 1355.

[44] Ibid., pp. 422–3, 652, 688; Warwickshire County Record Office, MI 278.

[45] I.S.W. Blanchard, 'Population change, enclosure, and the early Tudor economy', *Econ. Hist. Rev.*, 2nd ser., 23 (1970), pp. 436–8.

lands'.[46] No Burton Dassett court rolls survive, but those of other manors in the region confirm the general tenor of Belknap's story of a shortage of tenants, even at the end of the fifteenth century.

These interpretations of the evidence of the 1517 commissions suggest that there were not two separate phases of desertion, with decay before 1450 followed by deliberate depopulation. Rather they support the argument that while villagers were being evicted or driven away in the late fifteenth or early sixteenth century, often from debilitated settlements, the process of natural wastage was continuing.

There is ample evidence that in the late fourteenth and for much of the fifteenth century landlords strove to preserve their villages by seeking to prevent the migration of tenants, and by attempting to maintain the attractiveness of holdings. An example of the use of lordly power in order to keep tenants was at Brailes (Warwickshire), a manor of Richard Beauchamp, earl of Warwick, in 1420. Two serfs, John Taylard and John Hastyng, were said to have caused by their 'incitement and instigation' the withdrawal of William Taylard from his three-yardland holding. They were required themselves to take over the tenancy.[47] A more common seigneurial action, both in villages which were to survive and in others which later foundered, was to order the return of serfs who had migrated. Such orders were ignored, and they were discontinued on many manors in the late fifteenth century because lords recognised the weakness of the manor courts in the face of the growing mobility of serfs.

Similarly, landlords did not welcome the dilapidation of tenants' buildings, but instead made efforts to keep them in repair. As early as 1385 John Catesby's officials found eleven holdings vacant at Ladbroke (Warwickshire) and their reaction was to calculate the cost to the lord of repairing the buildings.[48] Throughout the region it became common in the early fifteenth century for landlords to make financial contributions or to provide building materials for tenants' repairs, presumably with the aim of keeping existing tenants and attracting newcomers.[49] At Chapel Ascote (Warwickshire), a village that was to become deserted in the course of the fifteenth century, the ladies of the manor (the successive prioresses of Nuneaton) used every available method to keep tenants' buildings intact in the period 1411-45. Tenants were ordered in the manor court to carry out repairs, and if they failed to comply with the orders they were amerced, not

---

[46] E. Kerridge, 'The returns of the inquisitions of depopulation', *English Historical Review*, 70 (1955), pp. 212–28; N.W. Alcock, 'Enclosure and depopulation in Burton Dassett: a sixteenth century view', *Warwickshire History*, 3 (1977), pp. 180–4.

[47] Birmingham Reference Library, 167901.

[48] Birrell, *'Status maneriorum'*, p. 27.

[49] Hilton, *English Peasantry*, pp. 191–4; R.K. Field, 'Worcestershire peasant buildings, household goods and farming equipment in the later Middle Ages', *Medieval Archaeology*, 9 (1965), pp. 109–10.

the usual few pence, but substantial sums of as much as 6s. 8d., 20s. 0d. and 40s. 0d. Recalcitrant tenants with ruinous buildings were threatened with the forfeiture of holdings, crops and chattels. When a tenant surrendered a holding, it might be surveyed and any damages assessed. In one case in 1435 John Knight surrendered a holding with its buildings in ruins; his brother Edward had acted as his pledge, to guarantee the maintenance of the holding, and the unfortunate pledge was amerced 20s. 0d. New tenants were expected to carry out repairs as a condition of their tenancies, and on at least one occasion a prioress had had a house rebuilt at her own expense. These efforts were apparently unsuccessful, and by the 1470s action on specific cases had ceased, and instead generalised orders were addressed to all tenants, requiring that buildings be repaired under threat of such minor penalties as 1s. 8d. and 2s. 0d. Parallels for all these measures can be found in other court rolls of the period, but the unusual variety of methods of tackling the problem of dilapidation at Chapel Ascote (recorded in a relatively short series of documents) might suggest some desperation on the part of the authorities.[50]

Landlords were much concerned with the maintenance of their income from rents; they conceded to their tenants as little as possible, but became aware of the dangers of too intransigent an attitude, so that in the 1430s officials of the bishopric of Worcester foresaw the 'final destruction' of manors because rent demands would lead to tenant migration, and the managers of the Beauchamp manor of Lighthorne (Warwickshire) reduced rents when they found nearly half of the holdings vacant and the remaining tenants threatening to depart.[51] In the fifteenth century rents in the declining villages were sometimes drastically reduced to as little as 6s. 8d. or 10s. 0d. per annum for a customary yardland, and entry-fines were often waived entirely, while tenants of yardlands in more healthy villages might still be paying 20s. 0d. per annum and fines of a few shillings. Policies on migration, buildings and rents support the argument that most lords were reluctant to see tenants leave.

The theory that there were numerous deliberate depopulations supposes on the part of landlords a degree of entrepreneurial adventurousness which is at variance with all that we know of their behaviour in the late Middle Ages.[52] Landlords and their advisers seem to have been slow to make decisions, so that the enclosure of vacant lands might take decades to accomplish.[53] We would expect the gentry to be the most adaptable of landlords, as they exercised closer personal supervision of their manors, and with limited resources had to make the most efficient use of land.

[50] BL, Add. Rolls 49395–49400, 49418–49452.
[51] Dyer, *Lords and Peasants*, p. 261; Hilton, *English Peasantry*, pp. 66–7; SBT, DR 98/685a.
[52] For example see Harvey, *Westminster Abbey*, pp. 331–3.
[53] Dyer, *Lords and Peasants*, p. 245.

Hence the evidence already quoted that men like Richard Verney, faced with dwindling rent income from decaying villages, removed the remaining tenants to create enclosed pastures. However, if gentry acquisitiveness was a main cause of desertions, we might expect to find deserted village sites concentrated on gentry estates. In fact they are found on the manors of a cross-section of the landlord class, including the conservative lay and ecclesiastical magnates.

Another group capable of seeking deliberately to get rid of tenants were the demesne farmers, an influential but often obscure group in late medieval rural society. An example of a demesne farmer who threatened the existence of a village comes from Quinton (Warwickshire). In the 1480s the vicar of Quinton wrote to the lord of the manor, the President of Magdalen College, Oxford, to complain that 'our poor town . . . falls fast in decay' and was 'near to the point of destruction'. 'Your housing goes down: twenty marks will not set up again that is fallen within this four years.' The vicar blamed the farmer, who was driving the tenants out, and urged the President that it was 'more meritory to support and succour a community than one man'. An undated petition of about the same time criticised John Salbrygge, the deputy farmer, for turning cottars off parcels of demesne arable that they had customarily occupied, and 'for evil will that he had to the town' he ploughed up 30 leys 'that the town should be supported by' (presumably as common pasture). The court rolls of Quinton for the 1480s confirm the story of decay, with their presentments of ruined buildings and lists of vacant holdings. The vicar had urged that the farmer be replaced by a group of villagers as lessees. This happened in about 1490, and as Quinton still exists, the advice may have saved an endangered community. We are rarely so well informed about the activities of demesne farmers, who may have contributed to other village desertions.[54]

After Desertion

The great variety of uses made of the abandoned land of villages during and after their desertion indicates the range of pressures and trends that lay behind the process of decline. If a major cause of desertion was a deliberate policy of removing tenants, we would expect to find the holdings falling into the lords' hands, and then being quickly converted into a profitable pasture. In fact, sometimes the village fields reverted to a virtual waste, as happened at Wontley, which for many years produced a very small rent for the landlord of a few shillings. No doubt such areas of under-exploited grassland were used by the neighbouring villages. This is recorded in 1457 in the case of Hardwick (Warwickshire) because the men of Lower Tysoe

[54] Magd. Coll., Quinton 56, 60; court book no. 1.

paid a (relatively modest) rent of 50s. 0d. per annum for the pasture.[55] In villages of divided lordship there might be doubts as to which lord inherited the grazing rights. Evidently a dispute at Westcote (Warwickshire) led to an inquiry in the late fifteenth century, in which various lords claimed pasture rights, and people from nearby places were asked to recall the obsolete customs of the defunct village. [56]

Often the landlord was not the beneficiary of the departure of his tenants. The lands might be taken over by tenants from neighbouring villages, as at Craycombe (Worcestershire) in the fifteenth century. In many cases a few tenants remained and accumulated very large holdings. Multiple tenements containing two or three yardlands (60-90 acres) were not uncommon in the fifteenth century but in the declining villages, like Barcheston (Warwickshire), Goldicote (Warwickshire), Roel (Gloucestershire) and Thornton (Warwickshire) holdings of between four and five and three-quarter yardlands are recorded.[57] It is easy to envisage how, as neighbours moved away, such holdings could be acquired, but less easy to imagine how they were worked in view of the desperate shortage of labour. We might expect the holdings to be turned over to pasture, but at Thornton rents were paid partly in grain, suggesting the continuation of a good deal of arable cultivation. Some of these holdings we may suspect were under-exploited; certainly they do not always seem to have been desirable assets. At Roel, for example, when John Pyrton died in 1466, leaving his five-yardland holding, no one was willing to take it. It is possible that some of these engrossers were making effective use of their land; indeed, like the demesne farmers mentioned above, the activities of a dominant tenant, particularly one who developed large-scale pastoral activities, could have hastened the departure of the remaining villagers. Also the accumulation of lands by non-residents, as happened at Welcombe (Warwickshire), could damage the village.[58]

Finally, and sometimes after long periods as waste or in the hands of the few remaining tenants, the village sites could be turned into efficient and productive land units if the capital was available for enclosure. Some landlords took full advantage of the opportunity. As has already been seen, the Catesbys of Ashby St Ledgers consolidated their control of Radbourne (Warwickshire) in the early fifteenth century, and for much of the century used the resulting 1000-acre pasture as a centre of demesne stock farming. For example, in 1476 they kept 2,742 sheep and 183 cattle at Radbourne. The animals were used to supply meat and cheese for the household, and wool and some meat for sale; profits were high, as the labour force needed

[55] PRO, SC 6/1040/15.
[56] Magd. Coll., Westcote 17.
[57] Leadam, *Domesday*, p. 416; PRO, SC 2/210/4; GRO, D 678/95; PRO, SC 11/819.
[58] GRO, D 678/95; Dyer, *Lords and Peasants*, pp. 254–5.

consisted of only five or six hands. The valuation of Radbourne manor rose from £19 in 1386 to £64 in 1449.[59]

More commonly landlords left the management of the new enclosed pastures to lessees. They might be gentry, like Richard Dalby, Nicholas Cowley, and Robert Throckmorton, successively farmers of Westcote (Warwickshire) between 1444 and 1501, or butcher-graziers, such as Benedict Lee of Warwick who farmed the site of Heathcote (Warwickshire) in the mid-fifteenth century, Thomas Grene of Stratford-on-Avon at Fulbrook (Warwickshire) in the 1460s, or the famous John Spenser who leased many deserted village sites in Warwickshire at the end of the fifteenth century.[60] The profitability of these pasture farms is indicated by their high rentals, such as the £26 13s. 4d. per annum paid by John Lichfield of Coventry from 1437 for Kingston which had in its decline in 1393/4 yielded only £11 11s. 0d.[61] As an unenclosed pasture Westcote paid an annual rent of only £4 in 1444 but after enclosure this increased rapidly to £13 6s. 8d. at the end of the fifteenth century.

While these transformations into highly-profitable pastures were by no means the immediate or universal consequences of desertion, they should be appreciated as creating rationally organised and market-oriented units of production, very similar to modern capitalist farms.

Why Were Villages Deserted?

In explaining rural depopulation we must examine changes within the peasant community. All villages faced problems in the later Middle Ages; the villages that were eventually to be deserted experienced difficulties similar in kind to those of their neighbours that survived, but in a more acute form. The fall in population continued from the mid-fourteenth to the mid-fifteenth century, and there is little sign of real recovery until about 1520. Most villages lost a substantial proportion, often about a half, of their population during this long period, but a few, as we have seen, dwindled even more drastically in size. Differences in the intensity of plague epidemics are unlikely to explain these divergences. As has already been noted, very few settlements can be shown to have been wiped out in the most severe plague of all, that of 1348/9, and subsequent outbreaks of disease, though they varied in their local effect, rarely caused a death-rate of more than 20 per cent. Clearly the desertions are closely related to the general decline in population, as cases are found primarily within the period of demographic

[59] PRO, SC 6/1041/19; 1042/2–7, 1043/10.

[60] Magd. Coll., Westcote 2, 44, 118; Styles, *Ministers' Accounts*, pp. 148, 166; Thorpe, 'Lord and the landscape', pp. 97–9.

[61] Hilton, *English Peasantry*, pp. 169–70.

decline or stagnation, but the relationship seems to have been an indirect one. The key factor was migration. There had been a good deal of geographical mobility before the Black Death, and it intensified in the later Middle Ages, especially after 1400, as opportunities for movement opened up, and as seigneurial controls relaxed.[62] Even relatively stable villages experienced a turnover of 75 per cent of families every fifty years or so. The inhabitants of villages on the way to desertion moved with even great rapidity, so that at Chapel Ascote (Warwickshire) none of the families recorded in the mid-fourteenth century can be found in the early fifteenth, and at Kingston (Warwickshire) only one tenant surname out of eleven persisted between 1394 and 1430.[63]

The increasing discontinuity in land-holding of the later Middle Ages, so that tenements changed hands rapidly and relatively few holdings were inherited, is well known. None of our deserted villages is recorded in a sufficiently full series of court rolls to make valid statistical comparisons, but in the documents that have survived, at Chapel Ascote, Compton Verney and Woollashill, one cannot fail to notice the number of surrenders of holdings, often into the lord's hands, suggesting a transient tenant population. Of the twenty-six land transfers recorded at Chapel Ascote between 1349 and 1442, only three show sons taking over their father's holding.

The overall patterns of migration clearly favoured settlements in the woodlands or in such districts as the Severn valley around Worcester. Here few settlements were completely abandoned and village populations in general declined relatively slightly. The villages most vulnerable to desertion lay in such areas of champion husbandry as the Feldon of Warwickshire, and on the Cotswolds. In seeking an explanation of the unattractiveness of these villages we must turn to the open fields upon which they depended for their livelihood. These settlements had developed in their heyday a specialised system of farming that involved the cultivation of extensive arable areas under strict communal control. With the reduction in the demand for grain, especially marked after about 1375, the peasantry tended to adopt forms of mixed agriculture with a growing emphasis on pasture. In the woodlands or such districts as the Severn valley change was relatively easily accommodated because there was much enclosure and mixed land use already. A fully-fledged open-field system was less readily adapted to meet the new circumstances. The open fields were not inflexible, but the conversion of arable strips to pasture, piecemeal enclosure, and the increases in the numbers of animals kept on the commons inevitably led to strains and frictions, amply documented in by-laws and presentments of

[62] J.A. Raftis, *Tenure and Mobility* (Toronto, 1964), pp. 153–82.
[63] BL, Add. Rolls 49395–7, 49399, 49422–49432; SBT, DR 98/438, 463a.

offences against customary practices found in the court rolls.[64] The records of our villages *en route* to desertion contain some evidence that the pressures were felt more strongly than in most open-field villages. Customary disciplines and the complex boundaries of strips within the fields were being ignored. At Frampton (Gloucestershire) in 1442 'William Tracey accroached and appropriated for himself . . . $\frac{1}{2}$ acre of land in the tenure of William Tanndy and another $\frac{1}{2}$ acre of the tenure of John Reve . . . and a parcel of meadow lying in the close called Hammes'. In 1466 Henry Tracey was enclosing a large area containing nineteen selions and an acre of land in Frampton's fields.[65] John Knight of Chapel Ascote in 1426 'occupies . . . a selion of the lady's lying on the furlong called *Shortblachment* formerly held by William Churcheman'. By 1451 all Ascote tenants were being reminded to repair their boundary marks.[66] Similar problems of tenants taking over land to which they had no title are also recorded at Compton Verney.

Another threat to the open-field system came from the extension of livestock farming, often to a point when individuals were presented to the manorial courts for overburdening the common pasture. Such presentments are found throughout the region, but rarely for flocks of sheep greater than 300. The case of Henry Tracey, who with men from nearby Toddington, was accused in 1466 of keeping 1,400 sheep on the pasture of Frampton and Naunton, represented a serious threat to the survival of the already declining village of Frampton.[67]

Problems of migration and the strains of open-field farming were found in many villages. We have already seen that such open-field communities as Lighthorne and Quinton came near to the brink, but survived. Did a minority collapse completely because they suffered from inherent disadvantages which pre-disposed them to depopulation? There is no strong evidence that they lay on inferior soils – the majority of villages vulnerable to desertion farmed land of average quality, which had been settled for many centuries before depopulation. Their abandonment seems not to show a retreat from marginal lands, nor a response to any supposed climatic deterioration, as their soils would have been adversely affected by bad weather no more than those of the many clayland or upland settlements that survived.[68]

[64] C. Dyer, *Warwickshire Farming 1349 – c. 1520: Preparations for Agricultural Revolution* (Dugdale Society Occasional Paper, 27, 1981), pp. 31–2.

[65] GRO, D 678/94, 95.

[66] BL, Add. Rolls 49431, 49438.

[67] GRO, D 678/95.

[68] Beresford and Hurst, *Deserted Medieval Villages*, pp. 20–1; for an argument in favour of the climatic theory see G. Beresford, *Medieval Clay-land Village*, pp. 50–4, but this has been rightly criticised, see S.M. Wright, 'Barton Blount: climatic or economic change?', *Medieval Archaeology*, 20 (1976), pp. 148–52.

Some characteristics seem to have been shared by enough deserted villages to suggest common weaknesses. Their tendency, even in their prime, to have been smaller than average, has been conclusively demonstrated.[69] To this may be added the fact that many – 73 per cent in Warwickshire for example – can be regarded as settlements of lesser importance, not the chief village of their parish. The small size and low status of the vulnerable villages could have reduced their attractiveness to existing or potential inhabitants. As they declined yet further in size, they would quickly reach a point when the social balance in the community, for example between the tenants of large holdings and the smallholders they employed, would break down. Smaller communities would lack the facilities of village life; at Chapel Ascote the presence of only one brewer selling ale in the early fifteenth century, and the eventual cessation of ale-selling after 1451, can be regarded as both a symptom of decline, and a further cause of the departure of the remaining villagers. An additional factor promoting emigration was the close proximity of many vulnerable villages to neighbouring settlements so that 80 per cent of Worcestershire deserted villages, for example, lay within a mile of another village.[70] The settlements in some districts were so closely packed in the thirteenth century that desertion could be seen as the thinning-out of a countryside over-stocked with villages.

In view of the unattractiveness of customary tenure, we might expect deserted villages to have had a high proportion of villein tenants in the pre-depopulation period. This is a marked characteristic of the 'to-be-deserted' villages surveyed in 1299 on the bishopric of Worcester estate, and is shared by some of the villages included in the Oxfordshire and Warwickshire Hundred rolls in 1279, but was not a universal feature. We can be more certain of the predominantly agrarian character of the economies of the deserted settlements. Industrialised villages, for example those involved in cloth-making in Gloucestershire or in metal-working in south Staffordshire, do not figure among the deserted settlements.[71]

None of these characteristics provides a single or simple explanation of the vulnerability of villages to desertion, and as well as seeing villages subjected to a process of natural selection, in which the weaker settlements died out, we must also allow for elements of chance, such as the presence of an acquisitive landlord, demesne farmer, or 'kulak' tenant, who helped to seal the fate of some communities.

This investigation has been confined to a single region, and raises the obvious question of whether the deserted villages of the West Midlands were exceptional. Some support for the view that the patterns of

---

[69] Beresford and Hurst, *Deserted Medieval Villages*, pp. 21–6.

[70] Ibid., pp. 28–9, for similar findings in Oxfordshire and Northamptonshire.

[71] In other regions, however, villages involved in pottery manufacture were abandoned.

depopulation depicted here occurred in other parts of England comes from recent excavations of village sites, in which the last phase of occupation can often be dated to the first half of the fifteenth century or earlier, or the excavators have observed evidence of gradual abandonment over a long period.[72] Such archaeological evidence needs to be supported by more detailed documentary research on deserted villages throughout the country. The circumstances and trends that have been suggested here as leading to desertion seem to have been widespread in the period *c.* 1320–*c.* 1520 – the decline in population, the restless movement of people, the crisis in the open fields when the balance between arable and pasture changed, the tensions within village society, and the overall decline in seigneurial authority – so that parallels to the West Midland case histories may well emerge in other regions.

If the line of reasoning presented here is accepted, it should not be taken as evidence of unmitigated economic decline in the later Middle Ages. The grain-producing capacity of the abandoned fields was no longer needed, and the large expanses of grassland that marked the sites of the lost villages helped to increase much needed pasture resources, either for the small-scale producers of neighbouring villages, or for the graziers who developed them into large, specialised, enclosed farms, representing an important innovation in agrarian organisation.

---

[72] From a sample of nineteen sites abandoned before 1500, fifteen were deserted in the fourteenth or early fifteenth centuries; at least six others show evidence of gradual abandonment, mostly between *c.* 1400 and the seventeenth century. These figures are based mainly on interim reports in the *Annual Reports* of the Medieval Village Research Group.

4

Dispersed Settlements in Medieval England:
A Case Study of Pendock, Worcestershire

This is a local study of dispersed settlements in a single parish. It is however intended to contribute to a larger enquiry. How can we explain the variety of medieval settlement patterns? The answer will not be found if we confine our research too narrowly to the details of plan forms. Rather the settlement pattern should be seen as an ingredient in a package that gave each region its special character. The elements within each package include natural resources, agrarian methods, social structures and ties of lordship, which were locked together to form a coherent whole — 'an intricate complex of techniques and social relations' to quote Marc Bloch.[1]

As is well known, modern England can be divided into areas with nucleated villages and those without. The distinction goes back to the twelfth century and perhaps 200 or 300 years earlier. Village England runs down the middle of the country from Northumberland and Durham to Dorset and Wiltshire.[2] Areas of dispersed settlement lie on either side of that zone, though there are also pockets of hamlets and farms within the village-dominated regions, just as a scatter of nucleated villages can be discovered in every corner of the country. Occasionally nucleated villages are found in association with isolated farms. We are talking of predominant forms within each region; exclusive territories and sharp boundaries are sometimes hard to find. Settlement patterns were linked with distinct agrarian systems. The inhabitants of nucleated villages cultivated open fields, often of the two- or three-field type, while the people of the hamlets and isolated farms held land in enclosures or irregular field systems. These formed the lowland landscapes known to the early topographers as 'champion' and 'woodland'. To one modern observer, the neat pattern of enclosure hedges that has replaced the orderly lay-out of open field furlongs has resulted in a 'planned' countryside, while the preservation of old enclosures in the woodlands allows them to be dubbed an 'ancient' countryside.[3] Nucleated villages in their heyday in the thirteenth century depended on extensive arable cultivation; dispersed settlements were linked with a wide range of economic activities, from the intensive grain

---

[1] M. Bloch, *French Rural History: An Essay on its Basic Characteristics* (London, 1966), p.35.

[2] B.K. Roberts, *Rural Settlement in Britain* (Folkestone, 1977), pp. 15–17.

[3] O. Rackham, *The History of the Countryside* (London, 1986), pp. 4–5.

growing of parts of East Anglia to the pastoralism of the north and west, both in woodlands and on uplands.

Villages have attracted a great deal of research in the last forty years, yet the dispersed settlements deserve at least as much attention. After all, the village zone covers less than half of the country, and the high densities of population in the eastern counties meant that in the thirteenth century the majority of people lived in non-village areas. Before the ninth century most settlements were small. Nor is the desire to study dispersed settlements a matter merely of transferring interest from one geographical area to another. If nucleation came at a relatively late date, a study of the areas that resisted that tendency may throw light on the influences that made some regions succumb to village formation.

Four groups of questions can be posed of any settlement type:

1   What are they? What are their different forms?
2   When did they originate?
3   How did they change?
4   Why did they develop? How did they function, and what were they for?

Much progress has been made towards answering these questions in the case of nucleated villages. Firstly, their plans have been subjected to rigorous analysis, and the existence of villages with regular rows ranged along streets and greens has been recognised, especially in the north. Among the more irregular villages of the Midlands researchers have classified plans, and identified polyfocal types, apparently the result of the fusion of a number of smaller settlement nuclei.[4]

Secondly, the date of village origins has been narrowed to the period between the ninth and the twelfth century. There are still many chronological problems to be solved, such as the apparent gap between the abandonment of the small scattered settlements that preceded the villages in the seventh, eighth and ninth centuries, and the earliest period of large-scale occupation in the villages, which is often dated to the eleventh and twelfth centuries.[5] There are likely to have been many local variations in the pace of nucleation, which seems to have happened earlier in Northamptonshire (for example) than in Yorkshire.

Thirdly, after they had formed, villages often grew in size, and could be reorganised. Two nearby villages might fuse, or alternatively a large

[4]   B.K. Roberts, *The Making of the English Village* (London, 1987); idem, 'Village forms in Warwickshire: a preliminary discussion', pp. 125–46 in T.R. Slater and P.J. Jarvis (eds.), *Field and Forest: An Historical Geography of Warwickshire and Worcestershire* (Norwich, 1982); C.C. Taylor, 'Polyfocal settlement and the English village', *Medieval Archaeology*, 21 (1977), pp. 189–93.

[5]   T. Unwin, 'Towards a model of Anglo-Scandinavian rural settlement in England', pp. 77–98 in D. Hooke (ed.), *Anglo-Saxon Settlement* (Oxford, 1988).

settlement might split apart.[6] From the fourteenth century many villages shrank, sometimes changing their shape in consequence, and a significant minority were completely deserted.

Finally, the reasons for nucleation are still debated. Some argue that lords created the villages and also laid out the open fields, to enhance their power and profit. Another school of thought emphasises the environment, and especially the interaction of a growing population with limited resources, which drove the inhabitants to extend the arable, adopt common grazing of fallows, and settle in the midst of their territory to co-operate in the most equitable and efficient exploitation of the land. Such an explanation of nucleation is more likely to draw its protagonists to the conclusion that village communities played an important role in the organisation and planning of their own settlements and fields.[7] Neither view convinces fully. If lords created villages, why is there no strong correlation between the areas of nucleation and the estates of the most powerful lords? And if large rural populations precipitated nucleation, why did this not happen in Norfolk and Suffolk, two of the most densely populated counties in eleventh-century England?[8] Whatever the circumstance of their origin, there can be no doubt of the ways in which the villages functioned at their height, farming according to agreed routines, with a large section of the population holding standard units — bovates or virgates — which governed their share of the villages' resources, and on which rents and services were levied. The inhabitants of a village had to accept a specific balance between public and private space, and were limited by a community interest which could override the selfishness of the individual.[9]

In turning to the same four questions about dispersed settlement, the answers must be more tentative. First, we know that their form varies radically, from the straggle of houses along the lanes and greens of East Anglia, through the hamlet clusters of Devon, to the isolated farms of upland Somerset and West Yorkshire.[10]

[6] C.C. Taylor, *Village and Farmstead. A History of Rural Settlement in England* (London, 1983), pp. 126–65; R.A. Dodgshon, *The Origin of British Field Systems: An Interpretation* (London, 1980), pp. 108–50.

[7] T. Williamson and L. Bellamy, *Property and Landscape* (London, 1987), pp. 29–53; Chapter 1 above, pp. 10–11; P.D.A. Harvey, 'Initiative and authority in settlement change', pp. 31–44 in M. Aston, D. Austin and C. Dyer (eds.), *The Rural Settlements of Medieval England* (Oxford, 1989).

[8] T. Williamson, 'Explaining regional landscapes: woodland and champion in southern and eastern England', *Landscape Hist.*, 10 (1988), pp. 5–13.

[9] W.O. Ault, 'The vill in medieval England', *Proceedings of the American Philosophical Society*, 126 (1982), pp. 188–211.

[10] P. Wade-Martins, 'Village sites in Launditch Hundred', *East Anglian Archaeology*, 10 (1980), pp. 17–75; H.S.A. Fox, 'Contraction: desertion and dwindling of dispersed settlement in a Devon parish', *Medieval Village Research Group Annual Report*, 31 (1983), pp. 40–2; M. Aston, 'Deserted farmsteads on Exmoor and the lay subsidy of 1327 in west Somerset', *Somerset Archaeology and Natural History*, 127 (1983), pp. 71–104; M.L. Faull and S.A. Moorhouse (eds.), *West Yorkshire: an Archaeological Survey to AD 1500*, iii (Wakefield, 1981), pp. 585–613.

Secondly, their origins were once thought to lie entirely in the assarting and colonising movements of the twelfth and thirteenth centuries, as if they were additions to the older established village settlements. Now we know of the ubiquity of isolated farms and small hamlets both in the period 400-800 and in prehistoric and Roman times. It is therefore possible to see at least part of the medieval dispersed settlement pattern as an archaic survival, and it has been suggested that some farmsteads stand on or very near to their Roman predecessors.[11]

Third, early medieval settlements seem very unstable both in shifting their sites and in changing their forms. In East Anglia there appears to have been a change from small nuclei to elongated strings of houses along the edges of greens.[12] In the uplands of northern England and Wales permanent farms developed out of temporary shielings.[13] In the fourteenth and fifteenth centuries the contraction of dispersed settlements could lead to the total desertion of isolated farms and complete hamlets, or the dwindling of clusters down to a single farm.[14] In spite of the general shrinkage, some new isolated settlements were still being founded in the late fourteenth and fifteenth centuries.[15]

Lastly, some of the explanations of the origins and functions of dispersed settlements have to be abandoned in the light of modern research. They can no longer be regarded as 'Celtic' or 'British', as they are found in many parts of the country, not just in the areas where the indigenous population was most likely to survive.[16] Instead we can more fruitfully explore the relationship between the scattered settlements and their irregular and enclosed fields, which could have been carved out of the waste in the course of medieval colonisation, or alternatively might have been inherited from the Roman countryside. Often the farming system had a more pronounced pastoral element than was possible in the orthodox open field system. In the absence of strict communal restraints the farmers of the dispersed settlements could exercise more individual choice in their use of land. The woodlands had a different social structure also. They did not lack slaves in the eleventh century or villeins in the thirteenth, but they also

[11] T. Williamson, 'The development of settlement in north-west Essex: the results of a recent field survey', *Essex Archaeology and History*, 17 (1986), pp. 120–32.

[12] Wade-Martins, 'Village sites'; P. Warner, *Greens, Commons and Clayland and Colonisation* (Dept. of English Local History, Occasional Paper, Univ. of Leicester, 4th ser., 2, 1987).

[13] D. Austin, 'The excavation of dispersed settlements in medieval Britain', pp. 231–46 in Aston et al. (eds.), *Rural Settlements*.

[14] C.F. Tebbutt, 'A deserted medieval farm settlement at Faulkners Farm, Hartfield', *Sussex Archaeological Collections*, 119 (1981), pp. 107–16; R.L. Ellaby, 'A deserted medieval farmstead in Woodlands Field, Earlswood', *Surrey Archaeological Collections*, 75 (1984), pp. 195–205; G. Beresford, 'Three deserted medieval settlements on Dartmoor', *Medieval Archaeology*, 23 (1979), pp. 98–158; Fox, 'Contraction: desertion and dwindling'.

[15] A.J.L. Winchester, *Landscape and Society in Medieval Cumbria* (Edinburgh, 1987), pp. 48–51.

[16] Taylor, *Village and Farmstead*, pp. 110–12.

often contained a high proportion of freeholders. Departures from the rule of primogeniture, whether partible inheritance or inheritance by the youngest son, are more likely to be found outside the nucleated villages.[17] And the population of dispersed settlements in general appears to have been more heterogeneous when we have our most detailed evidence in the late thirteenth century. Many smallholders lived in the woodlands, as also did a large number of craftsmen and others with non-agricultural occupations.[18] The inhabitants of dispersed settlements participated more readily in rebellions in the later Middle Ages, and in later centuries tended to embrace non-conformity and radicalism. Those in authority complained that they were an 'ungovernable people'.[19] This individualistic and rebellious streak can be overstressed however, because the organisation of the vill is found throughout medieval England. Peasants in dispersed settlements had the same obligations as those in nucleated villages to arrange the collection of taxes, representation at the royal courts, and the upkeep of the parish church. Although their fields may not have been as closely regulated as those of champion villages, they still needed to control the grazing of the fallows and the use of common pastures.

Before clear answers can be given to these questions, much more work is needed on dispersed settlements, and the case study of Pendock is a contribution to that research.

Pendock (Worcestershire)

The parish of Pendock lends itself to archaeological fieldwork because it contains both pasture fields with well-preserved earthworks, and arable land suitable for fieldwalking. It is reasonably well-documented and the records of adjoining manors help to fill some of the gaps. The size of the parish (463 ha) made a study over a five-year period manageable; its location on the M50 motorway ensured its accessibility. The chief attraction lay in the supposition that it was an ordinary and unexceptional place — one might be tempted to say typical. It was not the centre of a great estate or minster parish; it was remote from any town; most of its land was of average quality. Its only peculiarity is the extraordinary shape of the parish, as from early times it has been divided into two parts, one a little larger than the other (see Fig. 4.1). These have been distinguished in the past by various names, including Upper and Lower Pendock, but for the sake of clarity they will here be called West and East Pendock. The research method has been

---

[17] G.C. Homans, *English Villagers of the Thirteenth Century* (Cambridge, Mass., 1941), pp. 109–20.

[18] R.H. Hilton, 'Social structure of rural Warwickshire in the Middle Ages', pp. 113–38 in idem, *The English Peasantry in the Later Middle Ages* (Oxford, 1975); J.R. Birrell, 'Peasant craftsmen of the medieval forest', *Agricultural History Review*, 17 (1969), pp. 91–107.

[19] J. Thirsk (ed.), *The Agrarian History of England and Wales*, iv (Cambridge, 1967), pp. 111–12.

to gather every available piece of evidence, from air photographs, earthworks on the ground, pottery and artefacts from the plough soil, standing
buildings, documents and place-names. Inevitably the investigation proceeds
from the known to the unknown, backwards in time, from the certainties
of the modern landscape and maps, through the more doubtful
documentation of the later Middle Ages to the hazardous reconstruction of
earlier settlement patterns. However, the results of the enquiry will be
presented here in proper chronological order from prehistory until modern
times.

Let us begin with the land itself. Champion country in medieval
Worcestershire was confined to the Avon valley in the south east and the
plain east of the county town (see Fig. 4.1). The rest consisted of woodland
landscapes, including the south-west corner of the county, the focus of our
attention, which is bounded by the Malvern Hills on one side and the river
Severn on the other. In relation to the steep slopes of the Malverns, the
district is low lying, though it has an uneven appearance with many small
hills interspersed with patches of former marsh. Pendock occupies rising
ground on the western edge of Longdon Marsh, once the most extensive
wetland in Worcestershire, which remained undrained until the 1870s.[20]
The edge of Pendock Moor, part of this marsh, coincided roughly with the
15 m contour, while the highest point in East Pendock reaches 37 m above
OD, and in West Pendock 53 m. This relatively high ground divides the
streams, which in the east and north run into Longdon Brook, while in the
west the Wynd Brook flows southward via the river Leadon (see Fig. 4.1).
Both stream systems empty ultimately into the river Severn. In the valley
of the Wynd Brook lies a notable landmark, a natural pool known as *Cran
mere* or *Croumere* in the Middle Ages, and now called Cromer Lake. Pendock
has reddish loamy and clayey soils over Triassic mudstones, which are
judged to be of average quality by the Ministry of Agriculture. The two main
soil series represented in the parish are rather similar in terms of modern
agricultural potential.[21] Local opinion rates the land of East Pendock more
highly, and there is more arable in the East and more grazing in the West,
but this may reflect different management, as well as the inherent quality
of the soils. In south-west Worcestershire generally there are small patches
of woodland, and some open grassland, notably at Castlemorton Common.
At the time of Domesday extensive woods are recorded in the area, and in
the twelfth century Pendock lay near the southern edge of the royal forest
of Malvern, which in *c.* 1217 became Malvern Chase, a private forest in the

[20] C.J. Bond, 'The marshlands of Malvern Chase', pp. 95–112, in R.T. Rowley (ed.), *The Evolution
of Marshland Landscapes* (Oxford Univ. Dept. of External Studies, 1981).
[21] Ministry of Agriculture, Fisheries and Food, *Land Classification Maps*, sheet 143; J.M. Ragg
et al., *Soils and their Use in Midland and Western England* (Soil Survey of England and Wales, bulletin
no. 12, Harpenden, 1984), pp. 319–23, 344–8.

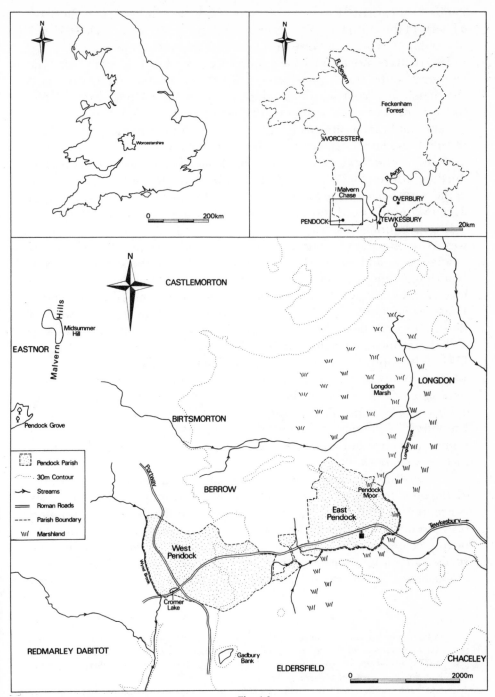

Fig. 4.1
Location of Pendock showing surrounding parishes, relief and selected features.

hands of the earls of Gloucester.[22] Pendock lay in the hundred of Oswaldslow, a liberty of the church of Worcester, though the laymen who held Pendock as tenants of Worcester were the effective lords of the manor.

Two roads of more than local importance passed through Pendock. The east–west route, which now connects Tewkesbury and Ledbury, crossed the marsh at a narrow point, which is now called Horse Bridge. The modern main road, straightened in *c.* 1800, runs through Sledge Green, but another branch (shown on Fig. 4.1) took a more southerly course along the modern Pendock Lane to join the two parts of Pendock. This was called a 'street' in the tenth century and could have been a Roman road. The north–south road which runs along the western edge of Pendock, known as the Portway, may also have been used in Roman times as it forms part of a route running northwards from Gloucester towards the Malverns.

In conventional historical writing settlement in the lowlands of south-west Worcestershire is believed to have begun in the early Middle Ages.[23] It appears as a blank on distribution maps of prehistoric and Romano-British sites, and is an obvious candidate to form part of the impenetrable forests and swamps which were once said to have deterred early settlers. However fieldwalking at Pendock has produced a thin scatter of worked flints, with finds from thirteen locations mainly in East Pendock (see Fig. 4.2). These include small scrapers, which are not closely datable, but are likely to be connected with use of the land in the Neolithic or Bronze Age. Barrows mentioned in a tenth-century charter boundary, preserved in the field name *Crokkeberowe* in the north-west corner of East Pendock (Fig. 4.3a), could be of prehistoric origin. In the Iron Age the minor hillfort at Gadbury and the major one on Midsummer Hill (see Fig. 4.1) provided points of defence and centres of power over rural territories that must have included Pendock.[24]

Romano-British pottery has been found in some quantity over the whole of the modern parish (Fig. 4.2). Two heavy scatters and three lesser concentrations indicate likely settlement sites, and a thinner distribution over twenty-seven sites could arise either from settlements buried too deeply below the modern plough soil for abundant finds to reach the surface, or more often the spreading of pottery with other refuse over arable fields in the course of manuring in antiquity. Almost every modern

[22] *Domesday Book* (Record Commission, 1783), i, fos., 173–4, 180. Domesday leagues have been converted to hectares according to the formula in O. Rackham, *Ancient Woodland* (London, 1980), pp. 113–17. For Malvern Chase see B.S. Smith, *A History of Malvern* (Leicester, 1964), pp. 25–40.

[23] E.g., Smith, *A History of Malvern*, p. 12.

[24] S.C. Stanford, *Midsummer Hill: An Iron Age Hillfort on the Malverns* (Leominster, 1981), pp. 165–6. A sherd of pottery from West Pendock could be Iron Age in date, but is more likely to reflect the survival of a native tradition in the Roman period.

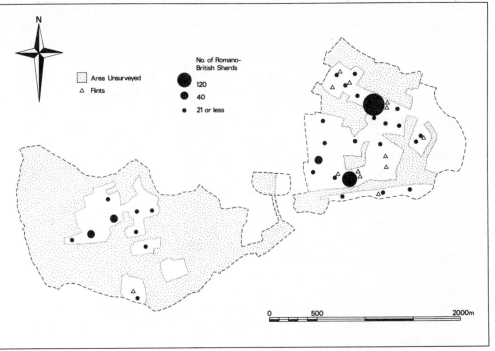

Fig. 4.2
Pendock before the Middle Ages, showing the fieldwalked areas and prehistoric and Romano-British finds.

ploughed field has produced Romano-British pottery; the only exceptions are either low-lying areas which are likely to have been used in Roman times, as they were in the Middle Ages, as moor or meadow, and which therefore would not have been manured, and three hilly fields in West Pendock. The pottery finds consist overwhelmingly (91 per cent) of Severn Valley ware, the locally made coarse pottery. Few specialist or fine wares have been found.[25] This poor ceramic assemblage, together with the absence of building materials, indicates low-status settlements, or native farms to use the customary term. The presence of a few sherds of black burnished ware from Dorset and mortaria from Oxfordshire points to market contacts which must have been directed towards such places as Gloucester to the south, and the wealthy regions of the Avon valley and the Cotswolds in the east. Although the finds from Pendock are not closely datable, their general character places them in the later part of the Roman period. The relatively small size of the concentrated spreads of pottery (which are less than $\frac{1}{2}$ ha), suggests single farms or very small hamlets which

---

[25] I am grateful for Paul Booth's comments on the Romano-British pottery.

lay at least 300 m apart, similar to the density of settlements revealed by aerial photographs in other parts of the region.[26] Population figures for the Roman period can scarcely be calculated on such slender evidence, as we do not know the size of the settlements under the pottery scatters, nor how many other Romano-British sites lie undiscovered under the modern pasture fields. Nor do we know if the sites that have been found were all occupied at the same time. However, it is worth remarking that the Romano-British pottery is more widely distributed, and much greater in quantity, than that of the twelfth and thirteenth centuries. Now all kinds of factors might influence this observation, such as the superiority of Roman mass-production techniques, the wider range of uses of pottery in the Roman period (as drinking vessels, for example), different methods of rubbish disposal and manuring, and finally the durability and visibility of Roman pottery which meant that it is more likely to be discovered in the modern plough soil. Nevertheless we are drawn to the inescapable inference that Pendock could have been at least as extensively cultivated and even as full of people in *c*. 250 as it was to be in *c*. 1250.[27] Even if such an equivalence between the two periods is thought to press too hard on flimsy evidence, there can be no doubt that the Romano-British period and the later Middle Ages mark peaks in the material culture with a considerable trough in the intervening centuries.

The cessation of mass production of pottery at the end of the Roman period removes an important source of evidence for settlement. A British population is likely to have survived in south-west Worcestershire, who came under Anglo-Saxon domination in the late sixth or early seventh century. The place-name Pendock was apparently formed around this time by Welsh-speaking people.[28] Its elements mean a hill and a barley field; the most likely candidate for the eponymous hill is the prominent ridge on which stands the medieval church in East Pendock (defined by the 30 m contour in Fig. 4.1). This hill, though lower than those in the West, would have made a greater impact on the visitor as it loomed dramatically over the marshes. Barley still grows on the plateau formed by the rising ground, and this land has a better claim than any other part of Pendock to have been under continuous cultivation since Roman times.

The overwhelming impression of Pendock's history in the post-Roman centuries, as in Feckenham Forest in north Worcestershire, Wychwood in Oxfordshire and Rockingham Forest in Northamptonshire, is of a retreat

[26] E.g., G. Webster and B. Hobley, 'Aerial reconnaissance over the Warwickshire Avon', *Archaeological Journal*, 71 (1964), pp. 1–22.

[27] For general observations on this problem, P. Salway, *Roman Britain* (Oxford, 1981), p. 544. The field-walking evidence is based on investigation of all land under the plough in 1985–8. The blank areas of Fig. 4.2 were under grass in those years.

[28] E. Ekwall, *The Concise Oxford Dictionary of English Place-Names* (Oxford, 1936), p. 344. I am grateful to Dr Margaret Gelling for advice on Pendock's place-names.

in cultivation and of woodland regeneration.[29] There is a strong contrast between the evidence for extensive settlement and cultivation in the Roman period, and Domesday's testimony to Pendock's large area of wood, which cannot be given a precise area, but might even have covered 400 ha. It was stated in 1086 that the manor of Pendock held of the church of Worcester by Urse D'Abetot contained wood measuring $\frac{1}{2}$ league by $\frac{1}{2}$ league, to which should be added the bulk of an area of wood one league by one league attached to the manor of 'Overbury cum Pendock'.[30] The changes in land use can be demonstrated for individual fields, like Newland in West Pendock and Ruddings in the East, where we find much Romano-British pottery, but which had to be cleared of trees in order to extend the area of cultivation in the twelfth and thirteenth centuries (see Figs. 4.2 and 4.3a).

Pendock and its neighbours in the tenth and eleventh centuries served as wooded appendages of more intensively cultivated manors of the Avon valley. Two belts of wood at the foot of the Malverns, one at Welland and Little Malvern, and another at Berrow and Pendock, were attached to Bredon and Overbury respectively, at distances of 15 and 17 km (see Fig. 4.1).[31] The Pendock-Overbury link is recorded in a charter of 875, but as this is a fabrication it tells us about the administrative arrangements when the forger was at work in the eleventh century.[32] A note in Worcester's early eleventh-century cartulary states that a lease of Pendock of 967 'belongs to Ripple', another Worcester manor in the Severn valley 6 km west of Bredon, and therefore much nearer to Pendock. This might refer to administrative supervision of leased land, but could record a temporary transfer of the management of the woods.[33] Indeed the charter itself helps to strengthen the evidence for the link with the Avon valley (to be strictly accurate, the valley of its tributary, the Carrant Brook), because the land

[29] C. Dyer, *Hanbury: Settlement and Society in a Woodland Landscape* (Dept. of English Local History, Occasional Paper, Univ. of Leicester, 4th ser., 4, 1991); B. Schumer, *The Evolution of Wychwood to 1400: Pioneers, Frontiers and Forests* (Dept. of English Local History, Occasional Paper, Univ. of Leicester, 3rd ser., 6, 1984); Taylor, *Village and Farmstead*, p. 121; see also P.T.H. Unwin, 'The changing identity of the frontier in medieval Nottinghamshire and Derbyshire', pp. 339–51 in B.K. Roberts and R.E. Glasscock (eds.), *Villages, Fields and Frontiers* (British Archaeological Reports International Ser., 185, 1983).

[30] *D.B.*, i, fo. 173; *Evesham A, a Domesday Text*, ed. P.H. Sawyer (Worcs. Hist. Soc., Miscellany, 1960), p. 32 shows that the wood was partly in Berrow.

[31] For Welland see C. Dyer, *Lords and Peasants in a Changing Society: The Estates of the Bishopric of Worcester, 680–1540* (Cambridge, 1980), pp. 70–1. Berrow's connection with Overbury is suggested by the dependence of its chapel on Overbury church: *Victoria County History of Worcestershire* (henceforth *VCH Worcs.*), iii, p. 260; and by the Domesday satellite, *Evesham A*, p. 32.

[32] W. de G. Birch, *Cartularium Saxonicum* (London, 1885–93), no. 541; H.P.R. Finberg, *Early Charters of the West Midlands* (Leicester, 1961), pp. 105–76; P.H. Sawyer, *Anglo-Saxon Charters* (London, 1968), no. 216.

[33] *Hemingi Chartularium Ecclesiae Wigorniensis*, ed. T. Hearne (Oxford, 1723), i, p. 185. The best text of the charter is Birch, *Cartularium*, no. 1208.

leased consisted of two hides at Pendock and one at Didcot, near Overbury. These connections between the arable lands of south-east Worcestershire and the woods of the south west were duplicated on the Pershore estate; this Avon valley monastery held Longdon with its members Castlemorton, Chaceley, Eldersfield and Staunton, places with plentiful woods which surrounded Pendock on three sides. The links between valley and woodland persisted, but not under Pershore's lordship, because much of its estate, including Longdon, was granted by Edward the Confessor to his newly refounded abbey of Westminster.[34] Territorial links over considerable distances are found throughout early medieval England, and are well-known features of counties such as Warwickshire, Kent and Sussex which were divided sharply between arable and wooded districts. The system encouraged regional specialisation: the people in the parent settlements concentrated on grain growing, confident that they could obtain fuel, building timber, and pasture at a distance. It is sometimes alleged that the arrangements linking arable and remote woods were primeval in origin.[35] However, the abundant Romano-British finds from Pendock would not support the idea that there was much wood there in that period, and the whole system of territorial linkages looks like a response to the collapse of marketing after the fall of the Roman administration. There is even a hint, unfortunately contained only in notes of the contents of a now lost charter, that King Alfred was granting Pendock in 888 to an unnamed party, so the association with Overbury may have formed only in the two centuries before Domesday.[36]

Pendock's woods were presumably managed for the benefit of the Overbury manor, with coppicing to yield poles and fuel, and areas of wood pasture for the production of timber. The road system of the area would have included, not just the main route to the east for the carriage of timber and wood and the droving of stock, but also a network of local access tracks for the use of woodmen and herdsmen. The boundary clause probably written in 967 refers to the road to Overbury as a street, and tells us that a bridge had been built to take it over the Longdon Brook.[37] Much of the circuit follows streams and refers to pools and trees in what could be regarded as a 'natural' landscape, but the references to hedges, open land (*feld*), an enclosure (*haga*) and a clearing (*leah*), suggest a wood/pasture landscape, with grazing land and fencing for stock management. The number of personal names mentioned attached to boundary points —

---

[34] B.F. Harvey, *Westminster Abbey and its Estates in the Middle Ages* (Oxford, 1977), p. 360–4; *D.B.*, i, fo. 174.

[35] D. Hooke, 'The Anglo-Saxon landscape', pp. 79–103 in Slater and Jarvis (eds.), *Field and Forest*.

[36] Finberg, *Early Charters*, p. 106.

[37] Birch, *Cartularium*, nos 542 and 1208. I am grateful to Dr Della Hooke for showing me her comments on the boundaries.

Aelfstan's bridge, Osric's pool, and Ealdred's *feld* — gives the reader the impression of a man-made countryside, parts of which were already in the hands of tenants. Clearly by 967 Pendock had embarked on the familiar process, found in woodland dependencies everywhere, by which the former colony became an independent village. Of course, there is no reason to believe that permanent settlement and at least small-scale cultivation ever ceased in East Pendock, so the development did not start from scratch in the early Middle Ages. A stage in growth was marked by the leasing of land to laymen, documented in 967. Haehstan, the first known tenant, was followed by Aethelwyn and Aefod. Northmann in the eleventh century acquired it by inheritance after the church of Worcester had lost control, but handed it back. By the time of Domesday Pendock was held by the powerful sheriff, Urse D'Abetot. A near contemporary source tells us that Pendock was divided between Warner and Walter, presumably Urse's subtenants.[38] Throughout this period we must doubt if Pendock was very populous or profitable. Land at Didcot was included in the 967 lease, presumably so that its fertile fields would supplement Pendock's limited arable resources. In 1086 part of the land, mostly wood and pasture we must suppose, still belonged to Worcester's manor of Overbury, and Urse D'Abetot's manor contained only two plough teams manned by four slaves (three male and one female) with three bordars apparently without ploughs. So, unless Domesday has omitted some category of tenant, such as those paying rents, Pendock's cultivated area attained no more than 200 acres (80 ha), and its population could have been in the region of twenty to forty, depending on whether slaves are regarded as isolated individuals or the heads of households.

Can these historical abstractions be given a topographical reality? It must be supposed that after the post-Roman regeneration, Pendock formed part of a larger area of woodland, including the area now called Berrow (see Fig. 4.1). At an unknown date in the early Middle Ages Berrow and Pendock were separated. Both needed access to the meadow on the Longdon Brook, and it must have been after some complex bargaining that the lion's share went to Berrow. Pendock was split in two, but was compensated with a large piece of meadow connected to West Pendock by a narrow corridor. The maps still oversimplify Pendock's territory, because later documents show that the manor included parcels of land in Berrow, Birtsmorton, Longdon, Redmarley and Corse, though some of these may have been acquired in the later Middle Ages.[39]

[38] *Hemingi Chartularium*, i, pp. 183, 249–50; *D.B.*, i, fo. 173; *Evesham A*, p. 30.
[39] Hereford and Worcester County Record Office (henceforth HWCRO), (Worcester branch), ref. 705: 101, BA 882/2 and BA 1097/1 (rentals of 1464 and 1490).

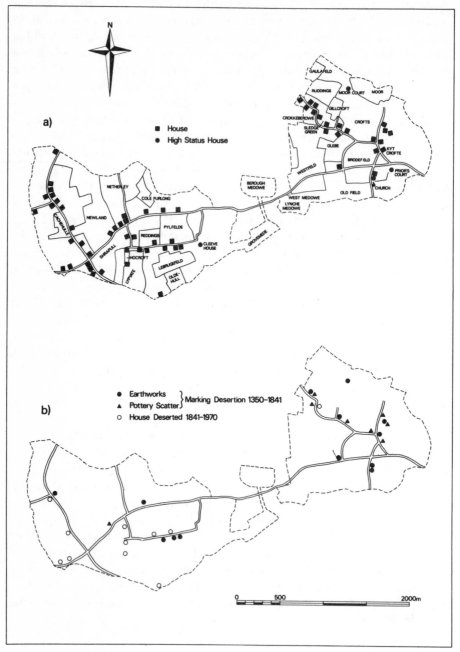

Fig. 4.3
Medieval landscape and settlements, before and after desertion. *a*. Reconstruction of the
houses, fields and roads of Pendock in *c*. 1300, based on a combination of
archaeological and documentary evidence;
b. Known deserted settlements, all periods.

Do the two parts of Pendock represent the tenurial division at the time of Domesday, with West Pendock containing the woods attached to Overbury? All the evidence supports the view that the lay manor of the tenth and eleventh centuries was based on East Pendock where a small nucleus of settlement had always survived. The earliest type of medieval pottery found in fieldwalking, a Saxo-Norman ware probably made at Haresfield (Gloucestershire), comes from the centre of East Pendock, from Broadfield and the Crofts (see Fig. 4.3a).[40] It was in the East that the church was built, probably as part of the wave of parish churches founded by secular lords from the tenth century onwards. The earliest datable stonework is of the twelfth century; if this was not the first building on the site, it is unlikely that its predecessor was built much earlier.[41] The manorial centre presumably lay in the East, so this was the logical place for the new church. It would be tempting to see the curved shape of Broadfield edged to the north and west by a deep holloway (see Fig. 4.3a) as an early seigneurial enclosure.[42] However, while the nucleus of the first manor lay in the East, a reference to ploughed land near Berrow Meadow in the tenth-century charter boundary, and the possession by later lords of demesne lands in West Pendock, make it dangerous to assume that there was a simple division between wooded church property on one side and a lay manor practising mixed agriculture on the other. At least a small amount of cultivation is likely to have continued in the early Middle Ages in the West as well as the East.

To sum up the state of Pendock's development by the late eleventh century: a heavily wooded area had been divided at least a century earlier, and Pendock emerged in two parts which are likely to have consisted of a wood and pasture enclave of the manor of Overbury and a small lay manor. The East would have contained the houses of peasant tenants, accommodation for slaves and the residence of local officials or subtenants of the absentee lay lord. If there were any permanent inhabitants in West Pendock, they are likely to belong to categories commonly omitted by Domesday — administrators protecting the wood and supervising grazing, or tenants paying cash rents.[43]

[40] I am grateful to Dr Alan Vince for his advice on this and other identifications of medieval pottery.

[41] The church is described in *VCH Worcs.*, iii, pp. 480–1. I have benefited from Mr Allan Brodie's comments on the architecture of the church; on the general point on the dating of churches, J. Blair, 'Local churches in Domesday Book and before', pp. 265–78 in J.C. Holt (ed.), *Domesday Studies* (Woodbridge, 1987); idem, 'Introduction: from minster to parish church', pp. 1–19 in idem., (ed.), *Minsters and Parish Churches: The Local Church in Transition* (Oxford Univ. Committee for Archaeol. monograph no. 17, 1988).

[42] For similar shapes, see Roberts, *Making of the English Village*, p. 75.

[43] For Domesday omissions, J.F.R. Walmsley, 'The "censarii" of Burton Abbey and the Domesday population', *North Staffs. J. of Field Studies*, 8 (1968), pp. 73–80; S.P.J. Harvey, 'Taxation and the economy', pp. 249–64, in Holt (ed.), *Domesday Studies*.

In the twelfth and thirteenth centuries Pendock was transformed by the extension of cultivation at the expense of the wood and pasture. This was not 'new settlement' as the *Agrarian History* calls it, but renewed occupation of land that had been under the plough in the Roman period, if not earlier.[44] We know of large-scale clearance in other parts of Malvern Forest in the late twelfth century, and it was in the 1170s that members of the de Pendock family were fined for forest offences, probably assarting.[45] The movement was still going on in 1189 and probably into the thirteenth century.[46] In East Pendock the existing cultivated area was pushed northward into the Ruddings and the Crofts (see Fig. 4.3a). A medieval field name, probably located near Moor Court, *Moor Old,* preserved the memory of former woodland.[47] Colonisation was conducted on a wider scale in West Pendock with the clearance of such large areas as Newland and Netherley in the north. The division of lordship and tenure increased in complexity. The manor held by Urse D'Abetot in 1086 descended in the family of minor gentry called the de Pendocks whose manor house lay near the church (see Fig. 4.3a). In about 1240 part of their land was granted to Little Malvern Priory and its centre was subsequently known as Prior's Court, lying to the north east of the church. The lordship over the lands of Worcester Priory (which had previously been attached to Overbury) by the thirteenth century came into the hands of the Abetot family of Redmarley (who were not the direct descendants of Urse), and their manor was apparently based in East Pendock also, at the moated site of Moor Court (Figs. 4.3a and 4.4d). Also in the early thirteenth century Westminster Abbey acquired a small group of holdings in West Pendock.[48] The de Cleeve family built up a large enough holding in the West in the thirteenth century to enable them to surround their house with a moat, but whether this accumulation can be described as a manor is uncertain (Figs. 4.3a and 4.4c).

The proliferation of small manor houses and moated sites itself contributed to the growth of settlement in Pendock. Peasant holdings also multiplied and the number of messuages (that is, a house and associated buildings standing in a small enclosure or toft) can be estimated from the documents at a little under forty.[49] This could be too low a figure, as it is notoriously

[44]   H.E. Hallam (ed.), *Agrarian History of England and Wales,* ii (Cambridge, 1989), passim. The use of the term was an editorial policy.

[45]   Dyer, *Lords and Peasants,* pp. 63, 91–3; *Great Roll of the Pipe . . . 1175–6* (Pipe Roll Soc., 35, 1904), p. 39; *Great Roll of the Pipe . . . 1176–7* (Pipe Roll Soc., 26, 1905), p. 66.

[46]   *Cartae Antiquae,* ed. J.C. Davies (Pipe Roll Soc., 76, 1957), pp. 189–90.

[47]   Public Record Office (henceforth PRO), C 134/74/11.

[48]   *VCH Worcs.,* iii, pp. 478–81; the location of the de Pendock manor house is implied by the 1322 survey cited in note 47 above.

[49]   If 40 per cent of households paid tax, a common estimate, the fifteen taxpayers of 1327 would imply a total of thirty-four: *Lay Subsidy Roll for the County of Worcester 1 Edward III,* ed. F.J. Eld (Worcs. Hist. Soc., 1895), p. 9; the later rentals (cited in note 39) list thirty-seven messuages and tofts which are likely all to have been occupied in *c.* 1300.

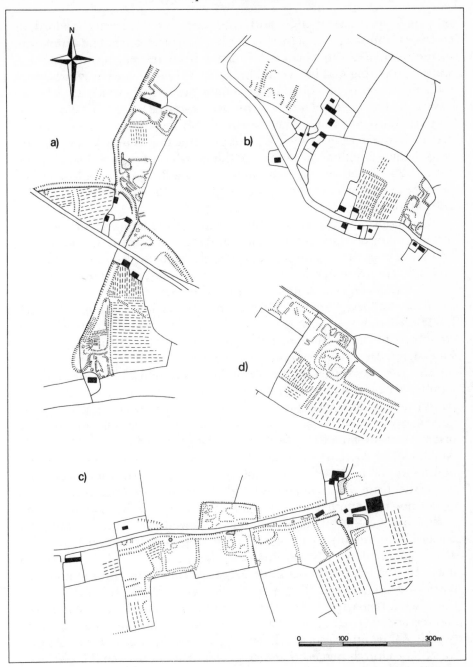

Fig. 4.4
Medieval settlement earthworks at Pendock. *a.* To the north of the church, in East Pendock;
b. At Sledge Green, in East Pendock; *c.* Along Grafton Lane, west of Cleeve House, in West
Pendock; *d.* At Moor Court, in East Pendock. Sketch plans drawn between April 1984 and
February 1988.

difficult to trace either subtenants, who paid no rent directly to a lord, or cottagers who were too poor to contribute to royal taxes. The number of medieval houses can also be calculated from the earthworks, pottery scatters, standing buildings containing early timbers, and by a hazardous estimate of houses inhabited in the nineteenth century which are likely to have stood on the sites of medieval predecessors (see Fig. 4.3a).[50] This yields a figure in excess of sixty, but may inevitably include some new sites not occupied until modern times. We can presume that Pendock's population at its medieval high point in the late thirteenth century stood at between 170 and 250. It had increased dramatically in the 200 years after Domesday, perhaps by as much as tenfold. For comparison, the parish's population in 1801 amounted to 211.[51]

The overall impression of Pendock's medieval topography is of a network of lanes, many of which are still in use, and are characteristically marked by holloways bounded by multispecied hedges, along which houses stood at 100 or 200 metre intervals. Their layout can best be appreciated where the houses have been abandoned and survive as earthworks.

A major holloway runs north from the church in the direction of Pendock Moor (Fig. 4.4a). It now appears to end at the church but originally continued to the south across the parish boundary in the direction of Eldersfield. An area of settlement earthworks immediately to the north of the church could represent the site of the manor house of the de Pendock family, or the rectory, or both. There appear to be two areas of hollows and platforms separated by a small holloway. Further north is a patch of ridge and furrow, a modern house and road, and then the junction with the original east–west road, the two roads merging briefly in a curving holloway. North-east of the curved section are the well-preserved platforms of a house site, and to the west the almost ploughed out earthworks of another house site, from which much medieval pottery has been recovered. Again to the north is another area of faint ridge and furrow, and then more earthworks, including a prominent and well-preserved rectangular enclosure, to the south east of a modern long stable. Another house site, again ploughed away, stood immediately to the north of the stable, on the crest of a hill overlooking the Moor. At the north end the holloway is very deeply marked. This was the droveway along which the village cattle were taken to graze on the Moor when dry summer conditions allowed access. The pottery from the northern house-sites is dated to the twelfth to fifteenth centuries; sherds of earlier pottery from the field to the west of the church suggest that medieval settlement here could have been

[50] *Christopher Greenwood, County Map-Maker, and his Worcestershire Map of 1822*, ed. J.B. Harley (Worcs. Hist. Soc., 1962); HWCRO (Worcester branch), APS 760/516, BA 1572 (tithe map of 1841); ref. 850 BA 2373 (enclosure map of 1843).

[51] *VCH Worcs.*, iv, p. 469.

established by the eleventh century.

Sledge Green (Fig. 4.4b) is now a small hamlet, but its clustered appearance is mainly a product of changes in the eighteenth and nineteenth centuries when the main road was straightened and new houses built. The original medieval features were (running from east to west on the north side of the main road) the sites of one or two houses marked by earthworks and a pottery scatter, followed by a patch of ridge and furrow, part of which lay in an enclosed croft, and then another house, which is a standing timber-framed structure called Broadstock House. Another piece of agricultural land and a group of largely modern houses are followed by the eroded earthworks in plough soil of one or two houses, a site which has produced much medieval and post-medieval pottery. On the south side of the road there is documentary evidence of a messuage, and a fairly dense scatter of pottery near the modern road junction. One or two of the modern houses probably stand on medieval sites. So the medieval Sledge Green was a linear settlement containing nine or ten houses extending over about 800 m. It illustrates both the slow process of decay and the tendency for modern houses to congregate. The house(s) marked by earthworks to the east were abandoned before 1500, but those to the west in the seventeenth century.

Grafton Lane in West Pendock (Fig. 4.4c) runs east–west from Cleeve House, with the medieval holloway slightly to the south of the modern road, though with earthworks suggesting alternative routes on the north side also. Starting in the east there are two moated enclosures, one surrounding Cleeve House. To the south of the lane are two apparently empty crofts defined by ditches, and then a croft containing a large oval platform. This is divided by a modern hedge and an early holloway from a more conventional medieval settlement earthwork, that is a rectangular enclosure with two building platforms. Opposite this to the north of the road is another enclosure with a number of platforms, in which a house stood in the early nineteenth century. Continuing on the south side an apparently empty space is followed by a croft with another building platform, and then two patches of ridge and furrow. The modern house opposite probably stands on a medieval site. About seven houses were spread over a distance of about 800 m.

Moor Court (Fig. 3.4d) lies in a valley bottom, with a complex system of ridge and furrow to the south west and low-lying meadow leading toward the Moor to the north east. The moat, which is still water-filled in winter, was fed from the north east and an overflow leat marked by earthworks ran along the headland of the ridge and furrow to the south east. There is earthwork evidence of buildings on the platform of the moat (with pottery suggesting that it was occupied into the eighteenth century). A platform for a building lay surrounded by ploughing to the south west (a barn?). More platforms and sunken rectangular areas suggest a considerable complex of agricultural buildings, yards and perhaps gardens stretching for almost 200 metres north west of the moat. Moor Court was the centre of a manor which seems to have come into existence after 1086, held by the Abetot family in the thirteenth century.

The main settlement form of Pendock is best described as an 'interrupted row', the term 'row' being borrowed from the vocabulary used to describe nucleated villages, but 'interrupted' because each house or messuage was separated by a piece of land in agricultural use. Houses were sited on both sides of roads, but rarely faced one another. The settlement pattern of Pendock consisted of five interrupted rows, three of which are illustrated in Fig. 4.4, and the others lay along Pendock Lane and the Portway, the main east–west and north–south routes in West Pendock. There were also isolated houses, like Moor Court; it lies on a land use frontier between arable and moor. The same may be true of some of the interrupted rows, as Sledge Green, Grafton Lane, Pendock Lane and Portway all ran beside assarts, and their settlements may have originated as rows of houses on the edge of an open pasture common, like the green edge settlements in East Anglia.

As settlements grew in number the cultivated land was extended in the thirteenth century until it filled almost the whole of the parish. The documents show that much of the area lay under the plough in fields, crofts and furlongs. Extensive ridge and furrow is preserved in the fields now used as pasture, and more was recorded in aerial photographs taken in 1946.[52] The exact date of use of the ridge and furrow must be uncertain though much of it is likely to be medieval, in view of its close relationship to the earthworks of abandoned medieval sites. It belongs to the narrow type, only 3 m to 5.8 m wide, which is characteristic of the woodlands of Worcestershire. The thin scatter of medieval pottery over the modern ploughsoil is a further indication of the areas of manured arable, which complements the evidence of the ridge and furrow. Taken together, these three sources of information show that, with the exception of low-lying meadows on the banks of streams, and the marshes where cultivation would have been impossible, practically the whole of Pendock was ploughed at some time in the Middle Ages (see Fig. 4.5). The land then assarted may not all have been of good quality. It certainly includes fields that have been used as pasture in recent times, and a medieval judgement of the quality of one field, Gaula Field, is conveyed by its name, which means barren and wet.[53] Very little common pasture remained after the expansion of arable apart from greens along road sides, and the important summer grazing on Pendock Moor. Late medieval documents contain no reference to woodland

[52] R.A.F. Sortie no. 106 G/UC 1488/1946 and UC 1652/1946.
[53] J. Field, *English Field Names* (Newton Abbot, 1972), p. 89.

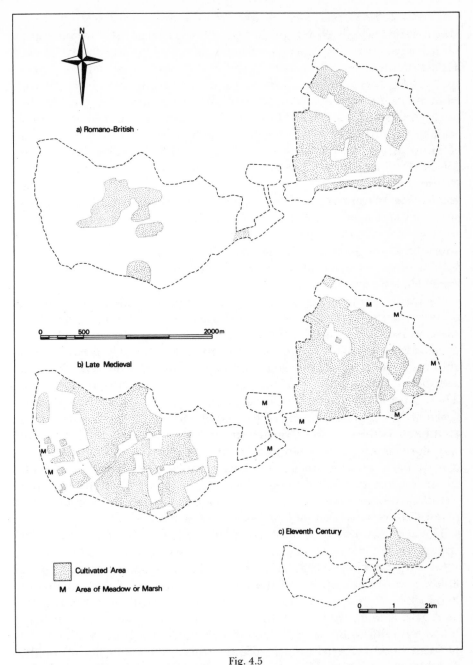

Fig. 4.5

Pendock: land use. *a*. Area of Romano-British pottery scatters, indicating the minimum area that was settled and cultivated; *b*. The cultivated area in the later Middle Ages (twelfth to fifteenth century) reconstructed from documents, ridge and furrow, and pottery scatters; the areas without stipple may have included some arable also, but simply lack evidence; *c*. The possible area of cultivation in the eleventh century, based on a little documentary and archaeological evidence.

at Pendock. Trees probably grew as they do now, on the steep slope of Berrow Hill (east of Cole Furlong on Fig. 4.3a). The names Grovemede and Grafton Lane recall the former existence of a wood to the east of Cleeve House, but this was probably removed in the assarting movement. Trees grew along the many hedgerows around the crofts and fields. In the fifteenth century Pendock's main woodland resources lay outside the parish, in a small wood called Lukes Grove in Birtsmorton, but on a larger scale at Pendock Grove (see Fig. 4.1) which lay in the parish of Eastnor (Herefordshire) on the edge of the Malvern Hills 2 to 3 km from West Pendock.[54] The size of this wood was variously assessed at 23 and 31 acres (9 and 12 ha) when it was surveyed in the early nineteenth century. The earthworks of internal subdivisions now visible show that it has changed size and shape over the centuries, but it could well have been large enough to provide for Pendock's timber and fuel needs. No better demonstration could be found of the completeness of the transformation of a former woodland dependency into a village devoted to cereal cultivation, so that it needed a detached wood of its own.

We can attempt to assess the changing area of cultivation over a period of more than a thousand years. In the Roman period a high proportion of the land available for study, and so by inference most of the territory, was under some form of settlement and cultivation (Fig. 4.2). The area of arable shrank in the early Middle Ages, perhaps as much as is indicated in a speculative reconstruction of the cultivated area in 1086 (in Fig. 4.5b). Then the ploughed area expanded once more until in about 1300 it reached the high level shown in Fig. 4.5a, which was probably similar to the attainment of the Romano-British farmers. In other parts of England there was more continuity between Roman and early medieval cultivation, and consequently a much smaller expansion in the twelfth and thirteenth centuries, but Pendock's story, which may not be so untypical of the woodlands, causes us to be wary of assuming that continuous exploitation of agrarian resources should be found everywhere.

The medieval arable lay in an irregular set of fields, of varying size, and apparently not integrated into any conventional rotational system (see Fig. 4.3a). Whereas in the regular system of champion Worcestershire each holding would be evenly distributed between the two fields, tenants in Pendock held parcels scattered apparently haphazardly over the various fields. For example in 1464 Philip Taylor had $1\frac{1}{2}$ acres (0.6 ha) 'in the field called Shrapull' and $\frac{1}{2}$ acre (0.2 ha) in Lebrugefeld.[55] There was no clear difference between a field and a croft, and some crofts could, like the fields, contain selions cultivated by a number of different tenants. The demesne

---

[54] For Lukes Grove, see rentals cited in note 39; for Pendock Grove, British Library, Add. Ch. 73751 (dated 1450); HWCRO (Hereford branch), OS. 179; Q/R1/17.

[55] HWCRO (Worcester branch), ref. 705:101, BA 1097/1.

of the de Pendock manor in 1322 included seventeen selions and four butts in Jakkescroft, presumably alongside or mingled with selions occupied by others.[56] Most crofts were small, an acre or two (0.4-0.8 ha), and held by a single person in severalty. A holding was often described as 'a messuage with croft adjacent', and this can be seen in the interrupted rows, where the gaps between the messuages were filled with crofts, used either as arable or pasture. So the land of Pendock peasants lay both in small enclosures and in parcels intermixed in the large crofts or fields. The largest of the open fields, Newland and West Field, were not finally enclosed until the nineteenth century.[57]

Without the regular divisions of an orthodox Midland field system, farming at a place like Pendock must have required complex management, in which neighbours in groups (rarely the whole vill) would have had to make some agreement on rotations and the fallow grazing of the fields in which they shared. They lacked the advantage often enjoyed by woodland cultivators that each was 'dwelling in the midst of his own occupying' because although most holdings had the convenience of the adjacent croft, their other lands often lay in remote fields.[58] John de Pendock's demesne in 1322 stretched over both East and West Pendock, and Robert Sandy was not alone among the tenants of 1490 in holding land in both parts of the village, in his case in Kyt Croft and Crokkeberowe in the East and Pylfelde in the West.[59] Cultivation of the land and supervision of grazing stock must have involved Pendock people in as much travel as was needed for the inhabitants of nucleated villages.

Pendock's society enjoyed relative freedom from seigneurial control, but at the same time it was sharply stratified. The eleventh-century manor appears to have depended for its labour on four slaves and three smallholders. Perhaps the descendants of these slaves and bordars became the handful of customary tenants paying high rents of about 1s. per acre later in the Middle Ages. The great increase in Pendock's population after 1086 came from an influx of free tenants, who acquired lands at low rents of between 1d. and 6d. per acre. It was they who occupied the majority of the scattered houses of the village, and in consequence many of them were given surnames deriving from the places where they lived — atte More, de Croumere, atte Cleve, Underhill and so on. They cleared the land, or bought from others newly created fields, and so their surnames became linked with assarts, such as Bykerudyng or Waxmonsrudyng.[60] Those who

[56] PRO, C 134/74/11.

[57] HWCRO (Worcester branch), ref. 850, BA 2373.

[58] The quotation is from William Harrison's *Description of England*, cited by Homans, *English Villagers*, p. 21.

[59] PRO, C 134/74/11; HWCRO (Worcester branch), ref. 705:101, BA 882/2.

[60] Westminster Abbey Muniments (henceforth WAM), 32817 (rental of 1442); Worcester Cathedral Library, B660–B662 (deeds of late thirteenth century, 1309, 1319).

either assarted on a large scale, or who took advantage of the land market, were able to build up substantial holdings. In the decades around 1300 certain names recur paying a large share of the vill's subsidy to the crown, witnessing deeds, or acting as jurors for inquisitions — atte Cleve, Waupol, Wasp, Archer, Danyel and atte More. At the other end of the social spectrum, numerous smallholders, who are hidden from view in the thirteenth century, appear in plenty in the fifteenth when their numbers elsewhere were usually shrinking. At least twenty of them held a messuage and a croft, or a couple of acres of land, or can be assumed to have held little land from the fact that they paid very low rents. Above them were a few middling tenants with between 8 and 22 acres (3 and 9 ha) of land, but they were dwarfed by two very large holdings based at Moor Court and Prior's Court, paying leasehold rents of £3 and £3 6s. 8d. respectively, which must have between them controlled the bulk of the agrarian resources of the village. There is a strong impression in the Pendock records, more so than in those of most manors, that the tenants held land from other lords in nearby villages. This is true of the major tenants like the late thirteenth-century John Waupol who held land at Welland as well as Pendock, and also of the smallholders, who may not have been as poor as their meagre Pendock holdings would suggest.[61]

The differentiation of the Pendock peasants between a few wealthy farmers and the many smallholders resulted from their involvement in the market, which often had a stronger influence in woodland than champion villages. The records of neighbouring Longdon show that its tenants in the late fourteenth century had commercial links with the towns of Tewkesbury and Gloucester, and in 1423-4 John Persones of Pendock paid the substantial fine of 3s. 4d. for trading in Gloucester, presumably for selling agricultural produce. A John Persons, perhaps his son, appears in the rental forty years later as a tenant of 10 acres (4 ha).[62] The high rents paid for the large holdings of Prior's Court and Moor Court could only have been paid out of the profits of selling substantial amounts of surplus produce in distant markets. The medieval pottery tells much the same story as that of the Roman period, in that the bulk of it was made locally, at Hanley Castle, and therefore reflects trade over a very short distance, though pottery from the Forest of Dean and Worcester indicates wider contacts. Pendock peasants also bought the local services of specialist carpenters, judging from the good quality cruck-based timber frames of a barn still standing on Pendock Lane, and a cottage on the parish boundary in Sledge Green.

---

[61] *Lay Subsidy Roll for the County of Worcester circa. 1280 (recte 1275)*, ed. J.W. Willis Bund and J. Amphlett (Worcs. Hist. Soc., 1893), p. 44.

[62] WAM, 21119, 21125; Gloucestershire Record Office (henceforth GRO), GBR, C 9/4 (I am grateful to Dr Richard Holt for this reference); HWCRO (Worcester branch), ref. 705:101, BA 1097/1.

Neither the inequalities of Pendock society, nor its commercial character, nor the divided village territory, would have prevented the necessary growth of some community organisation. The leading villagers assessed and collected the sums of money needed to meet Pendock's quota of taxes for the king. They elected and supported churchwardens who looked after the fabric and material goods of the church, which at a place like Pendock must have been an important unifying focus. Like the people of the nearby vills of Castlemorton and Chaceley, they would have been expected collectively to repair roads and clean ditches. And like the men of Castlemorton in 1377, they would no doubt have mounted resistance to encroachments on their common grazing from other villages.[63]

The people living in woodland landscapes were by no means immune from the late medieval crises: the catalogue of disasters mounted inexorably at Longdon, adjoining Pendock, in the accounting year from September 1348 to September 1349. At least eighteen tenants (a majority) died in the plague epidemic, and the wet weather flooded the meadows and rotted the corn. Two messuages and three cottages burnt down, and the sergeant of the manor had to pay 3s. 10d. in bribes to royal officials who intended to purvey (purchase compulsorily) corn. Tithe corn receipts dropped from 108 qrs in 1340-1 to 67 qrs in 1354-5.[64] But these were merely transient episodes in a long-term decline in population and shift in agriculture from arable to pasture. In 1428 Pendock was listed for tax purposes among the villages which had less than ten households, imprecisely suggesting that a majority of its population had gone.[65] In 1490 twenty-four tenants were listed as holding messuages, which would indicate a total population of just over 100. Rather less than 100 are implied by the fifteen taxpayers in 1525 and the eighteen families listed as resident in 1563.[66] So in the last two centuries of the Middle Ages the numbers of people living in Pendock had diminished by more than a half, very much in line with the national trend. Many of the previously inhabited messuages were abandoned. The 1490 rental lists five tofts (former messuages without buildings) and at least six other messuages were threatened with decay because they were held by tenants with more than one holding. Two others belonged to absentee tenants with homes in other villages. The retreat of settlement is indicated directly by the earthworks of a dozen house sites, and eight concentrated scatters of medieval pottery (see Fig. 5.3b). The material evidence reminds us that the desertion of house sites has been an almost continuous process,

[63] WAM, 21120, 21124, 21123.

[64] WAM, 21019, 21037–21045; the calculation of the rate of mortality depends on GRO, D 1099/M37; Harvey, *Westminster Abbey*, p. 433.

[65] *Feudal Aids*, v, p. 314.

[66] HWCRO (Worcester branch), ref. 705:101, BA 882/2; PRO, E179 200/136; T.R. Nash, *Collections for the History of Worcestershire* (London, 1781–2), ii, pp. 241–2.

as, judging from the pottery, occupation ceased at one site (to the north of the church) in the fourteenth century, and at others in the fifteenth, whereas another (at Sledge Green) produced finds of both medieval and post-medieval pottery and was not abandoned until after 1600. Desertion continued in recent times; two of the sites now visible as earthworks were marked as standing buildings on early nineteenth-century maps, and a total of ten buildings existing in 1841 have now gone.

Settlement desertion clearly affected places such as Pendock, but did not result in the departure of all the tenants. Nor were arable lands converted wholesale to pasture, as some of Pendock's fields remained in cultivation in the later Middle Ages. We are discovering more than just shrinkage and decay. The later Middle Ages saw much tenurial consolidation at Pendock, in which formerly separate holdings merged. Waupol's tenement, for example, was absorbed by its neighbours in the fifteenth century, and above all the various manors — those of the de Pendocks, the Abetots, and Little Malvern Priory, were united in the fifteenth century under the lordship of a branch of the Throckmorton family.[67] All of this made messuages redundant, including the manor house of the de Pendocks. In modern times the chief mansions of the village were to be Moor Court and Prior's Court. A process of migration within the parish has quickened in pace in the last 150 years. This has partly reflected the consolidation and enclosure of land holdings, and the arrival of growing numbers of villagers whose living did not depend directly on agriculture. Some areas, near the church for example, have lost inhabitants, and clusters of houses have developed at Sledge Green in East Pendock, and at the cross roads near Cromer Lake in the West. In 1889 so far had the centre of gravity shifted to the west that a wooden church was built near Cromer Lake, and after another century the medieval church has been declared redundant.

Conclusion

Can any better answer be given to the questions posed at the beginning of this essay, in the light of the study of Pendock? First, the arrangement of roads, houses and fields at Pendock amounts to a specific settlement type, the interrupted row. Similar patterns recur in other parts of west and north Worcestershire, and published plans show interrupted rows as far apart as South Wales and East Anglia.[68] Many other forms of dispersed settlement

[67] *VCH Worcs.*, iii, pp. 479–80.

[68] H.J. Thomas and G. Dowdell, 'A shrunken medieval village at Barry, South Glamorgan', *Archaeologia Cambrensis*, 136 (1987), pp. 94–137; D. Dymond and E. Martin (eds.), *An Historical Atlas of Suffolk* (2nd edn., Ipswich, 1989), pp. 70–1, For a description of the type, A. Davison et al., 'Six deserted villages in Norfolk', *East Anglian Archaeology*, 44 (1988), p. 59.

are known (see p.50) and the next stage of research must be to gather more data and compile distribution maps of the different plan types.

A contrast is often drawn between the regularity of the nucleated village and the informality, even the disorder, of the dispersed settlements, but patterns such as the interrupted row cannot have formed without some degree of organisation. This should not surprise us, because 'irregular' field systems are often found to have been worked in practice on a regular rotation.[69] As in the laying out of a nucleated village, so in the allocation of house sites in a dispersed settlement, both the lord and the community would have had an interest. In particular in the case of an interrupted row each new messuage and croft (we presume that they were added piecemeal) encroached on the common pasture of the existing inhabitants, and the community of the vill could therefore have had a view on the development of sites. The lord claimed rights over the common also, and expected the newcomers to recognise his superiority and pay a rent.[70]

Secondly, the origin of the occupation of the land, at Pendock as in many other woodland areas, goes back into prehistory. But that should not imply a precise continuity in settlement sites. In only one example at Pendock does a concentration of Roman finds coincide with a medieval pottery scatter. Indeed the Romano-British sites in East Pendock lie well apart from the later medieval houses, on land used in the Middle Ages as open fields and arable crofts. It is possible, but unlikely, that Romano-British sites are hidden under the pasture fields containing medieval earthwork sites; nearby arable fields have produced only thin scatters of Roman sherds. Woodland regeneration over a large area in the post-Roman centuries guaranteed an interruption in settlement continuity. Although no pottery of the period 400 to 1000 has been found at Pendock, analogy with Frocester and Roel in nearby Gloucestershire, where grass-tempered pottery has been found on sites that were not occupied in the later Middle Ages, and with eastern England where pottery scatters of the period are more abundant and more closely datable, would lead us to expect that the settlements of that period were subject to instability.[71]

Pendock's interrupted rows were mainly created in the twelfth and thirteenth centuries, but the road with its houses running north of the

[69] Hallam (ed.), *Agrarian History*, pp. 370–4.

[70] A good example of the regularisation of a new house is in the Longdon court roll for 1373 (WAM, 21116). John Muchegros was reported to have built a house 'of two couples' (i.e. of one bay) on the common of Chaceley. The villagers knew first, and perhaps had consented. They reported it to the lord's court, which accepted the new encroachment on payment of a fine of 6d.

[71] For Frocester, H.S. Gracie, 'Frocester Court Roman villa, Gloucestershire', *Transactions of the Bristol and Gloucestershire Archaeological Society*, 89 (1970), pp. 15–86, especially pp. 50–2; for Roel, finds by the author and D. Aldred; for the general instability, Taylor, *Village and Farmstead*, pp. 120–1.

church could well have been laid out before the Conquest. Evidently the notion that dispersed settlements were formed in the post-Conquest assarting movement is not the whole story. Interrupted rows could have originated as a settlement form in the tenth and eleventh centuries, or even earlier, judging from their existence at places with much better evidence for a large pre-Conquest population than Pendock.[72] There is always the possibility, familiar from the work on nucleated villages, of wholesale reorganisation and replanning of dispersed settlements in the eleventh and twelfth centuries. Only extensive excavation will resolve the problem.

The third conclusion is that dispersed settlements experienced change and decay just like the nucleated villages. In the case of the interrupted rows growth could have been accommodated by extending the houses along the road system with only limited damage to agricultural activity. Documentary evidence suggests that the crofts and tofts were infilled by cottages for subtenants and relatives, though this is not readily apparent in the earthworks of abandoned sites.[73] One could imagine, as has been argued for similar German settlements, that a progressive nucleation could occur as the gaps between houses filled up, but such a far flung pattern as is found in places like Pendock could only form a compact village through wholesale abandonment of outlying houses.[74]

In decline from the fourteenth century the interrupted row could be thinned by the loss of individual houses avoiding the traumas that affected many nucleated villages. The associated agrarian system was both resilient and adaptable. An example would be Forncett (Norfolk), which lost a half of its bond tenants by 1565 but without a collapse of the village economy.[75] The desertion of a whole settlement, and the total conversion of its fields from arable to pasture, was much more commonly experienced in the champion than in the woodland settlements. Nucleated villages, with their specialised and unified agricultural systems, were vulnerable to adverse changes.[76]

And finally we should not regard dispersed settlements as failed nucleated villages, or think of them as marking a primitive evolutionary survival of a proto-village. They were a very successful and long-lived settlement type, and the combination of scattered houses and irregular fields gave the inhabitants many economic advantages. At some stage in the pre-Conquest period different regions embarked on different paths of development. To

[72] E.g., Frocester, Glos.: M. Aston and L. Viner, 'The study of deserted villages in Gloucestershire', pp. 276–93 in A. Saville (ed.), *Archaeology in Gloucestershire* (Cheltenham, 1984), especially fig. 10.

[73] Z. Razi, *Life, Marriage and Death in a Medieval Parish* (Cambridge, 1980), pp. 51–7.

[74] E. Eigler, 'Regular settlements in Franconia founded by the Franks in the early Middle Ages', pp. 83–91 in Roberts and Glasscock (eds.), *Villages, Fields and Frontiers*.

[75] D. Dymond, *The Norfolk Landscape* (London, 1985), pp. 140–1.

[76] See above, Chapter 3, pp. 42–4.

continue with the biological analogy, they are the equivalent of sheep and goats, different branches deriving from a common ancestor.

The problem lies in explaining why they diverged. It may be that the common ancestor is an illusion. The Romano-British settlements that preceded the nucleated villages of Northamptonshire, for example, seem to have been fewer and larger than those that underlie a woodland settlement like Pendock. The distribution of Roman industries dependent on wood fuel, notably pottery-making and tile-making, suggests the presence of woods in such areas as west Worcestershire and north Warwickshire, in the same places where they existed in the Middle Ages.[77] But such a line of argument would merely push the problem back into an earlier period, not resolve the reason for the differences. In the Middle Ages the environment of the champion areas undoubtedly differed from that of the woodlands. The people of Pendock may have eventually cleared its woods and extended arable cultivation over a high proportion of the village's territory, but this came late, a century or more after the period of village formation elsewhere. And even at the end of the colonization Pendock retained the grazing of the moor and a general flexibility in the use of land that most champion villages lacked. But variations in land use form part of the package of differences between champion and woodland landscapes. Did contrasts in geology and soils determine the type of rural landscape? Environmental factors had some influence, but the differences in soils cannot always be judged to have been very great, and the same soil type can be found in districts with divergent settlement patterns.[78] The argument that increasing population densities forced the champion into nucleation cannot be the sole explanation, as the woodland areas did not necessarily support lower densities of people. At the time of Domesday, for example, south-east Worcestershire, a land of nucleated villages either in formation or completed, had as many people per sq. km as parts of east Suffolk, which probably had a dispersed settlement pattern then, and certainly did later.[79] Perhaps in any case the demographic characteristics of a region depended on its agrarian regime, and did not independently determine the settlement and farming system.

If 'natural' factors such as soils or population densities do not solve the problem, neither can ethnic or social differences provide an easy explanation. Pendock belonged to a sphere of British influence, but no close coincidence is apparent between settlement types and the assumed distribution of

[77] On the larger Northants. nucleations see the plans by D. Hall, e.g. in 'The late Saxon countryside: villages and their fields', pp. 99–122 in Hooke (ed.), *Anglo-Saxon Settlements*; on Roman woodland, G. Webster, 'Prehistoric settlements and land use in the West Midlands and the impact of Rome', pp. 31–58 in Slater and Jarvis (eds.), *Field and Forest*.

[78] The soil series of Pendock, for example, Whimple 3 and Worcester, extended into champion areas of the E. Midlands, see Ragg, *Soils and their Use*.

[79] H.C. Darby, *Domesday England* (Cambridge, 1977), pp. 90, 127.

ethnic groups. Pendock's lordship was divided and weak, but a similar lack of powerful lords is found in many nucleated villages. Pendock's neighbours, with a similar pattern of settlement and fields, lived under the powerful rule of Westminster Abbey. The suggestion that the circumstances in which the Germanic conquest took place had a profound influence on the subsequent pattern of development seems unlikely, in view of the remoteness of the conquest from the period in which the different settlement types were formed.[80]

Rather than seeking a single explanation of local differences, we must expect to find that regional cultures, then as now, were forged from a complex combination of environmental and social factors. Soils, social structures and lordship may not on their own have determined the distinction between champion and woodland, but acting in combination they may have had a cumulative effect. We need to do more groundwork in describing and analysing the variations in regional cultures.

---

[80] For the suggestion, Williamson, 'Explaining regional landscapes'.

5

Changes in Diet in the Late Middle Ages:
The Case of Harvest Workers

For generations knowledge of medieval agriculture has advanced, yet still we have hazy notions of the consumption of foodstuffs, especially by the lower ranks of society. A greater awareness of eating patterns can help our understanding of the social structure, so that such categories as 'wage-earners', 'peasants' and 'gentry' can be visualised in terms of their different material standards of life.[1] If we can learn more about diet we will be better able to test the hypothesis that the low nutritional status of large sections of the population in the early fourteenth century ended a century or more of increasing numbers and began a long period of demographic stagnation.[2] Finally, information about the use of crops should provide new insights into the aims and methods of agricultural production.[3]

The search for information about diet leads us to employ a great deal of indirect evidence, by analysing the grain allowances made to retired peasants for example, or by examining the grain liveries given to full-time servants on manors (*famuli*), or by sifting through bones and plant remains found as accumulated rubbish on archaeological sites. These and other areas of study are valuable sources of data, but they all tend to throw light on sections of the diet only, and often their use must be surrounded with uncertainties of interpretation.

The records contained in manorial accounts of the food and drink given to harvest workers provide a sample of lower-class diet over a long span of time, from the mid-thirteenth to the mid-fifteenth century. For this reason harvest workers' diets are worth investigating, and the first part of this essay will contain a survey of their food consumption. However, the harvest workers were not typical of the whole labour force, and the later part will attempt to define their position within the social hierarchy of living standards, and to explore the wider implications.

[1] For a continental example see L. Stouff, *Ravitaillement et Alimentation en Provence aux XIVe et XVe siècles* (Paris, 1970).
[2] M.M. Postan, *The Medieval Economy and Society* (London, 1972), p. 34; J.Z. Titow, *English Rural Society 1200–1350* (London, 1969), pp. 64–96; G. Bois, *The Crisis of Feudalism* (Cambridge, 1984), pp. 268–9.
[3] E.g. I. Blanchard, 'The continental European cattle trades, 1400–1600', *Econ. Hist. Rev.*, 2nd ser., 39 (1986), pp. 427–60.

Most manors paid their harvest workers a cash wage. On the minority of manors which are the subject of this enquiry, mostly in southern and eastern England, the labour force was given both cash and food. The group of workers who brought in the harvest included the *famuli*, the permanent staff of the manor, who for the 'autumn' (a period of four to seven weeks) received an enhanced cash wage and meals instead of the usual combination of cash and grain. They were joined by workers hired specially for the harvest (both for the duration, and for shorter times), and by administrators. For example, at Sedgeford (Norfolk) in 1273 thirty-four people were said to be 'resident at table', including the supervisors, that is, a sergeant, reeve, hayward and tithe collector, and the *famuli*, including the herdsmen and two dairymaids. Eleven extra hands were hired for the full 'autumn' of thirty-nine days, and four for ten days only.[4] A dairymaid *(deye)* did some of the food preparation, but usually a cook was employed full-time.

Before analysing the food issued on these occasions, we must consider the nature of this important part of the farming year. The participants worked hard over long hours cutting corn with sickles, binding the sheaves, tossing the sheaves into carts for carriage back to the manorial *curia*, and there 'pitching' the corn onto stacks. The work sometimes had to be hurried, 'for fear of rain' as the accounts say in justifying an extra tip given in encouragement. The intensity of pre-mechanised harvest work has been recorded by nineteenth-century observers, and the illustrator of the early fourteenth-century Luttrell Psalter, with his eye for the grotesque, has captured in the bent backs and strained faces of his figures some of the harsh toil involved.[5]

The harvest was a time of high labour productivity, when workers could keep up the pace better if they ate plenty of food, and employers gained from generous treatment of the workers. It was also a period of intense competition for labour, when the lords of manors, demesne farmers, rectors, and better-off peasants all needed hired hands. Labour mobility reached a peak in August, as people left their homes and normal occupations in search of good pay in the harvest fields. Even in the years around 1300, when labour was relatively abundant before the epidemics of 1348–9, village by-laws were requiring the able-bodied to accept employment in the harvest at 'a penny a day with food', instead of running off to other villages, or making a living by gleaning.[6] After 1349 the struggle for labour intensified, and many harvest workers came before the justices for offences under the Statute of Labourers, accused of demanding and receiving excessive rates of pay, and of breaking contracts in order to take the

[4] Norfolk RO, DCN 60/33/4.
[5] B. Bushaway, *By Rite* (London, 1982), pp. 107–38; G. Ewart Evans, *Ask the Fellows who Cut the Hay* (London, 1965), pp. 85–93; E.G. Millar (ed.), *Luttrell Psalter* (London, 1932), pp. 97–9.
[6] W.O. Ault, *Open-Field Farming in Medieval England* (London, 1972), pp. 29–34.

opportunities of the season. The cases show that daily wages doubled at harvest time, and that workers were also offered high lump sums (such as 6s. 8d.) and inducements in kind to work for the whole season.[7]

Because harvest workers were a special case, their diet, which formed an important element of their total pay, was superior to that of wage-earners in other occupations. The employers had the resources to provide ample supplies, in return for which they were able to recruit a large, willing and efficient workforce; they no doubt hoped that if well treated the workers would return in subsequent years.

Although the peculiar characteristics of the season and its workers should be borne in mind, they should not undermine entirely the value of studying the harvesters as a group of medieval wage-earners. We are not dealing with a single and exceptional day, like the reaping boon when all tenants turned out to do a day's labour service and were rewarded with a special meal. The autumn normally lasted for about five weeks, or a tenth of the year, more than an insignificantly transient episode in people's lives.

And the harvest workers formed a wide cross-section of the lower ranks of medieval society. Among the *famuli* some were no doubt youths labouring in the early years of their life-cycles, and others included married smallholders like Henry le Driver, the ploughman at Cuxham (Oxon) who was still working on the demesne at the age of about fifty in 1348, and widowed cottagers like Chaucer's *deye*, with her two daughters, three pigs, and three cows, who is of course fictional, but was recognisable as a type to an audience of the 1390s.[8] The temporary employees would also have included smallholders without the ties (or the security) of full-time work on a demesne, and members of their families. Workers in such industries as building and textiles abandoned their jobs for higher pay in August.[9] Temporary migrants came from towns, like the forty-six 'cokeres' from King's Lynn, who worked at Sedgeford in 1378.[10] Itinerants travelled from further afield, notably the bands of Welshmen who worked in the midlands in the autumn. At Brancaster (Norfolk) in 1368 three 'flemynges called Pekkeres' (presumably from Picardy) were hired.[11] All sources agree that both sexes joined in the harvest, for example at Appledram in Sussex in

[7] S.A.C. Penn, 'Wage-earners and wage-earning in late fourteenth century England', Research Report for the ESRC (Birmingham, 1986), p. 51.

[8] M.M. Postan, *The Famulus*, Economic History Review Supplement, 2 (1954); A. Kussmaul, *Servants in Husbandry in Early Modern England* (Cambridge, 1981); P.D.A. Harvey (ed.), *Manorial Records of Cuxham, Oxfordshire, c. 1200–1359* (Historical Manuscripts Commission, JP 23, 1976), p. 763; idem, *A Medieval Oxfordshire Village: Cuxham, 1240–1400* (Oxford, 1965), pp. 77, 125; F.N. Robinson (ed.), *The Works of Geoffrey Chaucer*, 2nd edn. (London, 1957), p. 199 (Canterbury Tales, vii, lines 2821–46).

[9] Penn, 'Wage-earners and wage-earning', pp. 17–31.

[10] Norfolk RO, Le Strange MSS 1B 3/5.

[11] PRO, SC6 931/8.

1450 wages were paid to 'various men and women harvesting, at the lord's table'.[12] A few better-off peasants (who would generally have been busy bringing in their own crops) would have been present at the demesne harvest by virtue of their tenure of such offices as reeve and hayward. By an unusual arrangement at Lullington (Sussex) the supervisors only were fed at the manor and the workers fended for themselves.[13] The sergeant or bailiff, often recruited from the lesser gentry, was the highest ranking of the residents, though monks or senior administrators sometimes stayed on the manor for a few days to keep an eye on the work. These fleeting visits did not usually have much influence on the types or quantities of food consumed.[14] In short, the main body of the harvest workers ranged from the upper peasantry to landless servants, with the great majority at the bottom end of the social spectrum. They included young and old, men and women, townsmen and villagers, householders and itinerants, English and foreigners, people working normally in both industry and agriculture, and those in both continuous and intermittent employment; they represent a varied sample of the whole medieval labour force.

Wealthy monasteries figure prominently among those known to have been employers of harvest workers who ate at the lord's table; they include Norwich Cathedral Priory, Battle Abbey, and St Swithun's Priory Winchester. Also the harvest is associated with paternalistic customs, like the many perquisites granted to customary tenants performing labour services in the autumn.[15] Is it therefore possible that the accounts which contain harvest diets are very unrepresentative, recording the generosity of 'good' lords, well in excess of normal provisions? This is unlikely, first because documents from the manors of minor landowners – gentry and very small monastic houses – show a similar autumn dietary regime; and secondly because great lords were very cost-conscious, and employed auditors to make sure that workers did not receive pay greatly in excess of the going rate. Peasant and seigneurial employers were competing in the same labour market, and both gave workers in the late thirteenth century a daily wage of '1d. with food', and presumably there was some comparability between employers in the payments in kind as well as in cash.

[12] Millar, *Luttrell Psalter*, p. 97; S.A.C. Penn, 'Female wage-earners in late fourteenth-century England', *Agricultural History Review*, 35 (1987), pp. 1–14; PRO, SC6 1018/24. See also M. Roberts, 'Sickles and scythes: women's work and men's work at harvest time', *History Workshop*, 7 (1979), pp. 3–28.

[13] PRO, SC 6 1024/1–2, 4–5, 8, 15; 1016/1.

[14] At Mildenhall (Suffolk), in 1323–4, the visitors included the cellarer of Bury St Edmunds, his entourage, and the estate steward, so wine appears among the harvest expenses: Bodleian Library, Suffolk Rolls, no. 21.

[15] A. Jones, 'Harvest customs and labourers' perquisites in southern England, 1150–1350: the corn harvest', *Agricultural History Review*, 25 (1977), pp. 14–22; Bushaway, *By Rite*, for a general discussion.

Feeding the Sedgeford Harvesters

Sedgeford has been chosen as an example because of the manor's remarkably long series of accounts, and the detailed information that they contain. They were compiled for Norwich Cathedral Priory, a house famous for its thorough accounting methods.[16] The form of the paragraph in each document headed 'Costs of the Autumn' is ideal for this analysis because the use of cash is given in detail. Many of the foodstuffs came from the manor's own resources, and are recorded twice, under the autumn costs, and on the dorse of the account. The information is imperfect in ways that are common to all medieval accounts. The officials in charge of the manors inevitably cheated the lord, by claiming more than the real expenditure. The harvest costs seem to have been subject to frequent disputes between officials and auditors, judging from the number of alterations on the documents. The vigilance of the auditors is our guarantee that the amounts are not ludicrously over-stated, and our trust in their professionalism receives some reassurance from the marginal notes in which they checked the figures by calculating the number of people receiving bread from a bushel of grain, or the daily cost of food issued to one employee.[17] The quantities are likely to be somewhat exaggerated, but were not fictitious. An administrative complication at Sedgeford arises from the existence of two manors, Easthall and Westhall; the former may have provided goods for the Westhall employees without any reference appearing in the accounts, but this is unlikely. Some items are absent from the accounts because they involved no expenditure of money, notably the vegetables from the manor's garden. Also the documents are silent about the distribution of foodstuffs among the workforce. For example, the meat included such delicacies as doves and poultry, which were likely to have been reserved for the supervisors and not shared equally among the workers. The main problem in using the accounts, however, is that they do not record the actual recipients of the foods. Judging from the vast quantities, the workers must have been handing over much of the food either to assistants or to their families. We know that in later periods harvest workers sometimes worked as teams with wives and children.[18] It is also possible that some food was sent out of the temporary harvest household to dependants. Certainly the diets that we are investigating must have been consumed by a much wider circle of people than the accounts reveal.

[16] E. Stone, 'Profit-and-loss accountancy at Norwich Cathedral Priory', *Transactions of the Royal Historical Society*, 5th ser, 12 (1962), pp. 25–48.

[17] This type of checking calculation was recommended in auditors' text-books; e.g. D. Oschinsky (ed.), *Walter of Henley* (Oxford, 1971), pp. 417–45.

[18] D.H. Morgan, 'The place of harvesters in nineteenth-century village life', in R. Samuels (ed.), *Village Life and Labour* (London, 1975), pp. 29–72; idem, *Harvesters and Harvesting* (London, 1982), pp. 23–5, 59. Cf. K.D.M. Snell, *Annals of the Labouring Poor* (Cambridge, 1985), pp. 52–3.

Sedgeford lay in the 'good sand' district of north-west Norfolk.[19] The sown acreage of the demesne sometimes exceeded 400 acres before the Black Death, and shrank to 268 acres by 1424. The land was used to grow barley with some wheat, rye, peas and oats. Stock kept on the manor included a dairy herd of about two dozen cows in the late thirteenth century, together with pigs and poultry, and a large flock of sheep.

Every year between twenty and fifty full-time workers appear on the harvest pay-roll of Sedgeford.[20] The content of the diet issued to them is indicated by Table 5.1, which gives the percentage of each type of food calculated by value. In the thirteenth century the bulk of the supplies was produced on the demesne, so the values have been estimated from current prices, mostly given in the Sedgeford accounts or from accounts of manors as near as possible to Sedgeford. In the fourteenth and fifteenth centuries more food was purchased, and the accounts themselves provide valuations for the products of the manor. Long-term and short-term variations in prices have influenced the figures, but they reflect changes in quantity rather than prices. Violent short-term fluctuations did not occur in the years chosen for analysis, and the long-term decline in grain prices was to some extent offset by the substitution of wheat for cheaper grains in the

Table 5.1
Analysis (by value, in percentages) of foodstuffs consumed by harvest workers at Sedgeford
(Norfolk), 1256–1424*.

Year	1256	1264	1274	1286	1294	1310	1326	1341
Bread	41	48	49	47	48	43	39	34
Pottage corn	1	1	2	2	1	1	1	1
Ale	13	7	11	12	16	14	17	21
Meat	4	4	7	14	8	8	11	9
Fish	13	16	12	12	9	10	10	17
Dairy produce	28	24	19	13	18	24	22	18

Year	1353	1368	1378	1387	1407	1413	1424
Bread	31	19	15	14	17	20	15
Pottage corn	1	1	1	1	1	1	1
Ale	26	28	22	20	33	29	41
Meat	15	25	24	30	28		28
Fish	14	13	15	23	10	} 50	6
Dairy produce	13	14	23	12	11		9

* All columns total 100%

[19] J. Williamson, 'Norfolk', in P.D.A. Harvey (ed.), *The Peasant Land Market in Medieval England* (Oxford, 1984), pp. 84–102.
[20] Norfolk RO, DCN 60/33/1, 2, 4, 5, 7, 10, 14, 19, 25, 30, 31; Le Strange MSS 1B 1/4, 3/5.

Table 5.2
Food allowances at Sedgeford (Norfolk) in
1256 (1443 man-days).

Food		Amount per man-day (imperial)	Amount per man-day (metric)	Kcal (%)	
Bread	1 qr 7 bu.wheat ⎱ 27 qrs 2 bu.barley ⎰	6.99 lbs	3,171 g.	9,602	(74%)
Pottage	1 qr 2 bu.oats	2.49 oz.	71 g.	285	(2%)
Ale	8 qrs 4 bu.malt	2.83 pt	1.61 l.	513	(4%)
Meat	1 pig ⎱ 20 fowls and ⎬ 6s. 8¼d. spent ⎰	3.68 oz.	104 g.	243	(2%)
Fish	170 mulwell ⎱ 1,050 herrings ⎰	15.52 oz.	440 g.	694	(5%)
Dairy produce	120 eggs	0.12 oz.	3 g. ⎱		
	602 lbs cheese	6.67 oz.	189 g. ⎬	1,630	(13%)
	518 gall milk	2.87 pt	1.63 l. ⎰		
				12,967	(100%)

1424 (906 man-days)					
Bread	3 qrs 4 bu. wheat	1.97 lbs	894 g.	1,994	(40%)
Pottage	4 bu. oats	1.59 oz.	45 g.	180	(4%)
Ale	12 qrs malt	6.36 pts	3.61 l.	1,154	(23%)
Meat	3 pigs ⎱ 1 bullock ⎪ 8 sheep ⎬ 8 geese and ⎪ 10s. 0d. spent ⎰	16.87 oz.	478 g.	1,169	(23%)
Fish	30 cod	3.46 oz.	98 g.	135	(3%)
Dairy produce	Cheese, milk, butter eggs – calculated as 224 lbs cheese	3.96 oz.	112 g.	336	(7%)
				4,968	(100%)

later part of the period. Therefore the main reason for the trends shown in Table 5.1 is the change in the actual quantity and quality of different foods issued, not movements in prices. The information is provided in approximate ten-year intervals, so far as the uneven survival of the documents allows. The figures usually derive directly from the documents. Estimation has been used only in the case of the oatmeal for the pottage, for which the accounts usually give the quantity only for the whole year, and for milk which is often stated to be the product of the cows during the autumn, which has to be calculated from the yield before and after the harvest period.

Table 5.2, which attempts to quantify the diet in two sample years by giving the items provided, and the share of each person per day, is much more speculative than Table 5.1. Meat and fish have been put together, though in reality they would have been eaten on separate days according to the church's rules. The figures for shares rest on questionable assumptions about the weight of foods, the translation of medieval into modern measures, the amount of waste in preparation, and the calorific values of medieval foods (the assumptions behind the calculations are given in Appendix 1). As noted above, the very large quantity of food allowed for each person, much in excess of the 2000–3600 calories now regarded as a normal adult's daily intake, must be explained by assuming that helpers and families were being fed out of the harvest allowances, and consequently no certain judgements can be made of the actual quantity eaten by individuals each day. Nor should the reduction in the size of the shares between the late thirteenth and early fifteenth century be taken as evidence of a decline in food intake. Over the period the method of payment shifted; at the beginning the average pay of individual workers for the harvest period was a little over 2s. in cash, with food allowances worth about 2d. per day, while in the 1420s the cash wage for the season had risen to about 7s. each and food allowances were valued by the auditors for the accounts at around 1½d. per person per day. So workers after the Black Death were receiving a higher proportion of cash, and food allowance of lower quantity and value, but of generally higher quality. The valuations of the individuals' allowances in both cash and calories suggest that in the thirteenth century (when skilled workers were paid about 3d. per day) the harvest workers were getting enough to feed a whole family, while after the Black Death they received a good proportion of a household's needs and the rest would have come from any land held by them or from purchases. The mechanics of food distribution among assistants or families are not known. The accounts insist that the grain was milled and baked and the malt brewed, so the workers were receiving prepared food and drink, not sacks of grain. Medieval bread was often kept, even in aristocratic households, for days, even a week, before consumption, so it could have been sent out occasionally to dependants. Liquids, like pottage and ale, were more difficult to transport in quantity, so it seems likely that they were consumed by the harvest workers themselves.

The diet of the thirteenth century revealed by these accounts is characterised by a high proportion of bread, with a great deal of dairy produce in the form of cheese made from the manorial cows earlier in the summer, and milk from the cows during the harvest season. Together these two elements totalled about four-fifths of the calorific value of the food issues. The malt could have provided a share of two or three pints (1.3–1.7 litres) of strong ale, in which case, in view of the heat and sweat of the harvest field the workers must have drunk much milk and water. A more likely way of using the malt would have been to brew a larger quantity of thinner ale (four or five pints?), though even then some other drink would have been needed to quench the thirsts of these active workers, especially in view of the unrecorded numbers of assistants or relatives receiving some of the ale.

Changes in the diet are apparent in the early fourteenth century (see Table 5.1), when the percentage spent on bread declined, and the value of the ale increased. By 1341 enough malt was provided to give as much as five pints (2.8 litres) of strong ale for each worker on the pay roll. After 1349 these trends were emphasised, with the value of bread corn, once a half of the total spent, falling to only a fifth, while the brewing malt rose from about an eighth to a quarter of the budget. By the early fifteenth century the quantity of malt would have been sufficient to give shares of six pints (3.4 litres) of the best ale, or a gallon of thinner stuff (4.5 litres), though each person, allowing for undocumented helpers, may have received a smaller amount. Perhaps Hillman's advice to farmers brewing for the harvest, written in 1710, indicates earlier practice: 'make three sorts of beer, the . . . strongest for your own use, the second is what is called best beer, whereof each man ought to have a pint in the morning before he goes to work, and as much at night as soon as he comes in. . . . Small beer they must also have in the field.'[21] Meat increased greatly in importance in the late fourteenth century, from a tenth or less of the food budget to a quarter or a third of the total, while dairy produce, and at a later stage, fish, declined. In terms of nutritional values, the allowances of the fifteenth century contained much fewer calories deriving from cereals consumed in the form of bread. Meat, which contributed a negligible proportion of calories two hundred years earlier, was now a source of a fifth or more of the total.

Another way of expressing the changes in the balance of the diet would be to set the ale aside and concentrate on solid foods. In that case, bread in the third quarter of the thirteenth century accounted for about a half of the total cost, and meat between 4 and 8 per cent, while in the early fifteenth century a quarter of the expenditure went on bread, and 42–47 per cent on meat. For every 2 lb of bread that they ate in the thirteenth century, the workers received an ounce or two of meat and about 5 oz. of fish. A century and a half later, for every 2 lb of bread workers were allowed a pound of meat and 3–4 oz. of fish.

The quality of the foods also changed. Bread was baked mainly from barley in the thirteenth and early fourteenth century. Wheat accounted for less than 8 per cent (by volume) of the bread corn, and probably the sergeant and other supervisors ate the wheat bread, along with other 'luxuries' such as poultry. An increase in the proportion of wheat and rye

---

[21] T. Tusser, *Five Hundred Points of Good Husbandry* (Oxford, 1984), p. 305.

at the expense of barley is apparent in 1341, and continued rapidly until the wheat and rye amounted to almost a half by 1353, and by 1387 barley bread had disappeared completely from the harvest food allowances. Then the proportion of wheat increased until it replaced rye entirely in 1407. In this year, the bread which was purchased for holidays when the Sedgeford baker took a rest was described as 'white', suggesting the use of flour with a high extraction of bran. When wheat replaced barley as the main bread corn the daily quantity dropped sharply to about 2 lb per head, so presumably the workers were exchanging quality for quantity, and gave a much smaller proportion to assistants.

The meat provided in the thirteenth century consisted mainly of bacon. Fresh beef was included from as early as 1286, and after the mid-fourteenth century the proportion of beef rose until three cattle were being slaughtered in some years; also in the fourteenth century fresh mutton was being added to meat supplies. Towards the year 1400 the allowance of meat for each officially listed worker had reached a level near to a pound per day, counting only the carcass meat, and a chance statement in the account for 1387 makes it clear that the offal was also consumed. Fish supplies consisted mainly of salt cod and preserved herring throughout the period, though its unpopularity is suggested by the diminishing quantities issued in the late fourteenth century, and fresh fish (that is, fresh sea fish) is mentioned for the first time in the early fifteenth century. Presumably the harvest workers kept the same pattern of meat and non-meat ('fast') days as did aristocratic households, observing fast days on Fridays and Saturdays, on the vigils of feasts, and perhaps also on Wednesdays, in which case it might be expected that the average quantity of meat would be equal to, or rather greater than, the weights of fish. Before 1349 fish exceeded meat, suggesting that cheese was eaten, either with the meat, or instead of meat on non-fast days. After the mid-fourteenth century the situation was reversed, and as the meat increased and the fish dwindled the cheese would have supplemented the fish. However, the quantities of dairy produce declined in the long term, being displaced by meat and perhaps (for liquid milk) by ale. No change in the types of milk-products is known, though butter is specifically mentioned for the first time in 1309 and regularly thereafter.

The physical arrangements for the harvest workers' meals can be glimpsed from hints in the accounts. At least one meal each day was eaten *ad mensam*, at the lord's table, set out in the hall of the manor house. A canvas tablecloth five ells long was bought in 1378, but a longer table would have been needed to seat all of the workers of that year, and perhaps only the supervisors enjoyed the privilege of a covered board. Expenditure on candles suggests that either some eating or food preparation took place in the dark, leaving the daylight hours for work in the field – unless such work as carting or stacking sometimes continued after dusk.[22] The morning meal, *prandium*, was eaten out-of-doors, judging from the employment of a servant to carry food and drink *versus campum* (to the field). The food was eaten from dishes, plates and bowls of wood bought for the purpose, together with wooden spoons; the brewing required the purchase and maintenance of large vessels. The custom of feeding harvest workers helps to explain why estates maintained manor houses which were used only rarely as residences for the lords.

To sum up, the Sedgeford records give a picture of harvest workers and their dependants of the thirteenth century sitting down to heavy meals of barley bread and cheese, accompanied by a little salt meat or preserved fish, with ale, milk and water to drink. Their successors of the fifteenth century were issued with ample quantities of wheat bread, nearly a gallon of ale per day, and (except on fast days), large portions of fresh meat.

Harvest Diets from Other Manors

The custom of feeding harvest workers at the lord's table was especially common in Norfolk, but is found sporadically in the records of manors in other counties. Information for comparison with Sedgeford has been obtained from seventeen manors, five in Norfolk, four in Hampshire, two each in Suffolk and Sussex, and single manors in Huntingdonshire, Lincolnshire, Oxfordshire and Warwickshire. There are broad similarities between the general trends at Sedgeford and these other manors, and some important variations.

First a general tendency can be recognised for the balance of the diet to shift from cereal-based foods (bread, oatmeal pottage and ale), towards meat, fish and dairy produce, which the accounts sometimes call *companagium* (literally, 'that which goes with bread'). At Hindolveston, another Norfolk manor on the same estate as Sedgeford, the bread element amounted to about a half (by value) in the mid-thirteenth century, and was reduced to 28 per cent in 1362 and 15 per cent by 1412.[23] At Martham in north-east Norfolk, in a much more fertile, intensively cultivated district, the proportion of expenditure on bread fell in a similar way from 48 per cent in 1266 to 16 per cent in 1389.[24] At both of these places the amount of meat increased markedly over the same period, from a tenth to more than a quarter of the food budget. On a different estate (that of Merton College, Oxford), at Cuxham (Oxon) the value of the cereal-based foods amounted to 69 per cent of the total in 1297, and by 1357 had fallen to 58 per cent, with a

---

[22] Night harvesting in Norfolk is attested in *c.* 1710; ibid., p. 305; see also Ault, *Open-Field Farming*, pp. 36–7.

[23] Norfolk RO, DCN 60/18/1, 14, 30, 38, 59.

[24] Norfolk RO, DCN 60/23/3, 23; NNAS, 5899/20 D1.

corresponding increase in the proportion of *companagium*.[25] The importance of the change in the mid-fourteenth century is indicated by the figures from Thurlby (Lincs) where the proportion of meat in the harvesters' food budget increased from 8 per cent in 1341 to 26 per cent in 1362, and the ratio between cereal-based foods and *companagium* changed from 77:23 to 56:44.[26]

Secondly, as at Sedgeford, there was a tendency for a greater proportion of cereals to be used for brewing rather than baking, with ale accounting for 16 per cent of the value of the supplies in 1287 at Appledram (Sussex), but 30 per cent and above in many years between 1341 and 1450.[27] A more modest increase is found at Cuxham, from 30 per cent in 1297 to 37 per cent in 1357.

Thirdly, the content of the *companagium* changed, the proportion of meat rising while that of dairy produce decreased. This was especially marked at Hindolveston and Martham. At Appledram in 1375 an explanation to the auditor shows that fresh meat was being deliberately substituted for dairy produce: 'and no more [cheese and butter] because six wethers and ewes were expended in the autumn, and three geese'.[28]

Variations from the Sedgeford example are mainly apparent in the types of food eaten. In Norfolk in the thirteenth century barley and rye were the main bread corns, though in the early fourteenth century the Hunstanton harvest workers were given maslin bread (wheat and rye).[29] Elsewhere the move towards wheat as the main or sole bread corn was a marked development of the fourteenth century, and the change had often been completed by the 1380s. The workers at Mildenhall, a Suffolk manor of Bury St Edmunds Abbey, advanced slowly and the proportion of wheat issued to them rose from a third in 1324 to below a half in 1382, when maslin and rye bread still accounted for much of the total.[30] In other counties, notably in Hampshire, Oxfordshire and Sussex, harvest workers were given wheat bread even in the late thirteenth and early fourteenth centuries. An exception is Combe (Hants) where 39 per cent of the harvest bread in 1307 was baked from *beremancorn* and the rest from wheat, and the harvesters at another Hampshire manor, Chilbolton, ate mainly wheat bread but a quarter or a third of the bread was baked from barley in the

[25] Harvey (ed.), *Manorial Records*, pp. 281–588.

[26] PRO, SC 6 914/6, 7.

[27] PRO, SC 6 1016/5, 7, 9, 12, 13, 14, 15, 18; 1017/1, 4, 5, 6, 8, 10, 11, 14, 16, 18, 20, 24, 25; 1018/22, 24.

[28] PRO, SC 6 1017/8.

[29] Norfolk RO, Le Strange MSS BG 4; NH 4a; G.H. Holley, 'The earliest roll of household accounts in the Muniment Room at Hunstanton for the 2nd year of Edward III', *Norfolk Archaeology*, 21 (1920–2), p. 95.

[30] Bodleian Library, Suffolk Rolls, no. 21; British Library, Add. Roll 53, 116.

decades around 1300, and the barley was replaced by wheat in the course of the fourteenth century.[31]

On southern manors before 1349 cider often provided a major part of the drink supplied to harvest workers, even exceeding the quantity of ale supplies. On such manors as Appledram, Lullington and Chilbolton in the late fourteenth century cider was replaced by ale, though at the first manor it continued to make an intermittent appearance after 1370.[32]

In Norfolk the meat mainly eaten by harvest workers changed from bacon to fresh beef. Similarly at Cuxham bacon figured prominently in the diets of the 1290s, and fresh mutton was added during the fourteenth century. Mutton appeared for the first time in the Appledram accounts in 1354 and then became a normal feature of the harvest workers' diet for at least the next century. At Manydown (Hants) mutton already figured prominently among the types of meat in 1338, and the innovation of the late fourteenth and fifteenth centuries was the introduction of quantities of fresh beef.[33] Poultry, especially geese, formed a fairly consistent minor element in harvest food supplies throughout the later Middle Ages. Traditionally geese were fattened on the grain that lay among the autumn stubble, and then slaughtered for a celebratory feast, called the *ripgoos*; they may also have been served on the 'high table' of the bailiff and supervisors throughout the whole season.[34]

While recognising the improvement in the meat allowance, some reservations should be made about the quality of the provisions. While medieval taste did not entirely share our preference for young animals, some appreciation of such meat in aristocratic households is indicated by the calves, piglets and lambs served in addition to predominantly mature animals. The harvest workers were generally given animals too old or too inadequate to perform their normal functions on the manor; the accounting officials were anxious to impress this on the auditors who might have questioned the use of high quality stock for this purpose. Hence the procession of ancient bulls, enfeebled oxen, sterile cows, and *kebb* (culled) wethers and ewes slaughtered for the harvest workers. When those at Mildenhall (Suffolk) were supplied with two heifers, the auditors were informed that the beasts were thought to be diseased – perhaps the harvest

---

[31] M. Chibnall (ed.), *Select Documents of the English Lands of the Abbey of Bec* (Camden Society, 3rd ser, 73, 1951), pp. 149–52; J.S. Drew, *The Manor of Chilbolton (Hants)*, Typescript in the Institute of Historical Research, University of London.

[32] See notes 13, 23, and 31 above.

[33] G.W. Kitchin, *The Manor of Manydown, Hampshire* (Hampshire Record Society, 1895), pp. 150–8; Winchester Cathedral Library, box 29, nos 47, 49.

[34] Tusser, *Five Hundred Points*, p. 178.

workers were not told of this.[35] As at Sedgeford, on other manors they consumed the offal of animals killed for the harvest.

The fish purchased for the autumn meals usually included some type of salted white fish and either red or white herrings. At Appledram after 1370 and in 1384 at Boarhunt (Hants) the harvesters ate fresh fish as well as the preserved kinds.[36]

Harvest workers were provided with pottage, which was also given to the full-time *famuli* all year round, when they received no other food apart from their liveries of grain. Oatmeal, and sometimes peas and beans, provided the basis of this dish. The other ingredients to some extent remain a mystery, except that at Catton (Norfolk) in 1274 5d. was spent on *olera* (vegetables) for pottage.[37] Normally such crops as onions and leeks were grown in the garden of the manor, and because they involved little expenditure, were not mentioned in the accounts. There is direct evidence at Lakenheath (Suffolk) where in 1329–30 the garden of the manor was leased out on condition that vegetables were still supplied for the pottage of the *famuli*.[38] In view of the relatively small effort that went in general into manorial gardening, certainly in terms of payments of cash, the production of vegetables must have been severely limited in quantity. Their virtual omission from the documents was not just accidental – it is a measure of their small importance in the eyes of lords and their officials. The vegetables contributed flavour to the meals, like the garlic supplied to the Cuxham harvest workers in 1357.[39] Salt is mentioned as a separate item in some accounts, but more often it came from the manors' general supply.

The domestic arrangements of the other manors resembled those of Sedgeford. At Catton, because the harvest workers collected rectorial tithes as well as bringing in the demesne crops, in 1274 they were 'at table' both in the hall of the manor, and in the 'church house'. Treen utensils were in use everywhere, and the purchase of a linen tablecloth at Wibtoft (Warw) in 1377 shows that Sedgeford was not unique in providing such a refinement.[40]

The detailed chronology of dietary change deserves closer investigation. Clearly the pattern of consumption changed most rapidly when the size of

[35] Feeding old animals to the harvest workers was advised by Hillman in the early eighteenth century: 'a cow or two, some fatted crones (old ewes) may be timely provided . . . and if you have but plenty, and fat, provided it be sweet, your guests will ask no further questions: for at this time they do expect a full diet': Tusser, *Five Hundred Points*, p. 302.

[36] Hampshire RO, 5 M50/72.

[37] Norfolk RO, DCN 60/4/5.

[38] Cambridge University Library, EDC 7/15/11/1/8 M5, M13. (Transcript by Miss J. Cripps in the School of History, University of Birmingham).

[39] Harvey (ed.), *Manorial Records*, p. 577. Saffron and pepper were provided, probably because a fellow of Merton College was visiting.

[40] British Library, Add. Roll 49,748.

the whole labour force fell precipitously in 1348–9, but the diets cannot be simply resolved into those prevailing before and after the plague. The Sedgeford figures show a definite downward movement in the proportion of the budget devoted to bread in 1341, and the beginning of the substitution of wheat and rye for barley. Another Norfolk manor, Catton, has more plentiful documents for the early fourteenth century, and they confirm a decline in expenditure on bread and an increase on meat long before the Black Death, even beginning as early as the 1290s.[41] Rye generally replaced barley on this manor in the early fourteenth century, and by 1339 wheat and rye together accounted for more than half of the corn used for baking bread. Similarly the introduction of fresh meat appears everywhere in the early fourteenth century, in 1317 in the case of mutton at Cuxham. So in diet, as with other indices of economic change, the Black Death appears as intensifying and accelerating processes that had begun in previous decades – it was not an initiator of trends.[42]

Nor did the first major epidemic lead to an immediate transformation of harvest workers' dietary standards. The shift in the balances of the diet between cereal-based foodstuffs and *companagium*, the rise of fresh meat to become the most important non-cereal food, and the emergence of wheat as the main bread corn, all worked their way through the system for fifty years and more after 1349. The peak of dietary improvement seems not to have been reached until the fifteenth century.

In addition to the long-term trends, food consumption was affected by year to year fluctuations in grain production. At Catton in 1322–3, a bad year, the price of barley had risen from the usual 3s. or 4s. per quarter to 8s., 9s. and 10s., and rye cost 10s. per quarter.[43] The quantity of grain allocated to the harvest workers did not change, but the estate managers stopped providing rye for bread as they had done regularly for more than twenty years, and the bread was therefore made entirely from the less-costly barley. They economised slightly on ale, meat and dairy produce, but still provided foodstuffs worth 64s., compared with a normal 30s. to 50s. The extra expenditure was perhaps judged to be profitable because of the high value of the harvested grain. In extreme shortages like the great famine of 1315–17 in Yorkshire, monastic employers did not scruple to lay off servants to save cash and grain.[44] The managers at Catton did not choose the harsh option of beating their workers down to a bare minimum when there must have been a queue of potential employees. Instead they

[41] Norfolk RO, DCN 60/4/1, 5, 6, 11, 15, 22, 25, 36.

[42] M.J. Hatcher and E. Miller, *Medieval England: Rural Society and Economic Change, 1086–1348* (London, 1978), pp. 240–51.

[43] Cf H.E. Hallam, 'The climate of eastern England, 1250–1350', *Agricultural History Review*, 32 (1984), pp. 124–32.

[44] I. Kershaw, *Bolton Priory* (Oxford, 1973), pp. 52–8.

responded predictably by switching to cheaper cereals, by using cereals for bread rather than for ale, and by economising on non-essential animal products. Independent wage earners and peasants presumably changed their consumption in years of shortage, but in much more extreme ways, for example by cutting out completely ale and animal products.

Medieval Diet in Relation to Harvest Workers

The study of the food given to harvest workers ought to have wider implications. Can we simply state that a normal lower-class daily diet throughout the Middle Ages contained thousands of calories with ample quantities of bread and *companagium*, and that the balance between cereals and meat improved considerably over the period 1250–1450?[45] The answer must be decisively negative. We must attempt to define the relationship between harvest workers' diets and those consumed by wage-earners of all kinds, especially in the nine-tenths of their lives when they were not working in the harvest field, and also to see how the harvest diets may have compared with those of peasants who consumed their own produce.

It is a simple task to show that some of the people who worked in the special circumstances of the harvest ate less well at other times. Some of those 'at the lord's table' on Norfolk manors were the demesne *famuli*, and the allowance of grain that they normally received was consistently inferior in both quantity and quality to the grain consumed in the autumn. The *famuli* received barley as their livery throughout the period, while the harvest workers were given a growing proportion of rye and wheat. The livery outside the harvest season increased in quantity during the upheavals of the fourteenth century, from a quarter every ten weeks (about $4\frac{1}{2}$ qrs. per annum) to a quarter every eight weeks ($5\frac{1}{2}$–6 qrs. per annum). This was marginally inferior to the allowance in the harvest season which often exceeded a bushel per week. For most of the year the *famuli* cannot have consumed much drink and *companagium*, as the 4s. per annum cash wage of a *famulus* in the early fourteenth century , rising to 13s. 4d. per annum a century later, would not have bought ale, meat, fish and cheese on the same scale as in the autumn. The same inequality between harvest provisions and daily fare is found throughout the country: the Cuxham *famuli* were given a mixture of 'currall' (low grade wheat), dredge (barley and oats), and peas, while the harvest workers ate wheat bread; and at Manydown (Hants) in the 1440s, where the harvesters were similarly well-fed, the *famuli* received barley and *berecorn* (winter barley). The *famuli* did not necessarily live entirely off their wages and liveries, as some of them had smallholdings,

---

[45] H.E. Hallam, *Rural England, 1066–1348* (London, 1981), p. 15, apparently supports this view.

but it seems likely that their liveries reflect the types of grain eaten by agricultural wage-workers generally.

Nor is it likely that the householding peasantry would have eaten as well as the harvest workers. There is some similarity between the types of grain issued to harvest workers and the allowances of grain made to retired peasants (including better-off peasants) under the terms of maintenance agreements. So, for example, in the early fourteenth century retirement allowances in Hampshire contained wheat as a third or a half of the total, not unlike the breadcorn consumed by the harvest workers of Chilbolton, Combe and Manydown.[46] Sedgeford peasants in the 1260s agreed to accept for their maintenance combinations of rye and barley, similar but rather superior to the mainly barley bread eaten by the harvest workers.[47] Also the emphasis on dairy produce and bacon in the pre-1349 harvest diet would have been typical of the peasantry. There, however, the resemblance ends, because only an extreme optimist would expect peasants to eat as much dairy produce, fish, or meat as did the harvest workers. At Sedgeford in the late thirteenth century forty or so harvest workers had the use of the products of twenty or more cows, whereas the better-off peasants who had a cow or two would only have drunk a little milk and would have made as much cheese as possible in the summer and autumn for consumption during the winter.[48] The wealthiest peasants may have consumed more food than usual in the harvest time, and offered workers a share that was comparable with that provided by their rival employers in order to obtain labour, but they would have eaten more frugally at other times. Peasants were better off than harvest workers overall because of the relative security of their source of income, while the harvesters taken on in August would not all have had a guaranteed job from October to July. To quote a fourteenth-century poem, in words attributed to a herdsman, 'Better were meles many than a mery nyghte.'[49] The smallholding peasantry were especially disadvantaged in the bad harvest years, because they would not have produced enough from the land to feed themselves, and their meagre earnings would not have bought much extra food.

The ratio between cereal-based foods (bread, oatmeal, ale) and *companagium*, measured in terms of value, provides a means of comparing diets. After the advance of the fourteenth century the harvest workers achieved a ratio of about 50:50. This places them well above the paupers of

---

[46] I am grateful to Dr J.Z. Titow for letting me see his transcriptions from the pipe rolls of the bishopric of Winchester (in Hampshire RO) of maintenance agreements.

[47] Norfolk RO, DCN 5282; I am grateful to Dr J. Williamson for this information.

[48] M.M. Postan, 'Village livestock in the thirteenth century', in *Medieval Agriculture and General Problems of the Medieval Economy* (Cambridge, 1973), pp. 214–48; R.H. Hilton, *A Medieval Society* (2nd edn, Cambridge, 1983), pp. 109–10.

[49] I. Gollancz (ed.), *Winner and Waster* (Oxford, 1921), l.365.

Sherborne hospital, Dorset, in 1439–40 (78:22) and somewhat superior to the carters employed by the same institution (62:38), or building workers at Bridgwater, Somerset, in 1420 (63:37), or building workers at Wyre Piddle (Worcs) in 1377–8 (58:42).[50] Before the Black Death the harvest workers' provisions were markedly inferior to those of minor aristocrats. The accounts of Thurlby (Lincs) of 1341 (see Table 5.3) record both the harvest costs and the household expenses of the prioress of the poor nunnery of Stamford.

Table 5.3
Expenditure on food at Thurlby (Lincs),
1340–1[51].

	Harvest workers	Prioress and companions
Bread	7s. 1d. (22%)	3s. 4d. (21%)
Pottage	6d. (1%)	—
Ale	17s. 8d. (54%)	3s. 2d. (20%)
Meat	2s. 8d. (8%)	8s. 2d. (53%)
Fish	3s. 6d. (11%)	3d. (2%)
Dairy Produce	1s. 2d. (4%)	3d. (2%)
Spices	—	4d. (2%)
TOTAL	32s. 7d. (100%)	15s. 6d. (100%)

Not only are the differences indicated by the ratios of cereal foods to *companagium* (77:23 for the harvest workers, 41:59 for the prioress), but the prioress also consumed such luxuries as spices and piglets. In the 1450s however, the ratio of 50:50 is found in the budget of the chantry priests of Bridport (Dorset), and is comparable with the harvest workers of the same period.[52]

So the autumn diets that we have been examining can be located at the apex of the wage-earning classes, suggesting that the harvest workers formed an aristocracy of labour, much better off than agricultural workers in normal seasons, wealthier than some building workers, having similarities with the standards of the peasantry, and, as the period developed, closing part of the gap between themselves and the lower ranks of the clergy or gentry.

[50] Dorset RO, D 204/A14; R.H. Hilton, 'Pain et cervoise dans les villes anglaises au Moyen Age', in *L'Approvisionnement des villes de l'Europe Occidentale*, 5e Flaran Journées Internationales d'Histoire (Auch, 1985), p. 222; PRO, SC6 1071/5.

[51] PRO, SC 6 914/6.

[52] K. Wood-Legh, *A Small Household of the Fifteenth Century* (Manchester, 1956), passim.

Although the quantity and quality of their diet put the harvest workers into a special category, the changes in their food allowances reflect more widespread developments throughout the lower ranks of society. The *famuli*, especially those who did not receive the bonus of meals at the lord's table in the autumn, were given a higher proportion of wheat in their liveries in the late fourteenth and fifteenth centuries, though they rarely achieved the privilege of an entirely wheat diet. *Famuli* and servants generally were criticised by late fourteenth-century clerical and gentry writers for their demands for good ale, and fresh meat that was well-cooked and hot. Evidence after 1349 for a shift in agricultural production from arable to pasture suggests a general increase in meat consumption, and the professionalisation of brewing may point to a greater volume of ale-drinking.[53]

Conclusion

The changes in diet so precisely measurable in the case of the harvest workers, and arguably affecting a wide section of society, seem to be capable of a simple demographic explanation. The quality of foodstuffs varied in inverse proportion to the size of the population, with cheap cereals being issued during the period of high and growing numbers of people in the late thirteenth century, and a switch to wheat and meat eating after the famines and plagues of the fourteenth century. However, closer examination of the changes suggests that more complex explanations are necessary. The early fourteenth century poses a problem, because there is clear evidence then, especially in Norfolk, of improvements in the diet of harvesters, very much in line with the general tendency for both cash wages and real wages to creep upwards in the three decades between the agrarian crisis of 1315–22 and the first outbreak of plague in 1348–9.[54] This would be compatible with the controversial argument that the population had reached a ceiling by 1315, and that decline was beginning before the Black Death. However, direct evidences of population movements are few and contradictory. Essex figures support the view that population declined, while in a Norfolk example a continued increase up to 1349 has been argued.[55] Real wages

[53] C. Dyer, 'English diet in the later Middle Ages', in T.H. Aston et al. (eds.), *Social Relations and Ideas* (Cambridge, 1983), pp. 210–14; P. Clark, *The English Ale House: a Social History, 1200–1830* (London, 1983), pp. 20–38.

[54] D.L. Farmer, 'Prices and wages', in H.E. Hallam (ed.), *Agrarian History of England and Wales*, ii (Cambridge, 1988), pp. 716–817.

[55] L.R. Poos, 'The rural population of Essex in the later Middle Ages', *Econ. Hist. Rev.*, 2nd ser., 38 (1985), pp. 521–3; B.M.S. Campbell, 'Population pressure, inheritance and the land market in a fourteenth-century peasant community', in R.M.Smith (ed.), *Land, Kinship and Life-cycle* (Cambridge, 1984), pp. 87–134.

may have increased in this period because of economic factors, notably the growing competition between industrial and agricultural employment, but with such a large agricultural workforce it seems difficult to believe that industry (such as cloth-making) could have generated enough employment to have a general impact on wages. The diet evidence – the most direct index of real earnings available to us – seems to support the view that population was declining and therefore causing a growing scarcity of labour, as is proposed by those who argue that population outstripped resources in the early fourteenth century. The discovery that individuals around 1300 were receiving food allowances in excess of 10,000 calories per day might seem to be incompatible with the idea that the same period suffered from problems of undernourishment. But, as has already been suggested, the allowances were in fact supporting whole families at perhaps 2000–3000 calories each per day, and the harvest workers were located at the top of a hierarchy that included at the bottom wage earners and smallholders who would have been much less well fed because of their low wages and intermittent employment. Above all, the harvest workers' food allowances were not much affected by the crises of subsistence, but the rest of society was not so insulated. Even the harvest workers who had lived quite well in August might have faced severe hardships at other seasons in such years as 1310 and 1323.

The changes in diet after 1349 took some time to have their maximum effect, in spite of the suddenness and the severity of the demographic catastrophe. This is partly because population levels, though reduced by 40 per cent or more in 1349, did not reach their lowest limit until after 1400. And the economy of the period 1350-75 had as one of its determining characteristics a succession of poor harvests and consequently high grain prices. Also the food allowances, as an element in wages, were subject to the complex combination of pressure and inertia that lay behind the increases in cash remuneration. The employees had to bargain for improvements, as at Appledram in 1354, where the provision of ale instead of cider was at issue. More ale was bought, explained the manorial officials to the auditors, 'because the reap-reeve would not drink anything but ale in the whole of the harvest time'. At any period of rapid social change time is needed to adjust to new circumstances, and the resistance of lords and employers provided a strong obstacle in the fourteenth century. As lords they had a grip on the *famuli* who were often also their serfs, and they could discipline them through the manor courts. Behind them lay the legal force of the kingdom, albeit inefficiently enforced, acting through the Statute of Labourers. The sense of shock felt by aristocratic employers at the new social climate was expressed in contemporary literature as well as legislation. For intellectuals to comment on such mundane matters as servants' eating habits is in itself an indication that an upheaval had taken place, which seemed to threaten the social order. The relationship between lords and *famuli* was informed by paternalism, signalled in the accounts by gifts and tips given at various times during the farming year. To demand more pay and food, the *famuli* had to overcome habits of deference, no doubt helped by the more mercenary attitudes of the temporary hired hands who joined them in the autumn. Custom acted as a brake on innovation, as is shown by the formalised rules under which labour services were performed, whereby boon workers ate barley bread long after the harvest hands had changed to wheat. Village custom, enshrined in by-laws, must have influenced the bargaining over the rewards of harvest workers when they were being employed by the wealthier peasants. [56]

So in the late fourteenth and early fifteenth century demographic factors influenced diet in the long term, but social pressures and institutional restraints slowed down the pace of change. Demography and nutrition interacted in very complex ways. Substantial improvements in food were achieved by the fifteenth century, most readily quantified in the case of the harvest workers, but clearly shown by the indirect evidence of plenty in falling grain prices and the relatively infrequent harvest failures between 1375 and 1520. This might have promoted earlier marriage, healthier children, and longer life expectation, so leading to population growth. On the continent, the diet of the lower orders improved in much the same way as in England, and in France and Italy the populations were growing in the second half of the fifteenth century.[57] In England stagnation continued well into the sixteenth century. Was this because the English were peculiarly vulnerable to epidemics, or because they adopted customs such as late marriage, which helped them to maintain their higher living standards? Whether we emphasise the influence of mortality or fertility at this period, there can be no doubt that this example shows that dietary improvement on its own could not promote population growth.[58]

Changes in diet of the fourteenth and fifteenth centuries have been treated here as improvements partly because they were so regarded by contemporaries. Wage-earners strongly favoured white bread, fresh meat and strong ale. The attractions of such a diet were largely social and

[56] On the general problems of this period, see R.H. Hilton, *The Decline of Serfdom in Medieval England* (London, 1969), pp. 32–43; A.R. Bridbury, 'The Black Death', *Econ. Hist. Rev.*, 2nd ser., 26 (1973), pp. 577–92.

[57] On continental diet, see e.g. B. Bennassar and J. Goy, 'Contribution à l'histoire de la consommation alimentaire du XIVe au XIXe siècle', *Annales ESC*, 30 (1975), pp. 402–30; D. Menjot, 'Notes sur le marché de l'alimentation et la consommation alimentaire à Murcie à la fin du moyen âge', in D. Menjot (ed.), *Manger et boire au Moyen Age*, I (Nice, 1984), pp. 199–210; on population, Bois, *The Crisis of Feudalism*, pp. 346–56; D. Herlihy and C. Klapisch–Zuber, *Les Toscans et Leurs Familles* (Paris, 1978), pp. 181–8.

[58] Cf. T. McKeown, 'Food, infection and population', *Journal of Interdisciplinary History*, 14 (1983), pp. 227–47.

cultural: in adopting this pattern of eating, the lower orders were aping the lesser gentry.[59] In nutritional terms the harvest workers' food of the thirteenth century contained the main elements of a healthy diet, including a combination of carbohydrates and animal protein, with vitamins A and D being provided by dairy produce, offal and herrings. Outside the harvest season however all of these foodstuffs may not have been consumed regularly by poorer people. As the diet changed in the fourteenth century the contribution of fish and milk products declined, but probably not to such a low point that the recipients would suffer vitamin deficiencies. The new diet with its growing proportion of fatty meat would not be regarded as an improvement by modern nutritionists. But there can be no doubt that in terms of palatability a variety of meats eaten with wheat bread was a great advance on the stodgy monotony of barley bread. Throughout the period the sources of vitamin C must remain a mystery. The supposition must be that the amount of green vegetables, although so small as virtually to escape reference in our documents, reached a minimum level sufficient to prevent serious deficiency diseases. The main nutritional problem in the later Middle Ages was not the lack of specific vitamins and minerals, or the excess of fats that causes concern in a modern affluent society, but simply that at certain times, and especially in the late thirteenth and early fourteenth century, those sections of the population who fell below the harvest workers' privileged standard of living survived on cereals with very little animal protein, and that in some years even the inferior cereals were scarce and expensive.

Finally, too simple a demographic explanation of agrarian history would suppose that agriculture could adjust itself easily to the new demands by shifting from arable to pasture. This was the trend, but it involved difficult structural changes for those peasant communities whose agrarian system was closely involved with grain production. The fifteenth century saw in the Midlands the development of specialised pastoral farms of a novel kind as landlords, lessees and wealthier peasants took advantage of the growing market for meat. In particular they were responding to an increased demand for beef. Cheaper grains and legumes, once grown largely for human consumption, must have been used more often as fodder crops. We are only beginning to appreciate the interaction between consumption and production in the medieval economy.

[59] On diet as a 'system of communications', and an element in social competition, see M. Montanari, *L'alimentazione contadina nell'alto medioevo* (Naples,1979), p. 461; S. Mennell, *All Manners of Food* (Oxford, 1985), pp. 40–61.

Appendix 5.1

The calculations in Table 5.2 are based on the assumption that 1 quarter (2.9 hls) of wheat made 510 lbs (231 kgs) of bread; that 1 quarter of barley made 336 lbs (152 kgs) of bread; that 1 quarter of oats made 180 lbs (82 kgs) of meal: E.J.T. Collins, 'Dietary change and cereal consumption in Britain in the nineteenth century', *Agricultural History Review*, 23 (1975), p. 108; D.W. Kent-Jones and J. Price, *The Practice and Science of Bread Making* (2nd edn, Liverpool, 1951), pp. 290–1; W. Tibbles, *Foods: Their Origin, Composition and Manufacture* (1912), p. 425.

Other assumptions are that 1 quarter of malt made 60 gallons (273 litres) of ale (in late medieval household accounts the figure ranges from 60 to 100 gallons, see Dyer, 'English diet in the later Middle Ages', p. 203), and that animal carcasses weighed as follows: cattle 250–450 lbs (113–204 kgs); pigs 70–90 lbs (32–41 kgs); sheep 31 lbs (14 kgs); geese 8 lbs (4 kgs); poultry 1–2 lbs (0.45–0.9 kgs). And that fish weighed: cod 6.6 lbs (3 kgs); herring $\frac{1}{2}$lb (0.2 kgs). Stouff, *Ravitaillement et Alimentation*, pp. 186–9, 301–19; Kershaw, *Bolton Priory*, pp. 157–8; H. Clarke and A. Carter, *Excavations in King's Lynn, 1963–1970*, Society for Medieval Archaeology Monograph, 7 (1977), pp. 403–8. Meat and fish weights have been reduced for waste, and calorific values have been calculated, from figures supplied in A.A. Paul and D.A.T. Southgate, *McCance and Widdowson's The Composition of Foods* (4th edn, 1978). For example, it is assumed that 74 per cent of a pork carcass was edible, and that in roast form its calorific value was 286 per 100 gs.

6

The Consumption of Freshwater Fish in Medieval England

Anyone who attempts to improve our understanding of the medieval past by combining both archaeological and documentary evidence knows the frustration of matching the two sources of information. Often there is an abundance of data on one side only, and connections are difficult to achieve. In the case of the problems posed by the production and consumption of freshwater fish there are plenty of archaeological sites, in the form of the earthworks of ponds, but the documentary references are rather scanty. Most historians writing about medieval society scarcely mention the subject, and perhaps in consequence some ill-founded myths have developed. When confronted with the substantial dams and complex networks of leats of medieval pond systems, we naturally seek a social or economic explanation. It is speculated that the ponds were built by villagers, and that the fish were eaten by peasants. Alternatively almost every pond is held to be the work of monks, who needed, we are told, ample supplies of fish because of their peculiarly restricted diet. It is commonly believed that fish production was necessary away from the coast because sea-fish could not be carried far inland. The regulation of diet by the church, especially compulsory fasting in Lent, is also said to have been the main reason for large-scale consumption of freshwater fish.

The purpose of this essay is to show how and why freshwater fish, especially pond fish, were consumed, and the conclusions will differ considerably from these speculations mentioned above. Freshwater fish must be regarded primarily as part of the diet of the aristocracy. This is indicated clearly enough by the frequency with which ponds are found in association with moated sites, castles and monasteries, or within parks. Although the costs of the construction of ponds appear only sporadically in manorial accounts, the formidable sums involved could clearly have only been borne by a wealthy minority. For example, in 1294–5 merely cleaning Westminster Abbey's pools at Knowle (Warwickshire) cost £7 14s. 11d.[1], and the enlargement, refurbishing and restocking by John Brome of ponds at Baddesley Clinton in the same county amounted in one year (1444–5) to

---

[1]   Westminster Abbey Muniments, 27694.

almost £5.[2] To provide a standard of comparison, the money spent on the Knowle ponds would have bought a herd of fifteen cattle or paid a skilled building craftsman for two years. Pond construction required an input of specialist labour, both the dykers (often of Welsh origin) who moved the earth, or the carpenters who made the pipes, sluices and other wooden fittings. Fish culture called for complexities of management, for example the supply of breeding stock over long distances, like the four bream carried 40 miles (64 km) from Turweston (Buckinghamshire) to be introduced into the pools at Knowle in 1301–2.[3] Peasants could not afford such investments, and the village ponds known from documents and archaeology are usually found to have been used not for fish culture but for watering stock.[4]

All sections of the landed upper classes constructed and used fishponds. Kings, who maintained numerous large pools, the higher nobility, knights and gentry, as well as bishops and monasteries were all involved in fish culture. Together these people and institutions represented about 2 per cent of the population, but enjoyed incomes (mostly in the range of £10 to £5,000 per annum) vastly in excess of the mass of peasants, artisans and wage-earners. An ample supply of food was one of the characteristics of their style of life, and especially the large quantities of meat and fish served to households of servants, retainers and guests. Animal protein accounted for between a third and half of their food consumption, calculated by value, and everyone in a magnate household would be allowed a pound or two by weight of meat or fish per day. The lower classes, who lived mainly on cereals in the form of bread and pottage, were not able to eat meat or fish regularly, and the poorest people, perhaps the bottom third of society, must have consumed only small quantities of these comparative luxuries, particularly in the period of low wages before the mid-fourteenth century.[5]

Fish played an important part in aristocratic diet partly because of the easy availability of some species, and partly because of the dietary rules enforced by the church that forbade meat consumption, not just during the six weeks of Lent, but also on Fridays and Saturdays in every week, in some households on Wednesdays too, and on the vigils of important festivals, such as Christmas Eve. These regulations caused no great hardship for the poor, who did not expect to eat meat every day anyway, but for aristocratic households large helpings of fish were regarded as necessary on every

[2]   B.K. Roberts, 'Medieval fishponds', *Amateur Historian*, 7 (1966–7), pp. 122–3; C.C. Dyer, 'A small landowner in the fifteenth century', *Midland History*, 1 (1972), pp. 1–14.

[3]   Westminster Abbey Muniments, 27701.

[4]   P. Wade-Martins, 'Village sites in Launditch Hundred', *East Anglian Archaeology*, report no. 10 (1980), pp. 110–12.

[5]   C.C. Dyer, 'English diet in the later Middle Ages', in T.H. Aston et al. (eds), *Social Relations and Ideas* (Cambridge, 1983), pp. 191–216.

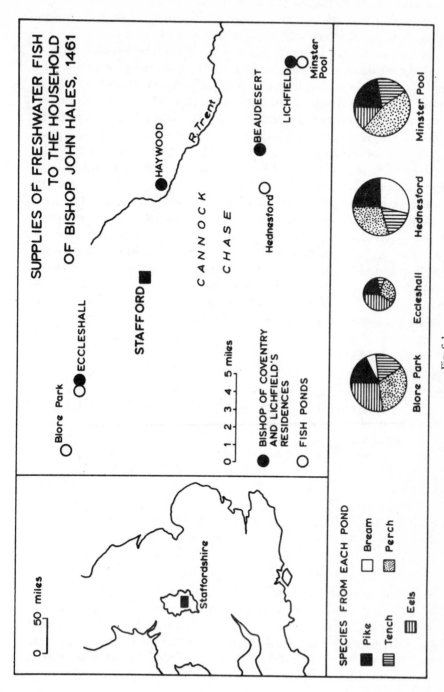

Fig. 6.1
Supplies of freshwater fish to the household of bishop John Hales 1461

non-meat day. The wealthier households in particular demanded a number of different dishes at the two major daily meals, and one of the functions of freshwater fish was to contribute to the variety of the menu.

Household accounts are our main source for the investigation of aristocratic consumption of freshwater fish. These accounts, which survive in their hundreds, vary in the amount of information that they give. In particular some foodstuffs, including game and fish, are intermittently recorded if they came from the parks and ponds of the estate, and were not purchased. When we are given no more than hints of fish consumption these documents can be very frustrating, like the reference in a 1392–3 account of John Catesby of Ashby St Ledgers (Northamptonshire) to expenditure on a 'flue-net'. The account gives no information about the fish which the net might have been used to catch.[6] Some records were sophisticated enough to value the freshwater fish which were obtained from any source, either from demesne ponds or as gifts. Such an account is that surviving from a four-month period in 1461 (24 May to 2 October) for the household of the bishop of Coventry and Lichfield, John Hales, when he was staying at his south Staffordshire residences at Lichfield, Beaudesert, Haywood and Eccleshall.[7] To give an example of the form of the document here is a translation of a characteristic day's entry:

Beaudesert

Friday, 28 August	
In 2 salt-fish bought by the steward,	15d.
In 2 stock-fish bought by the same,	5d.
In half fresh salmon bought by the same,	10d.
In butter bought by the same,	4d.

	Total	2s. 10d.

Stock

In 1 small pike (12d.), 1 tench (8d.), 1 small bream (4d.), 4 perch (2d.) from the lord's stock of Hednesford.

	Total	2s. 2d.

A few other late medieval accounts give some indication of the consumption of fish from ponds, and there are many which provide details of purchases of freshwater fish. Sea-fish were generally consumed in much larger quantities than freshwater fish. Distance from the coast did not prevent households based inland from buying both preserved and fresh sea-fish, as

---

6   PRO, E 101/511/15.
7   Staffordshire County Record Office, D1734/3/3/264.

is shown by John Hales's regular purchases of 'salt-fish' (white fish of some kind), stock-fish (dried cod), herrings described as fresh, white (salted) and red (smoked), and plaice or flounders. These were probably bought at Lichfield, an important local market for fish. Hales may also, like the near-by monks of Halesowen Abbey a century earlier, have bought in bulk direct from coastal suppliers – in their case at Boston (Lincolnshire).[8] Another Midland household, that of John Catesby of Ashby St Ledgers, made much use of the market at Coventry in the late fourteenth century, where a variety of fresh sea-fish could be obtained, including oysters, mussels, haddock and porpoise.[9] Hales's consumption is so fully recorded that the numbers of fish can be calculated. In four months he and his household ate their way through 639 sea-fish compared with 258 freshwater fish, which gives the latter 29 per cent of the total. We cannot really say if this is a typical pattern. From a much smaller sample of recorded days a proportion of freshwater fish as high as 36 per cent can be calculated for the household of Thomas Arundel, bishop of Ely, in the 1380s.[10] A high level of consumption should be expected there, because the bishop was living on the Isle of Ely, surrounded by fens that were teeming with fish. A much lower figure is found in the accounts of the household of John de Vere, earl of Oxford, in 1431–2, which apparently consumed only 215 freshwater fish and more than 26,000 sea-fish.[11] It is possible that proximity to the sea (the de Vere household spent most of its time in Essex) influenced the proportion of different types of fish, though we have to allow also for such imponderables as variations in the documentation and in the taste of individual lords.

We can only make crude comparison of numbers of fish of different types because our documents tell us nothing about weights. Value is a different matter, though, because the accounts were of course compiled in order to make financial reckonings. It should not surprise us to find that the high price of individual freshwater fish meant that though smaller in quantity, they could in total equal sea-fish in value. To take the Hales household again, in which fish accounted for 14 per cent of the value of foodstuffs consumed (compared with 35 per cent for meat and 47 per cent for cereals), the freshwater fish were worth £1 7s. 1d., as against £1 4s. 6½d. for sea-fish. The prices and valuations of different types indicate some relatively high prices for freshwater fish (see Table 6.1). The likely weight must be taken into account in assessing prices; from bones found at King's Lynn it has been calculated that medieval cod varied from 1.2 to 20 kg, and that many of them exceeded 6 kg in weight, so the price of Hales's purchases of sea-

---

[8] Society of Antiquaries of London, MS 535.
[9] PRO, E 101/511/15; 512/5 (a porpoise was thought in the Middle Ages to be a fish).
[10] Cambridge University Library, EDR D5/3, D5/5.
[11] Essex County Record Office, D/DPr 137.

fish may well have been less than 1d. per kg (or $\frac{1}{2}$d. per 1b).[12] Modern chubb and tench normally weigh less than 3 kg, so if their fifteenth-century ancestors were of similar size, they were being valued at more than 1d. per kg.[13] Pickerel, which usually weighed less than 1.5 kgs (3 lb), were evidently worth *c.* 5d. per kg (2$\frac{1}{2}$d. per 1b).

Table 6.1

Prices and valuations of fish (each) in south Staffordshire in 1461.

Sea-fish		*Freshwater fish*	
Species/type	*median price*	*Species/type*	*median valuation*
Salt-fish	8d.	Pike	12d.
Stock-fish	3d.	Pickerel	8d.
Herring	$\frac{1}{4}$d.	Bream	5d.
Plaice/flounder	$\frac{1}{2}$d.	Tench	6d.
		Perch	2d.
		Chubb	4$\frac{1}{2}$d.
		Eel	1$\frac{1}{2}$d.*
		* price	

The types of freshwater fish consumed depended on the local sources of supply. Salmon were eaten in varying quantities in almost every household though they may have come from sea as well as river fisheries. The main freshwater fish served in aristocratic households were eels, followed by bream, perch, pike, roach and tench. All could have been caught in rivers, though they were also the most common species to be kept in ponds. These six primary species are not found everywhere, so roach do not appear in John Hales's accounts, nor do bream in Thomas Arundel's. The most striking local variations are found in the case of river fish. In Staffordshire Hales bought chubb, dace, grayling and trout, which had probably been caught in the Severn or Trent, or their tributaries. Richard Mitford, bishop of Salisbury, whose household spent the year 1406–7 in Wiltshire, was able to indulge in trout and minnows from the downland streams.[14] The Stonor family in the fifteenth century, living in the Chilterns between the Thames and Thame, could buy only chubb, dace, gudgeon, minnows, ruff, trout and the occasional barbel.[15] In East Anglia Lady Katherine de Norwich in 1336–7 obtained ruff and burbot as well as the usual pike, eels, bream and

[12] A. Wheeler, 'Fish bone', in H. Clarke and A. Carter, *Excavations in King's Lynn, 1963–1970*, Society for Medieval Archaeology monographs no 7 (1977), pp. 403–8.

[13] A. Wheeler, *The Fishes of the British Isles and North-West Europe* (London, 1969), pp. 183, 210.

[14] British Library, Harley MS 3755.

[15] PRO, C 47/37/1/25; C 47/37/2; C 47/37/7.

roach.[16] Carp are absent from these documents because they were introduced into England in the late fifteenth century and took some time to become food species of importance.[17]

The consumption both of pond and river fish indicates the various ways in which supplies were obtained. In an ideal world of self-sufficiency we might expect to find the higher aristocracy planning their lives so that each manor would have foodstuffs, including the stocks of ponds, ready to keep the itinerant household for a required period before moving on to the next residence. A monastery might use its ponds in rotation through the year in order to meet its needs. If such arrangements ever worked this must have been in an early, undocumented period, because the late medieval sources show a considerable use of transport and the market. During the fourteenth and fifteenth centuries households became less mobile, their lords preferring to spend long periods at favoured residences. Fish-ponds might still be maintained in the less-used manors, and their stock could be carried for some distance to the consuming household. So when bishop Hales was living at Haywood, fish were brought from Blore and Eccleshall, 10 miles (16 kms) away. Bishop Mitford obtained fish from his pools at Sherborne (Dorset) to be eaten at Potterne (Wiltshire), a distance of 35 miles (56 km). The royal household in the thirteenth century had an elaborate system of supply by which fish from ponds as far apart as Brigstock (Northamptonshire), Feckenham (Worcestershire), Marlborough (Wiltshire) and Woodstock (Oxfordshire) were carried to Westminster and other palaces in response to written orders.[18]

The better-documented households were able to provide themselves with about three-fifths of their freshwater fish supplies from their own ponds, and the rest came from purchases. Aristocratic consumers became increasingly reliant on the market as they leased out their ponds and fisheries along with other demesne assets after the late fourteenth century. One important group of consumers, the wealthy townsmen, who in their tastes in food as in so many other aspects of their lives, aped the landed aristocracy, depended entirely on the market. Lords who kept their ponds under their own management sometimes sold surpluses of fish, an enterprising example being Sir Richard Verney, lord of Compton Verney and Kingston (Warwickshire), who held two 'shambles of fish' in the Northampton fish-market.[19] More commonly ponds were rented out to farmers who paid cash rents that reflected in some measure the profits that could be made from fish sales. River fisheries, which were generally more

---

[16] British Library, Add. Roll 63,207.

[17] C.F. Hickling, 'Prior More's fishponds', *Medieval Archaeology*, 15 (1971), pp. 120–1.

[18] J. McDonnell, *Inland fisheries in medieval Yorkshire 1066–1300*, University of York Borthwick Papers, 63 (1981), pp. 19–20; *Calendar of Liberate Rolls*, I–V.

[19] Shakespeare's Birthplace Trust Record Office, DR 98/504a.

productive than ponds, judging from their higher rents, were invariably in the hands of tenants who sold the bulk of their catch. The details of a river fishery's operations are revealed to us by an unusual account relating to Warkworth (Northumberland), which yielded 578 salmon and 2,640 trout in the accounting year 1471–2, of which only one fish in thirty went to the household of the lord, the earl of Northumberland, and the rest were either sold or salted.[20]

The farmers of fisheries evidently sold their catch to fishmongers. These included specialists in freshwater fish, like John Gere, 'pikemonger', who supplied both pike and tench to Humphrey, duke of Buckingham in 1452–3 and William Walis of London from whom pike were bought in some quantity by Ann, duchess of Buckingham in 1465–6.[21] A substantial trade in freshwater fish was centred on London, and in the provinces Cambridge clearly acted as an important distribution point for the abundant catches of the fenland.

Judging from the high prices paid for freshwater fish, supply could not keep pace with demand. It is true that some river fish could be bought quite cheaply, like the roach and dace from the River Severn that cost as little as $\frac{1}{4}$ d. each, the same price as herring, in the early fifteenth century, and small eels and lamperns which were sold for even less. These low prices put these fish within the reach of poorer consumers, so it would be a mistake to assume that the consumption of freshwater species was an exclusively aristocratic privilege. The customs of Alrewas (Staffordshire), in 1342 presume that peasants, who were forbidden to sell river fish, ate their catches themselves. And the busy trade in local fish in fenland villages and towns like Lakenheath and Ely shows that consumption was widespread.[22] There is still no doubt that the larger and choicer specimens were very expensive luxuries indeed. A mature pike at 2s. or 3s. in the fifteenth century cost as much as a skilled craftsman's wage for a week: a tench at 6d. was equivalent in value to twenty-four loaves of bread or 6 gallons of good ale. Perhaps the high prices reflect the labour-intensive methods of fish farming, demonstrated for example in Prior More's journal.[23] They may also have resulted from the low levels of productivity of the ponds, in which were kept such slow-growing species as tench, and which seem to have been managed unsystematically, for example without regular feeding. That there was room for improvement is suggested by the plentiful advice to

[20] J.C. Hodgson (ed.), *Percy bailiffs' rolls of the fifteenth century*, Surtees Society, 131 (1921), pp. 56–62.

[21] M. Harris (ed.), 'The account of the great household of Humphrey, first Duke of Buckingham, for the year 1452–3', *Camden Soc.*, 4th ser., 29 (1984), p. 13; British Library, Add. MS 34,213.

[22] Northamptonshire County Record Office, Westmorland (Apethorpe) 4.xx.4; British Library, Stow MS 880, fo. 29; Cambridge University Library, EDC 7/15/11/2/15; EDR C6/1.

[23] Hickling, 'Prior More's fishponds', pp. 118–23.

pond owners given in the post-medieval treatises.[24] Finally, a factor in the high price of fish was their undoubtedly high status. For example, chubb is described by a modern authority as 'poor eating', and is said to be 'nowhere regularly caught for food', yet in the Stonor accounts we find them being bought for as much as 7d. and 8d.[25] This must mean that they were being valued far in excess of their gastronomic qualities or nutritional worth, because of the place assigned to them in the prevailing aristocratic culture, rather as the modern monied classes have invested rarities such as truffles and caviar with a special luxury status.

An indication of the high regard with which freshwater fish were held is their frequent use as presents. Foodstuffs were often given in order to reinforce social bonds – at a high social level these would be such luxuries as wine and game, with freshwater fish as another common choice. Kings rewarded important subjects with bream from the royal ponds, sometimes for breeding purposes.[26] Clients of great lords would give them pike or other valuable fish in order to secure 'good lordship'.[27] Important churchmen would demonstrate their mutual respect with 'great eels'.[28] Towns often used gifts of fish to curry favour with the powerful and influential: the mayor of Leicester in 1346 gave the overlord of the town, the earl of Lancaster (among other good things) a dozen pike, bream, lampreys, eels and salmon.[29] Hull (not the place where we might expect to find much freshwater fish) in 1464, anxious to have the 'favour' of the officer in charge of the king's customs, gave him two pike and two tench worth 10s. 6d.[30]

Freshwater fish were often served at feasts or special occasions in contrast with the everyday staples of white fish and herrings. For example Bishop Hales invited sixty guests on 15 August 1461 to celebrate with him the feast of the Assumption. The festival fell on a Saturday, so the meal consisted entirely of fish, including two salmon, twenty-four eels, two chubb, three pickerel, twenty-four grayling, six trout, four perch and six dace. Relatively expensive freshwater species were also served in other households on Christmas Eve, or the even more important celebration of 1 January, when it fell on a fish day.[31] The arrival of a special guest on a fish-day also led to

[24] M. Aston, 'Aspects of fishpond construction and maintenance in the sixteenth and seventeenth centuries with particular reference to Worcestershire', in T.R. Slater and P.J. Jarvis (eds), *Field and Forest* (Norwich, 1982), pp. 266–77.

[25] Wheeler, *The Fishes of the British Isles*, p. 208; e.g. PRO, C 47/37/7.

[26] *Calendar of Close Rolls, 1264–8*, p.8.

[27] Longleat, MS Vol. XI.

[28] J.A. Robinson (ed.), 'Household roll of Bishop Ralph of Shrewsbury (1337–8)', in *Collectanea 1*, ed. T.F. Palmer, Somerset Record Society, 39 (1924), pp. 87–8.

[29] M. Bateson, *The Records of the Borough of Leicester*, 2 (London, 1901), p. 67.

[30] R. Horrox (ed.), *Selected rentals and accounts of medieval Hull, 1293–1528*, Yorks. Archaeological Society Record Series, 141 (1981), p. 97.

[31] PRO, C 47/37/7/.

the serving of freshwater fish, as on Saturday 24 August 1465, when Edward IV visited the duchess of Buckingham at Writtle (Essex), and sat down to a meal that included eight pike and six tench especially purchased in London for the occasion.[32] The royal household itself put on some magnificent fish feasts, like the celebration of St Edward's Day by Henry III on 13 October 1257, when 250 bream, 15,000 eels and 300 pike were collected from all over the country.[33] Freshwater fish figure prominently in surviving medieval recipe books, which is a further indication of their luxury status, as these writings were designed for use on special occasions in the wealthiest establishments. Fish were often served in piquant sauces, like galantine, which was a mixture of wine and vinegar flavoured with onions and spices. More elaborate dishes like fish blancmange involved cooking fish with rice, almond milk, sugar and ginger.[34] The accounts for a guild feast held in Coventry in 1458 show that the recipes were followed, the ingredients and equipment purchased indicating that the menu included 'Pike in Galantine' and 'Jelly of Fish'. The bream and tench for this celebration were brought from nearby Temple Balsall, where a large fishpond is still a feature of the modern landscape.[35] When freshwater fish were served in smaller quantities as part of a normal fish-day's menu they were often accompanied by eggs, butter, milk, cream, mustard and vinegar. On such occasions the accounts make it clear that the 'top table', sometimes called 'gentry' or the *libera familia*, received the freshwater fish, while the servants were served with large quantities of cheaper stockfish or herrings (see the example on p.104).

Food cannot be separated from the society in which it was produced and consumed. The apparently simple process of eating involves many complexities of social behaviour and social psychology far removed from the mere satisfaction of nutritional needs. Social anthropologists stress the connection between the development of a cuisine and the emergence of a differentiated social hierarchy.[36] This link can be seen in medieval England, where the production of freshwater fish involved the assertion of the social exclusiveness of the aristocracy. The ponds, located behind park pales or joined to moats, were associated with the physical barriers that helped to separate the aristocracy from the rest of society. Poaching was of course an offence punished in the seigneurial courts. Hunting and fishing rights became a symbol of social privilege, and there is good reason to see more

[32] British Library, Add. MS 34,213.

[33] *Calendar of Liberate Rolls*, iv, pp. 346–415.

[34] T. Austin (ed.), *Two fifteenth-century cookery books*, Early English Text Society, old series (1888), pp. 24, 101.

[35] G. Templeman (ed.), *The records of the guild of the Holy Trinity, St Mary, St John the Baptist and St Katherine of Coventry*, Dugdale Society, 19 (1944), pp. 180–1.

[36] J. Goody, *Cooking, Cuisine and Class: A Study in Comparative Sociology* (Cambridge, 1982).

than simple criminality in the mass assaults on parks and ponds frequently recorded in the fourteenth century. A typical case in 1376 involved sixty people taking thirty deer, and fish worth 100s., from the park of Evesham Abbey at Ombersley in Worcestershire.[37]

Freshwater fish also played a part in the subtle definition of the distinctions within the aristocracy. That acute observer, Geoffrey Chaucer, satirised the social climbing of the Franklin, a man of non-gentle origins, by emphasising his acquisition of the outward signs of aristocratic status. He was wealthy, and entertained lavishly. He also had 'many a bream and many a luce in stuwe'.[38] Here was clear evidence of his material prosperity and his pretensions, because such a well-stocked pond would normally have belonged to the well-established landed nobility. The aristocracy always recruited new blood from below its ranks, but in the late fourteenth and fifteenth century there was a new consciousness of the threat posed to the privileged classes by parvenus like Chaucer's Franklin. The leasing out of demesnes, and with them many ponds, provided just one of the changes threatening the traditional aristocratic way of life. A growing number of peasants and townsmen held and managed ponds, from which they derived both profits from sales, and also some fish for their own consumption. Still, the status symbol of freshwater fish remained until the end of the Middle Ages and beyond. When and why did this feature of the English aristocratic lifestyle die out? Another historian, with a more profound knowledge of the seventeenth and eighteenth centuries, ought to be able to provide the answer.

[37] B.H. Putnam (ed.), *Proceedings before the Justices of the Peace in the Fourteenth and Fifteenth Centuries* (London, 1938), p. 403

[38] F.W. Robinson (ed.), *The Works of Geoffrey Chaucer* (2nd edn, Oxford, 1957), p. 20 (*Prologue to the Canterbury Tales*, line 350).

7

Gardens and Orchards in Medieval England

The English are now a nation of gardeners, and the history of gardens has been written by enthusiasts, who have tended to exaggerate a little their past importance.[1] This essay, written by a rather reluctant gardener, will present a more objective picture of horticulture in the Middle Ages, and my purpose will be to assess the real economic importance of gardens and orchards in both production and consumption, for lords, peasants and townsmen.

Medieval horticulture is not easy to investigate, because it has left only slight traces in our documents. The garden was a commonplace feature of daily life: many people had access to one, and took it for granted. Because gardening did not involve much expenditure or administration, even the famous series of seigneurial accounts which provide English historians with so much information about agriculture in the thirteenth to fifteenth centuries contain only sporadic mentions of gardening. Gardens were embedded in the interstices of the domestic economy, and were bound up in a cycle of autoconsumption which is often hidden from our view.

The language of our sources provides a further barrier to our understanding of the subject. In their everyday speech medieval people employed the various versions of the English word 'yard' for gardens and orchards, and the clerks who were writing in Latin had to search for the appropriate word to translate this generic term. The words *gardinum, ortus* and *virgultum* all apparently meant a piece of land containing grass, trees and cultivated plants, often surrounded by a wall, hedge, fence or ditch. Words such as *pomerium* and *vinea* imply land devoted to fruit trees and vines. Contemporaries also used various terms for enclosed parcels of land, such as *clausum, croftus, curtilagium, pightellum* and *placea* many of which may have functioned as gardens. Also the complex of buildings and pieces of attached land called *cottagium, curia, messuagium* or *tenementum* often must have included gardens. An unspecialised vocabulary was also used to describe garden products, and words like 'apple', 'herb' and 'leek' in English, or *fructus* and *olerum* in Latin covered a wide range of species.

---

[1]   J. Harvey, *Early Nurserymen* (Chichester, 1974), pp. 15–26; idem, *Medieval Gardens* (London, 1981); idem, 'Vegetables in the Middle Ages', *Garden History*, 12 (1984), pp. 89–99; T. McClean, *Medieval English Gardens* (London, 1981).

Before turning to more detailed analysis, a general point must be made about the small scale of gardening activity. By every method of measurement, the same conclusion must be reached: gardens occupied in many regions a maximum of 1 or 2 per cent of the area of land in productive use; the income generated by horticulture, certainly judged in terms of cash, was minute; very few people, less than one in a hundred of the labour force, were employed in gardening full-time or even for the majority of their working time; the internal trade in garden products was of such minor importance that our documents scarcely mention it. In the late seventeenth century, making various social and economic calculations, Gregory King produced figures suggesting that in his day the cultivation of fruit and vegetables, together with industrial crops such as flax, hemp and dyestuffs, accounted for almost a tenth of agricultural production.[2] King wrote after two centuries of 'improvements' in horticulture, and medieval gardening is very unlikely to have contributed as much as a twentieth of total output from the land. Grain, wool, meat and cheese were vastly more important. And yet in spite of the limited *quantity* of gardens, they contributed much to the *quality* of life, and many people spent a significant amount of time in gardens, and derived either pleasure or material benefits from the experience.

Seigneurial Gardens

The lord's garden formed part of his outward display of wealth and exclusiveness. It was enclosed, sometimes very strongly with a moat or stone wall, and it was often attached to a fortified house or included within a walled precinct.[3] In many cases the garden was linked to a park, a fenced area set apart for the lord's private use. Gardens were intended as locations for the enjoyment of leisure, and the practice of a courtly style of life. Some lords and ladies took a personal interest in the garden, almost as a hobby.

As centres of production, seigneurial gardens were most actively exploited by their lords in the thirteenth and fourteenth centuries, at the same time as demesnes were being directly managed by the lords' officials. Most gardens were of 2 acres or less, though individual gardens of 5-8 acres were not uncommon. The 'old vineyard' at Clare (Suffolk) extended over 12 acres, and one of the largest medieval gardens known, that of the monks of Westminster, later called Covent Garden, covered at least 27 acres.[4] There

---

[2]   J. Thirsk, *Economic Policy and Projects* (Oxford, 1978), pp. 163, 174; J. Thirsk and J.P. Cooper, *Seventeenth-Century Economic Documents* (Oxford, 1972), pp. 782–3.

[3]   C. Taylor, *The Archaeology of Gardens* (Princes Risborough, 1983), pp. 33–40.

[4]   Harvey, 'Vegetables', p. 97; PRO, SC 6 992/25; Westminster Abbey Muniments (WAM), 18837.

is some evidence of expansion in the thirteenth century, like the bishop of Winchester's garden at Rimpton (Somerset) in 1264-6, when a new garden of 4 acres replaced one of a tenth the size; the knightly lord of Harlestone (Northamptonshire) acquired a parcel of arable land to extend the area of his garden in 1293.[5]

Large gardens commonly lay near to residential centres – royal and episcopal palaces, monasteries, and the castles and manor houses of the secular aristocracy. Sometimes a number of gardens were attached to a single centre, particularly in monasteries like Beaulieu (Hampshire) and Durham Priory where a number of officials each cultivated a small vegetable patch.[6] Over a large estate with many dispersed manors, whether under a monastic or a lay lord, the main gardening activity was concentrated on perhaps one manor in three.[7] This was evidently the result of coherent estate policies, which also led to central cider-making from the apple crops of a number of orchards, as happened at Glastonbury Abbey with a total of 257 qrs. in 1333–4, and on a smaller scale for the Percy estate centred on Petworth (Sussex).[8] Some manors with large gardens like that at Mildenhall (Suffolk) were expected to satisfy the internal needs of the manor itself (mainly vegetables for the servants' pottage), and produce a cash profit (at Mildenhall from the sale of madder), and to supply the monastic kitchen 10 miles away at Bury St Edmunds with leeks.[9] Another feature of the management of horticulture on a large estate was to designate a manor or two to grow vines, such as Ledbury (Herefordshire) which supplied the bishop of Hereford in 1289-90 with 7 tuns (1,680 gallons) of white wine.[10]

Lesser landowners – knights, gentry, parish clergy – tended to occupy a single residence and therefore perhaps to supervise gardening more closely. As some of these gardens were comparable in size with those found on magnate manors, they represented a higher proportion of the resources of a small estate.

The profits of gardens cannot be judged in a conventional way. When manors were assigned a cash value, the garden usually accounted for only

[5]   T.J. Hunt and I. Keil, 'Two medieval gardens', *Proceedings of the Somerset Archaeological and Natural History Society*, 104 (1959–60), pp. 92–3; D. Willis (ed.), *The Estate Book of Henry de Bray*, Camden Soc., 3rd ser., 27 (1916), p. 57.

[6]   S.F. Hockey (ed.), *The Account Book of Beaulieu Abbey*, Camden Society, 4th ser., 16 (1975); J.T. Fowler (ed.), *Extracts from the Account Rolls of the Abbey of Durham*, Surtees Society, 99, 100, 103 (1898, 1899, 1901), pp. 34, 84, 92, 101, 209, 228, 271, 272, 611, 719.

[7]   Northants RO, Fitzwilliam Milton, 2389 (Peterborough Abbey); British Library, Add. Roll 29794 (archbishopric of Canterbury); PRO, SC 6 827/39 (Isabella de Fortibus); L.M. Midgley (ed.), *Ministers' Accounts of the Earldom of Cornwall, 1296–1297*, Camden Soc., 3rd ser., 66, 67 (1942, 1945).

[8]   Hunt and Keil, 'Two medieval gardens', pp. 99–100; L.F. Salzman (ed.), *Ministers' Accounts of the Manor of Petworth, 1347–1353*, Sussex Record Society, 55 (1955), pp. 43, 58.

[9]   Bodleian Library, Suffolk roll no. 21.

[10]   J. Webb (ed.), *A Roll of the Household Expenses of Richard de Swinfield*, Camden Soc., 59, 62 (1853, 1854), p. 59.

1 or 2 per cent of the total.[11] But most gardens did not yield much money, because, when we have more detailed evidence of the use of garden produce, the bulk was consumed in the lord's household, and only the surplus was sold. Larger gardens could turn in a modest cash income, like the £3 left after the deduction of production costs at Norwich Cathedral Priory in 1387-8.[12] The earl of Lincoln's Holborn gardener in 1295-6 sold produce for £12, but labour alone cost almost £5.[13] These were tiny sums compared with the hundreds of pounds of income enjoyed by these magnate landlords. And many lords' gardens made no profit at all, like that of the bishop of Ely (also in Holborn), which in 1372-3 generated produce sales of about £4, for labour costs of £6.[14] It was of course the hidden consumption of produce by the households that justified the gardens' existence – they gave a convenient source of supply, under the direct control of the lord. The accounts give the impression that gardening was an intermittent, episodic activity, depending perhaps on short-term economic circumstances, but also on the personal interest of the lord. Sometimes a garden might cease production, and be grassed over, only to be revived later. Parcels of seigneurial gardens were often let out to tenants for rents in cash or kind. Informal leasing arrangements must lie behind the statement in accounts that the 'fruit of the garden' yielded some suspiciously round sum such as 5s. or 10s., and many lords gave up the trouble of organising a garden long before other assets were leased out, and let the land to tenants either as a garden or as a pasture.

Peasant Gardens

We must assume that the gardens and orchards held by peasants had a more practical and serious function than those of the lords. Sometimes peasants are recorded as holding a distinct area of land called a 'garden', which was often subdivided, so that individuals held a 'parcel', 'plot' or 'piece' of a garden, having some resemblance to a modern English allotment. As Table 7.1 shows, these specialised garden plots could be very small. Some originated either as fragments of former seigneurial gardens, or as the sites of former peasant houses.

Most peasants grew vegetables and fruit on a part of the messuage or cottage, in an enclosure at the back of the house and farm buildings. Some idea of the potential size of the garden can be gained by calculating the area of the whole messuage, and this can be done for villages in East Anglia and

[11] S.J. Madge (ed.), *Inquisitions Post Mortem for Gloucestershire*, British Record Society, 30 (1903).
[12] Norfolk Record Office, DCN 1/11/2.
[13] PRO, DL 29 1/1.
[14] Cambridge University Library, EDR/D6/2/12.

Table 7.1
Some peasant gardens.

Place (county)	Date	Garden dimensions	Source
Crondon in Stock (Essex)	1374	2 dayworks (8 perches)	Essex CRO, D/DRM780
Henbury (Gloucestershire)	1376–7	21 ft x 20 ft	Hereford & Worcester CRO, ref. 009:1, B.A. 2636/116
East Bergholt (Suffolk)	1383	1 rood	Suffolk CRO (Ipswich Branch), HA6:51/4/4.7
Stepney (Middlesex)	1442	5 dayworks (20 perches)	PRO, SC 2 191/62
Eaton (Norfolk)	1457	40 ft x 20 ft	Norfolk RO, DCN 60/9/13

Note: 40 perches make 1 rood; 4 roods make 1 acre

Table 7.2
Size of 'messuages' and 'cottages' – the plots within which buildings,
yards and gardens were sited

Manor (county)	Date	Number of examples	Maximum	Minimum	Median
Harlow (Essex)	1431	19	3 acres	$\frac{1}{8}$ acres	$\frac{1}{2}$ acre
Palgrave (Suffolk)	1361–79	37	1 acre	78 square yards	$1\frac{3}{4}$ roods
	1438–9	19	$3\frac{1}{2}$ acres	10 perches	3 roods
Sedgeford (Norfolk)	1454–5	9	2 acres $1\frac{1}{2}$ roods	1 rood 25 perches	2 roods 30 perches

Sources: Harlow: Cambridge University Library, Add. 5847, fos. 40–72
Palgrave: British Library, Add. MS 45,951, fos. 16–26; Add. MS 45,952, fos. 1–26
Sedgeford: Norfolk Record Office, DCN 52/8
Note: 40 perches make 1 rood; 4 roods make 1 acre

Essex where estate surveys provide precise measurements. Table 7.2 gives some examples, which suggest that messuages in eastern England averaged half an acre. Further west the documents are less informative, but we can measure the messuage sites (tofts) in deserted villages, now surviving as the earthworks of the banks and ditches that once surrounded the buildings, yards and gardens. This suggests a much smaller messuage, in the region of a quarter acre.[15] In a recently studied village in Wiltshire the tofts were as small as 400 to 700 square yards.[16] The proportion of the messuage or toft available for gardening was limited by the space needed for buildings, farmyards and animal pens. In the north barns are found built 'in the garden' on peasant holdings.[17] Peasants had to make economical use of the limited space available, and many cases of illicit tree felling show that fruit trees grew, not in an orchard, but in the boundary hedges of the messuage.

This difference in messuage size points to regional variations in the importance of horticulture. In East Anglia in the later Middle Ages arable holdings were small, commonly in the region of 5 acres, while Midland peasants were more often in possession of 10–15 acres. If we assume that half of the messuage was used for horticulture, this would amount to 5 per cent of the East Anglian peasant's landed resources, compared with only about 1 per cent of those of his Midland contemporary. As in the Low Countries, horticulture may be more commonly found in areas with high population densities, which therefore were supplied with an abundance of labour for intensive cultivation.[18] The general link between smallholdings and horticulture is confirmed by the common association in our documents of plots specifically described as gardens with cottage tenements. Local variations in peasant horticulture depended also on the suitability of the soils and climate, the proximity of markets, and the extent to which land was held in enclosures – it was difficult to plant any crops other than cereals and legumes in a highly developed open-field system. Thus we find in Gloucestershire that gardens and orchards are mentioned more frequently in the mild, fertile, enclosed west of the county (the 'Vale'), which lay near to the towns of Bristol and Gloucester, than on the corn-growing and sheep-rearing uplands of the Cotswolds in the east of the county. Individual villages developed gardening more than their neighbours, presumably

[15] *Medieval Village Research Group, Annual Reports,* 1971–1985.

[16] J. Musty and D. Algar, 'Excavations at the deserted medieval village of Gomeldon', *Wiltshire Archaeological and Natural History Magazine,* 80 (1986), p. 133.

[17] M.L. Faull and S.A. Moorhouse (eds), *West Yorkshire: an Archaeological Survey to A.D. 1500,* vol. 3 (Wakefield, 1981), pp. 822–30; PRO, DUR 3/14, fo. 303 (transcript by R. Britnell).

[18] M.-J. Tits-Dieuaide, 'Les campagnes Flamandes du XIIIe au XVIIIe siècle, ou les succès d'une agriculture traditionelle', *Annales: Économies, Sociétés, Civilisations,* 39 (1984), pp. 590–610; B.M.S. Campbell, 'Agricultural progress in medieval England: some evidence from eastern Norfolk', *Economic History Review,* 2nd ser., 36 (1983), pp. 26–46.

influenced by the combination of factors mentioned above. An example is Erdington (Warwickshire), which lay near to small towns and areas of rural industry, or Ewell (Surrey), perhaps under the stimulus of the London market.[19]

A guide to the level of horticultural production is provided by tithe receipts from individual parishes (Table 7.3). If we compare the tithe paid on apples, onions, flax and hemp, with the total receipts from tithes on corn, wool and other agricultural crops, we should understand better the importance of garden produce in the total production of the village. There are many dangers in these calculations, not least the selective evasion or exemption of tithe payment on the minor horticultural products. Different crops may also have rendered varying proportions as tithe. The resulting figures presented here suggest considerable local differences, but reinforce the general picture of a relatively small horticultural sector. Only in the examples from the southern counties of Sussex and Hampshire does the percentage of garden tithes rise above 5 per cent. The East Anglian parishes included in Table 7.3 do not support the suggestion that the region had a higher proportion of horticultural crops, but these parishes may not be typical. Analysis of the garden tithes in Suffolk (Table 7.4) from a larger sample of parishes in 1341 suggests that, though still on a small scale, flax, hemp and other crops from 'curtilages' made a significant contribution to the local economy.

Tithe records mention most commonly flax, hemp and apples as garden crops because these were the most valuable. Other sources, such as legal disputes over trespass, often caused by straying animals, refer to damage to vegetables and apples, but most commonly mention grass.[20] Maintenance agreements, made when old people gave up their holding to a younger tenant, often describe the resources of a messuage in some detail if the retired peasant was being assured a share of the tenement. Again gardens were sometimes promised to the retired peasant 'for herbage'. The other product most commonly reserved for the old peasant who was relinquishing the main holding was fruit, especially apples. From such sources emerges a picture of a typical peasant garden containing an area of grass under a group of trees. Peasants had to give a high priority to feeding livestock, for the sake of their pulling power and saleable produce as well as food, and so they needed to maximise the area of grazing. The fruit trees may not have been very numerous. The largest number mentioned on a peasant holding

---

[19] C. Dyer, *Warwickshire Farming, 1349–1520: Preparations for Agricultural Revolution* (Dugdale Society, Occasional Paper, 27, 1981), p. 40; C. Meekings and P. Shearman (eds.), *Fitznells Cartulary*, Surrey Record Society, 26 (1968), pp. 49–66.

[20] Faull and Moorhouse, *West Yorkshire*, pp. 824–5; Dyer, *Warwickshire Farming*, p. 23; J.R. Birrell, 'Medieval agriculture', *Victoria County History of Staffordshire*, vi, p. 30; New College Oxford, MS. 3912; Staffordshire County Record Office, D 1734/2/1/176, 427 (transcript by J. Birrell).

Table 7.3
Tithes on horticultural produce.

Parish (county)	Date	Tithes on horticultural produce		Tithes on agricultural produce	Source
Stoneham (Hampshire)	1341	Flax & hemp Apples	6s. 8d. 13s. 4d. £1 0s. 0d. (4.5%)	£21 6s. 8d. (95.5%)	*Inquisitiones Nonarum*, p. 126
Exton (Hampshire)	1341	Flax & hemp Apples	2s. 6d. 6s. 8d. 9s. 2d. (8.2%)	£5 2s. 0d. (91.8%)	*Inquisitiones Nonarum*, p. 127
Sompting (Sussex)	1341	Flax & hemp Cider	13s. 4d. 5s. 0d. 18s. 4d. (7.4%)	£11 8s. 0d. (92.6%)	*Inquisitiones Nonarum*, p. 351
Holme (Norfolk)	1400–1	Hemp Apples	1s. 6d. 6d. 2s. 0d. (0.4%)	£23 11s. 8d. (99.6%)	Bodleian Library, Shopshire Charter 27B
Newton (Cumberland)	1401–2	Flax & hemp Leeks Apples	4d. 3d. 1s. 2d. 1s. 9d. (1.1%)	£7 11s. 8½ d. (98.9%)	Cumbria RO, DRC/2/7
Downham (Suffolk)	1516–17	Garden Apples	6d. 2d. 8d. (0.2%)	£14 3s. 4d. (99.8%)	PRO, E 101/517/27
Helmingham (Suffolk)	1509–10	Apples	3s. 11d. (2.2%)	£8 11s. 3d. (97.8%)	BL, Add. MS 34,786
Warwick St Mary & St Nicholas (Warwickshire)	1465–6	Flax Hemp Garlic Onions Apples Saffron 'Gardens'	7s. 6d. 3s. 0d. 1s. 10d. 15s. 5d. 1s. 3d. 1s. 0d. 7s. 0d. £1 17s. 0d. (5.9%)	£29 12s. 11d. (94.1%)	D. Styles (ed.), *Ministers' Accounts of the Collegiate Church of St Mary, Warwick* Dugdale Soc., 26 (1969), pp. 78–85

Table 7.4
Tithes on horticultural produce: some parishes in Suffolk, 1341 (*Inquisitiones Nonarum*).

	Total of parish revenues	Total of tithes on horticultural produce
Colneis hundred (8 parishes)	£66 12s. 8d.	£4 3s. 8d.* (6.3%)
Blackbourne hundred (14 parishes)	£154 10s. 0d.	£4 14s. 4d.+ (3.1%)
Loes hundred (14 parishes)	£184 6s. 2d.	£10 5s. 8d.* (5.6%)

* hemp and flax
+ hemp, flax and curtilages

I have found is six (at Thornbury, Gloucestershire, in 1439).[21] Two examples hint at rather larger orchards. Firstly in 1415 at Marham (Norfolk) John Robyn complained that two neighbours had broken into his close and stolen apples and fruit worth 11s. 8d., which would imply that he had a dozen trees, unless we suspect that the injured party exaggerated the damage.[22] Secondly, when John atte Dene and Isabella his wife gave up their half-yardland (15 acres) holding at Bishop's Waltham (Hampshire) in 1457 they were promised a half of the cider, the total being 240 gallons.[23] Six trees would have produced enough apples for this (9–14 qrs.) only if the trees were an unusually high-yielding variety.

Peasants valued their gardens: they surrounded them with fences, hedges and ditches, and brought law suits against trespassers. Old people showed their attachment to the garden of their holding by insisting in written retirement contracts that a share (a quarter, third or half) be guaranteed for their use. One Huntingdonshire widow retained the fruit of a specific, named tree.[24] Gardens were clearly a useful asset to the peasantry, even if they did not constitute a major source of income.

Urban Gardens

Some of the earliest recorded gardens lay in or near to towns. An Old English riddle in a manuscript of the late tenth century describes a garden 'blooming and growing' in a *burh*.[25] Analysis of the pollen from the ninth- and tenth- century deposits excavated at York suggests the presence near the town of extensive hemp cultivation.[26] Many of the gardens *(orti)* mentioned in Domesday Book were situated on the fringes of towns, both provincial centres like Grantham, Oxford and Warwick, and at Fulham and Westminster to the west of London.[27] One of the earliest detailed urban surveys, that for Winchester of *c.* 1110, mentions gardens in the western suburb of that city.[28]

The abundant evidence of the later Middle Ages allows more detailed investigation of urban and suburban gardens, and this confirms Professor Irsigler's modification of von Thünen's theory, that horticultural activity

[21] Staffordshire County Record Office, D 641/1/4c/7.
[22] Norfolk County Record Office, Hare 2199, 194X4.
[23] Hampshire County Record Office, 11M59/Bp/BW80 (transcript by J.Z. Titow).
[24] A. Dewindt and E.B. Dewindt (eds), *Liber Gersumarum of Ramsey Abbey* (Toronto, 1976), p. 350.
[25] W.S. Mackie (ed.), *The Exeter Book*, ii, Early English Text Soc., O.S., 194 (1934), pp. 124–5.
[26] H.K. Kenward et al., 'The environment of Anglo-Scandinavian York', in R.A. Hall (ed.), *Viking Age York and the North* (Council for British Archaeology Research Report, 27, 1978), p. 61.
[27] H.C. Darby, *Domesday England* (Cambridge, 1977), pp. 135–6; See below, Chapter 12, pp. 246–51.
[28] M. Biddle (ed.), *Winchester in the Early Middle Ages*, Winchester Studies, i (Oxford, 1976), p. 49.

was concentrated in an inner zone around the medieval city.[29] Most of the largest and most productive seigneurial gardens lay in the London suburbs, serving the double purpose of supplying the lord's kitchen on his frequent visits to London to attend parliament or the king's court, and to make a profit from the sale of produce in the London market. Small-scale horticulture was also practised in the nearby villages such as Fulham, Lambeth and Stepney.[30] The largest concentration of gardens in the whole of England lay in the 2 square miles to the south-west of the city, from Holborn and the Strand to Charing Cross and Westminster, where the abbey maintained gardens in its precincts and to the west on its manor of Eye (now Hyde Park).[31] Here were gardens both small and large, kept by townsmen of London and Westminster, and by the nobility. South of the Thames lay more great aristocratic gardens, notably that of the archbishops of Canterbury at Lambeth, and in Southwark that of the bishops of Winchester.[32] The zones of gardens also extended into the eastern and northern suburbs.

The gardens of the larger provincial towns could not compete with those of the great magnates around the capital, though there were some individual monastic gardens, like that in the precinct of Norwich Cathedral priory, which can bear comparison. Also major towns like Norwich and York attracted the local gentry to set up town houses with appropriate gardens. In large towns gardens were often concentrated in suburbs. At Bristol they lay in some numbers to the south-west of the town at Billeswick.[33] A large garden area lay in the district of Southampton called Newtown immediately to the east of the walls, and was the cause of controversy in 1360 when royal officials sought to improve the defences by clearing gardens which would give shelter to potential French attackers. One regulation forbade the growing of any fruit tree tall enough to make a scaling ladder.[34] Gardens are also found in the centre of towns, because the standard 'burgage plot' was often large enough to provide some open space as well as the buildings, workshops and privies that occupied the front of the property. Sometimes whole plots were given over to gardening, either because the town had failed to expand over all of its designated area, or more commonly because

[29]   F. Irsigler, 'L'approvisionnement des villes de l'Allemagne occidentale jusqu'au XVIe siècle', in *L'approvisionnement des villes*, Centre Culturel de l'Abbaye de Flaran, Cinquièmes Journées Internationales d'Histoire (Auch, 1985), pp. 117–44.

[30]   PRO, SC 2 188/65; SC 2 191/62; SC 2 205/12

[31]   A.G. Rosser, *Medieval Westminster, 1200–1540* (Oxford, 1989), pp. 75–6, 133–7; WAM, 26851, 26855–26861, 26873.

[32]   M. Carlin, 'The urban development of Southwark, *c.* 1200–1550' (unpublished Ph. D. thesis, University of Toronto, 1983), pp. 96, 106–7, 289, 328–9, 350; Lambeth Palace Library, ED 545–548.

[33]   C.D. Ross (ed.), *Cartulary of St Mark's Hospital, Bristol*, Bristol Record Soc., 21 (1959), pp. 42, 60–82, 95–105.

[34]   C. Platt, *Medieval Southampton* (London, 1973), pp. 122–3.

in the fourteenth and fifteenth centuries the built-up area shrank and left gaps where houses had formerly stood. Again, distinct zones with a number of adjacent gardens can be identified – in Southampton within the wall in the south-west corner, and near the royal castle in the north-west. In the walled city of Norwich most of the gardens lay in the south-eastern district called Conesford; and in Leicester there were a number in the north-east section of the city called Torchmere.[35]

Numerous gardens seem to have been one feature that distinguished small towns from the surrounding countryside. Harlow in Essex, for example, was a small borough founded in the thirteenth century which was known locally as 'the market', which lay in one corner of a large parish containing at least seven rural settlements.[36] A survey of 1431 mentions a total of fifty-four gardens at Harlow (among hundreds of other pieces of land), twenty-two of which lay in the 'market', including nine of the thirteen separate gardens which were not mere appendages to messuages and dwellings. Some of the gardens in the market were large (by non-seigneurial standards), being a half or even a full acre.[37] Another town with a pronounced concentration of gardens was the Yorkshire borough of Pontefract, which is revealed in a rental of 1425 to have had thirty-eight, thirty-one of them detached from houses, which generated a total of £2 5s. 9d. per annum in rent, a tenth of the total value of the urban property listed.[38] Small towns stimulated horticulture in their vicinity. The seigneurial gardens of two manors on the edge of the Worcestershire town of Kidderminster were notably productive in the thirteenth and fourteenth centuries, and the only specialised peasant garden on the large Gloucestershire estate of Winchcombe Abbey in the mid-fourteenth century lay in Coates, a village on the edge of the town of Winchcombe itself.[39] Even a small town like Stratford-on-Avon had by the fifteenth century a specialised zone of gardens on its north-western boundary.[40]

All kinds of townsmen held garden property, whether the large pleasure gardens of officials and wealthy merchants (Paradise was a name sometimes

[35] L.A. Burgess (ed.), *The Southampton Terrier of 1454*, Southampton Record Series, 15 (1976), pp. 96–9, 110–11; Norfolk Record Office, DCN 45/22, 34, 37, 38; W. Hudson and J.C. Tingey, *Records of the City of Norwich*, i (London, 1906), pp. 235–6; W. Hudson (ed.), *Leet Jurisdiction in the City of Norwich*, Selden Soc., 5 (1892), pp. 70–1; M. Bateson (ed.), *Records of the Borough of Leicester*, i, (London, 1899), pp. 410, 427, 433, 436; *Victoria County History of Leicestershire*, iv, p. 341.

[36] *Victoria County History of Essex*, viii, pp. 132–3; J.L. Fisher, 'The Harlow cartulary', *Transactions of the Essex Archaeologcial Society*, 22 (1940), pp. 239–71.

[37] Cambridge University Library, Add. MS 5847, fos. 40–72.

[38] G.D. Lumb, 'A fifteenth century rental of Pontefract', *Thoresby Society*, 26 (1924), pp. 253–73.

[39] PRO, SC 6 1070/5; Bodleian Library, Worcestershire Rolls no. 2; survey of Winchcombe Abbey 1355, transcribed by D.M. Styles, in the possession of R.H. Hilton who kindly showed it to me; Gloucestershire County Record Office, D 678/96.

[40] Shakespeare's Birthplace Trust, Stratford-upon-Avon, BRT 1/3/127; Calendar of medieval deeds of Stratford borough, iii, pp. 818, 822.

used for them), or the small plots held by craftsmen and small traders and used no doubt as a source of food. A plot in Charing Cross near Westminster, for example, measured 55 feet by 42 feet and was leased to a 'yeoman' in 1486.[41] Some garden plots were capable of yielding much produce. An aggrieved property holder in the Oxford suburb of Holywell complained in 1340 that he had lost 40s. in corn, vegetables and herbs destroyed when animals had strayed into his garden through the neighbours' failure to maintain fences.[42] Perhaps the sum was exaggerated, but is unlikely to have been a complete fiction. The tithes from Warwick parishes (Table 7.3) show what the combined efforts of urban gardeners could achieve; their 11,000 heads of garlic, 50 qrs. of onions, and £5 worth of flax far outshone the horticulture of rural parishes of comparable size, and again indicate the importance for the development of gardening of a combination of a high volume of market demand and an abundance of labour.

Production and Sale

Most gardening was unspecialised, carried out by peasants and townsmen in their own plots in the slack periods between more remunerative work. The seasons for gathering and processing flax and apples, for example, did not clash with the main grain harvest.

The earliest specialised gardeners were peasant tenants on manors in the twelfth and thirteenth centuries who were expected to tend the lord's garden as an obligation of tenure.[43] They were probably the descendants of slaves who had done the work before the eleventh century. In the thirteenth and fourteenth centuries lords increasingly employed full-time farm servants (*famuli*) as gardeners, but such specialists were rare, and nine-tenths of manorial gardens were left to the part-time labours of servants normally employed on other duties (as carters or dairymaids, for example), assisted by occasional tenant services, or casual hired hands. No special skills were required: the full-time gardeners were paid at the same rate as a ploughman, and the casuals received a low labouring wage. Often lords economised by employing boys and women. Two notable exceptions were the highly rewarded officials in charge of the prestigious gardens attached to magnates' London houses, and the skilled vineyard managers (*vineatores*) who received at least four times the pay of a farm servant.[44]

[41] WAM, Register Book 1, fo. 6.

[42] Merton College, Oxford, 4546.

[43] Queen's College, Oxford, MS 366, fo. 25 (transcribed by D. Postles); M. Hollings (ed.), *Red Book of Worcester*, Worcestershire Historical Soc. (1934–1950), p. 341.

[44] PRO, DL 29 1/1; Cambridge University Library, EDR/D6/2/12; British Library, Add. Roll 29794.

Horticulture involved little capital expenditure, apart from the construction and maintenance of the enclosure – a new one cost £8 in Northamptonshire in 1300-1, built for the abbot of Peterborough.[45] Spades and other tools cost a few pence, and the only piece of equipment that required much money was a cider press – one at Clare (Suffolk) in 1330-1 involved a wage bill for carpenters of 19s.[46] A great deal of labour was needed, not just for the time-consuming digging, manuring, weeding and gathering, but also for the labour-intensive tasks of processing flax and hemp. Hire of labour was therefore the main expenditure of the managers of large gardens.

The level of horticultural technique cannot be judged from our scanty sources. The range of crops in many gardens seem to have been limited to onions, garlic, leeks, cabbage, peas, beans and parsley, among the vegetables, and apples, pears, cherries, plums and grapes among the fruits (with filberts and walnuts also). However, a wider range was grown in urban gardens. The seigneurial gardens near London contained dozens of varieties, with such plants as cucumber, borage and fennel, and citizens of Winchester grew hyssop and sage.[47] Seeds and pollen found by archaeologists in urban deposits include vegetables scarcely recorded in documents, such as parsnips and celery.[48]

In theory we ought to find that medieval horticulture was especially intensive in its methods, and therefore enjoyed higher levels of productivity than conventional arable farming. There are hints of this in the dense sowing of garden beans, for example, as compared with the field crop.[49] Gardens seem also to have received much manure. Gardeners developed special skills, like the grafting of trees about which didactic treatises were written in the fifteenth century.[50] Intensive production may also be implied by the high rents paid for some gardens, with leasehold rents and entry fines for garden ground in the country often exceeding arable land by two or three times, while some small urban plots were paying rents at astronomic rates such as £1 per acre (compared with 1s. per acre as a high rate for arable).[51] And yet there is much contrary evidence for a lack of intensity in cultivation, with large areas of gardens, even in towns, put down to grass.

[45] Northamptonshire County Record Office, Fitzwilliam Milton 2389.
[46] PRO, SC 6 992/20.
[47] D. Keene, *Survey of Medieval Winchester*, Winchester Studies, ii (Oxford, 1985), pp. 151–2.
[48] B. Ayers and P. Murphy, 'Waterfront excavation at Whitefriars Street car park', *East Anglian Archaeology*, 17 (1983), pp. 38–44.
[49] Salzman, *Accounts of Petworth*, p. 13.
[50] A.M.T Amherst, 'A fifteenth-century treatise on gardening by Mayster Ion Gardener', *Archaeologia*, 54 (1894), pp. 157–72; British Library, Sloane MS 686.
[51] For example, Norfolk Record Office, DCN 45/38/14; WAM, Register Book 1, fo. 6; Suffolk County Record Office (Bury St Edmunds Branch), E3/1/2.7.

In the fourteenth century much of the great Covent Garden was used to grow grain.[52]

High labour costs, and a general trend away from direct management of production, forced lords to hand over their gardens to lessees in the fourteenth and early fifteenth century. In the case of London this led to the emergence of the entrepreneurial gardeners. Those who managed gardens on behalf of the magnates had, one suspects, always traded on their own behalf as well as for the profit of their lord. A famous petition of 1345 tells us of the gardeners 'of the earls, barons, and bishops, and of the citizens' standing by St Augustine's church near St Paul's, 'selling peascods, cherries, vegetables and other wares'.[53] When the great gardens were leased out, the new breed of independent gardeners must have made considerable profits from produce sales in order to pay the rents of 40s. (at Norwich), 50s. and 60s. (for the Ely gardens in Holborn), and £5 for Covent Garden.[54]

Part of the profits of garden management lay in the trade in seeds and young plants. Again, the concentration of these products in urban centres is noticeable. In the late fifteenth century Durham Priory bought onion seed at Newcastle-upon-Tyne, and a gentry family from Derbyshire, the Eyres, obtained onion and leek seed at Rotherham and Sheffield, two modest Yorkshire market towns.[55] Plants of all kinds, including young trees and hedging quicksets were bought by the hundred, again often in urban markets. And the garden produce – cut flowers, fruit and vegetables – found a ready market in the towns. The profits were not high enough to give much opportunity for middlemen in the trade. At the top end of the market the London fruiterers supplied the wealthy London consumers, and complained in 1463 at unfair competition from foreign (non-citizen) traders, and above all of the activities of hucksters who travelled the streets selling from baskets.[56] These retailers of greengroceries are found in other large towns, such as Bristol, where fourteen to eighteen of them, called 'regraters' are recorded between 1282 and 1303 paying $\frac{1}{2}$ d. each in order to trade.[57]   Hucksters might originate in the country, like those from Kensington and Hammersmith who sold in the streets of Westminster in the early fifteenth century.[58] Huckstering was an occupation for poor

---

[52] WAM, 18836–18839.

[53] H.T. Riley (ed.), *Memorials of London and London Life* (London, 1868), pp. 228–9.

[54] Norfolk Record Office, DCN 1/11/16; Cambridge University Library, EDC 5/2/9, EDR/D6/2/13; Rosser, *Medieval Westminster*, p. 136.

[55] Fowler, *Abbey of Durham*, p. 101; Bodleian Library, MS D.D. Per Weld C19/4.

[56] R.R. Sharpe (ed.), *Calendar of the Letter Books of the City of London: Letter Book L* (London, 1912), pp. 30–4.

[57] M. Sharp (ed.), *Accounts of the Constables of Bristol Castle in the Thirteenth and Fourteenth Centuries*, Bristol Record Soc., 34 (1982), pp. 11, 23, 30, 38, 57; R.H. Hilton, *A Medieval Society* (Cambridge, 1983), p. 226.

[58] A.G. Rosser, 'London and Westminster: the suburb in the urban economy in the later Middle Ages', in J.A.F. Thomson (ed.), *Towns and Townspeople in the Fifteenth Century* (Gloucester, 1988), p. 52.

people, especially women, who made a meagre living from an uncertain and seasonal trade. The poor had to be warned at the Gloucestershire village of Weston Subedge in 1398 not to take for sale in the town the green peas that they were allowed to pick from their wealthier neighbours' land – they were only for their own consumption.[59] A rather better living was evidently available to the settled dealers in garden produce, called cabbage-mongers, garlic-mongers and leek-mongers, who are found in the suburbs of larger towns such as London and Oxford, and even in such small places as Godmanchester (Huntingdonshire).[60] Again, it must be stressed that for every known dealer in garden produce there were dozens who sold the major foodstuffs – bread, ale, fish, cheese and poultry.

The cheapness of garden produce must be appreciated to explain its low profile in the market place. Apples, at 4d.–8d. per qr. in the late thirteenth century were much cheaper than wheat which was often priced at 6s.[61] Cider, at $\frac{1}{2}$d. per gallon, compares with 1d. for ale. Onions were sold for a price similar to that of wheat. But English wine at 1d.–$1\frac{1}{2}$d. per gallon in the 1270s and 1280s cost much less than Gascon wine at 3d. and 4d., perhaps reflecting the lower quality of the English product. The only way that a gardener could raise his profit margin in these conditions was to exert himself to grow special varieties that appealed to the luxury market. Some kinds of apples and pears, such as 'warden' pears, could command a price as high as 6s. per qr., six times the price of the common kinds. And 'green' peas could be sold for 9s. per qr., three times the price of ordinary field peas.[62]

The English gardeners failed to meet the home demand, so that in the fourteenth and fifteenth centuries imports flowed steadily in, of onions and garlic, madder and woad, teasels and hemp. Even onion seeds and cabbages were imported, together with hops in the fifteenth century that were needed to make the ever more popular beer.[63] Horticultural produce came from Flanders and the Low Countries, and also from northern France, where gardens were evidently cultivated with more success than in England.

---

[59] Dorset County Record Office, DIO/M229/1–5.

[60] E. Ekwall, *Two Early Subsidy Rolls* (Lund, 1951), pp. 159, 160; J.E. Thorold Rogers, *Oxford City Documents, 1268–1665*, Oxford Historical Society, 18 (1891), p. 33; J.A. Raftis, *A Small Town in Late Medieval England, Godmanchester, 1278–1400* (Toronto, 1982), p. 135.

[61] J.E. Thorold Rogers, *A History of Agriculture and Prices in England*, i (Oxford, 1866), pp. 223, 418–19, 445–50; ii (Oxford, 1866), pp. 175–7, 379–82.

[62] Northamptonshire County Record Office, Westmorland (Apethorpe), 4xx4, fo. 2v.

[63] W. Childs (ed.), *The Customs Accounts of Hull*, Yorkshire Archaeological Soc. Record Series, 144 (1984), pp. 50, 51; D.M. Owen, *The Making of King's Lynn*, British Academy Records of Social and Economic History, new ser., 9 (1984), p. 354–77; B. Foster (ed.), T*he Local Port Book of Southampton for 1435–6*, Southampton Record Ser., 7 (1963), pp. 2, 10, 12, 38, 40, 64, 66, 68, 70–2.

Consumption

Gardening enthusiasts maintain that fruit and vegetables were consumed in large quantities by all sections of the medieval population. The fact that our documents, such as household accounts, refer so seldom to the purchase of greengroceries is seen as an irrelevance – the produce came directly from the seigneurial gardens, and so escaped mention in financial documents. However, we do have some accounts for produce, which allow us to calculate daily consumption. Glastonbury Abbey was supplied with 8,000 bulbs of garlic in a year, which seems a great deal unless we remember that there were a hundred consumers who could, if none was wasted or decayed, have a quarter of a bulb each per day.[64] It is true that the 10 qrs. of apples delivered to Maxstoke Priory (Warwickshire) in 1462–4 would have given each canon, servant and guest an apple each day, but this was an unusually prolific year, and in *c.* 1485 the thirty consumers of the priory had to share $1\frac{1}{2}$ qrs., enough to give them a weekly apple each.[65] Monasteries such as these, fixed in one place, were better able to organise regular supplies than the peripatetic households of the secular nobility. In the fifteenth century the magnates adopted a more settled life in perhaps two or three residences each year. Such prolonged stays by a large group of people (50-80 for the larger households) must have strained the resources of even a well-run garden, but there is no evidence even in the detailed accounts of these households of large-scale purchases of fruit and vegetables, even though they bought almost every other foodstuff in enormous quantities.

Recipe books designed for use in aristocratic households mention frequently fruit and vegetables, and there were some dishes based on these garden products, such as 'porray', a leek pottage, and an apple purée called 'appulmoy'.[66] But the overwhelming emphasis in medieval high cuisine was on the preparation of meat and fish dishes, flavoured with spices, which included dried fruits, the bulk of which were imported from the Mediterranean, not home-grown. Fresh fruit and vegetables were regarded as poor men's food, or as suitable for those doing penance. There was a suspicion that raw greenstuff was not good for the health. In aristocratic households there were seasonal patterns of consumption, with increased purchases of onions and leeks in Lent, as part of the ascetic diet of that time.[67] Some garden products were treated as delicacies, and purchased in small quantities, notably strawberries in June, peascods also in the early

---

[64] Hunt and Keil, 'Two medieval gardens', p. 100.

[65] Bodleian Library, MS Trinity College 84, fos. cclvi, cclxxxvi.

[66] C.B. Hieatt and S. Butler (eds.), *Curye on Inglysch*, Early English Text Society, S.S. 8 (1985), pp. 98–9, 116.

[67] Somerset County Record Office, DD/L P37/7.

summer, and apples and pears at Christmas.[68] The fact that some fruits were regarded as treats is shown by their use as gifts, including the presentation of apples, pears and cherries to visiting dignitaries by the governing bodies of large towns.[69] As regular items of consumption garden produce was probably used more in gentry households. A fifteenth-century treatise on domestic economy recommended that a knight should use 720 gallons of cider each year from his garden, while the higher nobility drank only ale and wine.[70] Garden produce was not regarded as an essential element in diet in the way that modern fashion decrees. When royal officials budgeted for the victualling of ships in 1340, they included every variety of foodstuff, but no fresh fruit and vegetables.[71] The warden of Merton College, Oxford went on an eleven-day journey in October/November 1299, far from the gardens of his college and his manors, and accounted in detail for his daily purchases: these included fruit on four days only.[72]

Poorer people ate more garden produce, as contemporary observers like the poet, William Langland, noted in detail.[73] Their basic foods were of course those which yielded most nutritional value at the lowest cost – bread, porridge, ale. But the garden provided valuable supplements, albeit in limited quantities. Farm servants on manors, the *famuli*, who were recruited from the poorer peasants, were given regular supplies of pottage, based on oat meal, but including vegetables from the manorial garden. This element in the dish is not often recorded, except when at Lakenheath (Suffolk) a lessee failed to maintain supplies as he had agreed. Occasionally elsewhere lords had to buy in supplies of leeks if the garden was deficient.[74] From the cooking utensils of peasants it is evident that variants of this cereal and vegetable pottage provided one of the basic ingredients of the popular diet. Garden produce also served as a valuable cushion for the poor in times of hardship, shown by the by-laws in many villages that allowed the poor to pick green peas in the fields for their own consumption during the 'hungry time' of the early summer before the grain harvest.[75] The only evidence of

[68] Northamptonshire County Record Office, Westmorland (Apethorpe), 4xx4; British Library, Add. MS 34213.

[69] Bateson, *Leicester*, ii, p. 25; Hudson and Tingey, *Norwich*, ii, p. 41; R.B. Dobson (ed.), *York City Chamberlains' Account Rolls, 1396–1500*, Surtees Society, 192 (1980), pp. 24, 25, 93.

[70] A.R. Myers (ed.), *The Household of Edward IV* (Manchester, 1951), p. 109.

[71] PRO, E 101/22/25.

[72] J.R.L. Highfield (ed.), *The Early Rolls of Merton College, Oxford*, Oxford Historical Society, 18 (1964), pp. 176–7.

[73] D. Pearsall (ed.), *Piers Plowman by William Langland* (London, 1978), pp. 158–9; C. Dyer, 'English diet in the later Middle Ages', in T.H. Aston et al. (eds), *Social Relations and Ideas* (Cambridge, 1983), pp. 206–8.

[74] Cambridge University Library, EDC 7/15/11/1/8, M5, M13; Northamptonshire County Record Office, Finch-Hatton 519; H.M. Briggs (ed.), *Surrey Manorial Accounts*, Surrey Record Society, 15 (1935), pp. 34–50.

[75] W.O. Ault, *Open-field Farming in Medieval England* (London, 1972), pp. 39–40.

the quantities consumed by peasants comes from maintenance agreements for retired peasants, and the most informative Hampshire example already cited suggests that a peasant couple could each have a daily pint of cider from their own orchard.

Towns, as we have seen, were centres both of production and consumption of garden produce. This must be partly because consumers from outside the town, especially the aristocracy, bought their supplies in urban centres, where they knew that goods of all kinds were available of the right quality and price. It was also true that towns, especially the larger ones, contained people who were cut off by their environment from direct access to a garden, and so relied on the market for supplies. It may also be argued that urban civilisation led to the cultivation of more sophisticated tastes, as a wider range of garden produce was eaten by the urban rich. This is supported by the varied plant species that we know to have grown in town gardens. Above all, varied consumption of fruits is implied by the most direct evidence for diet that we could hope to have – the contents of latrines, drains and cesspits. Analysis of the microfossils of plants, especially stones and pips, found in such deposits by archaeologists, has revealed, besides the expected cereal bran from bread and porridge, a mass of remains of apples, pears, plums, cherries, grapes, damsons, gooseberries and strawberries. Mixed with these are also seeds and stones from wild fruits such as blackberries and sloes. The profusion has led one botanist to refer to 'medieval fruit salad'.[76] Unfortunately, valuable as this evidence is for indicating the types of fruits eaten, it cannot tell us which social groups ate these garden products, or how frequently. The material could have accumulated over months or years. By the nature of their economies, towns also stimulated demand for industrial crops, especially teasels and dye-stuffs for use in cloth-finishing.

Conclusion – Change

The best known change of the later Middle Ages involves a general decline in self-sufficiency in favour of the reliance on the market. Seigneurial vineyards, which had multiplied in the late eleventh and twelfth centuries, shrank in the fourteenth century, and the English drank the wines of Gascony and the Mediterranean instead.[77] Of course, the potential area for

[76] J. Greig, 'The investigation of a medieval barrel-latrine from Worcester', *Journal of Archaeological Science*, 8 (1981), pp. 265–82; idem, 'Plant foods in the past', *Journal of Plant Foods*, 5 (1983), pp. 179–214; Ayers and Murphy, 'Waterfront excavations', pp. 38–44; M. Atkins, A. Carter, and D.H. Evans, 'Excavations in Norwich, 1971–1978', *East Anglian Archaeology*, 26 (1985), pp. 68, 228–34.

[77] E.M. Carus Wilson, 'The effects of the acquisition and of the loss of Gascony on the English wine trade', in *Medieval Merchant Venturers* (London, 1967), pp. 267–9.

use as gardens increased in the later Middle Ages, especially with the population decline after the plagues of 1348–9. Peasants took over neighbours' gardens along with their messuages; and in the towns the open spaces were extended, for example in Oxford and the northern and western areas of Winchester, as the built up area declined.[78] Yet active garden production may not have increased at this time. References to gardens and orchards used as pastures are many, and this need not surprise us in view of the shortage of labour. People could make a good living without the drudgery of horticultural work. The new demands for dyestuffs and teasels for the expanding cloth industry, and for hops in the brewing trade were met from the Continent. Only saffron cultivation seems to have been an area of growth and innovation in English horticulture. [79] The English were far from being a nation of gardeners at the end of the Middle Ages; expansion was to come from the 'improvements' in production, growth in labour supply, and new consumer demands in the sixteenth and seventeenth centuries.

[78] H.E. Salter (ed.), *Survey of Oxford*, i, Oxford Historical Society, 14 (1960), pp. 49–50; Keene, *Winchester*, pp. 154–5.
[79] *Victoria County History of Essex*, ii, p. 360.

8

English Peasant Buildings in the Later Middle Ages
(1200–1500)

Any appreciation of the nature of medieval peasants, their economic activities, their style of life and their standard of living must involve an assessment of the quality of their buildings. Although much research has gone into aspects of this subject, it has resulted in a dispersed literature, and has led to many contradictory judgements.

Historians, or rather the few who have written on the subject, tend to hold very low opinions of peasant housing conditions: 'hardly more than crude huts' is one view; a widely read text book states that 'Housing was primitive . . . for the most part (houses) were small, with one or two rooms for people and animals alike'.[1] These impressions are derived from archaeologists, who have in the past tended to emphasise the less sophisticated aspects of the peasant house. One village site has been said to have had buildings that were 'flimsy', 'slight', and built of 'poor timber'; the peasants, it is said, lacked both the materials and the incentive to build more solidly.[2] The conventional wisdom among those who study vernacular architecture is also to see 'impermanent buildings' being replaced by more durable types towards the end of the Middle Ages.[3] There is an evident reluctance to date good timber-framed buildings in peasant contexts much earlier than *c.* 1400.[4] These opinions have been challenged by some archaeologists and architectural historians,[5] and the purpose here is to re-examine the subject, firstly by means of a detailed regional study of the documentary evidence for the West Midlands in the period 1350–1500, and then through an extension of the investigation to other regions and earlier periods, using a

---

[1]   R. Roehl, 'Patterns and structure of demand 1000–1500', in C.M. Cipolla (ed.), *The Fontana Economic History of Europe*, i (London, 1972), p. 118; J.L. Bolton, *The Medieval English Economy 1150–1500* (London, 1980), p. 13.

[2]   J.G. Hurst, 'The Wharram research project: results to 1983', *Medieval Archaeology*, 28 (1984), pp. 77–111.

[3]   E.g. R. Machin, 'The Great Rebuilding: a reassessment', *Past and Present*, 77 (1977), pp. 33–56.

[4]   E.g. E. Mercer, *English Vernacular Houses* (London, 1975), pp. 3–4.

[5]   M.W. Barley, 'Houses and history', *Counc. Brit. Archaeol. Annual Rep.*, 31 (1981), pp. 63–75; S. Wrathmell, 'The vernacular threshold of northern peasant houses', *Vernacular Architecture*, 15 (1984), pp. 29–33.

combination of information deriving from documents, architecture and archaeology.

Before turning to the detailed evidence, some preliminary comments are needed on the term 'peasant', which has in the past created some difficulties and misunderstandings. To English-speaking people of the twentieth century the word conveys a picture of downtrodden masses, capable only of leading a meagre existence in wretched living conditions, at the mercy both of their physical environment and their social superiors. Given this perception of the peasantry, it is understandable that they should be expected to have lived in houses (or huts) that were rough, temporary and inadequate.

Peasants can be defined simply as small-scale rural cultivators, occupying a relatively subordinate social position, and having relatively low incomes. Their material and legal conditions vary today, and varied in the past, from country to country, and from individual to individual. The differences between peasants depended on the resources available to them, the level of technical development, and the prevailing social system.[6] The peasants of late thirteenth-century England, to take a much-studied case, are normally thought to have included everyone from smallholders with an acre or two of arable land (plus common rights) who gained much of their living from craft work, wage-earning or small-scale retailing, up to a well-endowed minority (perhaps a twentieth of the land-holding population), who had 40 or 50 acres (16 or 20 ha) of land. Most of the recorded rural population in England held between 5 and 30 acres (2–12 ha), except in the eastern counties, from Kent to Lincolnshire, where in many villages a clear majority held 5 acres or less. If peasants are defined in this way, with their families and dependents they formed a majority of the English population, in excess of 80 per cent, so their households according to current estimates numbered about a million.

A half of all peasants in the late thirteenth century suffered the disadvantage of holding in villeinage, that is, by a customary tenure regulated in the lord's court. Villeins (serfs), when compared with free tenants, owed heavier obligations to their lords in terms of labour services and rents, and they were also subject to restrictions on migration and marriage. Freemen had their share of deprivation, however, because their holdings were often smaller than those of villeins. In one sample of 22,000 peasants from the East Midlands in 1279, 29 per cent of villein holdings contained less than 7 acres, while 47 per cent of free tenants came into this smallholding category.[7] Both villeins and free tenants had some independence, in the

---

[6]   For a definition of peasants, with reference to the sociological and anthropological literature, see R.H. Hilton, *The English Peasantry in the Later Middle Ages* (Oxford, 1975), pp. 3–19.

[7]   E.A. Kosminsky, *Studies in the Agrarian History of England in the Thirteenth Century* (Oxford, 1956), pp. 197–229.

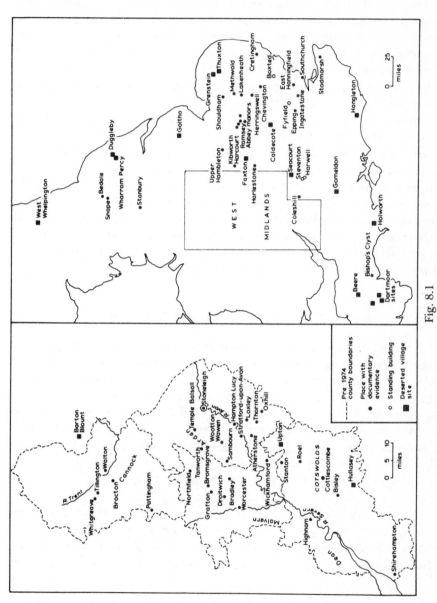

Fig. 8.1

Map of buildings, settlements and manors mentioned in text.

sense that they were responsible for the management of their own holdings, and the control exercised by lords, directed mainly to ensuring rent-payments, fell a long way short of complete dictatorship. The sharing of interests by customary and free tenants is shown by co-operation between neighbours within the village community, primarily in the use of common pastures and fields. Late medieval English peasants were much involved in the market, with the upper ranks selling surplus produce and hiring labour, while the less well-off had to earn wages and buy food. The penetration of buying and selling into peasant society is shown by the market for land, already active in the thirteenth century,[8] and the development of money rent, which was far advanced in 1250, and had almost entirely replaced labour services by c.1400.[9] This definition and characterisation of the peasantry is reflected in many ways in their material culture. Survey and excavation of village sites show the small defined territory (toft) of each household, often closely associated with neighbours in collective groupings. Comparison between the material remains of the village and those of aristocratic residences indicates the extent of social divisions between the peasant majority and the lordly elite. The import-ance of market contacts is demonstrated by the numerous finds of pottery and metal-work originating from outside the village.[10]

West Midland Peasant Buildings, 1350–1500

The documentary evidence for peasant buildings in much of England in the late fourteenth and fifteenth centuries is abundant, because of a special combination of circumstances. With the social and economic changes of the fourteenth century, and particularly after the collapse of population associated with the epidemics of 1348–75, there were important readjustments in the relationship between lords and tenants. Buildings became a point of friction, because tenants were amalgamating holdings and therefore wished to demolish redundant houses; they were also changing methods of farming, which required modification in accommodation for crops and animals. They might even wish to raise cash by selling surplus buildings or their materials. On the other hand the landlords correctly judged that the amalgamation of holdings and the decay of buildings would reduce their rent incomes, which were already declining. They seem to have lived in expectation that in the near future the

---

[8]   E.g. P.D.A. Harvey (ed.), *The Peasant Land Market in Medieval England* (Oxford, 1984), pp. 19–28.

[9]   E.g. R.H. Hilton, *The Decline of Serfdom in Medieval England* (London, 1969).

[10]   J.G. Hurst, 'A review of archaeological research', in M.W. Beresford and J.G. Hurst (eds), *Deserted Medieval Villages* (London, 1971), pp. 76–144.

population would recover, and that the holdings would again be rented out separately. The loss of buildings threatened this hope, as well as wasting what the lords saw as *their* assets, although the erection and maintenance of buildings had been the responsibility of the tenants as far back as our documents go.

Landlords in the late fourteenth and early fifteenth centuries were having to adjust to new and adverse circumstances, which involved them in abandoning the direct management of agriculture, and depending more than ever on rents. Thus their minds were concentrated on the problem of conserving tenant holdings. In the West Midlands they took a variety of measures to protect buildings, acting mainly through their chief instruments of discipline over tenants, the manor courts. From the court records of the region we find that, especially from the 1370s, tenants who demolished or stole buildings, or allowed them to decay, were amerced (fined). Tenants were ordered to carry out repairs, sometimes in such precise terms that the building or even the part of a building requiring attention was named. Those failing to comply with the orders were threatened with financial penalties. When a holding was surrendered, the lord could have a survey carried out with an assessment of the cost of repairs, sometimes with the intention of recovering the money from the outgoing tenant. When new tenants took up a holding, an obligation to carry out maintenance would commonly be inserted in the formal record of the tenancy. If decay was already far advanced, the new tenants might be required to put up a new building or buildings, often of a size fixed in the agreement, and with a time limit (usually a year or two) for the completion of the work. Tenants might be helped to repair or rebuild by remissions of rent, arrears of rent, or entry fines. More rarely they received grants of cash. Gifts of timber or straw were much more common, and these formed part of the building agreements between lords and and new tenants. A last resort would be for the lords themselves to carry out rebuilding, paying directly for the materials and the hire of labour.[11]

The lords were fighting a losing battle. The tenants, who sensed their improved bargaining position, were generally becoming more assertive. If a lord pressed them too hard, they could leave the manor, and many did. Lords might demand large amercements for failing to carry out repairs, as high as 3s. 4d. or 6s. 8d. instead of the normal 4d. or 6d.; they might warn tenants with huge penalties of £2 or £3; they could insist that the tenants be bound by pledges (sureties) to guarantee that they carried out orders or agreements to do building work. If a tenant resolutely refused to comply, he could be evicted, but this would have been an admission of defeat,

---

[11] B.F. Harvey, *Westminster Abbey and its Estates in the Middle Ages* (Oxford, 1977), pp. 273–4; see above, Chapter 3, pp.37–8; Hilton, *English Peasantry*, pp. 192–3.

because the whole idea was to keep as many tenants in well-ordered holdings as possible. Tenants could call their lord's bluff, because they knew that in the circumstances of the generally low demand for land a tenant with a decaying building was usually preferable to no tenant at all. Many buildings fell down, and perhaps a half of all of the occupied messuages of the 1340s had become empty tofts within a hundred years. Everywhere were ruined and abandoned buildings, not only concentrated in the deserted village sites, but also scattered over the many shrunken villages. Gradually the lords accepted the situation. Even at the height of their campaign individual tenants were occasionally given permission to remove a building or were excused compliance with a building agreement; by about 1480 most lords had given up the struggle for repairs, and stopped making building agreements or individual court orders. Instead they issued bland and ineffective general injunctions to tenants to maintain their holdings.[12]

These conflicts involved customary tenants only, as lords had no direct interest in the buildings of freeholdings. Occasional references in deeds and rentals suggest that the housing stock of free tenants declined also, but we cannot tell if the process was on a smaller scale. The selectiveness of the sources does not seriously diminish the value of their evidence, because customary tenants were numerous, and they give us a good sample of different economic strata within the peasantry. The lords, no matter how ineffective their measures, were unconsciously creating as a by-product of their attempts at conservation a mass of information for posterity.

In using this material I am extending the original work of Mr R.K. Field, who published a remarkable collection of building agreements for Worcestershire.[13] He showed that the agreements enable us to analyse the size of buildings because they often specify the number of bays ('spaces', *intersticia*, 'rooms') or the numbers of pairs of crucks ('forks', 'couples') to be built. As the dimensions of the bay, approximately 15 ft by 15 ft (*c.* 4.6 m x 4.6 m), are known from standing buildings, we can conclude that 84 per cent of the 113 Worcestershire buildings whose sizes are recorded, were either of three bays, 15 ft by 45 ft (*c.* 4.6 m x 13.8 m), or of two bays, 15 ft by 30 ft (*c.* 4.6 m x 9.2 m), with three bays in a majority. The remaining sizes were of one bay (2 per cent), four bays (11 per cent) or five or six bays (4 per cent). Research extending into Worcestershire's neighbouring counties of Gloucestershire, Staffordshire and Warwickshire repeats Field's findings

---

[12] C.C. Dyer, *Lords and Peasants in a Changing Society* (Cambridge, 1980), pp. 167, 294–5.
[13] R.K. Field, 'Worcestershire peasant buildings, household goods and farming equipment', *Medieval Archaeology*, 9 (1965), pp. 105–45.

in that 80 per cent of buildings were recorded as of two or three bays.[14] A Worcestershire agreement that has come to light since Field's publication gives contemporary confirmation of the size of the bay; at Grafton in 1435 Thomas Davys was to 'build anew a bay sixteen feet long annexed to his hall'.[15] In the light of the new research into the whole region a slight modification should be made to Field's argument that three-bay houses belonged to the better-off, thriving peasants. Three-bay buildings – being the commonest – are found on holdings as small as a quarter-yardland (*c.* 7 acres or 3 ha) and as large as a full yardland (*c.* 30 acres or 12 ha) or even larger. Similarly the four- or five-bay buildings that were sometimes built by wealthier tenants also occurred on quite modest tenements, so there does not seem to have been an exact correlation between the size of individual buildings and the acreage of their builders' holdings (this apparent anomaly will be discussed below). Critics of these sources may object that the sizes of buildings should not be taken too seriously because they generally refer to future constructions, and the agreements were not carried out; so the documents tell us about theory, not practice. It is true that tenants often did not keep their side of the agreement, but the sizes of the buildings were those that contemporaries thought appropriate and reasonable, in the light of their experience of existing buildings. In any case some of the buildings envisaged in agreements are known to have been completed.

In considering the nature of peasant buildings, our attention must be focused on the small piece of land, often as little as a quarter-acre (0.1 ha), that served as the centre of each holding, either arranged next to its neighbours along a village street, or, in an area of dispersed settlement, beside an access road. It was usually of rectilinear shape and bounded by banks, hedges, fences or walls, with an external ditch. Archaeologists customarily call this plot a toft, and in some parts of the country this is the word found in the documents. In the West Midlands the contemporary sources use the term 'messuage', 'toft' being reserved for an empty plot after the removal or decay of the buildings.

Throughout the West Midland region, as in Worcestershire, there are few references to two-storey buildings. Field's one example came from near

---

[14] The new figures, deriving from the counties of Gloucestershire, Staffordshire and Warwickshire, and a few manors in Worcestershire not available to Field, are as follows:

one bay	two bays	three bays	four bays	five bays	TOTAL
5	27	39	10	1	82

These figures, and the generalisations that follow on the West Midlands, are based on research into the records of 75 manors in the region, deposited in the nine archive repositories named in subsequent footnotes (15–45).

[15] Hereford and Worcester County Record Office (henceforth HWCRO), ref. 705: 100, BA 1120/12.

Bromsgrove (Worcestershire), in 1474. A clear reference to a rural building with an upper floor ('a lower and upper chamber in the upper part of the hall') is found in a maintenance agreement from Shirehampton (Gloucestershire, now Avon) in 1483.[16] At Loxley (Warwickshire) in 1488 a house was equipped with a *gryce* (ladder) and trap door, which implies the presence of a loft.[17] There is also architectural evidence for floored end-bays of cruck buildings of *c.* 1500 at Stoneleigh (Warwickshire) and there may have been a movement towards upper floors in rural houses in the region towards the end of the fifteenth century, as has been noted in Devon.[18]

People and animals were usually accommodated in separate buildings. The long-house, in which dwelling and byre came under the same roof, which is known from excavations in Gloucestershire in a thirteenth-century context,[19] had evidently become a rarity after 1350. Only two unambiguous references to dwelling houses and byres built in line were discovered by Field, to which another Worcestershire example can be added, at Northfield in 1440, where a tenant agreed to build 'a hall . . . and a chamber at the front end of the hall with a byre at the rear end'.[20] Normally peasants had a separate dwelling house, called a hall *(aula)*, or a hall and chamber *(aula et camera)*, or an *insethouse*. The most common arrangement was for a three-bay house to be divided into a hall and one or two chambers, separated by screens or walls which are called *speres* in a court roll from Hampton Lucy (Warwickshire) in 1457.[21] Kitchens are mentioned as free-standing buildings, though they may sometimes have occupied an end-bay of a dwelling house.

One problem that has been considered by both archaeologists and historians is the likelihood of a holding containing more than one dwelling house. Under the pressure of population increase in the twelfth and thirteenth centuries we know that holdings were divided, with yardlands and bovates being split into halves and quarters. Ultimately each fraction became a completely separate entity, but it is possible that at an intermediate stage two households would share the holding, and so two separate dwellings might be found occupying the same messuage. Subletting, a

[16] Dyer, *Lords and Peasants*, p. 318.

[17] Shakespeare's Birthplace Trust Record Office, Stratford-upon-Avon (henceforth SBT), DR18/30/15/8.

[18] N.W. Alcock, J.G. Braithwaite, and M.W. Jeffs, 'Timber-framed buildings in Warwickshire: Stoneleigh village', *Trans. Birmingham Warwickshire Archaeol. Soc.*, 85 (1971–3), pp. 178–202; N.W. Alcock and M. Laithwaite, 'Medieval houses in Devon and their modernisation', *Medieval Archaeology*, 17 (1973), pp. 100–25.

[19] R.H. Hilton and P.A. Rahtz, 'Upton, Gloucestershire, 1959–64', *Trans. Bristol and Gloucestershire Archaeol. Soc.*, 85 (1966), pp. 70–146; P.A. Rahtz, 'Upton, Gloucestershire, 1964–8', ibid., 88 (1969), pp. 74–126.

[20] Birmingham Reference Library, 518080. For Field's long-houses see E. Mercer, ' "*Domus Longa*" and "Long House" ', *Vernacular Architecture*, 3 (1972), pp. 9–10.

[21] HWCRO, ref. 009:1, BA 2636/164 91282.

clandestine activity and therefore only partially documented, might also have led to an extra house being built on a holding for a sub-tenant. A very well-documented occasion for the co-existence of two households would arise from retirement arrangements. An elderly couple, or a widow, would surrender land to a new tenant and sometimes a formal agreement for the maintenance of the old tenant would be registered in the court roll. The retiring peasant might be allowed a share – perhaps one bay – of the main dwelling house. More often a separate 'chamber' or 'house' was provided in the messuage, either a converted existing building, or a purpose-built dwelling. Because of the generally low expectation of life these arrangements would have been temporary and occasional.[22]

Peasant holdings were normally provided with agricultural buildings as well as dwelling houses. Even a cottage tenement might have a house, a granary and a byre, though perhaps only two buildings, a house and barn, would be found on some smallholdings.[23] Throughout the region, when for various reasons manorial juries listed all of the buildings on a holding, in villages such as Cottlescombe in Elkstone (Gloucestershire) and Stoneleigh, Oxhill, and Wootton Wawen (all in Warwickshire), three or more buildings are mentioned, such as a hall, granary, bakehouse and byre in 1438 at Cottlescombe, and a hall, chamber, kitchen, granary, oxhouse and bakehouse at Stoneleigh in 1481.[24] The basic structures were those to provide living space for people, one building for animals (a byre or sheepcote were the most common), and another for crop storage, either a barn *(grangia)* or granary *(horreum)*, terms which were apparently interchangeable.[25] Frequently an additional building was a free-standing bakehouse, which may have been also used for brewing. There are occasional references to the presence on peasant holdings of brewhouses, malt-kilns, stables, pigsties, dovecotes, cart-houses, wain-houses, shops and forges. Buildings must often have served more than one function, whether by using the same space for a number of purposes, such as storing a cart in a barn, or by dividing a building into sections, as must have happened in the case of the '*horrium cum* shepehouse' that needed roofing at Thornton (Warwickshire) in 1472.[26]

As peasants, particularly those who were better-off, clearly possessed a number of buildings, we can envisage the messuage as containing a

---

[22] R.M. Smith, 'Some reflections on the evidence for the origins of the European marriage pattern in England', in C. Harris (ed.), *The Sociology of the Family* (Sociological Review Monograph, 28, 1979), pp. 74–112.

[23] Dyer, *Lords and Peasants*, p. 317. This does not rule out the possibility that some cottage holdings supported one building only.

[24] Dorset County Record Office, D10/M227/1–2; SBT, DR18/30/24/17; PRO, SC 2 207/59–60; SC 6 1040/15.

[25] Repairs were ordered after the burning of '*orrii vel grangie*' at Atherstone-on-Stour, Warw., in 1450, Bodleian Library, Warwick ch.a1.

[26] Warwickshire County Record Office, CR 1911/13, for the 'granary with sheep-house'.

grouping, even a cluster of structures, often around a yard. This layout is familiar from the physical remains, whether revealed by surveys as at Hullasey (Gloucestershire) or by aerial photographs (to take an example from outside the West Midlands region) as at Duggleby (Yorkshire) or from excavations at sites such as Barton Blount (Derbyshire).[27]

Perhaps variations in the wealth and status of peasants were reflected in the number of buildings rather than in their size, or in a combination of number and size that would give a better-off peasant a total of a dozen bays, while a cottager would have only four or so. The quality of construction may also have varied with the social rank of the tenant. Certainly functional differences might lead to differences between buildings, like the timbers called 'forklegs' or 'hovel-forks', found in agricultural buildings, which indicate their relatively insubstantial construction.[28] Our suspicion that some buildings were very slight is aroused by the sale of their materials for sums as small as 1s. 6d. or 2s. 0d., unless of course the timber being sold had once been of good quality but had deteriorated badly through neglect. No doubt some of the minor structures, such as pigsties, were both small and flimsy, hence their rare appearances in our documents, because lords were concerned to maintain the more important buildings. One type of agricultural building, the 'helm', was in use at Bisley (Gloucestershire) in the late fourteenth century. The name was applied to poor quality cartsheds or stack-stands in some regions in later centuries, but at Bisley helms stood on staddle stones, to protect the crops stored in them from damp and vermin. Their timber-framed superstructures, designed to sit on four or twelve stones, would have been quite sophisticated, even if on a small scale.[29]

The bulk of the West Midland evidence relates to dwelling-houses or barns, and there can be little doubt of the substantial nature of these buildings. They normally had stone foundations, usually no more than a low plinth wall, but higher walls, even up to the eaves, are implied by some Cotswold records. The timber superstructures were invariably based on crucks, called 'forks' or 'couples', so peasants were using a building technique that could have been sturdy. Other major timbers, such as ground sills, wall-plates and studs are also mentioned, commonly made of oak, elm, or ash. The walls were infilled with wattle and daub, and can be

[27] P. Ellis, 'The medieval settlement at Hullasey, Coates', *Trans. Bristol and Gloucestershire Archaeol. Soc.*, 102 (1984), pp. 210–12; M.W. Beresford and J.G. Hurst, 'Wharram Percy: a case study in microtopography', in P.H. Sawyer (ed.), *Medieval Settlement* (London, 1976), plate 11.8; G. Beresford, *The Medieval Clay-land Village: Excavations at Goltho and Barton Blount* (Soc. Medieval Archaeol. Mono. 6, 1975), pp. 12–18.

[28] N.W. Alcock and R. de Z. Hall, 'Documentary evidence for crucks', in N.W. Alcock (ed.), *Cruck Construction: An Introduction and Catalogue* (Counc. Brit. Archaeol. Res. Rep. 42, 1981), pp. 28–36.

[29] C. Dyer, 'Evidence for helms in Gloucestershire in the fourteenth century', *Vernacular Architecture*, 15 (1984), pp. 42–5.

shown from some sources to have been plastered and lime-washed.[30] Thatched roofs of straw were normal, though reed thatch is recorded in two cases, and a peasant's barn at Sambourn (Warwickshire) mentioned in 1480, is known to have been tiled.[31] This example is by no means unusual in demonstrating a relatively high standard of construction for the more important agricultural buildings. Barns, when their structure is recorded, were invariably built with crucks. The agreements for maintaining retired peasants might provide for the conversion of an agricultural building into a dwelling, like the cart-house on a yardland holding at Stanton (Gloucestershire) in 1405, that was to be used to house an elderly couple.[32] This implies that an agricultural building, although in need of alteration to make it habitable, was not markedly inferior to a dwelling in its basic structure. Maintenance agreements have as a common theme the honourable treatment to be accorded to the outgoing tenants, and the comparability of their new style of life both with their life before retirement and with that of their successors, so they could not be fobbed off with a shed.

The quality of peasant buildings was very much dependent on the availability of suitable timber. In the special circumstances when the lords were encouraging or threatening tenants to do repairs they were given trees from the lords' woods. When timber was not available in the immediate vicinity, more remote sources could be used; so tenants on the bishop of Worcester's manors adjacent to the city of Worcester were supplied from Malvern Wood, 9 miles (*c.*15 km) away.[33] This leaves the problem of the source of timber for peasants who were putting up buildings in normal circumstances, either customary tenants acting on their own initiative (because most building work was *not* carried out under pressure from the lord), or free tenants whose buildings were not subject to control by landlords. Some tenants would have had trees growing on their land: in wooded districts like the Forest of Arden in Warwickshire peasants might have a small acreage of woodland as part of their holding; in champion districts there would have been at least some hedgerow timber around the messuages or in the boundaries between furlongs in the open fields.[34] The use of such trees by customary tenants was subject to seigneurial control, and illicit felling or the sale of timber led to amercement in the manor court. Presumably permission would have been given to customary tenants who wished to use the timber for building on their own holdings, and again free

[30] Field, 'Worcestershire peasant buildings', pp. 109–11.

[31] SBT, DR5/2358.

[32] Gloucestershire County Record Office (henceforth GRO), D678/61.

[33] HWCRO, ref. 009: 1, BA 2636/175 92474.

[34] For peasant groves, C. Dyer, 'A note on the economic environment of Sydenham's Moat, Tanworth-in-Arden', *Trans. Birmingham Warwickshire Archaeol. Soc.*, 90 (1980), pp. 63–4; on hedgerow timber in open fields, P.D.A. Harvey, *A Medieval Oxfordshire Village* (Oxford, 1965), pp. 23–5.

tenants would have encountered no restrictions. However, the amount of such timber, especially in champion areas, must have been quite small; for major timbers, like cruck blades, peasants needed access to the products of mature woods. A tenant's common rights often included 'housbote', entitling him to take some building timber from the lord's wood. On the rare occasions when this custom was given any definition, it was clearly supervised by the lord's officials, and we may doubt if large numbers of trees could have been taken.[35] Peasants also took timber without permission, and were then fined in the lord's court on the report of a woodward in an exercise designed to collect revenue rather than to deter offenders. The quantities recorded were usually small, often single trees, and certainly not enough to build complete new houses.

It therefore seems likely that peasants often obtained their timber on the market. We know that this happened in towns: for example, the Guild of the Holy Cross at Stratford-upon-Avon purchased timber together with other building materials for work on its properties in the fifteenth century. The guild records give information about prices, like the small oak trees which cost 3d. each. In a survey of Tanworth-in-Arden (Warwickshire) in *c.* 1500 'great' oaks, suitable for major building timbers, were valued at 8d. each.[36] If a three-bay cruck-built peasant house needed perhaps twenty trees of varying sizes the cost of buying timber could have been as much as 10s. 0d.[37] The employment of labour for felling, preparation and transport added to the expense, but this cost would have been incurred even if the trees were obtained freely. Expenditure could have been kept down by re-using timber from older buildings, and there is much evidence that this was a common practice. Other materials posed fewer problems, as straw, clay and (less certainly) withies or hazel rods for wattles would have been obtained either on the peasant's holding or on the commons. However, the

[35] R.H. Hilton (ed.), *The Stoneleigh Leger Book* (Dugdale Soc., 24, 1960), p. 103, gives a restrictive definition of 'housbote, heybote and fuyrbote': oaks and other trees could only be taken with the permission of the foresters, if the need was genuine and no waste was caused. Occasionally the right was enjoyed without restriction, as stated in a Little Packington, Warw., charter of the late twelfth century: R.R. Darlington (ed.), *The Cartulary of Worcester Cathedral Priory (Register 1)* (Pipe Roll Soc., new ser., 38, 1962–3), p. 167. Specific references to 'housbote' are rare because the right was customary, subsumed in charters and other documents in the phrase 'with appurtenances'.

[36] T.H. Lloyd, *Some Aspects of the Building Industry in Medieval Stratford-upon-Avon* (Dugdale Soc. Occasional Paper, no. 14, 1961), pp. 16–17; L.D.W. Smith, 'A survey of building timber and other trees in the hedgerows of a Warwickshire estate, *c.* 1500', *Trans. Birmingham Warwickshire Archaeol. Soc.*, 90 (1980), pp. 65–73. See also O. Rackham, *Trees and Woodland in the British Landscape* (London, 1976), pp. 73–84.

[37] O. Rackham, 'Grundle House: on the quantities of timber in certain East Anglian buildings in relation to local supplies', *Vernacular Architecture*, 3(1972), pp. 3–8 estimates for a modest East Anglian 3-unit house of *c.* 1600 the use of 79 trees. A cruck house of similar size needed less timber, as shown by J. Blair, 'Two early cruck houses in south Oxfordshire', *Oxoniensia*, 44 (1979), pp. 55–61, but his example was unusually economical in its construction. The figure of 20 arises from a tentative suggestion by D.Hinton.

iron-work of houses – nails, hinges, locks and keys – would all have been purchased.

Observation of the structures of surviving peasant buildings has led to the conclusion that they were put up by specialist carpenters, often using a high degree of skill. The suggestion is sometimes made that this is true only of the very best buildings, those exceptional examples that have stood the test of time. However, the documents show that carpenters were normally employed by peasants on all kinds of buildings. Aggrieved peasant employers in law suits complained of poor service from carpenters, like John Bonde, who contracted to build a house at Temple Balsall (Warwickshire) working by the day, and was impleaded in 1415 by Thomas Bloxwych, because 'sometimes he came to his work around prime (early morning) and sometimes around sext (midday)'.[38] Carpenters were too numerous to have all found employment in upper-class building projects. For example, thirty-two were listed among the tax-payers of sixty villages and towns in south Staffordshire in 1380–81. They sometimes lived in groups, like the three carpenters who were recorded at Brocton in Baswich, a village of about twenty-three households.[39] Contemporaries assumed that a professional carpenter would be employed to put up peasant buildings, as is shown by a grant of 9s. 10d. made to a tenant of Pattingham (Stafford-shire) in 1444 to pay a carpenter.[40] Litigation over contracts, and prosecutions under the Statute of Labourers in the late fourteenth century, record the employment by peasants of other building specialists, notably masons, thatchers and daubers. We cannot know the size of the contribution that the peasant or his household made to building work, especially in the less skilled jobs, such as preparation of the site, carriage of materials, and daubing, but in view of the evidence for the hiring of specialists, we should not assume that a great deal was done by the peasant. After all, the agricultural activities on the holding needed attention for much of the year, and some of the slack times of the farming calendar, like mid-winter, were not suitable for building work. Unskilled labour would certainly have been used in the 'rearing' of the timbers, recorded in seigneurial building projects when ale was supplied to the often large groups of volunteers who came to lend a hand. In this operation at least the idea that house building was a 'communal' activity has some justification.

The argument then is that peasants bought materials and employed labour, leading inevitably to the conclusion that they spent a good deal of money on their buildings. How much did a completed building cost? One

[38] Warwickshire County Record Office, CR 112, Ba 519.

[39] W. Boyd (ed.), 'The poll tax of 1379–81', *Collections for a History of Staffordshire*, 17 (1896), pp. 157–205.

[40] Staffordshire County Record Office (hereafter SRO), D1807/72 (I am grateful to Miss J.R. Birrell for this reference, and for the two subsequent Staffordshire examples below).

indication comes from the accounts of landlords who took on the construction of tenants' houses themselves. The most fully documented example is John Bromefeld's holding at Tillington (Staffordshire) where the earl of Stafford paid for a three-bay dwelling house and a three-bay barn in 1437–38.[41] He did this economically by dismantling two buildings at Whitgreave, about 2 miles away, transporting the timbers, and re-erecting them at the new site. This operation cost £2 5s. 4d., and together with extra timbers and laths, and the cost of wattling, daubing and thatching with reeds, the whole expenditure came to £3 18s. 2d., or about £2 per building. The job was evidently not completed at the end of the accounting year, as there is no mention of doors or fittings, so the £2 figure must be regarded as a minimum. Had the earl also paid the full cost of cutting and fitting new timbers, rather than recycling old materials, the completed buildings would surely have worked out at a minimum of £3 each. An estimate of this order is supported by the sum of £2 7s. $1\frac{1}{2}$ d. spent on extensive repairs (not a complete rebuild) on a three-bay house at Walton in Haywood (Staffordshire) in 1461–62, and an abbot of Evesham's claimed expenditure of £13 6s. 8d. on rebuilding a whole tenement (presumably three or four buildings) at Wickhamford (Worcestershire) in *c.* 1400.[42]

Is the cost of a tenant's building to a lord irrelevant in assessing a peasant's own costs? Lords built one in a hundred tenant buildings at most, and this minority could be unrepresentative as well as tiny. In particular it can be alleged that, because of their superior resources, lords built to a higher standard. There is probably some truth in this argument but it seems unlikely that their standards were very much better than those of the peasants. In the case of the Tillington buildings the original timber frames from Whitgreave are likely to have come from a peasant-built house and barn, and if these were acceptable to the earl of Stafford's officials they evidently did not expect that there would be great differences between a tenant house that they built, and one put up by a peasant. Incidentally, the moving of the buildings should not suggest their flimsiness, as is sometimes stated, but rather resulted from the flexibility of good quality timber-framing, which could be dismantled and reassembled, as is recorded on many occasions both for seigneurial and peasant buildings. A further indication of the portability and interchangeability of these structures is provided by the transfer in 1391–92 of two tenant buildings (most likely barns or dwellings) from Bradley (Worcestershire) to the town of Droitwich, a distance of 6 miles (9 km), and their re-erection as salt-houses by the estate managers of the bishopric of Worcester at a total cost of £7 12s. 0d.[43] Their

[41]   PRO, SC 6 988/12.

[42]   SRO, D 1734/3/2/2; W.D. Macray (ed.), *Chronicon Abbatiae de Evesham* (Rolls Ser., London, 1863), p. 305.

[43]   HWCRO, ref. 705:7, BA 7335/38.

timber-work was clearly of a sufficient standard to provide the basis for a seigneurial building, albeit one intended for industrial use.

If landlords had really been aiming to erect tenant buildings very much superior to those of peasant houses in general, they would surely have used techniques and materials familiar from their own manor houses: mortared ashlar foundations, for example, or glazed windows, or roofs of ceramic tiles. We should beware of idealising the motives of landlord builders. All of our knowledge of late medieval estate management suggests that they were reluctantly seeking to preserve wasting assets in a bleak economic climate. Unlike some builders of 'estate' cottages of the eighteenth and nineteenth centuries they were not making a far-sighted investment in the long-term future, because they had different concepts of investment, and they were unlikely to have been motivated by a spirit of paternalistic philanthropy.[44] They seem rather to have been providing at reasonable cost the sort of buildings that were appropriate for a peasant holding, so that tenants would be attracted to them. Accordingly we are justified in thinking that the costs of tenant buildings put up by lords provide some guide to the financial commitment of peasants paying for similar buildings. There are too many uncertainties to allow us to say that a peasant's costs would have been either higher or lower than those incurred by a lord. Any participation by a peasant in the work would have helped to reduce the labour bill; on the other hand many lords obtained timber free (or at least they did not pay for it directly), whereas the peasant who was putting up a building independently often had to buy his timber.

To some extent we do not need to speculate on the cost of building when the peasants themselves were paying, because there is direct evidence in the form of estimates made when a dilapidated tenement was inspected by a jury, and when sums of money were mentioned in building agreements. The bulk of assessments of dilapidation amount to a few shillings only, but they refer to relatively small-scale repairs, such as rethatching a roof. The largest sums, intended to pay for major repairs, are our best guide to the cost of a new building. Some examples are the 'waste and destruction' of Henry Channdeler's buildings at Roel (Gloucestershire) in 1400, said to be worth £4, or the assessment of £2 put on repairs to a cottage holding at Stanton (Gloucestershire) in 1442. In 1438 at Stoneleigh (Warwickshire) the lord gave a tenant £2 and 'sufficient timber' to repair a three-bay house. At Highnam (Gloucestershire) in 1351 a new tenant agreed to carry out building work worth £3 within a year.[45] These and other sums said to be needed to carry out major repairs on peasant buildings confirm the impression gained from the Tillington and Walton examples that a new

[44] Hilton, *English Peasantry*, p. 213; Harvey, *Westminster Abbey*, pp. 331–3.
[45] GRO, D 678/66A (Roel); D 678/94 (Stanton); PRO, SC 2 207/79 (Stoneleigh); GRO, D 936a/ M2 (Highnam).

house or barn of three bays would have cost at least £2, and a more likely sum would have been £3 or £4, especially if the timber had to be purchased. These are no mean sums: £3 approaches the annual earnings of a carpenter in about 1400, or the purchase price of six oxen or thirty sheep. Peasant houses were rather cheaper to build than modest town houses of the fifteenth century, which cost £10 or so, but these were two-storey buildings with tiled roofs.[46] Seigneurial buildings, superior to these houses in both size and materials, were very much more expensive. Taking into account the general levels of price and wages, these medieval rural houses were rather cheaper than modern houses. But they needed a considerable outlay of cash, and involved much greater expenditure than any 'crude hut'.

The documents summarised above accord well with the evidence of the surviving late medieval buildings. Dozens of well-carpentered houses, of two, three or four bays, based on cruck principals and erected on low plinth walls of stone, still stand in the West Midlands. The notion that these were superior buildings, exceptional in their ownership or craftsmanship, and were therefore given an unusual capacity for survival, has been countered by Alcock who has pointed to the 'cruck villages', like Stoneleigh, where cruck buildings exist in sufficient number to show that these were not just the houses of a small élite.[47] Also Charles's emphasis on the role of the carpenters working in the fifteenth century at the peak of their accomplishment within a well-established building tradition suggests that the surviving houses are representative of a once numerous type.[48] Many cruck buildings failed to survive, according to Alcock, not because they were flimsy in construction, but because their lack of height made them difficult to convert to two-storey dwellings in the sixteenth and seventeenth centuries. The documentary evidence allows us to glimpse hundreds of buildings that have now perished, which would appear to have been very similar in size and construction to those still standing.

To sum up: in the West Midlands in the period 1350–1500 peasant messuages generally contained a number of buildings, consisting frequently of a house and barn, and often one or two other buildings used for food processing and agriculture. The house and barn were commonly of two or three bays (about 9–14 m in length); they were built of large timbers, including crucks, by craftsmen at a cost of about £2 to £4. The other buildings may not have been as substantial as the houses and barns, but their quality should not be underestimated. Buildings were regarded by

[46] R. Machin, 'The mechanism of the pre-industrial building cycle', *Vernacular Architecture*, 8 (1977), pp. 15–19; Lloyd, *Some Aspects of the Building Industry*, pp. 23–4; D. Keene, *Survey of Medieval Winchester* (Winchester Studies, 2, Oxford, 1985), i, p. 172.

[47] N.W. Alcock, 'The origin and spread of cruck construction in Britain', in Alcock (ed.), *Cruck Construction*, pp. 56–60.

[48] F.W.B. Charles, *Cruck Construction and its Derivatives* (Soc. Medieval Archaeol. Mono. 2, 1967), p. 8.

landlords as such crucial elements of tenant holdings that they made strenuous efforts to keep them in good repair. Providing that they were maintained, buildings of this type were potentially durable: the tiny minority surviving until the present day were selected more by good fortune than by any unusual qualities in their original structure.

Documentary Evidence for Peasant Buildings outside the West Midlands, 1350–1500

Until other researchers are able to gather a similar quantity of documentary evidence for other regions, no more can be done here than to make brief excursions into the printed and manuscript sources to provide some comparative material. A starting point is Bishop's Clyst in Devon, where the bishops of Exeter built a number of cottages in the early fifteenth century, including one with the luxury of a roof of stone slates.[49] Devon, like the West Midland counties, lay within the cruck building area, though walls at Clyst were made of cob rather than the wattle and daub panels found further north. Two-bay thatched cottages built as part of a row (and therefore cheaper than a free-standing building), averaged £3 4s. 0d. each. Further east at Coleshill (Berkshire, now Oxon.) in the 1430s the lord was carrying out a major campaign of rebuilding, again including one building (a barn) roofed with slates.[50] A four-bay thatched dwelling house $21\frac{1}{2}$ ft (6.6 m) wide and $51\frac{1}{2}$ ft (15.7 m) long, with stone walls 9 ft (2.7 m) high at the sides and 16 ft (4.9 m) high at the gables, was built for £7 6s. 4d. The same yardland holding, known from a previous tenant as 'Feld's', was also provided with a barn *(orreum)* of at least two bays, which cost nearly £4 to repair over a two-year period.

In the East Midlands the building traditions were very different. Crucks were rarely used, and building stone was often scarce. On the Ramsey Abbey estate which was centred on Huntingdonshire, with outlying manors in Bedfordshire, Cambridgeshire and Northamptonshire, there were many building agreements between the abbey and its tenants in the first half of the fifteenth century.[51] The size of the buildings was described in terms of six or eight *byndyngstodis* or 'binding posts', that is of two or three bays; to confirm the expectation that these buildings were similar in size to those of the West Midlands the dimensions were sometimes given in feet, 30 or 40 ft (9.2 or 12.2 m) long and 14, 15 or 16 ft (4.3, 4.6 or 4.9 m) wide. Again each holding was equipped with a group of buildings. For example, a cottage at Wistow (Huntingdonshire, now Cambridgeshire),

[49] N.W. Alcock, 'The medieval cottages of Bishop's Clyst, Devon', *Medieval Archaeology,* 9 (1965), pp. 146–53.

[50] PRO, SC 6 744/17, 19, 22.

[51] E.B. Dewindt (ed.), *The* Liber Gersumarum *of Ramsey Abbey* (Toronto, 1976).

was described as consisting of an *insethouse*, a chamber and a bakehouse.[52] The first two were perhaps joined together, so the holding was provided with at least two separate buildings. A larger holding, at Little Raveley (Huntingdonshire) in 1428 had an *insethouse* of eight binding posts, a barn of eight, and a bakehouse of six, all in need of rebuilding after a disastrous fire.[53] On most Ramsey holdings buildings for animals are rarely mentioned, apart from the occasional sheepcote or stable. Long-houses were as rare as in the West Midlands, the only possible example being from a maintenance agreement at Chatteris (Cambridgeshire) in 1443 which allowed a widow to keep three animals 'at the east end of the *insethouse*'.[54] Animals were perhaps normally sheltered in yards. Most buildings were of one storey, except for a few with solars, notably at Warboys (Huntingdonshire).[55] The peasants of the Ramsey estate may have built less substantially and spent somewhat smaller sums on buildings than their contemporaries to the west: they did not build byres; judging from the absence of references to stone foundations they either built directly on the ground or on padstones; and the timbers needed for a structure without crucks could have been relatively slender. On the other hand the differences between the regions should not be over-rated: a tenant still had to maintain two or three buildings, totalling eight or more bays; he or she employed specialists for thatching and daubing as well as carpentry, to judge from references to these craftsmen in the building agreements; and because of its relative scarcity, timber cannot have been cheap to buy and transport. When Ramsey Abbey paid for repairs to tenant buildings at Hemingford Abbots (Huntingdonshire) in the mid-fifteenth century timber was purchased in parcels at prices varying from 2s. to 20s. A sum of 16s. bought the timber for a barn, and the 'making' of a barn in carpentry and roofing cost 39s. 4d.; £4 6s. 6d. was paid for repairs to a tenement (we are not told for how many buildings).[56] Further north, at Upper Hambleton (Rutland, now Leicestershire), an area where stone foundations were used, repairs to two tenant buildings in 1453 involved an outlay by the lord of £1 11s. 7d. and £2 2s. 11d.[57] That peasants would also have paid a minimum of £2 for a new building, and probably more, is implied by the reductions of rent and grants of cash made by Ramsey Abbey to its tenants, the sums of £1 or £2 evidently being intended to cover part of the cost only. One Ramsey document gives a clue about regular maintenance of buildings,

[52] Ibid., pp. 319–20.

[53] Ibid., p. 204.

[54] Ibid., p. 297.

[55] Ibid., pp. 101, 339–40.

[56] PRO, SC 6 877/4–8.

[57] H.B. Sharp, 'Some mid-fifteenth century small-scale building repairs', *Vernacular Architecture*, 12 (1981), pp. 20–9.

because in a contract to provide a retired peasant at Hemingford Abbots in 1444 with a 'chamber', the incoming tenant agreed to employ a thatcher for two days per annum.[58] If we assume that more time would be needed to look after the larger roofs of the three buildings of a medium-sized holding, then the ideal expenditure each year could have been as much as 2s. 0d. or 3s. 0d.

In the counties of Essex, Suffolk, Norfolk and in south Lincolnshire the documentary evidence for tenant buildings seems less plentiful. Buildings were certainly said to be falling into disrepair, and landlords enjoined new tenants to maintain them, but whether because the problem was less acute, or because different relationships prevailed between lords and tenants, detailed building agreements and direct subsidies for buildings seem to be recorded less frequently than in other regions. However, there is enough information to suggest that buildings were of the post or stud construction recorded in the East Midlands, without substantial stone foundations. Although some of the numerous cottage holdings may have been furnished with only one building, at Shouldham (Norfolk) in 1434 a cottager had two, and a one-acre tenement recorded at Herringswell (Suffolk) in 1371 was provided with three.[59] There are several statements, from Methwold (Norfolk), Cretingham and Chevington (Suffolk) and Epping (Essex) that the messuages of larger holdings contained three buildings.[60] Besides the dwelling houses, barns and bakehouses are most frequently mentioned. In Suffolk in the late fourteenth century bakehouses were sufficiently well-built to make them convertible into living accommodation for retired peasants.[61] Throughout the region, from the middle of the fourteenth century, two-storey houses (the upper rooms being called solars) are recorded in the context of divisions made on retirement.[62] Dimensions of buildings were evidently similar to those of the East Midlands. Retired people were given small chambers of 15 by 15 ft (4.6 x 4.6 m); the houses of active peasants were larger, like the building measuring 40 x 18 ft (*c.* 12.2 x 5.5 m) that a tenant of Methwold agreed to erect in 1432.[63] A hint of costs is provided by the grant of 20s. together with timber that was given to the same Methwold tenant, and the sum of 31s. spent by the lord of

[58] Dewindt, *The* Liber Gersumarum, pp. 302–3.

[59] Norfolk County Record Office (henceforth NRO), Hare 2453; British Library, Additional Charter 54072.

[60] NRO, Bantoft, P 190 B; Suffolk County Record Office, Ipswich Branch, HA 10: 50/18/5.1 (I); Suffolk County Record Office, Bury St Edmunds Branch (hereafter SROB), E 3/15.3/1.15; PRO, SC 2 171/72.

[61] E.g. at Walsham-le-Willows in 1378: SROB, HA, 504/1/8.

[62] E.g. at Ingatestone, Essex: Essex County Record Office, D/DP M15; Great Cressingham, Norfolk: NRO, R 187A; Forncett, Norfolk: F.G. Davenport, *The Economic Development of a Norfolk Manor* (Cambridge, 1906), pp. lxxviii–lxxix.

[63] NRO, Bantoft, P 190 B.

Southchurch, Essex, on a tenant's building in 1438.[64] These sums, together with the assessments of damage, amercements and penalties of £1 or £2 mentioned in connection with decayed or demolished buildings, suggest that the expenses of building may have been a little lower than in the west of the country, but were by no means negligible. The sums quoted above tend not to include the cost of buying timber, and high prices, in an area where demand was such that native timber supplies were supplemented by imports, may have been a factor in East Anglian building costs. The timber collected by a prosperous peasant of East Hanningfield (Essex) for building a house in 1381 was valued (after his execution for joining the revolt of that year) at £5 6s. 8d.[65]

In Kent, where informative manorial records are lacking, wills of the period 1460–1500 sometimes give an indication of housing arrangements when they specify the division of property between widows and heirs. The wills are useful because they confirm the evidence of standing buildings that the better-off peasants lived in wealden houses with their combination of open halls and two-storeyed end-bays. Robert att Wod of Stodmarsh, for example, in his will of 1497 left his wife access to 'the north chamberre ... and the chamber underneth'. In the course of describing the rights of widows and heirs references are made in various wills to kitchens, shops, a bakehouse, a barn and a stable, suggesting that in Kent messuages were often provided with subsidiary buildings, like their counterparts elsewhere.[66]

The documents of the south-eastern counties can be compared with the more tangible evidence of surviving buildings. In the north this is difficult, because few low-status buildings survive that can be dated before 1600. Does this mean that the medieval peasant houses of the region were of exceptionally poor quality? In their authoritative study of the vernacular architecture of north Yorkshire and Cleveland Mr B. Harrison and Mrs B. Hutton have refuted this suggestion partly through the use of documents. Accounts of Bedale of the second quarter of the fifteenth century show the lord building houses and barns for tenants with substantial timber frames on stone foundation walls and pad-stones. Because of the expense of providing some roofs with stone slates some of these houses cost more than most of those recorded further south at the same period: the construction

---

[64] J.F. Nichols, 'Custodia Essexae' (unpublished University of London Ph.D. thesis, 1930), p. 270.

[65] Essex County Record Office, D/DP M833.

[66] H.S. Cowper, 'A note on some fifteenth and sixteenth century wills', *Archaeologia Cantiana*, 30 (1914), p. 127; E. Melling (ed.), *Some Kentish Houses* (Kentish Sources, v, Maidstone, 1965), pp. 7–9. The latter publication, and L.F. Salzman, *Building in England down to 1540* (2nd edn. Oxford, 1967), p. 601, contain editions of a building contract for two buildings at Cranbrook *c.* 1500. If this was being built for a peasant it would show a complete transition to modernity, because the larger house, 44 feet by 18 feet, was to be entirely of two storeys, with 3 rooms above and below, and a chimney and two fireplaces.

of one house came to £11 3s. 9d. and another totalled £4 15s. 6d. Such sturdy and expensive structures were by no means universal in the north, and other documents like accounts for Snape apparently depict (despite difficulties with impenetrable dialect terms) some quite crude and cheap buildings. Judging from the number of references in north Yorkshire to two-bay buildings, houses could have been rather small but, as in other regions, they were invariably accompanied by barns.[67] At Stanbury in Bradford (W. Yorkshire) in 1421 it was agreed in a court judgement that three buildings were sufficient for a holding.[68]

This survey of documented buildings, although inevitably incomplete, confirms the wide variety of local constructional traditions already known from the material evidence. There are however some common characteristics:

1   Peasant messuages contained not just a house but a group of buildings. The long-house was a localised type, and over most of the country animals were either housed separately, or kept in yards. Of other buildings, barns were most common, followed by kitchens and bakehouses, and a variety of other structures.

2   Individual houses and barns were mostly of two or three bays, so measured from about 30 to 45 ft (9.2 to 13.7 m) in length.

3   Among the great variety of materials used, some seem to have been of high quality, including stone foundations, and even complete stone walls in the west and north; they used substantial timbers, and (more rarely) slated or tiled roofs. Buildings were not provided with such solid foundations in the east but they were still professionally built using expensive timber. The agricultural buildings included some very well-built barns, and even bakehouses and cart-houses were regarded as suitable for adaptation for use as dwellings. Surviving vernacular buildings seem to be characteristic of once more numerous types, and the absence or rarity of standing buildings in some regions should not necessarily be regarded as evidence of the flimsiness of the local methods of construction.

4   Buildings for peasants were erected by professional craftsmen, certainly in the case of the carpentry, and often for the stone work and thatching also. The wages, together with the costs of materials, meant that houses built by lords cost anything between £2 and £11, and when peasants were paying,

[67]   B. Harrison and B. Hutton, *Vernacular Houses in North Yorkshire and Cleveland* (Edinburgh, 1984), pp. 2–16.

[68]   M.L. Faull and S.A. Moorhouse (eds.), *West Yorkshire: an Archaeological Survey to A.D. 1500* (Wakefield, 1981), p. 815.

may be estimated at between £2 and £4. The involvement of the craftsmen has implications for the quality and durability of the buildings.

Peasant Buildings, 1200–1350

So far the discussion has concentrated almost entirely on the period 1350–1500, because so much of the documentary evidence belongs to that period. The decades after 1350 might be seen as a time of radical innovation in peasant building, and the situation in our documents regarded as the result of recent or current developments. This would accord with the view of the period as the 'golden age of the peasantry', when after the plagues, land and corn were relatively plentiful, rents and restrictions were reduced, and standards of living improved.[69] The evidence of standing buildings fits this theory particularly well, because so many are dated to the decades after 1400, when it is argued that standards of carpentry attained a high level of competence. Still-existing late medieval peasant buildings are numerous in the south-east and especially in Kent, with its impressive wealden houses, and where there is independent evidence of a concentration of peasant prosperity.[70]

However, we should be cautious in accepting this argument too uncritically. Historians always have to be wary of confusing a real change with a mere innovation in documentation. We know more about houses after 1348–9 because of the administrative responses to the fall in population. The changes in peasant society during the fourteenth century were real and important, but they should not be exaggerated. Peasants with larger holdings could have fared quite well in the thirteenth century because rising prices and low labour costs gave them the opportunity to profit from the market. Conversely the fifteenth century, with its low prices and high wages, posed problems for those who had acquired more land. Just as historians can recognise the perpetuation of many aspects of society through the fourteenth-century crises, the archaeological evidence suggests some continuity also in peasant buildings. The innovations revealed by excavation belong to the thirteenth century rather than to the period after 1350. The characteristics of late medieval peasant buildings indicated above can also be recognised in the period 1200–1350:

[69] E.g. M.M. Postan, *The Medieval Economy and Society* (London, 1972), pp. 139–42.

[70] Mercer, *English Vernacular Houses*, pp. 3–4; J.T. Smith, 'The evolution of the English peasant house to the late 17th century: the evidence of buildings', *J. Brit. Archaeol. Assoc.*, 3rd ser., 33 (1970), pp. 122–47; F.R.H. Du Boulay, *The Lordship of Canterbury* (London, 1966), pp. 191–2.

1   The typical layout of house, barn, and other buildings is found on many thirteenth-century sites. Long-houses were more widely distributed than after 1350, and perhaps all of the needs of a peasant holding could be served by a single long-house, though it is difficult to prove archaeologically that long-houses stood in isolation. On the Dartmoor settlements, or at Gomeldon (Wiltshire) long-houses were associated with other structures, interpreted as barns, byres, out-houses and ovens.[71] In the areas where long-houses do not occur, in much of the East Midlands and the south-east, houses and barns are found together, and with bakehouses or other structures.[72] In East Anglia we can appreciate the complex of buildings within a messuage from the excavations of Thuxton in Norfolk.[73] Maintenance agreements in East Anglian court rolls assign to old people access to a number of buildings on a holding, often as many as three, and retired peasants might be given the bakehouse for conversion into a dwelling. References to peasant barns are not infrequent in early series of court rolls such as those for Lakenheath (Suffolk).[74]

2   The dimensions of excavated thirteenth-century buildings are very much in line with those recorded in later documents. The great majority measured from 25 ft (7.6 m) to 50 ft (15.2m) in length, and from 12 to 16 ft (3.7–4.9 m) in width, similar to the two or three-bay buildings mentioned in post-1350 court rolls. Often those measuring 60 ft (18.3 m) or more accommodated both animals and people, and could have been long-houses in the true sense.

3   We can define a clear and important innovation in building construction in the thirteenth century when various forms of foundation were adopted instead of earthfast posts (visible archaeologically as post-holes) which had been a feature of building in rural settlements since prehistoric times. The new foundations ranged from the well-built and quite high dry-stone walls (surviving up to 4 ft, or l.2 m), using Dartmoor granite or Cotswold oolite, to the thinner but mortared flint walls at Hangleton in Sussex, or to the

---

[71]   G. Beresford, 'Three deserted medieval settlements on Dartmoor: A report on the late E. Marie Minter's excavations', *Medieval Archaeology*, 23 (1979), pp. 98–158; D. Austin, 'Excavations in Okehampton Park, Devon, 1976–78', *Proc. Devon Archaeol. Soc.*, 26 (1978), pp. 191–239; Hurst, 'A review of archaeological research', p. 111.

[72]   E.g. M. Biddle, 'The deserted medieval village of Seacourt Berkshire', *Oxoniensia*, 26–27 (1961–2), pp. 70–201.

[73]   'Medieval Britain in 1964', *Medieval Archaeology*, 9 (1965), p. 214.

[74]   R.M. Smith, 'Rooms, relations and residential arrangements: some evidence in manor court rolls 1250–1500', *Medieval Village Research Group Annual Report*, 30 (1982), pp. 34–5; Cambridge University Library, EDC 7/15/11/1/6–9, transcribed by Miss J. Cripps and deposited in the School of History, University of Birmingham.

relatively rough chalk blocks of Wiltshire and the Yorkshire Wolds.[75] In those areas in which stone was less easily obtained only the gables might have foundations (a phase at Faxton in Northamptonshire), or at Goltho (Lincolnshire) pad-stones allowed the main upright timbers to stand a few inches off the ground surface. Even when no stone was used (for example in Norfolk) walls of 'clay lump' were built.[76]

The significance attached to the new type of foundation depends on the reconstruction proposed for the superstructure. One temptation is to assume that the stone walls on some sites once stood to a sufficient height to carry the rafters, which may be supposed to have been no more than rough branches. Alternatively the stone walls can be seen as bases for walls of cob, or of timber infilled with wattle and daub of the kind known from vernacular buildings. The former theory found favour in the past, but now opinion among architectural historians is moving towards associating the beginning of stone foundations in the west with the development of cruck building. As it is thought that the use of crucks in peasant buildings developed in the thirteenth century, the simultaneous appearance of stone foundations seems more than a coincidence.[77] The foundations protected the timbers from damp, and provided a level base for a good quality roof. The crucks have left no archaeological trace because they were set into horizontal sill beams. Accordingly the buildings of the thirteenth century when excavated have a similar appearance to those of the succeeding three or four centuries because they were built on the same principles, in their superstructures as well as their stonework. Documentary references from the West Midlands to the use of crucks in the construction of small peasant houses as early as 1312 and 1325 add some support to this view.[78] Outside the regions where stone foundation walls and crucks were used, 'primitive' framing was evidently introduced in the late thirteenth and early fourteenth century, providing a structure with a longer life and more sophisticated carpentry than earlier earthfast construction.[79]

Small finds from excavations of peasant houses throughout the country provide clues to the character of the superstructure. They show that the

[75] Beresford, 'Three deserted medieval settlements', p. 138; Rahtz, 'Upton', p. 94; E.W. Holden, 'Excavations at the deserted medieval village of Hangleton, Part I', *Sussex Archaeol. Collections*, 101 (1963), pp. 54–181; J.G. and D.G. Hurst, 'Excavations at the deserted medieval village of Hangleton, Part 2', ibid., 102 (1964), pp. 94–142; J.G. Hurst, *Wharram, A Study of Settlement on the Yorkshire Wolds* (Soc. Medieval Archaeol. Mono. 8, 1979), pp. 37–54, pls III and IV.

[76] 'Medieval Britain in 1966', *Medieval Archaeology*, 11 (1967), p. 307; Beresford, *Medieval Clay-land Village*, pp. 41–2; P. Wade-Martins, *Village Sites in Launditch Hundred* (East Anglian Archaeol., no. 10, 1980), pp. 112–26.

[77] J.T. Smith, 'The problems of cruck construction and the evidence of distribution maps', in Alcock (ed.), *Cruck Construction*, pp. 5–24 believes that while crucks are older than the thirteenth century, they developed greatly in that century with the abandonment of earthfast foundations.

[78] Alcock (ed.), *Cruck Construction*, pp. 29–33.

[79] Beresford, *Medieval Clay-land Village*, pp. 40–1.

doors were hung on iron hinges or turned on stone pivots and were provided with iron locks and keys. Sometimes there is evidence also of fittings for wooden shutters. The number of such openings is suggested in an agreement to build a house for a widow at Halesowen (Worcestershire) in 1281 which specifies the provision of three doors (presumably one was internal) and two windows. Descriptions of crimes in late thirteenth-century court rolls show that doors could be considerable obstacles.[80] Carpentered doors and shutters with locks and hinges, fittings into frames and strong enough to frustrate robbers, must have been attached to high walls with strong timber uprights in the thirteenth as well as in the fifteenth century.

4   If we accept that the adoption of solid foundations was accompanied by the introduction of substantial timber superstructures, we may also suppose that professional building craftsmen were being employed by peasants in the thirteenth century. A rare reference to a peasant obligation to carry out building work on village houses appears in a custumal of Sturminster Newton (Dorset) of 1235–52, which states that 'if any building in the vill decays and ought to be repaired', a customary yardlander 'with his neighbours' ought to carry timber, 'make the wall', and make the wattling. This shows that peasants could play a major part in building work, co-operating in common under the lord's enforcement.[81] The relatively early date of the document, and its nature as a record of established customs, means that it recalls an old self-help system that was probably already giving way to the use of more specialised labour. In the absence of any occupational census an indication of the relative importance of rural crafts can be obtained from surnames. In Essex, for example, 'Carpenter' was becoming quite common in 1222, in the early phases of the formation of surnames. A century later contributors to the Lay Subsidy in the county included thirty-five people called Carpenter or Wright, who presumably practised the trade, or whose recent ancestors had done so. These were the fourth commonest craft surnames, after Smith (129), Tailor (47) and Baker (36). There were many more Carpenters and Wrights than Coopers, Turners or Dyers.[82] A conservative estimate (in view of those exempt from taxes, and those without an occupational name) would be that there were more than a hundred carpenters working in the county, and such a figure is plausible in the light of Edward I's ability in the late thirteenth century to recruit for

---

[80]   Door fittings occur on most sites, e.g. ibid., p. 43; for shutter hinges see Holden, 'Excavations', pp. 166, 169; J. Amphlett (ed.), *Court Rolls of the Manor of Hales, 1272–1307* (Worcs. Hist. Soc., 1910), i, p. 165; Faull and Moorhouse, *West Yorkshire*, p. 809.

[81]   E. Hobhouse (ed.), *Rentalia et Custumaria* (Somerset Rec. Soc., 5, 1891), p. 82.

[82]   W.H. Hale (ed.), *The Domesday of St Paul's* (Camden Soc., 1859); J.C. Ward (ed.), *The Medieval Essex Community, The Lay Subsidy of 1327* (Essex Historical Documents, i, 1983).

castle building in Wales large numbers of woodworkers, for example forty-seven carpenters from Oxfordshire on one occasion in 1277.[83] If they were to have all found peace-time employment, these craftsmen must have been employed by peasants as well as aristocrats, clergy and townsmen.

Labour could be hired more cheaply in 1200–1350 than afterwards, and prices of some materials may have been lower also, though there is little direct evidence for the cost of peasant buildings. Fragments of information can be gleaned from occasional court-roll references, usually arising from disputes among tenants. On the Suffolk manor of Lakenheath in 1326 Matthew Outlawe was said to owe half of the cost of trees needed to build a house, 5s. 0d., so the full price would have been 10s. 0d. When Adam le Grey of the same place was accused in 1331 of destroying parts of a house – doors, locks, a kiln, timber, and a (?) well – damages of 13s. 4d. were claimed.[84] If these sums are at all typical, materials and fittings could have cost a pound, and wages would have brought the total to at least double that sum. On the other hand, some cheap structures are known. Two lords of East Midland manors in the first half of the fourteenth century, Henry de Bray of Harlestone (Northamptonshire) and Merton College at Kibworth Harcourt (Leicestershire) built cottages, presumably to house full-time estate workers, at relatively low costs of 10s. 0d. to 30s. 0d. each in the first case, and 9s. 9d. each in the second.[85] Perhaps such buildings can be regarded as characteristic of those of the lower ranks of rural society? On the other hand cottages intended for living-in servants may well have been specialised structures untypical of the house-holding peasantry.

The main resistance to the idea that many peasant buildings were of substantial and professional construction is based on the study of the surviving architecture. If, as is now argued, the new stone foundations and pad-stones of the thirteenth century were designed to support well-carpentered timbers, including crucks in the west and south, why is it that such buildings are not still with us? Their inability to last is surely proof of their technical inadequacy? However, while it is true that the bulk of standing medieval peasant buildings are dated after 1350, there are a few examples from an earlier period, notably cruck houses at Harwell and Steventon in Berkshire (now Oxfordshire) both dated by radiocarbon and dendrochronology to the years around 1300. In explanation of these awkward dates the suggestion is made that the Harwell house belonged not to a peasant but to the tenant of a twentieth of a knight's fee, who, unlike

[83] A.J. Taylor, 'Castle-building in the late thirteenth-century: the prelude to construction', in E.M. Jope (ed.), *Studies in Building History* (London, 1961), pp. 104–33.

[84] Cambridge University Library EDC 7/15/11/1/6, 8.

[85] D. Willis (ed.), *The Estate Book of Henry de Bray* (Camden Soc., 3rd ser., 27, 1916), pp. 49–51; C. Howell, *Land, Family and Inheritance in Transition. Kibworth Harcourt 1280–1700* (Cambridge, 1983), p. 56.

a peasant, would have been capable of constructing a durable building.[86] In fact the status of the tenure may give an impression of grandeur, but the amount of land that these tenants held would not have been much greater than a peasant's yardland. The Steventon house, judging from a near-contemporary survey of the manor, is likely to have belonged to a villein with a yardland or so, who was burdened with substantial rents and services.[87] If Mr C. Hewett is right in his dating of houses at Boxted and Fyfield in Essex, then it is also possible to find in the non-cruck areas relatively humble rural dwellings of the thirteenth and early fourteenth century still standing. There are other candidates for early dates in Oxfordshire and Kent, and the extension of dendrochronological research will no doubt add to the numbers of houses known to survive from the pre-1350 period.[88]

The test of durability until the twentieth century is a very stringent requirement. That any peasant building should still be in use after seven centuries should rather be a matter for wonder. A more reliable yardstick of quality might be the observed period of use of excavated buildings. The successive houses at Wharram Percy's House 10 site were originally thought to have each lasted about thirty years, but now that the sequence has been re-interpreted to give each a life of perhaps seventy years, this has ceased to be the classic demonstration of ephemeral housing.[89] At Beere (Devon) and Holworth (Dorset) houses built in the thirteenth-century are thought to have been in use for a century or more.[90] These and other examples from deserted settlements were cut off prematurely by decay or depopulation. Indeed, a great number of thirteenth-century buildings must have been the subject of tussles between lords and tenants over dilapidations in the late fourteenth and fifteenth centuries, and collapsed more often through deliberate neglect or even demolition than because of inherent defects in the original construction. Many other medieval houses fell victim to the successive post-medieval rebuildings, mainly because of changing fashion and a desire for improvement in accommodation. The

[86] C.R.J. Currie and J.M. Fletcher, 'Two early cruck houses in north Berkshire identified by radio-carbon', *Medieval Archaeology*, 16 (1972), pp. 136–42; P.A. Legget et al., 'Tree ring dates for buildings with oak timber', *Vernacular Architecture*, 13 (1982), pp. 48–9; J. Hillam and J. Fletcher, 'Tree-ring dates for buildings with oak timber', *Vernacular Architecture*, 14 (1983), pp. 61–2.

[87] London, British Library, Add. MS 6164, fo. 19; Alcock (ed.), *Cruck Construction*, p. 60.

[88] C.A. Hewett, 'The smaller medieval house in Essex', *Archaeological Journal*, 130 (1973), pp. 172–82; Blair, 'Two early cruck houses'; E.W. Parkin, 'A unique aisled cottage at Petham', in A. Detsicas (ed.), *Collectanea Historica, Essays in Memory of Stuart Rigold* (Kent Archaeol. Soc., 1981), pp. 225–30.

[89] Hurst, *Wharram*, pp. 28–41.

[90] E.M. Jope and R.I. Threlfall, 'Excavations of a medieval settlement at Beere, North Tawton, Devon', *Medieval Archaeology*, 2 (1958), pp. 112–40; P.A. Rahtz, 'Holworth, medieval village excavation, 1958', *Proc. Dorset Nat. Hist. and Archaeol. Soc.*, 81 (1959), pp. 127–47.

expensive houses of Bedale, none of which have lasted, provide only one example of the failure of good-quality buildings to survive.

Supposedly temporary buildings have been linked with the peasants' insecurity of tenure and rapid migration, both of which would reduce, it is thought, any incentive to invest in expensive and long-lasting buildings. In fact, although lords had the right to evict customary tenants, they generally respected hereditary rights. Even the heirs of notorious rebels benefited from the assumption that holdings should stay in the family. There was a tendency for customary tenures to be converted into leasehold for a number of years or lives, especially in the fourteenth century, but the change did not happen everywhere, and sometimes even reverted back to hereditary tenures. All freeholds were hereditary. It seems unlikely that a peasant's fear that his investment would be taken away by his lord would be a major reason for erecting flimsy buildings. Perhaps peasants who often migrated, or who sold their holdings, lacked the motivation to build durable houses? This is an unconvincing suggestion because tenants would have benefited in the short term from solid buildings that gave them elementary comfort, dry shelter for animals and crops, and lower maintenance costs. As holdings were often sold for cash (that is, money paid by the new tenant to his predecessor, over and above the dues owed to the landlord), the outgoing tenant would presumably have gained from a price that reflected the good quality of the buildings. Migration became even more rapid after 1350, and as we have seen this led to much decay, but there is no evidence that new buildings became less substantial – rather the contrary is true.

Finally, it has been suggested that peasants would have had difficulties in building to high specifications in areas of timber scarcity. This problem must have been at its most acute in the thirteenth century because land clearance for agriculture then reached its greatest extent, and pressure on timber resources increased because of the demands of urban and seigneurial building. Although we are ill-informed about the details of common rights to take trees, it seems likely that much timber was purchased. There may be a link between the adoption of better standards for some peasant buildings in the thirteenth century and the rapid expansion of the market in that century. Peasants who had previously been dependent on sometimes inadequate local supplies, were able to buy timber more easily because of the proliferation of markets, the wider use of cash, and the development of the transport network. The peasant who had laid out money for materials would be anxious to avoid a future recurrence of cost, and would have favoured new building methods like the use of foundations that prolonged the life of the timber. The growth of a labour force of building workers would have been a natural accompaniment of the tendency away from self-sufficiency and towards economic specialisation.

Although enough has been said to counter the theory that thirteenth-century peasant houses were merely impermanent huts, their quality should not be over-estimated. One reservation must arise from regional variations, which make generalisations well-nigh impossible. In particular there are the districts where the post-medieval vernacular tradition, like that of Lincolnshire, includes such features as earthfast foundations and insubstantial mud and stud, pointing to the survival of older building methods through the later Middle Ages.[91] Also excavations of East Midland sites show that the abandonment of earthfast posts was followed by phases of building in which timbers simply rested on the ground surface without any foundation, which represents a very modest step forward in construction technique.[92] And finally there is the problem of reconciling a view that houses went through a significant general improvement with historical perceptions of the period (especially the years *c.* 1280 to *c.* 1320) as one of growing peasant poverty, in which small-holdings increased in number, and high rents and taxes exacerbated the problems of low agricultural productivity and bad harvests. Perhaps the changes in housing (which have not been closely dated anywhere) belong to periods of relative prosperity in the years before 1280, or after 1320? Should historians emphasise more strongly the benefits of the expanding market on the middling and upper peasantry? The groups who were especially vulnerable to the economic trends of the thirteenth century, the small-holders and cottagers, depended for their livelihood on wages of such a low purchasing power that they could not have paid for any but the cheapest building. Even peasant families with large holdings must have been periodically deprived of their savings by the swingeing entry fines and other exactions that some lords were able to impose at the height of their powers in the late thirteenth century.

Conclusion

We have tended, under the influence of Hoskins's 'Great Rebuilding' theory, to look for dramatic waves of innovation in rural building in the thirteenth and the fifteenth centuries as well as in the period 1570–1640. Now that the 'Great Rebuilding' idea is being revised and refined in terms of a series of regional movements at different times within the sixteenth, seventeenth and eighteenth centuries, we should also define the late medieval 'rebuildings' as a number of trends and processes rather than revolutions.[93] In the thirteenth century in many regions stone foundations

---

[91] D.L. Roberts, 'The vernacular building of Lincolnshire', *Archaeological Journal*, 131 (1974), pp. 298–308. Post-medieval architecture could of course have deteriorated from medieval standards.

[92] Beresford, *Medieval Clay-land Village*, p. 40.

[93] Machin, 'The Great Rebuilding', revising W.G. Hoskins, 'The rebuilding of rural England, 1570–1640', in *Provincial England* (London, 1963), pp. 131–48.

developed, and were probably accompanied by new types of timber-work that resulted by 1300 in some well-carpentered and durable structures. Some areas advanced more rapidly than others: while a thirteenth century peasant at Upton (Gloucestershire) could have a house founded on ten or more courses of excellent dry-stone walling, his equivalent of *c*.1400 at Grenstein (Norfolk) managed with walls of clay-lump. The carpenters employed by a peasant of Steventon erected a cruck framework that still stands, while those working at Goltho were developing a technique of 'primitive framing' with an estimated life of 'more than fifty years'. Archaeology has made us most conscious of regional variations, but we should also be aware of social differences. We can rarely link an excavated house with a particular type of tenant, though we can say with some confidence that the superior house at Upton belonged to a customary yardlander, as such people made up the overwhelming majority of the villagers there at the time; it is equally likely that the Grenstein buildings belonged to smallholders with less than 10 acres, which may be a factor in explaining the differences between the two settlements. Another approach to this problem might be to discover by excavation different standards of building in the same village at the same time, but no village has been excavated extensively enough to enable such variations to be defined. As has already been indicated, cheap cottages like those built by the lords of Harlestone and Kibworth Harcourt before 1350 may point to a sizeable substratum of housing for poorer people that co-existed with substantial buildings (see p. 158). A similar disparity between the better-off and the poor existed at the time of the 'Great Rebuilding', which began with yeomen's houses in the sixteenth century, but did not benefit the labourers of eastern England until the late seventeenth century.[94]

Turning to the layout and function of buildings, in the late thirteenth century the regions can be divided between those where the chief building of a messuage was a specialised dwelling-house, in the south and east, and those in which long-houses predominated. The pattern was already changing by the late thirteenth century on sites in Gloucestershire and Wiltshire where separate dwellings replaced long-houses. This trend was apparently continuing in the Midlands in the next two centuries, but it was not everywhere a one-way process, as at Wharram Percy at House 6 a long-house succeeded a smaller separate dwelling in *c*. 1400. Groups of buildings on peasant messuages are recorded throughout the period 1200–1500, and there is some evidence for an increase in the number and size of agricultural buildings in the later part of the period, for example at Faxton.[95] Peasant houses of two storeys were being built in eastern England from the mid-fourteenth century, and had become common by 1500. They

---

[94] M. Spufford, *The Great Reclothing of Rural England* (London, 1984), p. 3.
[95] 'Medieval Britain in 1968', *Medieval Archaeology*, 13 (1969), p. 279.

were in use in Berkshire before 1400,[96] and developed in Devon and the West Midlands in the fifteenth century.

In the late fourteenth and fifteenth centuries a general improvement in the standards of materials and workmanship increased the durability of buildings. Again this was a case of gradual change, not a sudden transformation, as the techniques of building foundations and the associated carpentry had originated before 1300. Perhaps a feature of the period after 1350 was the wider diffusion of standards of carpentry that had previously been confined to a minority of houses. The main roofing material continued to be thatch, though a few peasant buildings erected by lords were being given complete slate roofs in the fifteenth century.

Given these changes in the later Middle Ages, the 'Great Rebuilding' may now look like a further stage (or a succession of stages) in a continuing process. When a settlement that was occupied from the Middle Ages until the eighteenth century is excavated, as at West Whelpington in Northumberland, the 'Great Rebuilding' is revealed not as a revolutionary innovation but as the gradual adaptation of late medieval structures to the needs of a new age.[97] Throughout the country, as we have seen, most of the new features adopted after 1540 can be shown to have at least an ancestry before 1500.

Many wider implications flow from the study of peasant buildings. The detail of these would extend this discussion beyond the scope of a single article, and they will only be sketched here.

First, the rich variety of housing types and methods of construction across the country give only one indication of the heterogeneous peasant culture of medieval England. We are aware of many geographical variations in settlement forms, field systems, agricultural methods, diet, inheritance customs and dialect. Unfortunately the distribution of building types coincides exactly with none of the other variables in peasant society, so that for example, regional variety in buildings cannot be explained simply in economic or ethnic terms. Although the availability of materials and the needs of farming systems help to throw light on some of the differences in buildings, they do not provide all of the answers.

Secondly, the agricultural buildings must be seen as the major single investment that a peasant made. Erecting a three-bay barn in the fifteenth century could have taken a high proportion of a middling tenant's disposable income over many years. The proliferation of agricultural buildings in the fifteenth century, shown most dramatically at Caldecote (Hertfordshire) where on one holding two great barns dwarfed a dwelling house, points to the increased level of investment by peasants *en route* to becoming capitalist

[96] Biddle, 'The deserted medieval village', p. 111.
[97] Wrathmell, 'The vernacular threshold'.

farmers.[98] By giving better protection to crops, animals and equipment the peasants' expenditure on buildings made a contribution to the efficiency of their agriculture.

Thirdly, the dwelling house can be regarded as an important item of peasant consumption. Archaeology has made us aware of the peasants' role as buyers of metal goods and pottery, but, leaving aside food-stuffs, they are likely to have spent most on clothing, with housing accounting for a sizeable proportion of their expenditure. Once we accept that peasants lived in houses, not huts, we can make some judgement of the quality of life that the structures provided. They were hardly ideal residences, measured against later standards, because of their lack of built floors; also the small size of their unglazed windows, combined with open hearths, cannot have provided their occupants with a healthy environment. They can still be compared in size with working-class urban houses of the nineteenth century, which had much the same floor area (450–650 sq. ft, or 42–59 sq. m). They were superior to Indian housing of the 1960s which allowed less than 40 sq. ft (3.7 sq. m) on average per person, or peasant houses in late medieval Provence (65 sq. ft or 6 sq. m per person), as the average English peasant family of five had 90 sq. ft (8.3 sq. m) each in a two-bay house, and more than 100 sq. ft in a three-bay house.[99]

Fourthly, methods of paying for buildings deserve some consideration, because peasants depended on supplies of credit to raise sums as large as £3, and many of them must have spent years paying off the cost of a dwelling or barn. Pleas of debt in manorial court rolls show that facilities for borrowing cash existed in many peasant communities, and there are occasional references to mortgages. 'Starts' on building perhaps depended on short-term economic fluctuations, above all the variable quality of the harvest; cycles of building, as in more recent times, presumably moved in relation to long-term shifts in incomes, with relatively few 'starts' in, for example, the difficult years 1300–20. Also building activity can be assumed to have taken place at specific stages in the tenant's life-cycle, avoiding the years at the beginning when an entry fine had to be paid to the lord, and often a purchase price to a previous tenant. Perhaps the best time for building was in the peasant's early middle age.

Modern observers have tended to underestimate the capacities and the achievements of the medieval peasantry. Those who began research on

---

[98] *Medieval Village Research Group Annual Report*, 22 (1974), 22A; G.G. Astill, 'Economic change in later medieval England: an archaeological review', in T.H. Aston et al. (eds.), *Social Relations and Ideas: Essays in Honour of R.H. Hilton* (Cambridge, 1983), pp. 217–47.

[99] L.S. Burns and L. Grebler, *The Housing of Nations* (London, 1977), p. 11; S.D. Chapman (ed.), *The History of Working-class Housing* (Newton Abbot, 1971), pp. 107, 232–35; G. Demains d'Archimbaud, *Les fouilles de Rougiers, contributions à l'archéologie de l'habitat rural médiéval en pays méditerranéen* (Paris, 1981), p. 243.

peasant houses had low expectations of their subject, because they were understandably prepared to find the simplicity and extreme poverty usually regarded as the main peasant characteristics. As knowledge has advanced, peasant buildings appear to have been both more complex and in many cases more substantial than was originally supposed. Many questions remain unanswered, and it is hoped that this essay will help to indicate the problems that can only be resolved by further research, especially in the material evidence.

9

Wages and Earnings in Late Medieval England: Evidence from the Enforcement of the Labour Laws

with Simon A.C. Penn

At least one-third of the population of late medieval England gained all or a part of their livelihood by earning wages.[1] Ever since the days of Thorold Rogers's investigations, the evidence for a rise in both cash wages and real wages in the second half of the fourteenth century, coinciding with the sudden and sustained population decline after the Black Death of 1348-9, has been well established. Phelps Brown and Hopkins were able to calculate the figures with considerable precision – daily wages in cash of skilled building workers in southern England increased by 66 per cent between the 1340s and the 1390s, from 3d. to 5d. per day, and those of the unskilled almost doubled from around $1\frac{1}{2}$d. to 3d. per day. Real daily wages of craftsmen were 45 per cent higher in the 1390s than they had been 50 years earlier, and those received by unskilled workers rose by a larger margin.[2] The method of assessing real wages, by using a 'shopping basket of consumables' calculated from the records of a household of chantry priests, might now be criticised in the light of new knowledge of lower-class consumption. Building workers would have spent a rather higher proportion of their income on cereal-based foods than did the priests, especially in the period before 1349, but this would make only a small difference to the real wage figures. Wages should not be regarded as disposable income, as they were expected to cover such expenses as the cost of raw materials, tools, assistants and apprentices. We must allow also for the wage being supplemented by other sources of income, such as retail

---

[1]   R.H. Hilton, 'Some social and economic evidence in the late medieval English tax returns', in idem, *Class Conflict and the Crisis of Feudalism* (London, 1985), pp. 253–67; idem, *Bondmen Made Free* (London, 1973), pp. 170–7; P.J.P. Goldberg, 'Female labour, service and marriage in the late medieval urban north', *Northern History*, 22 (1986), p. 21.

[2]   J.E. Thorold Rogers, *A History of Wages and Prices in England* (7 vols, London, 1866–1902), i, pp. 252–325; W. Beveridge, 'Wages in the Winchester manors', *Econ. Hist. Rev.*, 7 (1936), pp. 22–43; idem, 'Westminster wages in the manorial era', *Econ. Hist. Rev.*, 2nd ser., 8 (1955), pp. 18–35; J. Hatcher, *Plague, Population and the English Economy, 1348–1530* (London, 1977), pp. 47–54; H. Phelps Brown and S.V. Hopkins, *A Perspective of Wages and Prices* (London, 1981), pp. 13–59.

trade and the cultivation of land.³ Research into wage rates, though valuable in itself, does no more than throw indirect light on earnings, and it is only when we have extended our knowledge of the latter that we can make judgements about standards of living, and explore the wider questions of the links between the wealth of individuals, changes in population, levels of productive activity, social relationships, and other dynamic elements in the economy.

The Evidence

Our main source of information about wage rates, seigneurial accounts, were compiled for the convenience of employers, but we need to reconstruct the world of work as it was perceived by the employees. The information, to pick an example at random, that the bailiff of Thaxted in Essex in 1380/ 1 paid '1 man for 10 days digging and collecting stones . . . 2s. 6d., at 3d. per day', shows the daily rate for unskilled work in that part of the country, and a little more research can indicate how much grain or other goods could have been bought for 3d.⁴ But we are in ignorance about the man's work for the rest of the year, when we must presume that he worked for other employers who have left no accounts of their own. No source can fill the gaps in our account evidence, but we can learn more about the variety of employers of wage labour, and the behaviour of the workers, from the proceedings under the Ordinance of Labourers of 1349, the Statute of Labourers of 1351, and the Statute of Cambridge of 1388.

The Ordinance and the Statute of Labourers marked the first attempts at national wage regulation. They were intended, at a period of severe labour shortage, not only to control wages, but also to restrict the occupational and geographical mobility of workers. Landlords, for example, were to have first claim upon the labour of their own tenants. Once employed, workers rendered themselves liable to imprisonment if they decided to leave their service before the end of the agreed term. The statute laid down maximum wage rates for various occupations, special concern being shown about the provision of food and drink in addition to a cash payment. Certain conditions of employment were also stipulated: servants, for example, were not to work by the day but on longer term contracts, normally lasting a year. This provision was made more specific in the Statute of Cambridge which laid down the maximum annual rates of pay

---

³   See above, Chapter 5, pp. 77–99; D. Woodward, 'Wage rates and living standards in pre-industrial England', *Past and Present*, 91 (1981), pp. 28–46; H. Swanson, 'The illusion of economic structure: craft guilds in late medieval English towns', *Past and Present*, 121 (1988), pp. 33–7.

⁴   K.C. Newton, *Thaxted in the Fourteenth Century* (Chelmsford, 1960), p. 96.

that various servants should receive. Prices charged by craftsmen for their wares were also regulated by the 1351 statute – shoemakers, for example, were not to ask for any more than they had done in the years previous to the Black Death.[5] The surviving indictments brought under the statutes are, therefore, concerned with such matters as the giving and receiving of excessive wages, and the breaking of employment contracts before the end of an agreed term.

A group of cases for Essex in 1389 were analysed effectively by Kenyon; she used them to show that workers preferred the freedom of short-term engagements to annual contracts, and thereby gained higher wages. She also detected a movement of workers from agriculture into crafts.[6] This investigation is based on the surviving judicial records of the late fourteenth and early fifteenth centuries which contain significant numbers of labour cases, and extends Kenyon's investigation with a special focus on the problem of earnings.

A total of sixty-two rolls of the period 1349–1415 have been identified and consulted.[7] It would appear that in most cases these rolls were only compiled in response to a visit by King's Bench to a particular county. All undetermined indictments were thereby handed over to the superior jurisdiction. The decline in the number of such rolls towards the end of the fourteenth century can therefore be explained by the fact that King's Bench had by then settled permanently at Westminster, which meant that it was no longer necessary for the rolls to be produced.[8] Thereafter, labour cases are found in other records such as King's Bench and Gaol Delivery rolls which survive in great quantity into the fifteenth century, though by the early fifteenth century those enforcing the law had begun to lose interest in an outdated piece of legislation. Further study of these records is clearly necessary for an understanding of the later working of the labour laws.

The records that have been consulted are of two types. In the 1350s proceedings were held before Justices of Labourers, who were specially appointed to hear cases relating to the receipt of excessive wages. These records normally consist of presentments of statute offenders by jurors of

---

[5] *Statutes of the Realm*, i, pp. 311–13; ii, p. 57.

[6] N. Kenyon, 'Labour conditions in Essex in the reign of Richard II', in E.M. Carus-Wilson, ed., *Essays in Economic History*, ii (London, 1962), pp. 91–111.

[7] The 62 manuscript rolls consulted are as follows: PRO, KB 9/3, KB 9/23, KB 9/30, KB 9/54a, KB 9/55a, KB 9/55b, KB 9/57, KB 9/61, KB 9/62, KB 9/63, KB 9/80, KB 9/99, KB 9/102, KB 9/104, KB 9/115, KB 9/131; JUST 1/32, JUST 1/33, JUST 1/76, JUST 1/101, JUST 1/107, JUST 1/125, JUST 1/170, JUST 1/195, JUST 1/266, JUST 1/268, JUST 1/293, JUST 1/297, JUST 1/298, JUST 1/312, JUST 1/313, JUST 1/472, JUST 1/529 (2), JUST 1/530, JUST 1/693, JUST 1/717, JUST 1/731, JUST 1/752, JUST 1/769, JUST 1/773, JUST 1/795, JUST 1/796, JUST 1/812, JUST 1/813, JUST 1/815, JUST 1/907, JUST 1/971, JUST 1/973, JUST 1/974, JUST 1/975, JUST 1/1018, JUST 1/1019, JUST 1/1134, JUST 1/1135, JUST 1/1136, JUST 1/1143 (2), JUST 1/1145 (3), JUST 3/221.

[8] B.H. Putnam, ed., *Proceedings before the Justices of the Peace in the Fourteenth and Fifteenth Centuries* (London, 1938), pp. lxv–lxix.

a village or hundred. The name and sometimes the occupation of each offender is recorded, but details of wages or other terms of employment are rarely provided. As will be seen presently, however, these rolls are useful in indicating the numbers of wage earners being presented in certain areas, and the work that they were carrying out. From the 1360s presentments of statute offenders were made at the county quarter sessions of the Justices of the Peace. These later rolls tend to provide much more information on the tasks performed, the place and period of employment, the mobility of the workers, and the wages which they were said to have received. During this period separate Justices of the Peace were also appointed for particular urban centres, though surviving records of their sessions are sparse and have not been included in this study.[9] The great variety of labour cases recorded in the county peace rolls is in contrast not only with the earlier Justices of Labourers' records, but also with local manorial or borough court records which, where available, appear to concentrate largely on breaches of contract.[10]

We must be very cautious in using the sample of employers, employees, wages and conditions of service that are described in the royal court records. They are hardly a representative cross section of the wage-earning sector of the economy, but must be regarded as the tiny minority of illegal contracts and payments that happened to find their way before the courts. Judging from the records in accounts of the universal payment of wages above the limits set in the Statute of Labourers, the law was broken each year by hundreds of thousands of workers, but after a very large number of cases were brought in some areas in the early 1350s, the justices in normal years dealt with only a few hundred offenders in each county for which we have information.[11] There is undoubtedly some justification for the argument that the gentry, who acted as justices and generally exercised a great deal of influence over the proceedings, manipulated the law by securing prosecutions in their own interest.[12] However this does not mean that the majority of the employers involved were necessarily gentry or their agents. The purposes of the gentry were best served by paying wages high enough to secure an adequate labour supply, while bringing the forces of the law to bear on workers who demanded higher rates, and on rival employers who lured them away with competitive offers. In this way they could hope

[9]   B.H. Putnam, *The Enforcement of the Statute of Labourers during the First Decade after the Black Death* (New York, 1908), pp. 9–17; E.G. Kimball, 'Commissions of the peace for urban jurisdictions in England, 1327–1485', *Proceedings of the American Philosophical Society*, 121 (1977), pp. 448–74.

[10]   E. Clark, 'Medieval labor law and English local courts', *American Journal of Legal History*, 27 (1983), pp. 330–53.

[11]   L.R. Poos, 'The social context of Statute of Labourers enforcement', *Law and History Review*, 1 (1983), pp. 44–8.

[12]   J.B. Post, 'Some limitations of the medieval peace rolls', *Journal of the Society of Archivists*, 4 (1973), pp. 645–8.

both to hire sufficient numbers of workers and to exercise some influence over the prevailing rates of pay. Certainly a proportion of the employers mentioned in the judicial records seem to have been peasants and artisans, and even a few labourers who were recruiting assistants. Such people would have had some opportunity to use the law in their own interest – after all, better-off peasants and artisans figured among the constables and jurors who were essential participants in the administration of the law.[13] This wide spectrum of employers had a common aim of limiting wage increases, and of controlling labour contracts. Many of them, for example, would have preferred annual terms of employment, which would have given them a regular source of relatively cheap labour.

The complaints and accusations that led to the cases coming to court must remain a mystery. We are sometimes conscious of a flood of accusations from one place or hundred, suggesting that someone in authority had mounted a campaign. The opposite is indicated by the refusal of local people to co-operate with the enforcement of the labour laws, notably when the constables of one Essex hundred were reported to have neglected to enforce the statute in 1378. This must be a signal of something more co-ordinated than coincidental forgetfulness.[14] And finally we must suspect that the existence of a law against which so many people offended provided golden opportunities for malicious accusations to be made in pursuit of quarrels and enmities of all kinds. The sources therefore are biased in a number of directions, but for the purposes of this enquiry we can regard as advantageous the variety of influences that brought the cases into court. The accused included employees of every kind, who worked for many different types of employer. The cases came from a wide geographical area, over a number of decades, and involved those engaged in both agricultural and non-agricultural work.

Patterns of Employment

All of our judicial evidence derives from the period after the Black Death of 1348–9. We have enough information from other sources to suggest that some aspects of the wage-earning scene were not post-plague novelties, but reflected normal patterns of employment in late medieval society. The onset of plague changed social conditions sufficiently to spur employers to react and initiate the changes in the law, but no overnight social transformation was involved. Many of the tendencies of the period 1349–1415 continued trends already begun in the early fourteenth century. Four

---

[13] Poos, 'Statute of Labourers enforcement', pp. 27–52; Clark, 'Medieval labor law'.

[14] E.C. Furber, ed., *Essex Sessions of the Peace, 1351, 1377–9* (Essex Archaeol. Soc., Occasional publications, 3, 1953), p. 169.

characteristics of wage earning will be identified, all of them revealed most plainly in the post-1349 documents, but not necessarily originating in the mid-fourteenth century.

The first conclusion that can be drawn from the records of the enforcement of the labour laws· is that in many parts of the country people pursued a great variety of occupations. This is a well-known feature of the published poll tax records of the eastern and northern counties of Essex, Suffolk and Yorkshire.[15] It was also true of the west, for example in Somerset in 1358, where the jurors of the five towns of Axbridge, Bath, Bridgwater, Langport and Wells named forty-seven offenders, who were said to follow eight occupations, including the vague descriptions 'common labourer' and 'common workman' which presumably covered people involved in a number of trades.[16] Among the 419 names presented by the hundred juries (drawn mainly from country dwellers), were people following nineteen occupations, including spinners, weavers, and many retailers of food stuffs and fuel who were presumably being fined for breaches of the price restrictions of the Statute of Labourers. One in four of the accused were women, who figured prominently and unsurprisingly among the spinners and brewers. There were also seven female weavers, and some women who were called 'common labourers'. Workers involved in a number of occupations are found in Wiltshire in the 1350s in districts of varied character.[17] In the 'cheese' country of the north-west of the county, with its pastoral rural economy and tendency to industrialisation, represented in our records by presentments from the hundreds of Chippenham and Kingsbridge, twenty-two occupations were named, twelve of them non-agricultural. In the eastern 'chalk' country, tending towards corn and sheep farming (the hundreds of Swanborough and Kinwardstone), of the twenty-three occupations mentioned, fourteen were non-agricultural. However, the more pronounced development of the cloth industry of the west of the county is represented by the presence there of twenty-eight textile workers, compared with fourteen in the east.

A more marked contrast is apparent from two districts of Herefordshire in 1355-6, one in the hilly border country in the north-west, near Pembridge and the other in the more arable area around Ross-on-Wye to the south-east.[18] Each contained a small market town and a group of villages, and their jurors produced approximately equal numbers of names – 138 in the

---

[15] C. Oman, *The Great Revolt of 1381* (London, 1906), pp. 168–82; E. Powell, *The Rising in East Anglia in 1381* (Cambridge, 1896), pp. 67–119; '*Rotuli collectorum subsidii . . . in Westrythyngo in comitatu Eboraci*', *Yorkshire Archaeological Journal*, 5 (1877–8), pp. 1–51, 241–66, 417–32.

[16] PRO, JUST 1/773, mm. 1–4.

[17] E.M. Thompson, 'Offenders against the Statute of Labourers in Wiltshire, A.D. 1349', *Wiltshire Archaeological and Natural History Magazine*, 33 (1904), pp. 384–409; PRO, KB 9/131.

[18] PRO, JUST 1/312, mm. 3, 5d, 7.

north-west, 134 in the south-east. Yet those in the south-east were grouped under only nine occupational descriptions, whereas in the north-west there were twenty-three. Most of the south-eastern occupations were agricultural, while the offenders in the north-west included twenty-nine textile workers, thirteen tailors, sixteen cobblers and tanners, six building workers and a scatter of other craftsmen such as glovers, wheelwrights, hoopers, sawyers and a smith.

The court records fall far short of full occupational censuses. The motives of jurors are unknown, but they could well have been influenced by prejudices and interests which meant that some trades were cited before the courts more often than others. We can safely conclude that the documents do not list a complete range of local trades and crafts. Similarly we cannot know if the proportion of women appearing in the records is representative of their presence in the labour force as a whole. It may be that all-male juries and benches found the prospect of women demanding more pay especially distasteful, or perhaps women's seasonal work at harvest time made their high pay rates peculiarly conspicuous. On the other hand, women workers may have escaped accusation because their work was judged in a masculine world to be less important and therefore to be unworthy of notice by the jurors. The fact that the proportion of women could be as high as 28 per cent (in the Herefordshire examples mentioned above) shows that the female contribution to the labour force deserves our attention; many women were able, if single, to keep themselves or, if married, to bring significant earnings to family budgets. Women were especially active in the food and drink trades, and the juries' habit of listing 'excess' profits of such retailing alongside 'excess' wages reflects the close association of the two sources of income for many households.[19]

The second notable feature of the late medieval labour force was its occupational flexibility. Lists of offenders of the 1350s commonly assign to groups of workers a combination of occupational descriptions: 'brewers and spinners', 'threshers and fishermen', 'carpenters and fishermen', 'threshers, mowers and carpenters', and so on. In the 1370s individuals could be called 'dauber, mower and thatcher' (in Norfolk), or 'labourer, ploughman and carter' (in Essex).[20] In the case of groups of workers this might have resulted from the hard-pressed clerks' attempts to describe as many people as quickly as possible, but in view of the references to two or three occupations for individuals, they seem also to have been recording

[19] S. Penn, 'Female wage-earners in late fourteenth-century England', *Agricultural History Review*, 35 (1987), pp. 1–14; R.H. Hilton, 'Women traders in medieval England', in idem, *Class Conflict*, pp. 205–15; M. Kowaleski, 'Women's work in a market town: Exeter in the late fourteenth century', in B.A. Hanawalt, ed., *Women and Work in Pre-industrial Europe* (Bloomington, Indiana, 1986), pp. 145–64.

[20] PRO, KB 9/80, m. 23; Furber, ed., *Essex Sessions of the Peace*, p. 176.

the jobs which a worker could do in the course of a year, compatible with one another because they could be pursued at different times. Thus the court records confirm the evidence for mining or forest crafts, of workers moving from one seasonal activity to another.[21] Many of those in jobs which were less dominated by the weather or the season, such as leather working or cloth making went into fishing or harvesting in the appropriate months.[22]

Agricultural production in particular demanded a degree of movement from one occupation to another. The full-time farm servants (*famuli*) who were hired on annual contracts as ploughmen or carters were expected to join in the hay making, corn harvest and threshing as need required. But most of the labour for those tasks came from hired hands who were taken on for a few days or weeks. Sometimes we know that these people worked in industry, such as building, and we can assume that many had small holdings of land.

Permanent, and sometimes radical changes in occupation are noted in the judicial records when the move from one job to another had led to an accusation of breach of contract, or of one employer luring workers from a rival. Ploughmen figure prominently among those cited, because they were the most numerous of the *famuli* who were supposed to work for the whole year. Even the smallest demesne needed a staff of two to man the plough, and many had six or eight. Ploughmen often left their normal employment to do short-term, unspecialised agricultural work as mowers and threshers, but individuals are also known to have taken, on a more permanent basis, such varied occupations as carpenter, weaver, fuller, butcher, fisherman, thatcher and shipwright.[23] Perhaps the most unexpected transfer was made by Richard Fouke of Shernborne, Norfolk, who 'withdrew from the craft of ploughman, out of the service of master Emere of Shernborne, and is received and hired by Ralph Pibel, crossing the sea in the craft of mariner'.[24] The succession of cases involving ploughmen gives the impression that almost anything was preferable to that arduous agricultural task, though the occasional move in the other direction, whereby a Norfolk thresher took up employment as a ploughman,

---

[21] I. Blanchard, 'The miner and the agricultural community in late medieval England', *Agricultural History Review*, 20 (1972), pp. 99–100; J.R. Birrell, 'Peasant craftsmen in the medieval forest', ibid, 17 (1969), pp. 96–101.

[22] Putnam, ed., *Proceedings before the Justices*, p. 216 (a skinner, tanner and weaver left their hundred in Hampshire to do harvest work in 1390).

[23] R. Sillem, ed., *Records of Some Sessions of the Peace in Lincolnshire, 1360–1375* (Lincoln Record Society, 30, 1937), pp. 63–4; E.G. Kimball, ed., *Records of Some Sessions of the Peace in Lincolnshire, 1381–1396* (Lincoln Record Society, 49 and 56, 1955 and 1962), ii, p. 208; PRO, KB 9/115, mm. 3, 24d; B.H. Putnam, ed., *Yorkshire Sessions of the Peace, 1361–1364* (Yorkshire Archaeological Society Record Series, C, 1939), p. 55; Putnam, ed., *Proceedings before the Justices*, pp. 122, 343–4, 357, 360, 361, 367, 370, 373, 376.

[24] Putnam, ed., *Proceedings before the Justices*, p. 114.

suggests that the trend was not wholly one-way.[25] Other *famuli* also left for alternative work, like the Bedfordshire shepherd in 1363 who was indicted for becoming a tiler 'contrary to the statute'.[26] It might be thought that lack of skill would have made the transition from agricultural to craft work a difficult one, and indeed John Persons of Yoxley in Suffolk, who refused to serve in his usual occupation as a ploughman, was said to be 'ignorant of any other trade'.[27] Some of his colleagues seem to have been more adaptable and adventurous, and the levels of skill required were doubtless declining after 1348-9.

On the basis of such reports Kenyon believed that there was a drift in the late fourteenth century from agricultural to craft work. The problem in accepting this from the evidence of the court cases is that annual contracts were especially common in agriculture, and the country gentry and demesne farmers who had strong influence on the courts were much concerned to bind their *famuli* to their obligations. The clause in the Statute of Cambridge that forbade young rural workers from taking up apprenticeships in towns reflects the fears of the same landowning interest. If there was a movement from the land in the period 1350-1400, which is possible because of the growth in the cloth industry and the urban boom around 1400, it was not an entirely new development, in view of the rising fortunes of textile manufacture and the large urban populations before the Black Death.

The third characteristic of late medieval wage earners was their capacity for geographical mobility. This is apparent from the fragmentary pre-1348 evidence, notably from the indirect testimony of locative surnames which reflect migration into towns, and the patterns of immigration and emigration that emerge from good series of manorial court records. Harvest by-laws of the early fourteenth century show the leaders of the village communities combating the tendency for wage earners to leave their homes in the autumn. Specialist craftsmen like masons travelled long distances from site to site.[28]

---

[25] PRO, KB 9/80, m. 23 (a thresher, Thomas Weston, came to serve Edward de Eston at Upton as a ploughman).

[26] E.G. Kimball, ed., *Sessions of the Peace for Bedfordshire, 1355–9, 1363–4* (Bedfordshire Historical Record Society, 48, 1969), p. 107.

[27] Putnam, ed., *Proceedings before the Justices*, pp. 362–3.

[28] P. McClure, 'Patterns of migration in the late Middle Ages: the evidence of English place-name surnames', *Econ. Hist. Rev.*, 2nd ser., 32 (1979), pp. 167–82; S. Penn, 'The origins of Bristol migrants in the early fourteenth century: the surname evidence', *Transactions of the Bristol and Gloucestershire Archaeological Society*, 101 (1983), pp. 123–30; L.R. Poos, 'Population turnover in medieval Essex: the evidence of some early fourteenth-century tithing lists', in L. Bonfield, R.M. Smith and K. Wrightson, eds, *The World we have Gained* (Cambridge, 1986), pp. 1–22; E. Britton, *The Community of the Vill* (Toronto, 1977), pp. 146–52; W. Ault, *Open-field Farming in Medieval England* (London, 1972), p. 33; D. Knoop and G.P. Jones, *The Mediaeval Mason* (3rd edn, Manchester, 1967), pp. 127–8.

Table 9.1 Geographical mobility of wage-earners.

Date	Name(s)	Occupation, type of work	County	From	To	Distance (miles)
1353	Elizabeth, dau. of Henry of Screffington (and 5 other women)	autumn work	Rutland	North Luffenham	Barrowden	2
1361	John Wlnard	carpenter	Suffolk	Cratfield	Flixton	7.5
1362	Simon Wygenhale	thatcher	Suffolk	Debenham	Letheringham	7
1362–3	William le Thresshere	—	Suffolk	Trimley	Ipswich	8
1362–3	Robert Russel	servant	Suffolk	Walton	Foxhall	6
1362–3	Margaret, wife of John le Bere of Wantisden	reaping	Suffolk	Wantisden	Ilketshall	20
1362–3	Philip Coffedok	thresher	Suffolk	Debenham	Ipswich	12
1363	Matilda Chanardeby	autumn work	Suffolk	Great Livermere	Great Fakenham	3.5
1363	Alice, wife of Peter Chauntrell	reaping	Yorks. (E. Riding)	Pocklington	Tibthorpe	10.5
1363–4	Alexander Cokerel	house-roofer	Suffolk	Stratford St Andrew	Blaxhall	2
1364	Richard de Queldryk	former ploughman	Yorks. (E. Riding)	Sutton upon Derwent	York	7.5
1370	William de Breton of Ingoldsby	thatcher	Lincs. (Kesteven)	Ingoldsby	Bitchfield	1.5
1372–3	John Perlica of Dunholme	thresher	Lincs. (Lindsey)	Dunholme	Scothern	1.5
1373	Alice Treu	autumn work	Lincs. (Lindsey)	Croxby	Swallow	3
1374	Ralph atte Car . . .	threshing	Lincs. (Lindsey)	Firsby	Thorpe	7
1374–5	John Sutor of Hagworthingham	mowing	Lincs. (Lindsey)	Hagworthingham	Aswardby	2
1374–5	Alice Milner of Heckington	—	Lincs. (Kesteven)	Heckington	Sleaford and Burton	4 2
1377	Matilda Gosse of Buxton	autumn work	Norfolk	Buxton	Burgh next Aylesham	2.5
1377	John de Banyngham of Thwaite	ploughman	Norfolk	Thwaite	Colby	2
1377–8	William Sesson of Little Barningham	thatcher of straw	Norfolk	Little Barningham	Forncett	24
1378	John Pykard	—	Norfolk	Thurne	South Walsham	3
1380–1	John Walker of Little Cotes	reaper	Lincs. (Lindsey)	Little Cotes	Stallingborough	3.5
1383	Roger Toke, tailor	autumn work	Lincs. (Lindsey)	Great Steeping	Salmonby	9
1392	Richard Styward	autumn work	Hants.	Kingsley	Lasham	8
1393	John Theker	servant	Lincs. (Kesteven)	Harmston	Lincoln	5.5
1393	Roger Schepherde	servant	Lincs. (Kesteven)	Navenby	Lincoln	8.5

1394–5	Richard Seman	—	Lincs. (Holland)	Moulton	Lynn (Norfolk)	20
1395	William and Thomas Thacker	common roofers	Lincs. (Holland)	Fleet	Gedney and Long Sutton	1 3
1395–6	John Tasker of Hagworthingham	—	Lincs. (Lindsey)	Hagworthingham	Oxcombe	5.5

Sources: PRO, KB 9/80, mm. 23, 25; KB 9/115, mm. 2d, 8; Kimball, ed., *Sessions of the Peace in Lincolnshire*, i, pp. 12, 75, 76–7; ibid., ii, pp. 78, 153, 238; Putnam, *Enforcement of the Statute of Labourers*, p. 198*; idem, ed., *Proceedings before the Justices*, pp. 215–6, 349, 358, 359, 360, 367; idem, ed., *Yorkshire Sessions of the Peace*, pp. 58, 69-70, 71; Sillem, ed., *Sessions of the Peace in Lincolnshire*, pp. 34, 63, 71, 92, 159, 206.

The records of the enforcement of the labour laws make it possible for us to calculate precisely the distances travelled by some workers, whose journeys were mentioned in the course of an accusation that they had broken a contract, or that they had refused to accept employment, or because they infringed the clause in the Statute of Cambridge which forbade them to cross hundred or wapentake boundaries without authorisation (see Table 9.1). On average they travelled a little less than 7 miles, though the longest distance recorded was the 24 miles covered by a Norfolk thatcher from Little Barningham to Forncett.[29] Many reported for moving were, like the thatcher, building workers, who must have served a number of towns and villages in the normal course of their trade, and another mobile group were the harvesters who habitually followed the ripening crops across England. Perhaps the longest movement of labour took Welsh harvest workers into the Midlands, and in some numbers, judging from the complaint that a single employer on the Worcestershire/ Gloucestershire border in 1396 had hired 119 of them.[30] Some of the journeys, for example from rural Norfolk into King's Lynn, demonstrate the continued drawing power of the large towns at this period. We have no certain way of judging the effects on migration of the late fourteenth-century labour shortage. It ought to have intensified the tendency of workers to travel, and this seems to be confirmed by contemporary complaints of increased vagabondage, and by calculations of migration made by modern students of manorial court rolls.[31]

The fourth feature of wage earning that is revealed by the enforcement of the labour legislation concerns employment practices and conditions of service. They must have originated at earlier periods, but appear in the post-1349 records in a state of controversy and stress. Servants and *famuli* normally began their annual contracts at Michaelmas (29 September) or Martinmas (11 November), which suggests some machinery for bringing

[29] PRO, KB 9/80, m. 25.
[30] Putnam, ed., *Proceedings before the Justices*, pp. 410–11.
[31] Z. Razi, *Life, Marriage and Death in a Medieval Parish* (Cambridge, 1980), pp. 117–24.

masters and servants together that was akin to the hiring fairs of later centuries.[32] Under the Statute of Labourers the constables took an active interest in the annual hiring process. There are various hints that the labour market was not a matter of simple negotiations between individual employers and individual workers. The accusation that one worker had persuaded or encouraged his fellows to leave the workplace, or had advised a fellow worker of the terms that he should accept, reveals collective links among the rural workforce. These were perhaps based on no more formal organisation than the teams of harvest workers, or the pairs of ploughmen who habitually worked together in the field. In towns at this time illicit conventicles and fraternities were being formed by journeymen, proof that medieval workers were capable of collective defence of their interests in the right circumstances.[33]

The activities of employment agents were especially sinister from the point of view of the employers. These 'enticers' or 'procurers' of labour would recruit assistants, and then hire them out to others. For example Robert Archer of Forncett in Norfolk was accused in 1378 of leading half a dozen labourers or more out of his village to work at harvest time.[34] This had the effect of both driving up wages, and leaving Forncett very short of workers. Some of these middlemen operating in the labour market were said (doubtless with exaggeration) to have secured a monopoly on a section of the workforce. Henry Maddy of Lincolnshire was described in 1381 as a 'common forestaller of labourers and servants so that no-one in the neighbourhood is able to hire any servant without his approval and aid'.[35] Similarly, anyone wishing to hire roofers in Lincoln in the mid-1390s was obliged to approach a certain Thomas Sees, a painter, who was said to be 'the chief engrosser of craftsmen in the city'.[36]

Once a worker had been engaged, the method of payment varied a good deal, which complicated the enforcement of the labour laws and meant that justices had to use local custom and practice in interpreting the regulations on rates of pay. Often a day's work was rewarded with a meal as well as a sum in cash. Workers on annual contracts received a combination of cash and food, sometimes with accommodation and clothing thrown in. In Wiltshire in 1364 we find that the primitive practice of paying harvest workers in sheaves of corn persisted.[37]

---

[32] *Statutes of the Realm*, i, p. 311 refers to public hiring in market towns.

[33] R.H. Hilton, 'Popular movements in England at the end of the fourteenth century', in idem, *Class Conflict*, pp. 152–64.

[34] Putnam, ed., *Proceedings before the Justices*, p. 109.

[35] Kimball, ed., *Sessions of the Peace in Lincolnshire*, ii, p. 150.

[36] Ibid., p. 221.

[37] Penn, 'Female wage-earners', p. 9; A. Jones, 'Harvest customs and labourers' perquisites in southern England, 1150–1350: the corn harvest', *Agricultural History Review*, 25 (1977), pp. 14–15.

Changes in Wage-Earning after the Black Death

Having considered those aspects of the wage earners' existence which continued throughout the later Middle Ages, though with some developments in the fourteenth century, it is time to examine the changes more fully.

Kenyon rightly stressed as a major theme of her research into the Essex cases of 1389 that workers had a strong desire to escape from the constrictions of annual contracts in order to work on a series of temporary jobs. In terms of the language of the poll taxes, they preferred life as labourers *(laborarii)* to that of servants *(servientes* and *famuli)*. Full-time service smacked of servility, and just as serfs left the manor to gain their legal freedom, so the former *famuli* went off to work where they pleased. They might have wished to do this before 1348–9, but were given more opportunity afterwards because of the ease with which work could be found. The employers who helped to enforce the labour laws saw this as a transition to a disreputable itinerant life, and as a threat to the social order. So in 1376, a 'common labourer' of Carlton in Lincolnshire was said to 'wander about idly', and a Norfolk ploughman who left his long-term employment was reported to have become a vagabond for the sake of taking excessive wages.[38] The statement that two female labourers from Messingham in Lincolnshire refused to serve according to the ordinance, but would only work 'at their own will', tells us a good deal about the disapproval of workers' independence shown by the juries.[39] Some workers enjoyed their leisure. There was an element of enforced idleness because of the church's insistence that about forty days of holiday should be observed each year, in addition to Sundays.[40] But many workers took much more time off than that. The most striking example is John Hogyn, presented before the justices in Hampshire in 1371 as a common disturber of the peace, and accused of leaving the county, refusing to serve anyone. He spent his time sleeping during the day and frequenting the tavern at night where he played 'penyprik'.[41] A Yorkshire labourer, John Moy, excused his failure to accept long contracts on the grounds that he was ill, but the jurors accused him of malingering: 'he would not serve by the year, because he was able to take more by the day.'[42]

---

[38] Sillem, ed., *Sessions of the Peace in Lincolnshire*, p. 90; PRO, KB 9/80, m. 9.

[39] Ibid., pp. 36–7; the desire to hold land 'at their own will' was attributed to rebels in 1381: see below, Chapter 10, p. 218.

[40] E.C. Rodgers, *Discussion of Holidays in the Later Middle Ages* (New York, 1940), p. 10; B. Harvey, 'Work and *festa ferianda* in medieval England', *Journal of Ecclesiastical Hist.*, 23 (1972), p. 292.

[41] Putnam, ed., *Proceedings before the Justices*, pp. 207–8.

[42] Putnam, ed., *Yorkshire Sessions of the Peace*, p. 25.

Workers often accepted employment for very short periods. Some who were persuaded to embark on long terms quickly changed their minds and broke their contracts. To take some Lincolnshire examples, ploughmen, carters, servants, fishermen and other wage earners departed after 2 days, 3 days, 2 weeks, 20 days, 21 days, 1 month, just over 11 weeks, 3 months, 6 months and 7 months.[43] Perhaps because they were conscious of the difficulty of persuading workers to serve for a whole year, employers would offer terms of half-years or even less, but these were rejected also – two Lancashire workers in 1349–50 refused to accept employment for 4 months and 6 months. Those in the same county who initially accepted such contracts left before the end of their period of service – so Alice daughter of John Robynsone of Chorley agreed to work for twenty-three weeks but went after sixteen weeks in 1350.[44]

Short-term employment seems to have been preferred by the workers, but many of the jobs on offer were also for short periods of time. Lords of manors needed a group of *famuli,* and both better-off peasants and artisans would employ a servant or two, but all employers, rich and poor alike, required a few days or weeks of a labourer's or craftsman's time much more often than all-the-year-round service. Take thatching, for example. Occasionally an employer with many large buildings could offer as much as three months of continuous work, as happened at Shifnal in Shropshire in 1410.[45] Much more typical would be the case of John Warmale of Suffolk, who in 1362 did a week's work for one employer, and in 1363 ten days for a different one.[46] The small size of peasant buildings, and the need for small-scale repairs on larger roofs, made short-term employment of this kind the norm for the trade, so he probably performed dozens of such jobs in the two-year period. Carpenters and masons in Lincolnshire in 1371 were being employed for only two or three days at once, according to the reports to the Justices of the Peace.[47]

Many seasonal tasks lasted for a limited amount of time. The harvest could have continued for as long as six to eight weeks, but workers need not have been active throughout that period. A Lincolnshire woman was said in 1383 to have worked for only twenty days in the autumn, and Ralph Kyng of Blickling in Norfolk in 1377 can be calculated from his 'excess' earnings to have been employed for twenty-four days.[48] Many craftsmen and labourers moved from one employer to another, the normality of the

[43] Sillem, ed., *Sessions of the Peace in Lincolnshire,* pp. 15–16, 20, 27; Kimball, ed., *Sessions of the Peace in Lincolnshire,* ii, pp. 14, 45, 183, 186, 217, 222, 226.

[44] PRO, KB 9/54a, m. 2.

[45] E.G. Kimball, ed., *Shropshire Peace Roll, 1400–1414* (Shrewsbury, 1959), p. 93.

[46] PRO, KB 9/115, m. 5d.

[47] Sillem, ed., *Sessions of the Peace in Lincolnshire,* p. 173.

[48] Kimball, ed., *Sessions of the Peace in Lincolnshire,* ii, p. 82; PRO, KB 9/80, m. 25.

situation being indicated by the formula that excessive pay had been taken from a named employer and 'from various other men'. Sometimes a number of employers are identified. In the autumn of 1378 a labourer of Skeyton in Norfolk earned 7s., plus food, from Geoffrey Pye. In the following year he divided his harvest season by working for both Pye and John Crane, and earned 2s. more.[49] A 'common thatcher' of Twyford in Lincolnshire, John Corby, took excessive wages in 1394 from John Yole of Corby and Thomas Wryght of Colsterworth.[50] The detailed documentation of this is unusual, but the habit must have been common. Workers who had a number of jobs in a year must have spent a good deal of their time both travelling from one employer to another, and negotiating for the best possible pay and conditions.

We are left wondering for how many days in an average year a worker actually earned wages. Two examples suggest a high degree of irregularity. Between 1 November 1363 and 2 February 1364 a Suffolk labourer worked for only forty days for one employer.[51] He could have attached himself to other employers in the gaps, but the combination of winter weather and the Christmas holiday may well have kept him idle for the other five weeks. Walter Wright, a 'common carpenter' of Messingham in Lincolnshire, was fined 20s. excess wages for his work over the previous two years.[52] As it seems likely that the excess amounted to 1d. per day, he can be calculated to have worked for 240 days, or an average of only 120 days in each year. This would not mean that his whole income was only 30s. per annum plus his meals. He could have had other resources, such as a holding of land, or the court may have let him off lightly by underestimating the number of his working days.

The emphasis in the records on the trend towards short-term employment may be misleading. The manorial accounts and the poll tax returns reveal the continuation in full-time employment of many thousands of *famuli* and servants. To take just one example, the Gloucestershire village of Kempsford, with a total tax-paying population of 157 in 1381, contained no less than sixty-nine servants.[53] Servants, however, did not form a homogeneous group. The term includes the young 'life-cycle' servants who worked for relatively small amounts of pay, and obtained most of their reward in the form of their keep. Their relationship with their employers, who evidently regarded them sometimes as child substitutes, would have differed considerably from that which existed between absentee lords of manors and adult *famuli*, who were often tenants of cottages, and were paid in a

[49] PRO, KB 9/80, m. 25.
[50] Kimball, ed., *Sessions of the Peace in Lincolnshire*, i, p. 7.
[51] PRO, KB 9/115, m. 8.
[52] Sillem, ed., *Sessions of the Peace in Lincolnshire*, p. 52.
[53] R.H. Hilton, *The English Peasantry in the Later Middle Ages* (Oxford, 1975), p. 32.

combination of cash and grain. 'Life-cycle' service was not lacking in contention, but it seems to have caused less formal dispute before the royal courts.[54] The records of the employment of *famuli* in the manorial accounts sometimes support the testimony of the indicting juries because they tell us of ploughmen or shepherds who left a lord's employ during the year and had to be replaced.[55] One piece of behaviour recorded before the justices shows that the wandering tendencies of wage earners also affected those who kept their contracts, in the sense that they changed employers at the end of the term. For example, Adam Godwyn, a ploughman from Upton in Norfolk, worked for a different employer in each of three successive years in the 1370s.[56] The search for a new employer presumably explains why some *famuli* left very near to the end of their terms, in two cases in Lincolnshire in 1379/80 and 1393/4, after service of eleven months.[57] This annual mobility – it seems in our period like an habitual restlessness among people who felt no strong attachment to any employer, and who perhaps always dreamt of greener grass in the next parish – continued to be a feature of the employment of farm servants in later centuries.[58]

Drawing on the analogy of farm servants in the seventeenth and eighteenth centuries, the suggestion has been made that in the later Middle Ages servants employed on annual contracts increased as a proportion of the labour force. This change reflected employers' desire for labour which was relatively cheap because of the low cost of food; also the demand for full-time workers grew as pastoral farming developed in importance.[59] However, much of our evidence suggests the weak bargaining position of the employers, to the point that their preferences may not have counted for much in the real world of negotiation with potential servants. The evidence of debts and broken contracts in manorial court records also indicates a growth in short-term employment.[60]

For the employee one of the attractions, and indeed probably the main attraction, of the short-term job was its higher rate of pay. In some of the indictments it is explicitly stated that the accused left an employer in order to take excessive wages elsewhere. A ploughman working full time for a

[54] Ibid., pp. 51–2; the poll taxes also reveal the existence of *servientes per dietam*, whose pattern of employment resembled that of labourers – see Hilton, 'Social and economic evidence', p. 261.

[55] E.g. Canterbury Cathedral Library, Beadles' rolls, East Farleigh, Kent, 1373/4: two ploughmen 'withdrew at the end of the season' after two and a half terms of the four that they should have worked.

[56] PRO, KB 9/80, m. 23.

[57] Kimball, ed., *Sessions of the Peace in Lincolnshire*, ii, pp. 185, 234.

[58] A.S. Kussmaul, *Servants in Husbandry in Early Modern England* (Cambridge, 1981), pp. 49–69.

[59] R.M. Smith, 'Human resources', in G. Astill and A. Grant, eds, *The Countryside of Medieval England* (Oxford, 1988), p. 210.

[60] Z. Razi, 'Family, land and the village community in later medieval England', in T.H. Aston, ed., *Landlords, Peasants and Politics in Medieval England* (Cambridge, 1987), pp. 388–90.

year in Suffolk in the early 1360s would receive less than 10s. in cash and about five quarters of grain, which in normal years would be worth £1 or so (though in a bad harvest year, especially if it included a high proportion of wheat, its value could rise above 30s.).[61] The *famulus* would be given additional gifts and perquisites amounting to a shilling or two. His earnings would therefore have reached a total of less than £2 in most years. According to cases coming before the justices in the same county at that time harvest workers were being paid 6d. per day, so that a labourer who was not tied down by an annual contract could hope to earn 15s. to 20s. in the autumn. In the shorter hay-making season he could obtain 3d. or 4d. per day with food, and at other times of the year would have no difficulty in finding such jobs as threshing for which the going rate was 2d. per day with food.[62] It would not be unreasonable to suppose that he could have worked for 200 days for £2 8s. 4d. (40 days at 6d., 20 days at 3d. and 140 at 2d.), plus meals worth at least 10s. Add to these material benefits his sense of well-being as an independent worker able to exercise some choice over the amount and type of work that he accepted, and the advantage of leaving the ploughman's job becomes clear.

The actual rates of pay recorded in the court proceedings throw new light on wages because they were paid by a wider range of employers than those recorded in manorial accounts. Not only were wages paid in very different forms – by the day, by the week, by the task, by the season, in cash, in cash and food, in kind – but the amounts, when they can be compared, varied greatly even within the same county. In the East Riding of Yorkshire, for example in 1362-3, harvest workers are recorded as having been given 3d., 4d. and 6d. per day, in each case with food. Wages for threshing in the same county in the same year varied from $1\frac{1}{2}$d. to 4d. per day, again in each case 'with food'.[63] The different rates presumably reflected variations in local demand, seasonal changes, differences in the arduousness or skill required for each task, and the quality of food. To give a single example in which a very high rate can be explained, Suffolk thatchers normally received 3d. to 4d. per day, but in 1362 William Champeneys was obtaining 12d., 7d. and 8d., probably for repairs in the aftermath of the great gale of 15 January 1362.[64] It was clearly well worth a worker's time on the road to shop around for the best rates. The general rule that the shorter the term of employment, the higher the rate of pay, can be shown to work within the different periods of short-term employment, as well as in the broad contrast between annual and daily rates. As table 9.2 indicates, Suffolk labourers working for ten to

[61] PRO, SC 6 1304/31; Suffolk Record Office (Bury St Edmunds branch), E 3/15.3/2.10d.
[62] PRO, KB 9/115.
[63] Putnam, ed., *Yorkshire Sessions of the Peace*, passim.
[64] PRO, KB 9/115, m. 4.

fifteen days seem in general to have gained more per day than those employed for twenty to forty days.

Table 9.2
Rates of pay for different periods of time worked by labourers[a] in Suffolk, 1360–4

Period of service	Number of labourers	Average daily cash wage (pence)
10 days	1	4.0
12 days	2	2.5
14 days	1	6.0
15 days	1	4.0
20 days	9	2.9
1 month	1	1.5
40 days	4	3.1

Note: [a] ie wage-earners described as either 'common labourer' or 'common workman'.
Source: PRO, KB 9/115, mm. 6, 6d, 7d, 8, 24, 24d.

The movement of daily rates over time was clearly upwards, though the rates quoted in the judicial records are incapable of forming a statistical series. Thatchers, for example, according to Thorold Rogers received on average 3d. per day in the 1340s and 4d. in the last three decades of the fourteenth century. If we take the highest figure recorded in sets of judicial records, we find some thatchers receiving 3d. with food, and others as much as 12d. with food, with 4d. (both with and without food) as a median figure. It may be significant that low figures are recorded in Shropshire and Nottinghamshire, while the highest are found in East Anglia, suggesting a tendency for rates to increase as one moved eastwards, but this is not an invariable rule, as the highest rate for thatching reported in Norfolk in 1378–9 was 3d. with food. There is nothing here to say that averages calculated from accounts are 'wrong', but they do show that the average may conceal some remarkably varied figures. Of course we must always bear in mind the nature of our source, and the tendency of the jurors to exaggerate the offence. This factor might explain the remarkable range of pay rates ascribed to the *famuli* who were paid by the year, though the deficiency of the source cannot wholly explain why the manorial accounts show ploughmen being paid around 10s., and only exceptionally 20s. per annum, in the late fourteenth century, while the justices heard of ploughmen in Essex, Suffolk, Norfolk and Lincolnshire who were receiving 20s., 24s., 26s. 2d. and even 30s.[65] One can only suppose that some employers were driven to desperate measures to attract and keep *famuli* in order to combat the growing *wanderlust*.

[65] On the lower rates, see M. Mate, 'Labour and labour services on the estates of Canterbury Cathedral Priory in the fourteenth century', *Southern History*, 7 (1985), pp. 55–67; a comment on the discrepancy between the sources is in Kenyon, 'Labour conditions in Essex', p. 99.

The exceptional nature of the labour market is implied by the many and consistent reports of employers giving rewards and perquisites to their *famuli*. An Essex ploughman in 1378, for instance, was offered a new tunic, and the use of the lord's plough on his own land as well as 20s. in cash and $4\frac{1}{3}$ quarters of grain per annum.[66] Others were tempted with extra gratuities in cash, and concessions that would not be apparent in the manorial accounts. In 1372 a canon of Sempringham (Lincolnshire) offered a shepherd both an illegal extra 2s. per annum in cash, and the right to keep on the lord's pasture four more sheep of his own than he had been allowed by his previous employer.[67] The most extreme example of the lengths to which employers would go concerns the abbot of Newbo in Lincolnshire and his ploughman, Roger Hert of Sedgebrook, in 1394. Roger was to receive 16s. in cash, a cartload of hay valued at 3s., pasture for his cow worth 18d., and instead of the usual livery of corn, a weekly fifteen loaves of bread (seven of them white, i.e. wheaten), and 7 gallons of ale, as if this farm worker was being treated as a domestic servant of the monastery.[68] The allowances of grazing for animals owned by the *famuli* are especially significant. They suggest the workers' aspiration to a degree of economic independence and perhaps a stepping stone to a new life as a tenant. These illegal perquisites were often linked with attempts to poach servants who were already engaged to another employer. It seems likely then that the whole package of rewards for servants employed by the year helped to push their wages up more rapidly than those of workers employed by the day. This did not prevent the drift into casual work, but it must have had some effect in view of the continued existence of a labour force of servants and *famuli*.

The judicial records reflect improvements in workers' conditions in general. They show a rise in the quality of food allowances, confirming the complaints by contemporaries like William Langland that employees demanded good ale, and hot dishes of fresh meat and fish. The growing proportion of meat, the greater quantity of ale, and the tendency for servants' bread to be baked from wheat rather than barley are recorded in accounts for the costs of feeding harvest workers. The justices in Lincolnshire heard of servants who took wheat and rye for corn allowances rather than peas; and a ploughman in 1353 insisted that fresh meat rather than salt meat should be served.[69] At the same time there is evidence that as a proportion of their total remuneration, payments in food diminished in

[66] Furber, ed., *Essex Sessions of the Peace*, p. 164.
[67] Sillem, ed., *Sessions of the Peace in Lincolnshire*, p. 195.
[68] Kimball, ed., *Sessions of the Peace in Lincolnshire*, i, pp. 32–3.
[69] See above, Chapter 3; Sillem, ed., *Sessions of the Peace in Lincolnshire*, pp. 173–4, 100; Putnam, *Enforcement of the Statute of Labourers*, p. 196*.

importance. Workers preferred payment in cash, and employers responded, in the case of manorial *famuli* by giving grain allowance of better quality but of only slightly greater value, while doubling (at least) their cash wages.

The length of the working day also provoked controversy, expressed most directly in the ordinances of urban 'craft guilds'. The problem appears in our records in terms of workers demanding the same pay throughout the year rather than the 'summer' and 'winter' rates that had prevailed before 1348–9. In Norfolk in the 1370s, for example, threshers were indicted for receiving 2d. per day during both summer and winter.[70] Payment for holidays was extended after 1348–9. Building workers seem not to have received holiday pay before the Black Death.[71] The situation evidently changed, because in the late fourteenth century some of the workers who appear in the judicial records had been employed by the week, which must have allowed them to take holidays with pay. Occasionally workers like David Denays of Coventry in 1379 were fined for taking excessive wages on feast days; presumably employers gave a bonus for those working 'unsocial hours'.[72]

Changes in conditions, as in the case of increases in pay, were secured by the assertiveness of workers. Their demands for improvements, strengthened by threats to move elsewhere if unsatisfactory rewards were offered, run as a continuous thread through all our sources, from the manorial accounts, through the court cases, to the comments of contemporary moralists.

Conclusion

The first general conclusion that can be drawn from this enquiry is an admission of our ignorance of many aspects of wage earning. Series of wage rates, and above all the Phelps Brown and Hopkins graphs, which appeared to students of the medieval economy to form firm islands of facts in a shifting sea of opinion, no longer seem so certain. They do not mark the end of our search for knowledge about the medieval wage earner, but rather the beginning of a new stage of investigation.

We must recognise the problem of defining the wage-earning population. There was no clear distinction between employers and employees. Those who paid wages did not form an homogeneous group, ranging as they did from the highest aristocracy to numerous artisans, peasants and labourers who were little better off than the people whom they hired. The workers

---

[70]   PRO, KB 9/80, m. 26.

[71]   Knoop and Jones, *Mediaeval Mason*, p. 106.

[72]   E.G. Kimball, ed., *Rolls of the Warwickshire and Coventry Sessions of the Peace, 1377–97* (Dugdale Soc., 16, 1939), p. 27.

were similarly diverse, including an element who relied on wages as their sole means of livelihood for all of their lives, and also large numbers of occasional workers.[73] A craftsman or peasant experienced life as a wage earner in early life, and eventually could have become an employer in later years as his workshop or holding grew in size. The prominence of many married women and young people in the workforce meant that employers and employees co-existed at close quarters in every village and street, and in a good number of households. There was likewise no monolithic employing interest. The Statute of Labourers and its successors became devices whereby individual employers could punish a rival or discipline individual workers. Conflicts of interest between employers and employees joined forces with friction between employers to create a complicated web of accusation. Wages often formed only one of a number of sources of income in complex household economies that depended also on the profits of retail trade, holdings of land and common rights. Changes in wage rates influenced the recipients' standard of living but did not determine it.

In the light of the evidence outlined above, we could adopt two approaches to the problem of earnings. The maximalist argument would take as a starting point the doubling of the wages of unskilled workers in southern England, from $1\frac{1}{2}$d. per day in the 1340s to 3d. in the years around 1400. Earnings would have risen by at least as much. More work was available, as the labour shortage abolished the unavoidable under-employment of the pre-plague era. Round-the-year jobs such as threshing and spinning helped to fill the gaps between seasonal tasks. Occupational flexibility kept workers from enforced idleness in any one activity or trade. Their mobility ensured that they could find work if there was any shortage of jobs in a single town or district. Their willingness to move from job to job and from place to place enabled them to select the most remunerative work. They were even able to take on higher paid skilled work as the labour shortage encouraged a degree of 'deskilling'. The improved conditions of work also raised earnings, by removing the lower winter wages, and ensuring that they were paid in holidays. In addition to the better pay of the unskilled male worker, each household would benefit from the increased opportunity for work, and the improved wage rates available to women. If wives chose to enter the retail food and drink trades, profit margins seem to have increased, judging from the prosecutions under the price clause of the Statute of Labourers in the 1350s. Exact figures are impossible to calculate, but we can envisage a labourer's household in *c.*1400 as having a total

[73] A. Hassell Smith, 'Labourers in late sixteenth-century England: a case study from north Norfolk (part one)', *Continuity and Change*, 4 (1989), pp. 11–52, shows a similar diversity in the early modern labour force.

annual income in excess of £4, at a time when a family's supplies of wheat bread, with some ale, could have cost as little as £2.[74]

A minimalist approach would begin by stressing the elements of continuity in late medieval wage earning. Even before the epidemics that began in 1348–9 there are signs of the beginning of an upward movement of wages, and there were multiple occupations and seasonal migrations well before they are exposed with such clarity by the cases brought under the statute. The balance of power between employers and employees shifted in favour of the latter group, but this did not leave the employer without any ability to bargain. The statute, for all its patchy enforcement, may have inhibited the demands of workers. Employers wished to hire full-time servants, and were evidently able to recruit large numbers of workers on annual contracts, as can be seen in the poll tax returns and the manorial accounts. Some workers evidently preferred security and were willing to accept lower pay in full-time work. Those who chose the wandering life did so partly to spend less time in work, and used their time for holidays and playing games in taverns. Also the constant changes of jobs and employers ate into their working time, hence the contemporary complaints of vagabondage. Some may have worked for as little as 120 days per annum. Annual earnings as low as £2 would not have allowed a household to buy wheat bread and drink ale every day, especially if there was to be some spending on clothing or household goods. Such people had low expectations of their living standards; they worked until they had provided themselves with a minimum, based on cheap food like barley bread, and then took time off. Leisure was regarded as a positive benefit, and there was a strong aversion to drudgery. As the historians who have adopted a behaviourist approach have argued, higher wage rates led to a reduction in number of days worked, and therefore earnings increased by much less than wage rates.[75]

The reality probably lies between these two extremes. The workers' behaviour would very much depend on their circumstances, so that youths are likely to have fallen into the minimalist mould, and older people with family responsibilities would have had more incentive to maximise their earnings. Cottagers with a few acres of land or an involvement in retail trade would have approached their wage work in a frame of mind that differed sharply from that of landless people entirely dependent on

---

[74] For the cost of a family's food, see C. Dyer, *Standards of Living in the Later Middle Ages* (Cambridge, 1989), pp. 226–7.

[75] I. Blanchard, 'Labour productivity and work psychology in the English mining industry, 1400–1600', *Econ. Hist. Rev.*, 2nd ser., 31 (1978), pp. 1–24; G. Persson, 'Consumption, labour and leisure in the late Middle Ages', in D. Menjot, ed., *Manger et boire au Moyen Age* (Nice, 1984), i, pp. 211–23.

earnings. Each worker, depending on his or her circumstances, could make a different decision in balancing the rival claims of freedom and income.

What were the implications of increased wages for the wider economy? If the greater spending power helped the boom in the manufacturing and urban economy at the end of the fourteenth century, why was this not sustained as wage rates continued at high levels in the fifteenth century? To what extent did the workforce go through a structural change in the successive generations after the Black Death, whereby a high proportion of the population acquired land holdings and craft workshops, and so were able to rise out of the dependence and insecurity of the wage-workers' existence? Or did the concentration of holdings in fewer hands spoil the chances of many servants and labourers of acquiring land and greater independence? And why did the increased earning capacity of young people not lead them to marry earlier, to produce larger families, and to begin a demographic recovery, which was in fact delayed until the early sixteenth century? The argument that life-cycle service became more prevalent and so prevented early marriage does not accord with the antipathy towards full-time service on annual contracts which is revealed by the proceedings under the labour laws. To explain the intractable problem of the length and persistence of the late medieval demographic trough, and the economic changes of the period, we must expand our understanding of these fundamental problems of social behaviour.

10

The Social and Economic Background to the
Rural Revolt of 1381

Was the revolt of 1381 merely a 'passing episode' in English history, an irrational aberration, or was it deeply rooted in the economic and social life of the later Middle Ages?[1] The frustration of historians who despair of finding a social explanation of the rising is understandable, as causes suggested in the past have been shown to be inadequate. There is little evidence to support the theory that labour services increased in the late fourteenth century, and we can no longer accept the view that the revolt was caused by the dissolution of the traditional feudal order by the advance of a money economy.[2] There is now general agreement that the conditions of peasants as well as wage-earners tended to improve after the plague of 1348–9, so that any economic explanation of the revolt must be expressed in terms of rising expectations. Did the actions of landlords frustrate these expectations? Was there a seigneurial reaction in the post-plague decades? In order to consider these problems it is necessary to define more closely the groups who made up the rebel ranks, and to examine their motives and aims. These questions are too numerous to receive a full answer in a single essay. In concentrating on them here, the political and religious aspects of the revolt, which deserve to be properly considered in any full assessment of the complex events of 1381, will be unavoidably neglected.

Much of the literature on the 1381 rising was published before 1907, when most of the chronicle sources were already in print, and many of the relevant classes of public records were available for research. The main sources for investigating the social and economic background, the manorial records, lay scattered in the muniment rooms of country houses and the offices of local solicitors. This study is based on the mass of this local material which is now more readily available. Such is its bulk that it has been

[1]   M.M. Postan, *The Medieval Economy and Society* (London, 1972), pp. 153–4.

[2]   For older interpretations, see J.E. Thorold Rogers, *A History of Agriculture and Prices in England*, 7 vols (Oxford, 1866), i, pp. 80–3; D. Petrushevsky, *Wat Tyler's Rebellion*, reviewed by A. Savine in *Eng. Hist. Rev.*, 17 (1902), pp. 780–2; this work is also discussed in P. Gatrell, 'Studies of medieval English society in a Russian context', *Past and Present*, 96 (1982), pp. 35–7. Roger's explanation was criticised effectively in C. Petit-Dutaillis, *Studies and Notes Supplementary to Stubbs' Constitutional History*, 3 vols (Manchester, 1914), ii, pp. 252–304. For more recent explanations, see *The Peasants' Revolt of 1381*, ed. R.B. Dobson (London, 1970), pp. 1–31; R.H. Hilton, *Bond Men Made Free: Medieval Peasant Movements and the English Rising of 1381* (London, 1973).

necessary to concentrate on the four counties of Essex, Hertfordshire, Kent and Suffolk. The method of research has been to compile an index of non-urban places affected by the revolt, and then to look for manorial records of those places or at least for manors in their vicinity. The manorial records were used to compile biographical studies of individual rebels (supplemented by some information from the archives of central government), and to examine the changes in rural society in the forty years before the revolt. The records of more than a hundred manors have been consulted, though many more sources for the four counties are known to exist.[3]

The Rural Revolt of 1381

Accounts of the revolt naturally concentrate on the events in London and, although we cannot be sure of the precise numbers involved, the large crowds of countrymen assembled there provide some indication of the mass support that the revolt received, particularly from Essex and Kent. Much of the rebellious activity took place outside the capital, and the numbers of villages involved can be calculated from sources in print as 105 in Essex, 35 in Hertfordshire, 118 in Kent and 72 in Suffolk. These are minimum figures, which will be greatly expanded when the results of research recently carried out in the public records are published.[4] The distribution of the places known to have been affected by the revolt reveals no clear geographical pattern, except for a concentration of rebellious villages in south-central Essex and central Kent, and a relative absence of recorded activity in north-west Hertfordshire and the extreme south-east of Kent.

---

[3]   The large St Albans Abbey estate in Hertfordshire has been excluded from this study because the large numbers of records involved, and the complexities of their interpretation, deserve separate study.

[4]   The printed records that have been used are: A. Réville and C. Petit-Dutaillis, *Le soulèvement des travailleurs d' Angleterre en 1381* (Paris, 1898), pp. 175–240, 288; J.A. Sparvel-Bayly, 'Essex in insurrection, 1381', *Trans. Essex Archaeological Society*, new ser., 1 (1878), pp. 205–19; W.E. Flaherty, 'The Great Rebellion in Kent of 1381 illustrated from the public records', *Archaeologia Cantiana*, 3 (1860), pp. 65–96; W.E. Flaherty, 'Sequel to the Great Rebellion in Kent of 1381', *Archaeologia Cantiana*, 4 (1861), pp. 67–86; E. Powell and G.M. Trevelyan, *The Peasants' Rising and the Lollards* (London, 1899), pp. 3–12; E. Powell, *The Rising in East Anglia in 1381* (Cambridge, 1896), pp. 126–31, 143–5; *Rotuli Parliamentorum*, 6 vols (Record Comm., London, 1783), iii, pp. 111–13; *Cal. Pat. Rolls, 1381–5, 1385–9; Cal. Close Rolls, 1381–5; Cal. Fine Rolls, 1377–83*. Some secondary sources also make references to otherwise unpublished documents, notably in Réville and Petit-Dutaillis, *Le soulèvement des travailleurs*, and in *VCH Herts.*, article on social and economic history by A.F. Niemeyer. Large quantities of information about the rebels remain unpublished in manuscripts in the Public Record Office (hereafter PRO). Professor A.L. Brown has helped me with additional names from these sources, and I have also received information, notably about the burning of records, from Mr A. Prescott. The new research mentioned is being carried out by these two scholars.

The total number of rebels can only be guessed. It is possible to extract the names of about four hundred rural rebels for the four counties from the printed documents. The new researches in the public records could well multiply this total tenfold. Even then we can expect that these were the leaders, or people who attracted the attention of jurors or informants by notorious acts, or perhaps some who were not involved in the revolt but who had enemies among the jurors. Even as a means of identifying the leaders these lists are inadequate, as the manorial records reveal the existence of local leaders unnoticed by the royal courts, like John Cok of Moze (Essex), who 'was the first in error, seeking and taking the court rolls', or the eighteen who burnt the court rolls of King's Langley (Hertfordshire), or John Cole who did 'damages or trespasses', and helped to burn the court rolls at Felixstowe (Suffolk).[5] The rank and file of the rebel bands must have been made up of many who will always remain anonymous. The indictments tell us of whole villages which rose, like 'all of the men' of three Essex vills assembled by John Geffrey of East Hanningfield.[6] The lords of manors were apparently sometimes willing to believe that their property had been attacked by outsiders, 'unknown malefactors', but at Great Bromley (Essex) 'all of the tenants of this manor in bondage' were accused of involvement, as also were the tenants of servile holdings at Bacons in Dengie (Essex).[7] At the latter place it was also stated that the revolt went on for a much longer span of time than is normally allowed – not the first three weeks in June, but from April to July.

The indictments in the royal courts and the chronicles tell us a great deal about the major acts of rebellion in 1381. Many of these had a partly or wholly political character, such as the attacks on royal officials, escheators, justices and tax-collectors, and the killing of the 'traitors', notably Sudbury, Hales and Cavendish, and the pillaging of their property, of which the best-known example was the destruction of John of Gaunt's Savoy. There were also the apparently xenophobic killings of Flemings, and the many acts of local banditry, usually involving blackmail and theft. Social grievances are more apparent in the demands presented to the king rather than in the actions of the rebels, though the attacks on the lawyers in London were presumably expressing an antipathy with a social basis, and the revolt of the tenants of St Albans Abbey is a well-documented assault on seigneurial power. Some of the indictments mention the burning of manorial documents, but many more cases are recorded in court rolls written after the revolt, and it appears that the burning of court rolls was one of the most widespread expressions of rural rebellion. Using both direct references, and the

[5] Essex Record Office (hereafter ERO), D/DGh M14; PRO, SC 2/177/47; Suffolk Record Office, Ipswich Branch (hereafter SROI), HA 119: 50/3/80.
[6] Sparvel-Bayly, 'Essex in insurrection, 1381', p. 218.
[7] ERO, D/DU 40/1; D/DP M1191.

indirect evidence of surviving series of court rolls that begin at the time of the revolt, it is possible to identify some 107 incidents of destruction, including the burning of central estate archives such as those of the archbishopric of Canterbury, Stratford Abbey and Waltham Abbey that affected the records of many manors.[8] Fortunately for modern historians, the rebels were by no means comprehensive in this form of rebellion.[9]

The burning of records was often combined with a variety of actions against landlords. At Berners Berwick in Abbess Roding (Essex) the rebels stole their lord's timber, firewood, hay, harrows and cattle, and drove their animals to pasture on the demesne lands. Major trespasses on the lord's demesne by tenants' stock, in one case with twenty cows and two hundred sheep, are also recorded at Bacons in Dengie (Essex), and wood was taken from the lady of the manor of Tolleshunt Major (Essex).[10] At King's Langley (Hertfordshire) and probably also at Knebworth in the same county, customary tenants felled timber growing on their holdings in large quantities, which normally required the lord's permission.[11] The rebels of Childerditch (Essex) asserted control over demesne land by seizing an enclosed croft which they may well have regarded as rightfully common. At the same place they made the lord's servants leave their work. The tenants of West Mersea (Essex) withdrew their rents and services at the time of the revolt.[12] Actions of individuals or small groups included refusals to pay rents, rejection of election to office in the manorial and village administration, and especially refusals to serve as chief pledge, that is, the headship of a tithing which carried the responsibility of informing the lord's view of frankpledge of the offences of the tithing-men. Individuals also rejected the jurisdiction of the courts, and made violent attacks on officials or other tenants. To take an example, the view of frankpledge at Holwell (Hertfordshire) held on 6 June, before the revolt had really penetrated into the county, showed signs of unusual agitation, with the chief pledges initially refusing to pay the common fine, a suitor contradicting a chief pledge, and another suitor

[8]   Réville and Petit-Dutaillis, *Le soulèvement des travailleurs*, pp. 188, 218; *Cal. Pat. Rolls, 1381–5*, pp. 71–2.

[9]   The success of the rebels in destroying documents depended on the place of deposit of their archives used by landlords. Records kept in the manor-house were most likely to be burned. Barking Abbey's archives were evidently kept at the abbey, so the rebels at Ingatestone were able to burn only the current court roll for 1381; W.M. Sturman, 'Barking Abbey: a study in its external and internal administration from the Conquest to the Dissolution' (unpublished Univ. of London Ph.D. thesis, 1961), p. 121. On some estates the steward kept the previous year's rolls with him, so that although the main series of court rolls were destroyed by the rebels, the records for 1380 and 1381 were preserved.

[10]   ERO, D/DHf M28, M45; D/DP M1191; PRO, SC 2/173/94.

[11]   PRO, SC 2/177/47; Hertfordshire Record Office (hereafter HRO), K3.

[12]   ERO, D/DP M1099; W. Gurney-Benham, 'Manorial customs in West Mersea', *Trans. Essex. Archaeological Society*, new ser., 13 (1915), pp. 307–9.

uttering threats against the constable.[13] At Fryerning (Essex), a Hospitallers' manor much nearer to the starting point of the revolt, a court and view session was begun on 4 June, but after a small amount of business had been transacted, the court roll states that 'William fitz Perys . . . was a rebel and would not do the steward's orders', and as this is the last item on the record we may speculate that the court ended prematurely.[14] It was a fortunate coincidence for the rebels that many lords in Essex and Hertfordshire traditionally held their annual view of frankpledge in the week after Whitsun, which in 1381 fell in the first week in June, just after the first outbreak in south Essex, so that officially summoned assemblies of all the adult males in many villages were meeting at a sensitive moment.

Serious personal violence against lords seems to have been unusual, with the important exception of the revolt at Bury St Edmunds (Suffolk), where among other casualties was John Lakenheath, a monk who had carried out a systematic reorganisation of the abbey's archives, and who also appears in the pre-revolt court rolls making decisions about the level of seigneurial dues.[15] The lady of Great Bromley (Essex) was 'insulted', but this was probably because the rebels encountered her in the manor-house when they broke in to take the court rolls.[16] The landlords who were killed otherwise are usually found to have been serving in some official position in local government, which led to their selection for harsh treatment.

To sum up, the rural revolt in the four counties involved large numbers of people in hundreds of villages, who attacked 'political' targets, indulged in some conventional crime, but also directed themselves in both petty and large-scale acts of rebellion against the goods, lands, privileges and judicial powers of landlords.

The Rebels

With the exception of the handful of gentry and clergy who participated in the revolt in our four counties, notably in Suffolk, the social status and economic position of the rebels is not easily defined. We know something about their material possessions from the escheators' valuations of the goods and lands of indicted individuals, and the records of the royal courts sometimes give the rebels' occupations. This evidence shows that 100 of 180 rebels from the whole area of rebellion owned goods valued at £1 to £5, and

[13] Guildhall Library, London, (hereafter GL), 10, 312/165.

[14] Wadham College, Oxford (hereafter WC), 44B/1.

[15] Réville and Petit-Dutaillis, *Le oulèvement des travailleurs*, p. 64; *The Archives of the Abbey of Bury St Edmunds*, ed. R. M. Thomson (Suffolk Records Society, 21, 1980), pp. 23–33; Suffolk Record Office, Bury St Edmunds Branch (hereafter SROB), E3/15.3/1.19(d), shows him dealing with the forfeited chattels of a felon of Chevington (Suffolk).

[16] ERO, D/DU 40/1.

15 of them were worth more than £5, including the very affluent Thomas Sampson of Suffolk and John Coveshurste from Kent.[17] The poorer rebels, and those with non-agricultural occupations, were especially numerous in Kent. This is sufficient to show that we are dealing primarily with people well below the ranks of the gentry, but who mainly held some land and goods, not the 'marginals' recently claimed as playing an important part in the revolt;[18] in other words most of the rebels were peasants and artisans.

By combing manorial and government records for the names of known rebels, it is possible to find out more about their backgrounds. This has been done for eighty-nine rebels, forty-eight from Essex, eighteen from Hertfordshire, thirteen from Suffolk and ten from Kent. Of them, forty-six are recorded as rebels in central government records, mainly indictments, and forty-three can be identified as rebels from the manorial documents. The Kentish rebels will be discussed separately because of the nature of that county's documents.

Of the remaining seventy-nine, we have information about the landholding of almost fifty of them. Thirty-eight are recorded as holding land by customary tenure; six held both free and customary land; and five are recorded only as free tenants. So the majority of our sample of rebels held land by disadvantageous tenures, often described as villein land, in a region where free tenants were very numerous. At least a tenth of our rebels (eight) were 'serfs by blood' *(nativi de sanguine)*.

The economic standing of our rebels is best indicated by the size of their holdings, of which we are given some indication in thirty-six cases. Of these, fifteen had holdings of 14 acres or more, of whom only two held more than 32 acres; nine held between 7 and 12 acres; and twelve were smallholders with 5 acres or less. In some cases the information is incomplete, so the figures represent minimum landholdings. Nor should the other rebels be assumed to have been landless – the great majority can be shown from references to rent payment or their attendance at manorial courts to have been tenants. An indication of the scale of the rebels' agricultural activities and of their wealth is provided by references to their animals. We find individuals owning flocks of as many as twenty-five, twenty-eight or eighty sheep; John Hermar of Havering atte Bower (Essex) had four oxen and a horse, while William Smyth of Ingatestone and Fryerning (Essex) owned six *avers* (draught animals), five calves and some pigs. Robert Wryghte from Foxearth (Essex), whose holding of land is not recorded, can be assumed to have had a strong interest in agriculture from references to his possession of three horses, two cows and six pigs.[19] Rebels with smallholdings, and some sizeable amounts of land, would have had alternative sources of

[17] Hilton, *Bond Men Made Free*, pp. 180–4.
[18] G. Fourquin, *The Anatomy of Popular Rebellion in the Middle Ages* (Amsterdam, 1978), p. 101.
[19] ERO, D/DU/102/1; WC, 44B/1; ERO, D/DK M58.

income from wage work or from the pursuit of crafts or trades. John Phelipp of Thorrington (Essex) was employed in fencing a park for $36\frac{1}{2}$ days soon after the revolt. At least three of the rebels from his village cut wood for sale.[20] Elsewhere individual rebels are known to have sold fish, and three are recorded as traders, as a fellmonger, draper and chandler. There were two carpenters, a miller, a cook and a barber. A subgroup among the rebels were brewers or close associates of brewers, for example one of the few women to be named as a rebel, Margaret Wrighte of Lakenheath (Suffolk), who helped to kill John Cavendish, the chief justice, appears in the court records before the revolt as breaking the assize of ale. The wife of Robert Wryghte of Foxearth brewed a good deal, and the father of William Metefeld junior was the chief seller of bread and ale at Brandon (Suffolk).[21] Perhaps ale houses were especially suitable breeding grounds for disaffection, so that their keepers were drawn easily into rebellion, or perhaps brewers, like others involved in crafts and trades, were likely to be independent, articulate and aware.[22] At the higher end of the scale of status and wealth was a franklin (Richard Baud of Moulsham, Essex), and two others who, judging from their wealth in animals and goods, clearly belonged to the top ranks of village society, perhaps on the fringe of the gentry.[23]

In general, the sample seems to represent a wide spectrum of rural society, with a slight bias towards the better off. This could reflect the nature of the government sources, which tend to give the names of leaders rather than the rank and file, and the manorial records, which will tell us more about tenants than servants. The gentry will not appear in the sample because manorial documents will refer to them rarely, but rebels from this group were few in any case. There is nothing here to contradict the traditional identification of the rising as the 'Peasants' Revolt'.

The most striking common characteristic of our sample of rebels is their prominence in the government of their manor, village or hundred, either at the time of the revolt or within a few years of 1381. No less than fifty-three of them, out of seventy where we might expect to find evidence, are known to have served as reeves, chief pledges, affeerers, ale-tasters, bailiffs, jurors, constables or in other positions of responsibility. These offices were numerous, so that even a small village had to find more than a dozen officials at any one time, and we cannot regard the occupants of these

[20] St John's College, Cambridge (hereafter St JC), 97.25(1), (2).

[21] Cambridge University Library (hereafter CUL), EDC/7/15/11/2 (I am grateful to Miss J. Cripps for lending me her notes of the Lakenheath court rolls); ERO, D/DK M57–8; SROB, J529/1–2.

[22] On radicalism among modern craftsmen, E.J. Hobsbawm and J.W. Scott, 'Political shoemakers', *Past and Present*, 89 (1980), pp. 86–114

[23] For Baud PRO, E 179/107/63. The other two are William Gildeborn and Thomas Sampson.

positions as a narrow oligarchy. None the less every village had an élite, and it was evidently from this group that the leadership in the revolt was drawn. Office-holders in normal times and leaders in revolt both tended to have some maturity of years, and we can show that many of the 1381 rebels were middle-aged. Some estimate can be made of the age of twenty-two of our sample, and seventeen of them, judging from their appearance in the court records in the years 1359–68, or from references to their mature children in the years around 1381, are likely to have been at least approaching forty at the time of the revolt.[24] Most of the rebels came from families well established in their villages, and only two can be identified as recent immigrants, of which one was a special case. This was John Geffrey, a serf who had moved (or rather perhaps had been moved) from a Suffolk manor of the earls of Pembroke, Badmondisfield, 35 miles across the estate to their Essex manor of East Hanningfield to act as bailiff, presumably because of his administrative skills and trustworthy character.[25]

It is typical of previous conceptions about the participants in the revolt that the editor of the *Essex Sessions of the Peace* has speculated that some of the criminals who were indicted before the JPs in 1377–9 would have joined the rising.[26] In fact none of those accused of felonies appear in the list of rebels; on the contrary, one of those helping to identify the criminals, a juror of Barstable Hundred in 1378, William Gildeborn of Fobbing, was hanged for his part in the revolt.[27] Similarly, we might expect to find among the rebels some of the many labourers hauled up before the justices for offences against the labour laws. There is one, James atte Ford of Takeley, who took excessive wages in 1378, but he was exceptional, as he bought a large holding of 18¾ acres in 1380, and so had transformed his social position by the time of the rising. The other Essex rebel known to have fallen foul of the labour laws was an employer, William Bette of Elmdon, who lured two ploughmen with high wages – he may have been acting as a bailiff at the time. Two Suffolk rebels are known to have employed servants in their own right in the decade before the revolt.[28]

The very different character of the Kentish manorial records makes similar analysis of our ten rebels from that county much more difficult. We can say no more than that three held office in seigneurial courts as borsholder (the Kentish equivalent of chief pledge), affeerer and juror; two

---

[24] It has recently been suggested that John Ball was aged about fifty in 1381: B. Bird and D. Stephenson, 'Who was John Ball?', *Trans. Essex Archaeological Society*, 3rd ser., 8 (1976), pp. 287–8.

[25] ERO, D/DP M833.

[26] *Essex Sessions of the Peace, 1351, 1377–1379*, ed. E.C. Furber (Essex Archaeol. Soc. Occasional Pubns., iii, 1953), p. 69.

[27] Ibid, p. 155.

[28] Ibid, pp. 162–4; PRO, KB 27/479; SROB, J529/1–2; SROI, HA 12/C2/19.

of them were active in the land-market, though the size of their holdings is not known; and three appear in the records in the 1360s, so in 1381 they were near to middle age. This suggests similarities with the rebels north of the Thames, but it must be said that rebels are more difficult to find in the manorial records in Kent. This could result from the peculiarities of Kentish customs and documentation, or may reflect the higher proportion of landless and poor among the rebels, already noted on the basis of the escheators' valuations.

In our concern to identify and learn more about the background of the named rebels, we are in danger of ignoring the participation of humbler and poorer men. For example, manorial *famuli*, full-time servants on the demesne, joined the rebel hands, like the servants of Coggeshall Abbey at Childerditch (Essex), who departed, supposedly against their will, on the encouragement of John Noreford, and at least five of the *famuli* at Wye (Kent) were 'ensnared by Rakestrawesmayne' according to the manorial official who had to justify extra expenditure on replacement labour for the hay-making.[29]

Although not all of the rebels were men of substance, occupying positions in seigneurial administration and as upholders of the law in their local communities, the presence of so many people of this kind must affect our assessment of the revolt. Experienced and well informed, they knew about the workings of law and government, and must have been aware of the risks of rebellion. In the event at least five of our sample were hanged, and another eight spent some time away from their homes as fugitives. Their revolt was not a temporary aberration, as some of them persisted in acts in defiance of authority long after the revolt, even to the point of personal ruin, like John Wylkyn of Fryerning (Essex), who lost his holding in 1382 for refusing to pay rent and carry out repairs after June 1381.[30] It is difficult to believe that these leading rebels were acting on mere impulse, or that they were affected by collective delusions. We must conclude that they had substantial grievances, and that their experiences of the real world drove them to embark on the revolt.

Changes in Social Relationships, c. 1340–81

The four counties had such diverse characteristics in their economy and social structure that it is difficult to identify features that made them ripe for revolt in the late fourteenth century. It should be noted that the area contained a good deal of woodland, marsh and pasture, that settlements were often dispersed, and that field systems were irregular, with much

[29] ERO, D/DP M1099; PRO, SC 6/901/5.
[30] WC, 44B/1.

enclosure.[31] The inhabitants of such areas in later periods have been characterised as being independent and nonconformist, and their radical tradition may well date back to the Middle Ages.[32] However, similar landscapes are found throughout England, and those outside the south-east were not in the forefront of the 1381 revolt. The counties are well known for their widespread rural industries, and craftsmen have often played an important role in rural revolts. In Essex and Suffolk there was an unusually high proportion of servants and labourers, who were vulnerable to the attempts to restrict wages, but as we have seen, landless wage-earners do not seem to have played a *leading* part in the rising.[33] The proximity of London may have been a factor in the rapid diffusion of news, rumours and ideas. The London market stimulated both industrial and agricultural producers in the surrounding countryside, so that those with a saleable surplus were acutely aware of opportunities for profit, and therefore perhaps particularly resentful of the restrictions imposed on them, such as the rents and dues that ate into their surplus.

The landlords of the four counties included the normal mixture of ecclesiastical corporations, lay magnates and gentry. Large church estates were prominent in western Suffolk, Hertfordshire and Kent, but not sufficiently to mark off these counties as very unusual. The peasantry of Kent enjoyed the unique privilege of the total absence of both serfdom and the normal restrictions of customary tenure. In the other three counties free tenants were numerous, but it is possible to find many manors where they were outnumbered by customary tenants, and most lords had at least a few serfs by blood *(nativi de sanguine)*. Customary holdings might carry heavy burdens of rent and services, though the distinction between free and customary tenure was blurred by the existence of tenements of intermediate status, like molland, and the land-market allowed many tenants – a quarter of those at Hadleigh (Suffolk) in the early fourteenth century, for example – to hold both free and customary land.[34] Did the presence of so much free tenure increase the customary tenants' consciousness of their disadvantages? And in Kent were the tenants so

---

[31]   O. Rackham, 'The medieval landscape of Essex', in D.G. Buckley (ed.), *Archaeology in Essex to A.D. 1500* (Council for British Archaeology Report no. 34, London, 1980); A.M. Everitt, 'The making of the agrarian landscape in Kent', *Archaeologia Cantiana*, 92 (1976), pp. 1–31; L.M. Munby, *The Hertfordshire Landscape* (London, 1977); P. Barton, 'Manorial economy and society in Shenley', in *The Peasants' Revolt in Hertfordshire, 1381* (Hertford, 1981); N. Scarfe, *The Suffolk Landscape* (London, 1972).

[32]   J. Thirsk (ed.), *The Agrarian History of England and Wales, 1500–1640*, series ed. H.P.R. Finberg (Cambridge, 1967), pp. 109–12.

[33]   Hilton, *Bond Men Made Free*, pp. 170–4.

[34]   J.F. Nichols, 'Custodia Essexae' (unpublished Univ. of London Ph.D. thesis, 1930), p. 251.

privileged that they resented even the light hand of lordship that they experienced?[35]

In the thirteenth and early fourteenth centuries a feature of the rural society of the south-east, noticeable especially in Essex and Suffolk, was the very small size of most tenant holdings. Generalisation is difficult; although a few manors, like Lawling (Essex) in 1310, had two-thirds of tenants with 30 acres or more, and on most manors the liveliness of the land-market allowed a small minority to prosper and accumulate very large holdings, it is often found that a half or even three-quarters of tenants held 5 acres or less.[36] The information available relates normally to the amount of arable land only, and the many smallholders must have made use of the pastures, wastes and woods, as well as supplementing their incomes from agriculture with wage and craft work.

The plague epidemic of 1348–9, judging from the Essex frankpledge payments, killed nearly half of the population, and no real recovery is apparent in the next three decades.[37] We might expect to find that the number of tenants was reduced, and the size of holdings increased; these trends can be discerned, but on a very limited scale. The holdings left vacant by the plague were filled by inheritance, or taken on by survivors who were prepared to accumulate greater quantities of land, either on the old conditions or on new leasehold terms. Formerly landless wage-earners could move into the ranks of tenants, like Edmund, servant of the rector of Ingatestone (Essex), who took a 7-acre holding for a term of seven years in 1359.[38] The reduction in the number of tenants could be a slight one, so that those listed in rentals of Fristling (Essex) declined from forty-four in *c.* 1340 to thirty-nine in 1369.[39] On some manors a potential force for change came from demesne leasing in parcels, which put further quantities of land in the

---

[35] Réville and Petit-Dutaillis, *Le soulèvement des travailleurs*, p. 55; F.R.H. Du Boulay, *The Lordship of Canterbury: An Essay on Medieval Society* (London, 1966), pp. 181–9.

[36] J.F. Nichols, 'The extent of Lawling, A.D. 1310', *Trans. Essex Archaeological Society*, new ser., 20 (1933), pp. 173–98; G.F. Beaumont, 'The manor of Borley, A.D. 1308', *Trans. Essex Archaeological Society*, new ser., 18 (1928), pp. 254–69; A.J. Horwood, 'A custumal, A.D. 1298, of the manor of Wykes', *Trans. Essex Archaeological Society*, new ser., 1 (1878), pp. 109–15; K.C. Newton, *Thaxted in the Fourteenth Century* (Chelmsford, 1960), pp. 10–16; idem, *The Manor of Writtle* (London, 1970), pp. 37–54; Sturman, 'Barking Abbey: a study in its external and internal administration from the Conquest to the Dissolution', pp. 244–51; A. Clark, 'Church Hall Manor, Kelvedon, in 1294', *Essex Review*, 19 (1910), pp. 139–49; J.L. Fisher, 'Customs and services on an Essex manor in the thirteenth century', *Trans. Essex Archaeological Society*, new ser., 19 (1930), pp. 111–16; M.K. McIntosh, 'Land, tenure and population in the royal manor of Havering, Essex', *Econ. Hist. Rev.*, 2nd ser., 23 (1980), pp. 17–31; E. Miller, *The Abbey and Bishopric of Ely* (Cambridge, 1951), pp. 113–53.

[37] A. Clark, 'Serfdom on an Essex manor, 1308–78', *Eng. Hist. Rev.*, 20 (1905), pp. 479–83; L.R. Poos, 'Population and mortality in two fourteenth-century Essex communities, Great Waltham and High Easter, 1327–89' (Fellowship Essay, Univ. of Cambridge, 1979), ch. 2; Newton, *Manor of Writtle*, pp. 78–82.

[38] ERO, D/DP M19.

[39] ERO, D/DP M1411, M1412.

hands of tenants.[40] It seems in spite of the undoubted shift in the balance between population and land after 1348 that smallholders remained an important element in society at the time of the 1381 rising. Of the 155 customary holdings on six Essex manors restored to their tenants after the burning of the court rolls in the revolt, eighty-one (52 per cent) contained 5 acres or less, and only thirteen were of 20 acres or more, not very different from the overall distribution of land before 1348.[41]

There is some evidence of growing prosperity among the peasantry. Smallholders would have enjoyed the benefits of rising wages. There seems to have been a general increase in the numbers of animals owned, judging from the tenant animals presented for trespassing on the lords' demesne lands. Flocks of eighty or a hundred sheep or herds of six or ten cattle were not uncommon, and occasionally even greater numbers are mentioned, appreciably larger than the flocks and herds appearing in the early fourteenth-century records. The value of land remained remarkably high, and tenants seem to have had large amounts of cash at their disposal. This is indicated by the occasional records of the sums paid for customary holdings by one tenant to another. Thomas Spryngefeld of Fristling (Essex) bought an $8\frac{1}{2}$ acre holding in 1379 for £20; at Fingrith (Essex) a tenant paid £12 for 20 acres in 1378, and just after the revolt land changed hands at Havering atte Bower (Essex) for 13s. 4d. per acre. A rare direct piece of evidence for an accumulation of cash concerns John Henne of Earl Soham (Suffolk), who had 20s. 0d. in money to be stolen in 1370.[42] Disputes recorded in court rolls reveal a lively trade in grain, wool, cheese, animals and timber, sometimes in large quantities, like the 160 sheep sold by an East Hanningfield (Essex) tenant in 1378.[43]

The evidence for the changes in peasant fortunes in the period is fragmentary and difficult to quantify. There is no certainty that their circumstances were improving decisively, but the trends were mainly in their favour.

The landlords of the south-east, in common with those in other regions, were already experiencing economic difficulties in the second quarter of the fourteenth century. The plague epidemic opened up the prospect of sharp reductions in their incomes. Before 1348 demesnes were being cultivated with much wage labour. The labour shortage and rising wages eroded the profits of the demesnes, but most landlords continued with the

[40] For example, at Layham (Suffolk) the demesne was leased in 1379 to nine tenants: SROB, E 3/1/2.7.

[41] ERO, D/DP M1191; D/DP M833; D/DFy M1; D/DGh M14; ERO (Southend Branch), D/DMq M1; ERO, T/B 122.

[42] ERO, D/DP M718; D/DHt M93; D/DU 102/1; SROI, V 5/18/1.2.

[43] ERO, D/DP M833. See also E. Clark, 'Debt litigation in a late medieval English vill', in J.A. Raftis (ed.), *Pathways to Medieval Peasants* (Toronto, 1981), pp. 247–79.

old system, reducing the area under cultivation, and gaining some benefit from the high grain prices of the period up to 1375.[44] Whole demesnes were leased in the 1350s and 1360s, and there was renewed leasing activity just after 1381, but at the time of the revolt most demesnes were still under direct management.

The landlords' attitudes towards their tenants, subordinates and employees must have been coloured by the high wages and signs of increasing peasant prosperity, however embryonic. Their resentments of the changes affecting the rest of society are reflected in such literature as *Winner and Waster* and Gower's *Vox Clamantis*, and, more forcefully, in legislation like the 1351 Statute of Labourers and the Sumptuary Law of 1363. They were naturally anxious to take what advantage they could of the new developments and to tap some of the growing wealth that they saw below them.

Lords hung on to their powers after the plague epidemic. Their hold over their serfs represented the most complete form of social control available to them. In the 1330s and 1340s the *nativi* appear in the court rolls paying marriage fines and less commonly leaving their lords' manors illicitly or on payment of chevage. The degree of control exercised by one lord is indicated by an inquiry at Birdbrook (Essex) in 1338, after a 4-acre holding fell vacant, as to 'which of the neifs who have no land are most capable of taking the said land', implying that a serf could be compelled to take on the tenancy.[45]

After 1349, marriage fines continued to be exacted, up to and beyond 1381. They declined in number at Ingatestone (Essex), but at Birdbrook (Essex) they were levied in the late 1370s more frequently than before.[46] There was no fixed rate of fine and after 1349, although some payments continued at the old level of 1s. 0d. or 2s. 0d., some lords demanded higher fines, 3s. 4d. or even 6s. 8d.

References to the emigration of serfs increase markedly after 1349, reflecting both the general *Wanderlust* of the period, and also the renewed concern of the lords to deal with the problem. Licensed departures might cost the serf a fine of 20s. 0d. or 40s. 0d., or a regular chevage payment which could be nominal, or as high as 3s. 4d. per annum. Permission to leave could be hedged around with conditions, to return once a year, or, in the case of a servile woman, not to marry without a licence. The lords' chief anxiety was to prevent illicit departures that might deprive them of their valuable assets. Pressure was put on relatives to bring the errants back,

---

[44] On pre-1348 problems, see Miller, *Abbey and Bishopric of Ely*, pp. 105–11; R.A.L. Smith, *Canterbury Cathedral Priory* (Cambridge, 1943), pp. 126–7. For post-1348 developments, see A.R. Bridbury, 'The Black Death', *Econ. Hist. Rev.*, 2nd ser., 26 (1973), pp. 580–6.

[45] ERO, D/DU 267/29

[46] ERO, D/DP M15–M22; D/DU 267/29, 30.

like the 20s. 0d. amercement demanded from Robert atte Chirch of Drinkstone (Suffolk) in 1377 because he failed to produce his two sons at the court, 'which he did not do, but refused'.[47] The lord of Aldham (Suffolk) imposed oaths on his serfs in 1369–71; Nicholas Mervyn, after a period of absence, came to the court and swore 'that he would be obedient to the lord and bailiffs and that he would come to serve the lord wherever and whenever the lord or his council wish'.[48]

Lords also attempted to control the acquisition of free land by their serfs, and to force them to pay extra rents and hold the land on customary tenure. An elaborately recorded case in 1374 at Crondon in Stock (Essex), a manor then held by Simon Sudbury as part of the estates of the bishopric of London, concerned one William Joyberd, who took a mare of his aunt's which the lord required as a heriot. It was then revealed that William, though a *nativus de sanguine*, held a messuage and 9 acres of free land which he had acquired by charter in the nearby village of Ramsden Bellhouse. An order was given for William, his family, lands, goods and chattels to be seized because 'he never gave to the lord an increment of rent, nor rendered the said lands to the lord as serfs ought'.[49] The danger of allowing such arrangements to go unchecked is shown by a discovery made by the officials of the countess of Norfolk at Walton (Suffolk) after the revolt, that two of her serfs had set themselves up as leading townsmen of Manningtree (Essex), one with $63\frac{1}{2}$ acres of freehold land, and the other with 21 acres and eleven messuages, shops and cottages.[50]

The lords had obvious financial reasons for maintaining control, but another motive in the post-plague labour shortage lay in the possibility of using their hold over serfs as a means of securing a supply of wage-labourers. This attempt to impose a sort of 'second serfdom' emerges from some agreements made when serfs were given permission to leave the manor. At Aldham (Suffolk) in 1368 an emigrant was required to return each year 'in the autumn to serve the lord', in other words to help with the harvest. A servile girl of Windridge (Hertfordshire) was allowed to leave providing that she should be 'ready [to serve] the lord when he pleased to have her'.[51] The coercive power of the lord could also be used to secure employees for the demesne through the election of *famuli* in the courts, recorded at Brandon (Suffolk) and Winston (Suffolk) in the 1360s and 1370s. The hapless employees were required to take an oath on election. Needless to say, the candidates were often recruited from the unfree. Such was the lord's claim on the employment of serfs at Iken (Suffolk) that in

[47] SROB, E 7/10/1.2.
[48] SROI, HA 68:484/135.
[49] ERO, D/DP M780.
[50] SROI, HA 119:50/3/17.
[51] SROI, HA 68:484/135; HRO, X.E.I.C.

1372–3 the parson paid a fine in order to obtain the services of Agnes Fenman, a *nativa domini*.[52] The families of servile employees were also vulnerable to pressure to enforce labour discipline, as is recorded at Thorrington (Essex) in 1381. William Phelipp, a serf, was employed by the demesne farmer, probably on an annual contract. He broke the contract and left, but revisited the village and stayed with his mother, brother and uncle. These three were distrained by the lord of the manor for the trespass of receiving and entertaining their relative.[53]

Perhaps the term 'second serfdom' can also be applied to agreements made between lords and non-serfs, who were bound to work on the demesne as wage-earners in return for a grant of land. John Dryvere of Foxearth (Essex) was granted in 1364 a cottage, curtilage and one acre of land for life, at a rent of 5s. 0d. per annum 'on condition that the same John will serve the lord of this manor for the whole of his life . . . as a common labourer', and at Birdbrook (Essex) in 1377 Thomas Whetelee was granted 5 acres of land 'as long as he remains in the service of the lord'. In a similar case at Iken (Suffolk) Roger Wisman took a holding in 1378 and promised 'to serve the lord as a labourer, taking for his wage what is just', which we may suspect in the circumstances involved a commitment to accept wages below the current rate.[54]

'Serfs by blood' formed a relatively small minority of the rural population of the south-east. Much more numerous were the customary tenants, many of whom still held 'servile land *(terra nativa)*', heritable by their family or 'brood *(sequela)*', and who received seizin of the holding 'by the rod *(per virgam)*'. The terminology is that of servile tenure, the obligations of which had been fixed in the very different economic circumstances of the thirteenth century. Increasingly after 1349 lords were letting customary holdings on short-term leases (ten years or less, or a single life), for a cash rent only, or for a cash rent and minimal labour service. The development of these forms of tenure affected only a minority of customary holdings, as they were more numerous than the old heritable tenures on only nine of a sample of thirty manors. For the tenants who were still in theory liable to heavy labour services the late fourteenth century saw a prevalent tendency towards commutation which meant that few tenants were expected by 1381 to perform week-work, though seasonal services and boons were commonly demanded. Kentish labour services had not been very onerous, but tenants there were sometimes expected to do their services in the late fourteenth century with little opportunity for commutation.[55] No doubt these continued

[52] SROB, J529/1–2; CUL, EDC7/17/25/3; SROI, HD 32:293/390.

[53] St JC, 97.25(1).

[54] ERO, D/DK M57; D/DU 267/30; SROI, HD 293/388.

[55] On the new forms of tenure, see B.F. Harvey, *Westminster Abbey and its Estates in the Middle Ages* (Oxford, 1977), pp. 244–67. On commutation in Kent, see Smith, *Canterbury Cathedral Priory*, pp. 126–7.

demands for service were resented, as is suggested by many references to their non-performance in court records, but we may suspect that the lords' demands for cash also caused a good deal of friction. The leasehold tenancies carried a heavy burden of rent, varying from 6d. to 2s. 0d. per acre for arable, and commonly at a shilling per acre, or three times the universal rent demanded by the rebels at Mile End.

The leasehold tenures often carried no more than a nominal entry fine, but the traditional tenures involved a liability to pay a variable fine on inheritance or transfer. Wide differences between rates of fine, such as 22s. 0d. for a cottage and 6s. 8d. for 19 acres, on the same manor in successive years in 1380–1, suggest their flexibility, influenced by the lord's calculation of the new tenant's capacity to pay and the variable quality of the land. There was no consistent trend in the rate of entry fines, which may reflect both economic differences between manors, and variations in seigneurial policy. New tenants at East Hanningfield (Essex) paid 11d. per acre before the plague, and 6d. per acre up to the 1380s. More commonly the rate fell after the plague, but then increased until by the 1370s it was very near to its pre-plague level. For example, at Bredfield (Suffolk) fines averaged 5s. 2d. per acre in the 1340s, 2s. 9d. in the 1350s, and 4s. 11d. in the 1370s. Ingatestone (Essex) shows an unusual pattern of consistent increase from a pre-plague 5d. per acre to 1s. 1d. in 1379–81.[56]

The growing variety of customary tenures in the late fourteenth century must have led tenants to make comparisons. Tenants on manors which did not see any significant move towards leasehold would have cause for resentment. Those who had access to land on the new terms could well have envisaged that one major change in traditional arrangements might be followed by others.

Landlords were much concerned with the control of the market in customary holdings. Land changed hands rapidly both before and after the plague, and the lords accepted this provided that the transfer was carried out through the manor court, so that a fine could be levied and the new tenant and the conditions of tenancy entered on the court roll. The numbers of illicit transfers recorded in the late fourteenth century, either sales by charter in the manner of freeholders or sublettings for terms of years, increased, and are commonly encountered in the 1370s. This could reflect a growth in attempts to bypass the lord, or renewed seigneurial vigilance, or both. On some manors one gains the impression of some

[56] The wide discrepancies in rates of fine are recorded at Fristling (Essex): ERO, D/DP M718. The other figures for fines come from ERO, D/DP M832–3; SROI, HA 91/1; ERO, D/DP M15–22. Parallels to Bredfield are Fingrith (Essex), with a rate of 1s. 10d. per acre in 1327–38, 11d. in 1362–4, and 1s. 3d. in 1377–81, and South Elmham (Suffolk), with rates of 2s. 10d. and 3s. 7d. before 1348, and 1s. 5d. in the 1350s, 1s. 2d. in the 1360s and 2s. 6d. in 1372–81; ERO, D/DK M108, D/DHt M92, M93; SROI, HA 12/C2/14–19. These rates are all calculated from fines paid on *ad opus* transfers.

administrative slackness in the two decades after the plague, followed by more stringent controls in the 1370s. This would explain the number of cases in which former illicit transfers were discovered, like the unlicensed marriage of a widow at Arkesden (Essex) of 1366 which was revealed to the manor court in 1378, or the remarkable discovery in 1379 at Earl Soham (Suffolk) that a serf, John Hamond, had enjoyed the profits of a free tenement for ten years by granting the land into the hands of feoffees, a legal device normally associated with a more elevated section of society.[57] A tightening of administration is suggested also by the number of new rentals made in the 1370s and in 1380–1, or the order in 1380 at Aston (Hertfordshire) 'to inquire who holds lands of the demesne and servile land, namely how many hold by copies because it is said that a great number of acres have been usurped'.[58] Unofficial transfers might lead to confusion over the exact status of particular plots of land, so that we find inquiries as to whether parcels were free or customary, again common in the 1370s.

The seigneurial courts were the key institutions for the maintenance of lordly control. They were used to enforce the obligations of tenants, such as the performance of labour services, or the repair of buildings on customary holdings. The courts disciplined manorial officials for slackness or corruption. They helped to maintain labour discipline, by amercing *famuli* employed on the demesne for poor work, and by assisting the higher courts in dealing with offences against the labour laws, ordering labourers to accept offers of work from the lord's officials, and occasionally punishing those who demanded high wages, like the three threshers at Chartham (Kent) who had obtained 2d. per day plus food in 1379.[59] The courts also provided lords with revenues from amercements and fines, including levies on brewers, and amercements on craftsmen such as potters and tilers for collecting their raw materials, that seem to have had the character of a seigneurial tax on trade and industry. Regular annual dues, like the common fine, or avesage (pannage of pigs), were collected through the courts.

The perquisites of courts made an appreciable contribution to seigneurial incomes; they rarely accounted for more than a tenth of manorial profits, but their value lay in the flexibility which allowed them to be increased when other sources of income were static or tending to decline. The normal pattern in the four counties was for court profits to increase between the 1340s and the post-plague decades. (See Table 10.1.) The amount of increase may seem unremarkable, but to expand such revenues when the numbers of people attending the courts was declining must have involved

[57] ERO, D/Ad 122; SROI, V 5/18/1.3.
[58] HRO, D/EAS 24.
[59] Canterbury Cathedral Library (hereafter CCL), U15/12 48480.

a considerable growth in the average *per capita* payments made by the suitors. Presentments of some offences increased in number; on some manors the quantity of brewing offences and public nuisances moved slightly upwards, and on all manors the failure to repair buildings became a repetitive item of business by the 1370s.[60] Another growth point was provided by amercements for trespass on the demesne; no doubt the quantity and scale of incursions by tenant stock really increased because of the growing emphasis on pastoralism in peasant farming, but lords probably also made efforts to ensure that as many cases as possible were reported to the courts and substantial sums levied in amercements. The number and size of amercements both rose, so that the total taken from tenants for trespass offences might double between the 1340s and 1370s. Individual very high amercements could be demanded, such as 26s. 8d. from an Ingatestone tenant for selling a building from his customary holding.[61]

Table 10.1
Average annual totals of court perquisites.

Wheathampstead (Herts.)		Chevington (Suffolk)	
1340–7	£6 10s. 1d.	1339–48	£2 8s. 10d.
1371–81	£7 1s. 2d.	1359–80	£4 3s. 8d.
Meopham (Kent)		East Farleigh (Kent)	
1340–7	£1 0s. 1d.	1334–43	£8 3s. $7\frac{1}{2}$ d.
1368–75	£2 6s. 5d.	1372–88	£9 2s. $9\frac{1}{2}$ d.

Source: Hertfordshire Record Office, D/ELw M144–MI85; Suffolk Record Office, Bury St Edmunds Branch, E 3/15.3/2.4–2.11; Canterbury Cathedral Library, beadles' rolls for Meopham and East Farleigh.

The rising trend in court perquisites made only a modest contribution to offsetting the overall downward movement in seigneurial incomes. The extent of that decline was surprisingly slight. Income from the rents is difficult to survey in the long term because of the changes in the form in which rents were paid, such as fluctuations in the commutation of services, and the advance of leasehold tenures. Nor can we be certain as to the amount of evasion of rent payment. These complications are least problematic on the Kentish manors of Canterbury Cathedral Priory, and we find there that the reduction of total rent income on individual manors between the 1340s and the 1370s rarely exceeded 15 per cent and could be as low as 3 per cent. The most adversely affected estate with manors in the

[60] D.A. Crowley, 'Frankpledge and leet jurisdiction in later medieval Essex' (unpublished Univ. of Sheffield Ph.D. thesis, 1971), chaps. 11, 12 (brewing offences declined after 1350 at Messing, but increased at Rickling; public nuisance presentments increased at Messing and Claret but may have declined at Rickling).
[61] ERO, D/DP M22.

region seems to have been that of Battle Abbey, which suffered a 30 per cent drop in income between 1346–7 and 1381–2. The normal experience seems to have been a decline in revenues considerably smaller than this.[62]

We must conclude that fourteenth-century landlords defended their interests and incomes with vigour in a period of economic adversity. To emphasise one aspect of their position in the late fourteenth century, they succeeded in retaining the initiative so that they were still capable of disciplining tenants and making arbitrary demands through fines and amercements. The tenants had gained access to more land, and presumably the growth in leasehold tenure represented a concession to them, providing greater certainty in obligations. They seem to have been constantly testing the regime: serfs successfully left their manors, attempted to conceal the marriages of their daughters, and secretly acquired free land. Customary tenants also sought to evade the restrictions on the sale and leasing of land, and neglected or wasted their buildings. They failed or refused to perform labour services, four cases of which are known involving a dozen or more tenants in the years 1379 and 1380. These could be seen as leading cumulatively to the subversion of lordly authority, or merely as actions to gain short-term advantage. However, the existence of a strand of open and self-conscious opposition to seigneurial control sometimes emerges from episodes recorded in even the most routine series of court records.

The first half of the fourteenth century provides examples of protests by tenants, such as the collective avoidance of suit of mill at Ingatestone (Essex) in 1346, or the complaint of a tenant of Polstead (Suffolk) in 1340 who accused the lord and his bailiffs of corruptly protecting the manorial *famuli*, who he claimed were robbers, or the well-known Bocking (Essex) petition, apparently made by free tenants to the prior of Christ Church, Canterbury, over the excesses of a steward. Actions against lords in the royal courts are most commonly found in the Midlands at this period, but the 'poor people' of the village of Albury (Hertfordshire) petitioned parliament in 1321–2 over the oppressions of their lord, Sir John de Patemore, who had imprisoned them and seized their cattle.[63]

Throughout the period examined here we find serfs seeking to assert their freedom, and being thwarted by their lords. Two South Elmham

---

[62] E. Searle, *Lordship and Community, Battle Abbey and its Banlieu* (Toronto, 1974), pp. 256–62; G.A. Holmes, *The Estates of the Higher Nobility in Fourteenth-Century England* (Cambridge, 1957), pp. 90–3, 109–20; Smith, *Canterbury Cathedral Priory*, p. 13; Harvey, *Westminster Abbey and its Estates in the Middle Ages*, pp. 66–7. On the demands of lords in general, see R.H. Hilton, *The Decline of Serfdom in Medieval England* (London, 1969), pp. 36–43.
[63] ERO, D/DP M16; BL. Add. Roll 27683; J.F. Nichols, 'An early fourteenth century petition from the tenants of Bocking to their manorial lord', *Econ. Hist. Rev.*, 2 (1929–30), pp. 300–7; *Rotuli Parliamentorum*, i, p. 189. On tenants' legal actions against lords, see R.H. Hilton, 'Peasant movements before 1381', in E.M. Carus-Wilson (ed.), *Essays in Economic History*, 3 vols (London, 1954–62), ii, pp. 73–90.

(Suffolk) men, John Clench and John Soule, claimed to be free in 1360. The 'whole homage' of the manor court stated that they were serfs, and they were put in the stocks. They did fealty as serfs to their lord, the bishop of Norwich, and were fined 3s. 4d. each 'for an unjust claim and rebellion'. Another tenant who had supported them (suggesting that the other villagers were by no means unanimous in their opinion) was deprived of his lands until he submitted to the lord's grace and paid a fine.[64] A similar case at Great Leighs (Essex) in 1378 concerned Joan Lyon, daughter of William Lyon, serf, who married without permission. William White and Richard Dryver, both servile tenants, and Richard Gardener, a born serf, 'conspired among themselves at Chelmsford to swear and give the verdict at the next court at Great Leighs' that Joan was free. They 'could not deny' the conspiracy, and the two tenants were amerced the large sums of 13s. 4d. and 20s. 0d. Needless to say, all three conspirators served as chief pledges at the time.[65]

A sharp reaction against a claim to freedom is revealed in the manor court of Earl Soham (Suffolk) in 1373. Alice Conyn, the daughter of John Bronnewen, was asked by what right she held land and married without licence. She produced a charter of manumission granted to her father by Thomas Brotherton, earl of Norfolk, in 1337. The court discovered a loophole in her claim to be free. Brotherton had held the manor in fee tail, by the terms of which he could not alienate property except in his own lifetime, so the charter carried no weight. Alice, and her sister, were each required to pay marriage fines at the punitively high rate of 13s. 4d.[66]

When at Flixton (Suffolk) Robert Borel denied his servile condition, 'with ingratitude', and committed a series of offences, marrying without permission, detaining a rent of a lamb, and wasting his holding, the lady of the manor, the prioress of Flixton, summoned an extraordinary tribunal in 1377, consisting of nuns, the prior of Aldeby (Norfolk), the steward and other lay advisers, who concluded an 'agreement' with Borel. He acknowledged his serfdom, swore an oath of servility 'without coercion', and agreed to render the old customs, to observe the rules governing marriage, and to reconstruct his buildings. He had to find pledges who were bound to see him carry out his obligations under penalties of £5 each. The prioress's side of the 'agreement' was to remit amercements totalling 53s. 4½ d. in exchange for a fine.[67]

All of these cases show the lords using their judicial authority to assert their interests against the claims of their subordinates. However, the seigneurial courts were somewhat ambiguous institutions, which depended

---

[64] SROI, HA 12/C2/14.
[65] PRO, LR 3/18/3.
[66] SROI, V 5/18/1.2.
[67] SROI, HA 12/C3/7.

on the participation of tenants who presented offenders, fixed penalties, and collected dues. These petty officials can be seen ideally as performing a mediating role, moderating the harshness of the lord's rule, and making the regime more acceptable to their neighbours. In reality, especially in a period of heightened tension, the officials found themselves assailed on all sides. They were under pressure from the lord to present more cases, reveal more misdemeanours, and to collect more cash; on the other side, their friends and neighbours expected some protection and favourable treatment. They received a good deal of criticism in the courts from people who 'contradicted the chief pledges', uttered threats, and showed contempt for the courts. For example, in February 1381 William Morkyn of Fingrith (Essex) had to pay an amercement of 12d. because his wife 'was a rebel and spoke badly of the affeerers'. In 1380 at Walsham-le-Willows (Suffolk) Edmund Patyl, who had just heard that his illicitly acquired customary tenement of 9 acres had been seized by the lord, was amerced 3s. 4d. 'for contempt done to the lord, abusing the whole inquest [jury] openly in full court', directing his anger, it should be noted, against the jurors who revealed his involvement in the secret sale of land.[68]

The village élite could attempt to act as spokesmen for the villagers in negotiations with the lord, as apparently happened at Ingatestone (Essex) in 1379 after a dispute over the allocation of services among tenants, when the homage offered the lord a sum of 40s. 0d. so that rents and services could be made 'certain'.[69] They might also conceal cases and shield their neighbours, but if they were found out by the lord they had to answer to him. We can sense the growing distrust between the lord of Winston (Suffolk) (a manor of the priory of Ely) and the jurors. In 1374 a jury which 'did not know' who had killed three of the lord's lambs was ordered to pay for the dead animals, and a chief pledge was amerced 1s. 0d. for concealing a case. In 1378 the reeve's failure to report the taking of wood cost him 1s. 0d., and the homage was ordered to investigate damage to the woods. In the same year a group of jurors told the steward after the court that the jury had concealed trespasses against the lord and the vill by animals belonging to the vicar, which led to another collective amercement of 3s. 4d. In 1379 the jury failed to report ruinous buildings and defaults of suit of court; in 1381 damage to the woods was concealed again.[70]

In view of the widespread difficulties arising from the ambiguous position of the officials it is hardly surprising that we find, particularly in the 1370–81 period, many refusals to serve in administrative positions, as rent-collectors, constables or ale-tasters. This could involve a collective refusal,

---

[68] ERO, D/DHt M93; SROB, HA 504/1/8.
[69] ERO, D/DP M22.
[70] CUL, EDC7/17/23/5; 7/17/25/4; 7/17/25/5; 7/17/25/7; 7/17/26/4.

like that of the homage of Fingrith (Essex) in 1375, to elect any rent-collector.[71] Such actions threatened the existing machinery of government, and lords reacted sharply with threats of high penalties and eviction from holdings. Similarly, refusals to take the oath as chief pledge, which occurred on a number of occasions, were regarded as acts of rebellion, and punished with such large amercements as 6s. 8d. That these amounted to more than an individual desire to escape the responsibility and expense of office is suggested by the collective denial of the common fine, paid over by the chief pledges at the annual view of frankpledge, which is found five times between 1370 and 1379.

Even if they accepted office, the chief pledges might 'spend all day making their presentments', which annoyed the East Hanningfield (Essex) steward in 1379, or not turn up to the view at all. The most remarkable case of this kind occurred at Fingrith (Essex) in 1376 when the June view was boycotted, and none of the fifteen chief pledges, and only ten of the (presumably) hundred or more tithing-men, attended, so that the business of the view had to be postponed until a court session held in the following December.[72]

Offenders against manorial discipline, such as those who failed to pay rents or other dues, might find that their goods or animals were seized in order to distrain them to pay up. At all times a reply might come in the form of a 'rescue', in which the tenant took back the distrained possessions, but cases seem to occur more frequently in the decade 1371–81. 'Rescue' was also sometimes accompanied by violence against the official concerned, like the minister of Canterbury Cathedral Priory who was assaulted in 1372 by Thomas Creake of Adisham (Kent), for which Creake was amerced 4s. 0d.[73] An extreme case of an attack on a seigneurial official was the subject of a complaint by the abbot of St Augustine's Canterbury to the court of King's Bench in 1380. Roger Manston 'with other malefactors' assaulted the estate steward and prevented him from holding the abbot's court at Minster in Thanet, leading to disruption in the manorial administration, and a loss of income for the lord.[74]

Many lines of continuity can be seen between the events of the pre-revolt period and the 1381 outbreak. The manifestations of discontent made before the revolt, notably the insubordinate acts in lords' courts, were repeated in local incidents in 1381. The protests made before the revolt concerned issues that figured in the rebel demands to the king in 1381 – the abolition of serfdom and servile tenure, the removal of service beyond a simple cash rent, and the curtailing of lords' judicial power. In the

[71] ERO, D/DHt M92.
[72] ERO, D/DP M833; DD/Ht M92.
[73] CCL, U 15/9 48357.
[74] PRO, KB 27/479.

agitations before 1381 and in the main revolt the local élite, such as the chief pledges, played a prominent role. Places that rose in the main revolt, such as East Hanningfield, Ingatestone and Thanet, had some experience of pre-revolt incidents.

Close links between the seigneurial policies of the years 1350–81 and the revolt itself can be substantiated if we return to our sample of eighty-nine rebels. In pre-revolt documents we can show that they experienced the routine incidents of manorial life: John Cok of Prittlewell (Essex) was in arrears with his rent; John Cok of Moze (Essex) was amerced for failing to repair a building; Edmund Gerneys and Thomas Gardiner of Little Barton (Suffolk), along with many others, allowed their animals to trespass on the demesne and were amerced.[75] Most of the rebels, especially those who were customary tenants, would expect to pay at least a few pence every year for such offences. Occasionally we can show that individual rebels had experienced especially harsh treatment before the revolt, notably from records of a court session held on 6 June 1381 at Thorrington (Essex), when two serfs were accused, in spite of their protests that they had already paid merchet, of having married off their daughters without permission, and Juliana and John Phelipp were punished for sheltering their own son and brother who had broken an employment contract, in an incident described above. All four people involved in these cases joined in the burning of the Thorrington court rolls a week later.[76]

Prominent among the rebels were those whose economic position was improving before 1381. John Philip of Brandon (Suffolk) accumulated at least five separate holdings of land in the 1370s as well as rising in his lord's service from warrener to bailiff.[77] Three Essex rebels, John Fillol, John Geffrey (both of Hanningfield) and James atte Ford of Takeley all acquired land in 1380. Geffrey, who had recently been appointed bailiff and moved into East Hanningfield from his Suffolk home, had bought a smallholding, and obtained the reversion of a further 15 acres. He was evidently about to build a new house, for which he had collected timber worth 8 marks. In the late 1370s Robert Wryghte of Foxearth was increasing the number of animals that he owned, and his wife became the chief brewer in the village. John Cole of Felixstowe (Suffolk) had bought a freeholding before the revolt, and John Herde of Berners Berwick (Essex) was leasing his lord's herd of cows.[78] The lords of these successful peasants were able to take advantage of their enterprise. John Fillol and James atte Ford both had to

[75] ERO, D/DU 190/6; D/DGh M14; SROB, E 7/24/1.3.

[76] St JC, 97.25(1), 97.25(2a).

[77] SROB, J529/1–2; PRO, SC 6/1304/31–36.

[78] ERO, D/DP M833 (Fillol and Geffrey); New College, Oxford (hereafter NC), 3697 (Ford); ERO, D/DK M57–8; PRO, SC 2/172/10 (Wryghte); SROI, HA 119:50/3/80 (Cole); ERO, D/DHf M28, M45 (Herde).

pay higher-than-average entry fines for their new purchase of land. Ford was actually in the process of paying at the time of the revolt a fine of 33s. 4d. for 18¾ acres of land (1s. 9d. per acre). Wryghte was being milked of large sums of money through the manor court; he was charged unusually high amounts for such offences as trespassing on the demesne, and his wife had to pay substantial brewing fines. Together they paid a total of 7s. 8d. in 1378, and 13s. 0d. in 1379, including an exceptionally high brewing fine of 10s. 0d. Here is direct evidence for the view that not just rising expectations, but actual achievements, were being exploited by a vigorous seigneurial administration, and that the victims were numbered among the 1381 rebels.

Rebels with a background of service in administrative positions, such as Godfrey Panyman of Mistley (Essex) and Thomas Gardiner of Little Barton (Suffolk), are known to have refused office, in the former case as a bailiff, the latter as a juror, before 1381.[79] It is tempting to see the involvement of so many local officials in the revolt as a development of such actions, leading to a widespread rejection of their ambiguous position, and an unequivocal siding with their neighbours against the constant demands of lords.

General Implications

To interpret the revolt solely in terms of lord–tenant relationships is to take far too narrow a view of the events of 1381. The horizons of the rebels extended beyond their own village and manor, of necessity, because of the intrusion of the state into the lives of every rural community. The operation of royal justice had become particularly evident to the people of Essex, Suffolk and Norfolk in 1379 when the court of King's Bench made one of its infrequent journeys out of Westminster and held sessions under Sir John Cavendish at Chelmsford, Bury St Edmunds and Thetford.[80] The business of the royal courts had expanded in the mid-fourteenth century with the attempts to enforce the labour laws. Labour cases still occupied the attention of the Essex JPs in 1377–9, and cases are also recorded on the King's Bench plea rolls of 1379–81; in 1380 a long list of Suffolk outlaws includes a number of servants. Two servants of the future rebel, Thomas Sampson of Kersey, were fined in 1380 by King's Bench for taking excessive

---

[79] PRO, SC 2/171/59, 60: the identification of Panyman is not entirely certain. The 1381 rebel was called Geoffrey, while the man who refused to act as bailiff is called Godfrey in the court rolls. If they were two individuals, they are likely to have been close relatives and the line of argument about attitudes to office-holding may still be relevant. For Gardiner's refusal see SROB, E 7/24/1.3.

[80] *Proceedings before the Justices of the Peace in the Fourteenth and Fifteenth Centuries*, ed. B.H. Putnam (London, 1938), p. 32.

wages. Sampson acted as pledge for them, suggesting that he did not regard himself as the injured party in the case, and indeed he may have resented this interference in the competitive labour market. A cursory examination of the King's Bench records of 1379–81 reveals the names of eight other future rebels who were involved in trespasses or land disputes.[81] Their experiences with the law may well have had some influence on their behaviour in 1381. A radical dissatisfaction with royal justice in Essex in 1378 is apparent from the refusal of the constables of Dunmow Hundred to make any attempt to enforce the labour laws, an incident that was still concerning the authorities three years later.[82] Some of the victims of the rebels also had dealings with King's Bench on the eve of the revolt, such as John Sewall and John Ewell, respectively sheriff and escheator in Essex, and no doubt the progress through the courts of cases involving influential figures was accompanied by rumours of partiality and corruption.

The king's wars also affected the lives of many people. Villagers might be involved in military activity, like the men from the hundred of Wye (Kent) who served in Calais and guarded the Kent coast in the early 1370s.[83] Taxes to pay for the war touched everyone, including the numerous smallholders and wage-earners after the introduction of poll taxes in 1377. A reluctance to pay the conventional lay subsidies as well as the new tax is suggested by the scatter of legal disputes between collectors and non-payers found in the records of manorial courts, peace sessions and King's Bench in 1379–81. In the 1380–1 poll tax that sparked off the revolt the lists show that future rebels contributed, no doubt with reluctance, but some rebels' names cannot be found in their village lists. Is it possible that they had evaded payment, almost as a first stage of rebellion? A specific example would be John Fillol, a miller of Hanningfield (Essex), who appears in a list compiled by the tax collectors in 1381 alone, without any reference to a wife. He had evidently concealed her, as after he was hanged for his part in the revolt, she recovered tenure of his holding.[84] The most important aspect of the poll tax was, however, not its effect on individuals but its universality, shifting financial burdens everywhere on to the less well off, and taking away from every village élite their almost fifty-year-old right to assess and collect taxes, all in the cause of paying for a futile war.

While it is possible to demonstrate that individual rebels had suffered at the hands of both their lords and officials of the state, these specific frictions

---

[81] PRO, KB 27/475, 479, 480, 481.

[82] *Essex Sessions of the Peace*, ed. Furber, p. 169; PRO, KB 27/481.

[83] PRO, SC 2/182/21; references to service in coastal defence are rare, and the main French threat affected the whole Channel coast from Kent to Cornwall, not primarily the south-eastern counties which rebelled, so it seems unlikely that invasion fears were a major cause of the revolt, as argued in E. Searle and R. Burghard, 'The defense of England and the Peasant's Revolt', *Viator*, 3 (1972), pp. 365–89.

[84] PRO, E 179/107/63; ERO, D/DP M833.

are inadequate to explain the whole rising. If, for example, the local tyranny of Thomas Hardyng of Manningtree and Mistley (Essex) provoked a rebellion in those places, why was it not directed solely against the offending lord?[85] The striking feature of the revolt is that it did not consist only of a mass of private vendettas; the rebels were willing to generalise their actions and demands. The rebels' behaviour was not always directly related to their personal grievances. To choose one example, Robert Wryghte of Foxearth, who had been so badly treated in his lord's court, went off in 1381 to plunder the property of the chief justice of King's Bench, Sir John Cavendish. One thinks also of the men of Kent, where there were no serfs, being provoked into revolt according to one account by the imprisonment of a serf from outside the county, or reviving the revolt in September 1381 on hearing a rumour that John of Gaunt had freed his serfs.[86] We may suspect that the rebels recognised the close connection between lordship and government, so that 'political' and 'social' grievances were linked in their minds. The seigneurial view of frankpledge enforced laws in the name of the king, including the labour laws; the royal courts were involved with social matters, villeinage cases or the enforcement of contracts between employers and employees; the same men acted as royal justices and estate stewards, and held manors of their own. Dr Maddicott has explored the long history of collusion between royal judges and landowners, represented at the time of the revolt by John Cavendish's association with the monks of Bury.[87] We can only guess at the suspicions caused by such arrangements as John Bampton doubling as an Essex JP, and estate steward of Barking Abbey.[88] Thomas atte Ook of Suffolk, like Cavendish and Bampton, was killed by the rebels in 1381, and his property was plundered. He combined employment as steward of the bishopric of Ely with service as Justice of the Peace and on many commissions in Essex, Norfolk and Suffolk. In his role of steward atte Ook had to deal with the difficult tenants of Brandon, who on one occasion in 1370 refused to appear before him in spite of a formal summons. As a royal official, he served on commissions with such figures as Cavendish, Bampton and Belknap, including one with Cavendish and others in 1378 to deal with a conspiracy of tenants to withdraw services and customs at Framsden (Suffolk).[89] Such

[85] A.J. Prescott, 'London in the Peasants' Revolt: a portrait gallery', *The London Journal*, 2 (1981), p. 127.

[86] *The Anonimalle Chronicle, 1333–1381*, ed. V.H. Galbraith (Manchester, 1927), p. 136; Flaherty, 'Sequel to the Great Rebellion in Kent', p. 76.

[87] J.R. Maddicott, *Law and Lordship: Royal Justices as Retainers in Thirteenth- and Fourteenth- Century England* (Past and Present Supplement no. 4, Oxford, 1978), pp. 63–4.

[88] Sturman, 'Barking Abbey: a study of its external and internal administration from the Conquest to the Dissolution', pp. 40, 212.

[89] SROB, J 529/1–2; PRO, SC 6/1304/31–6; *Cal. Pat. Rolls, 1370–4*, pp. 36, 239, 489, 491; *1374–7*, pp. 137, 276, 332, 486–7; *1377–81*, pp. 299, 305, 474.

men represented the power of government in its many guises, and it is understandable that the rebels should have seen their superiors as involved in a single system of corrupt authority.

It is not possible to attribute any single aim to a very heterogeneous group of rebels. We need to seek no profound motive behind acts of simple pillage. A complicating factor must have been the existence of feuds and conflicts within peasant society that helped to condition attitudes and alliances before and during the revolt. The chief pledges and other officials must have been involved in such rivalries, hence some of the dissatisfaction and violence expressed against them. An example would be William Draper and his son Thomas, both of South Elmham (Suffolk). William served regularly as chief pledge in the 1370s and 1380s, and was clearly quite prosperous. In 1372 the Drapers were involved in a bitter conflict with members of the Erl family, involving both personal violence and litigation over trespass in the manor court.[90] Such quarrels were frequent and other examples could be given involving individual rebels. While in no sense a cause of revolt, the decision to participate may well have been coloured by alliances and enmities created by feuds, so that the involvement of the Drapers ensured that the Erls stayed at home, ready to inform the authorities after the events had ended. Many inexplicable episodes in the revolt, especially apparently motiveless assaults and attacks, must owe their origins to long-remembered grievances and jealousies. Such factors might also solve such puzzles as the appearance of a King's Langley (Hertfordshire) man, John Marler, as both a participant in the revolt and the victim of a rebel from Berkhamstead![91]

However, while accepting the existence of many complexities of motive, to discuss 1381 primarily in terms of rivalries within villages would reduce the rising to the absurd. The demands made in London seem to indicate an ability to think in general terms, and there is some evidence to support the view that the leaders in the capital were voicing radical opinions widespread among the rebels. The rebels came from the manors of all kinds of landlord, not just from the estates where the regime was particularly harsh, like those of the countess of Norfolk or the bishopric of Norwich. For example, the revolt found support at Havering atte Bower (Essex), where the tenants enjoyed the extensive privileges of a royal demesne manor.[92] And then there is the problem of Kent. At first glance the freedom of Kentish peasants and the feebleness of seigneurial authority in the county, where the manorial courts lacked many powers normally found in their counterparts north of the Thames, might be thought to have prevented the

---

[90] SROI, HA 12/C2/14, 15, 18.
[91] PRO, SC 2/177/47; Réville and Petit-Dutaillis, *Le soulèvement des travailleurs*, p. 39.
[92] McIntosh, 'Land tenure and population in the royal manor of Havering, Essex', pp. 17–18.

tenants of Kent developing any strong sense of grievance against their lords. Yet frictions and insubordination are recorded in Kentish court rolls before 1381, and in the revolt itself manorial documents were destroyed, and services refused. Throughout the four counties it is therefore difficult to discern evidence of much discrimination in the rebels' attitudes towards landlords, which contrasts with their highly selective choice of 'political' targets. This could be taken to mean that many rebels were hostile to lordship in general, a view that found its ultimate expression in the well-known Smithfield demand for the division of lordship among all men.

The burning of court rolls, again involving no apparent selection of particular lords or types of lords, should not be underestimated as an act of radical rebellion. A view of the aims of the rebels of Wivenhoe (Essex) was given by the clerk who wrote the record of 'the first court . . . after the burning of all the court rolls'. He stated that the tenants claimed to hold land 'at their own will for ever, freely, and not at the will of the lord'. In short they wished to abolish all customary tenures, depriving the lord of a good deal of his power and wealth, 'in disinheritance of the lord' as the clerk put it.[93]

The Smithfield demands envisaged the removal of the machinery of government, so that the only law was to be the 'law of Winchester'. When we find that so many of the rebels had experience of government at village level, this aim does not seem as naive as is often assumed. The chief pledges of Holwell (Hertfordshire) were fully aware of the law mentioned at Smithfield when in 1377 they complained that the village constable did not summon the watch 'according to the statute of Winchester'.[94] They could imagine (as we know happened in the Flemish revolt of the 1320s) that local government of a kind could function without direction from above, with order enforced by the local militia provided for in the statute.

Finally we must allow for the millenarian enthusiasm that gave the revolt a strong impetus. The controversy over the collection of the poll tax helped to create the volatile atmosphere of the summer of 1381. Other events may have contributed to the sense of excitement, incidents which may seem trivial to us, such as the great storm of May 1381 – we know that the gale of January 1362 had a major impact on contemporaries, who saw in such happenings warnings of imminent catastrophe.[95]

---

[93] ERO, T/B 122; W.C. Waller, 'A note on the manor of Wivenhoe', *Trans. Essex Archaeological Society*, new ser., 10 (1909), pp. 320–2.

[94] GL, 10, 312/163.

[95] Newton, *Thaxted in the Fourteenth Century*, pp. 97, 99, on the 1381 storm. For reactions to the 1362 gale, see M.W. Bloomfield, *Piers Plowman as a Fourteenth-Century Apocalypse* (New Brunswick, 1962), p. 114.

Conclusion

Rural unrest in the late fourteenth century can be readily explained in terms of the tension between entrenched lordly power and the changes, or potential changes, in peasant society. These tensions were felt acutely in the south-east because of the importance of the market economy in the region. Dissatisfaction with the government, especially with the administration of the law, was bound up with resentment against landlords. The outbreak of a major revolt came when the poll tax provided the whole region with a single common grievance. The specific form taken by the revolt, in terms of its organisation and demands, reflected its origins in rural society. The village élite, acting from a position of confidence and authority, gave the revolt leadership and coherence. Out of the diversity of motives found in any popular movement emerged ideas and actions hostile not just to serfdom and servile tenures, but also to the very existence of lordship, championing the realisable goal of independent and self-governing village communities.

11

The Rising of 1381 in Suffolk: Its Origins and Participants

The revolt of 1381 still baffles historians, to the point that an authority on the subject confesses that to him it seems 'historically unnecessary'.[1] It is true that the rising cannot be explained in simple economic terms, because the conditions of the mass of the population had reached a low point three generations before 1381, between 1294 and 1325, when a succession of poor harvests culminated in famine, and lords' demands for rents and the state's collection of taxes weighed most heavily.[2] The economy changed during the fourteenth century, as the plague epidemics that began in 1348–49, combined with other factors, ensured a drop in the numbers of people. This helped the survivors and their successors to improve their material welfare, for wage-earners in particular were able to demand increased wages, and after some difficult harvests up to 1375 food became relatively cheap. Peasants, that is small-scale rural cultivators, benefited from the more easy availability of land, and the relaxation of pressure on pastures enabled them to increase the numbers of their animals.[3] We cannot therefore explain the rebels' behaviour as a reaction against impoverishment, but instead we must interpret the rising in a context of growing prosperity, or at least of an economic climate in which people could expect to better themselves. In bringing together the different strands of social and political change that lay behind the 1381 rising there are many advantages in concentrating on a single well-documented county, and Suffolk is ideal for this purpose.

As is well known, Suffolk in the Middle Ages was a county in which lay both good arable land and extensive patches of woodland, grassland, heaths and wetlands.[4] The county was relatively densely settled, supporting about

[1]   R.B. Dobson, 'Remembering the Peasants' Revolt, 1381-1981', in W.H. Liddell and R.G.E. Wood (eds), *Essex and the Great Revolt of 1381* (Chelmsford, 1982), p.20.

[2]   E. Miller and M.J. Hatcher, *Medieval England: Rural Society and Economic Change 1086-1348* (London, 1978), pp.139-64; J.R. Maddicott, *The English Peasantry and the Demands of the Crown* (Past and Present Supplement, no. 1, 1975), passim.

[3]   A.R. Bridbury, 'The Black Death', *Econ. Hist. Rev.*, 2nd ser., 26 (1973), pp.577-92; J. Hatcher, *Plague, Population and the English Economy, 1348-1530* (London, 1977), pp.31-5; R.H. Hilton, *The Decline of Serfdom in Medieval England* (London, 1969), pp.32-5.

[4]   N. Scarfe, *The Suffolk Landscape* (London, 1972), pp.149-91.

120,000 people in 1377 – many more before the plagues – partly through agriculture, but also by means of fishing and the exploitation of such natural resources as peat, and above all through an intense commercial and industrial development.[5] By 1350 at least ninety markets had a formal existence in the county. The settlements associated with these markets often showed the urban characteristics of a high concentration of population and a wide diversity of occupations, and by 1327 it is possible to identify more than forty places which possessed these features.[6] In 1327 many craftsmen in the cloth industry were working in the small towns and villages of Babergh and Cosford hundreds in the south-west of the county and cloth-making developed further during the century. The countryside was divided into vills which often coincided with parishes. However, most people did not live in nucleated villages but in straggling groups of houses and hamlets. From these dispersed settlements the inhabitants worked irregular subdivided fields or land held in 'severalty' (enclosures). Manors rarely coincided with villages: the total domination of a village by a single lord is most commonly found on the estates of large ancient churches, such as the monastery of Bury St Edmunds in the west of the county, and the priory of Ely in the east. But three-quarters of the manors in Suffolk were held by laymen, and then mainly by the gentry, and such lords tended to hold no more than a fraction of a village.[7] Although the church estates have left us more documents than those of lay lords, therefore tending to provide a slanted picture of society, lay manors are by no means lacking in evidence, and of the thirty-two manors whose records have been used in this study, nine belonged to members of the gentry.

Historians rightly think of Suffolk as a county of free tenants. They were plentiful at the time of Domesday, and continued to be numerous in the later Middle Ages. However, alongside the freemen, on lay manors as well as those of churches, customary tenants and serfs formed an important part of the population.

[5]   E. Powell, *The Rising in East Anglia in 1381* (Cambridge, 1896), p.123.

[6]   M. Duddridge, 'Towns in Suffolk and the urban crisis of the later Middle Ages' (unpublished B.A. dissertation, Univ. of Birmingham, 1983), pp.13-39, based on S.H.A. Hervey (ed.), *Suffolk in 1327, being a Subsidy Return* (Suffolk Green Books, 9, 1906).

[7]   D.C. Douglas, *The Social Structure of Medieval East Anglia* (Oxford, 1927) on the general character of tenures in the county. The calculation of manorial lordship is based on W.A. Copinger, *The Manors of Suffolk*, 7 vols (London, 1905-11).

Table 11.1: Analysis of tenants recognising new lords in Suffolk.[8]

Manor (date)	Free tenants	Tenants of servile holdings	Serfs by blood	Total
Bredfield (1361)	23 (42%)	19 (34%)	13 (24%)	55 (100%)
Iken (1363)	10 (29%)	12 (34%)	13 (37%)	35 (100%)
Earl Soham (1382)	2 (3%)	44 (70%)	17 (27%)	63 (100%)

Table 1 analyses three later fourteenth century lists of tenants who recognised, or who should have recognised their new (lay) landlords in eastern Suffolk. The lists distinguish between free tenants, tenants who were personally free but who held land on customary or servile tenures, and those who were 'serfs by blood' (*nativi de sanguine*). The proportions of the different categories vary, but the formidable numbers of the latter two speak for themselves: assuming that these manors were not untypical, there must have been many thousands of servile tenants and serfs in late fourteenth century Suffolk. From the landlord's point of view these tenurial and legal distinctions were all important, because of the heavier dues and rents (mostly in cash) that he could extract from the customary tenants and serfs. A distinctive feature of the Suffolk peasantry was their widespread practice of partible inheritance, and their involvement in a very active land market. Holdings varied greatly in size, with a majority, taking examples recorded between 1370 and 1383, having five acres or less. They must have relied on wage work or craft work to supplement the production of their land, as is shown by the 80 per cent of tax-payers in the incomplete 1380–81 poll tax who were identified as labourers or servants, or as having some non-agricultural occupation. At the other end of the social hierarchy were the very small number of substantial tenants. Only about one-eighth of the tenants held more than 20 acres of land, and an exceptional one in every thirty holdings exceeded 30 acres.[9]

The complexity of Suffolk's society seems to be reflected in the variety of incidents in the county in June, 1381.[10] Our main source, the indictments drawn up by juries after the revolt, leaves an impression of a fragmented series of episodes. Bands of rebels under a number of leaders moved around the county sometimes attacking the property of nationally recognised 'traitors' like Sir John Cavendish, chief justice of King's Bench, but also

[8] Suffolk Record Office, Ipswich Branch (henceforth SROI), HA 91/1; HD 32:293/390; V 5/18/1.3.

[9] R.M. Smith, 'English peasant life-cycles and socio-economic networks: a quantitative geographical case study' (unpublished Ph. D. thesis, Univ. of Cambridge); R.H. Hilton, *Bond Men Made Free. Medieval Peasant Movements and the English Rising of 1381* (London, 1973), p.171. The figures for holding size have been calculated from the records of 32 manors in the county.

[10] Powell, *Rising in East Anglia*, pp. 9-25, 126-31; A. Réville, *Le soulèvement des travailleurs d'Angleterre en 1381*, ed. C. Petit-Dutaillis (Paris, 1898), pp. 53-83, 121-8.

indulging in acts of extortion that the juries represented as simple criminal acts. Further consideration suggests, however, that these activities had a coherent pattern. The rebels concentrated in important places in the government of the county, not just the two largest towns of Bury and Ipswich, but also the administrative centre of Ely's liberty of St Etheldreda at Melton. The rebels often chose as their victims leading figures in local government, such as escheators, justices of the peace and a knight of the shire. There seem to be many similarities between the events of 1381 and those of Kett's Rebellion in 1549. At the latter date it has been argued convincingly that the rebels intended to create an alternative county government, and a number of actions by the 1381 rebels support the view at least that they saw themselves as taking charge of their localities.[11] How else are we to interpret the attempt to force the constable of Hoxne hundred to levy ten archers from the hundred for the rebel forces, at a wage of 6d. per day each? Or the accusation that the rebel band based on Brandon were 'assuming to themselves the royal power'? It would be a grave error to allege that the rebels were behaving lawlessly; rather they were establishing a new law. This form of rebellion, combined with the presence of some gentry and clergy among the leaders, might suggest that the revolt had a political rather than a social character. That the rebels had social grievances is indicated by the killing of Cavendish, who had personally enforced the Statute of Labourers in the county and was suspected of corruption in collusion with the monks of Bury. Two leading Bury monks, the prior and John Lakenheath, also lost their lives mainly because of the Abbey's old quarrel with the townsmen of Bury. The rebels revealed something of their aims by the burning of manorial court rolls, which happened in at least thirteen places in the county, and in dozens of other incidents throughout the south-east of England. This selective destruction was designed to remove the written records of customary tenure and servility, and to establish a new social order.

We can probe more deeply into the nature of the 1381 revolt and its causes by using the names of people indicted or pardoned after the rebellion, to investigate their lives and background. Fourteen biographies are included in the Appendix; the subjects were selected from the 150 or so known rebels simply because they appear in the manorial records which provide the main source of detailed local information. The sample is therefore a biased one. The indictments and pardons tend to contain the names of those accused of leading the rebellion. The manorial records tend to give more information about the upper ranks of peasant society. So rank-and-file rebels, and the village poor, cannot be so readily investigated. In spite of these drawbacks, this small sample is still a precious source of

---

[11] D.N.J. MacCulloch, 'Kett's rebellion in context', *Past and Present*, 84 (1979), pp.36-59.

evidence. Given the patchy survival of documents, the recovery of so much information about relatively humble fourteenth-century individuals is remarkable.

As the biographical details of the rebels are printed below no more than brief comments on their salient features are needed here. Most of the leading rebels came from the peasant élite. The amount of land that they held, the number of animals that they owned, and offices that they filled in the manorial administration, as bailiffs, chief pledges, jurors and affeerers, all point to this conclusion. In order to run their manors, landlords needed the services of men of substance who commanded respect among the tenants. In 1381 the same people continued to act as leaders, now in opposition to authority rather than as collaborators. There were also among the rebels, perhaps even in a majority, poorer people whose names are not commonly recorded, though they are represented among our fourteen by two landless youths, Thomas Draper and William Metefeld junior, and by the Lakenheath alewife, Margaret Wrighte. One of our fourteen stands out clearly above the others, Thomas Sampson. His lands, stock and wealth were much greater than those of Brightwold, Gardiner and the other rebels; whereas they were officials of manors, he held office at county level, as a tax-collector. He must be counted as a member of the lesser gentry. In examining the rebels as in our earlier survey of the rebellion itself, the similarity between the 1381 rebellion and that of 1549 is again apparent. Here indeed were 'substantial men with plenty of experience of petty administration'.[12] In judging the aims and motives of the rebels we should not, however, allow the presence of Sampson and a few other gentry to colour too strongly our assessment of the revolt. While we might speculate that Sampson and others of his class rebelled because of some antagonism towards the ruling group in the county, or because they imagined that the rebellion would lead to political changes, the great majority of the rebels were peasants, artisans and petty traders whose involvement must be explained in terms of their experiences at a much humbler social level.

The apparent suddenness of the 1381 revolt has created some of its mystery. A rising that breaks out without warning may indeed to a modern observer look 'unnecessary'. However, there is sufficient evidence of disturbances and agitations in Suffolk earlier in the fourteenth century to suggest that the 1381 rebels were acting within a tradition of opposition to authority.

A well-documented case is that of the long struggle between the powerful abbey of Bury St Edmunds and the people of Mildenhall. This large fen-edge manor brought the cellarer of Bury an enormous annual income, well

---

[12] Ibid., p. 45.

over £200 in one year in the 1320s.[13] In October 1320 Roger son of William Hervy of Mildenhall brought an action under the writ *Monstravit* against the abbot, alleging that as Roger was a tenant in ancient demesne, the abbot was not entitled to services beyond certain labour services. The disputed customs and services included the recognition fine (demanded by each new abbot), *merchet* (marriage fine) and entry fines at will, typical of the uncertain and variable dues demanded of servile tenants. The case was tried in 1321. Domesday Book was consulted and this showed that Mildenhall had indeed belonged to Edward the Confessor, conclusive proof of the manor's ancient demesne status. This in theory meant that Roger and his fellow villeins were exempted from the impositions of the abbot and could claim a special privileged status of 'villein sokemen'. However the abbot's lawyers argued that Roger was a villein, that he and his ancestors had owed tallage, service as reeve, *merchet* and entry fines, so that he had no right to bring a suit against his lord. Although two accounts of the case survive, neither tells us the outcome, but the fact that details were copied twice into Bury registers implies that victory, as was usual in such cases, lay with the landlord. The heading of the account in the *Pinchbeck Register* refers to the parties in the dispute as the 'villeins of Mildenhall', suggesting that Roger Hervy was acting as the representative of a group of tenants, the twenty-three holders of 15 acres each (of which Hervy was one) and the fourteen tenants with 30 acres who were all performing very heavy labour services in the early 1320s.[14]

A Mildenhall manorial account of 1323–4 hints at continuing troubles. A dispute with a tenant, William Everard, had led to the seizure of his cow. More seriously, legal expenses had been incurred in 'a plea between the lord and the homage of Mildenhall', indicating a collective dispute spreading more widely than the earlier villeinage case. Fines on customary tenants going back to 1320 (perhaps the original cause of the Hervy law-suit) were still partly owed in 1323. The presence of disgruntled tenants at Mildenhall in 1327 presumably explains the burning of an abbey barn there at the time when the townsmen of Bury rose against the monks.[15]

Troubles flared up again in 1341. Four Mildenhall tenants, Thomas Olyve (who held a sub-manor of considerable size), John Gernon, Simon Chapman and William Everard (all with more modest holdings) complained that their sheep folds had been broken down by the abbot, a monk and a

[13]   Bodleian Library, Suffolk Rolls, no. 21.

[14]   F. Hervey (ed.), *The Pinchbeck Register* (Brighton, 1925), pp.321-4; Cambridge University Library (henceforth CUL), Add. MS 4220, fos 121r-v; *Year Books* (1672), p.455; Bodleian Library, Suffolk Rolls, no. 21. Cf. similar cases in R.H. Hilton, 'Peasant movements in England before 1381', *Econ. Hist. Rev.*, 2nd ser., 2 (1949), pp.117-36.

[15]   Bodleian Library, Suffolk rolls, no. 21; T. Arnold (ed.), *Memorials of St Edmund's Abbey* (Rolls Series, 1892), pp.349, 352.

lay official. The abbot replied that the folds were illicit, and that these tenants would be allowed to have them only when the abbot wished. Also in 1341 a commission of *oyer* and *terminer* was sent by the crown in response to the abbot's complaint that a session of the court leet held on 25 June had been disrupted. Forty-eight people (all named) were said to have prevented the abbot's servants from executing the judgement of the abbot's court, namely that brewers who had broken the assize of ale should undergo the ritual humiliation of being placed in the tumbrel. The crowd rescued the brewers (probably all women), assaulted the lord's bailiff, and stole his goods.[16] There are elements of continuity between this riot and the earlier conflicts. Three members of the Hervy family, and all four tenants whose folds had been demolished were among the named forty-eight. Discontent with the abbey's exercise of leet jurisdiction, which lay behind the 1341 disturbances, also gave rise to a petition from the tenants of Mildenhall, undated but probably belonging to this period.[17] The petition appears to have come from the chief pledges who were also free tenants, as they asked that no villein or customary tenant should be a chief pledge, and that no customary tenant should act as affeerer with a free man. They sought to protect the privileges of the chief pledges, excluding the bailiff from their deliberations, and demanding that the steward 'ought not and could not take any inquest on the day of the leet ... unless by the chief pledges'. Another concern was the encroachments on the roads, including some made by the lord's officials. The petition bears some resemblance to a near contemporary one from Bocking in Essex, also directed by free tenants at another monastic landlord.[18]

Thus Mildenhall's tenants in the early fourteenth century seem to have been questioning the power of their lord, seeking the protection of the royal courts over villeinage, and quarrelling with the lord's monopoly over sheepfolds and his full use of his powers of jurisdiction. There were evidently differences of attitude between the leading free tenants (who merely asked for reforms of short-term and small-scale problems and who seem to have felt no common interest with the villeins), and men like Hervy. His ancient demesne case may have been a defensive response to increasing lordly demands, but it would be surprising if the dues mentioned really were novelties in the 1320s, and we may suspect that this law suit shows that the customary tenants had radical ideas about their ancient liberties and were prepared to dispute long-standing seigneurial demands like recognitions and marriage fines. Needless to say, the people of Mildenhall

---

[16] CUL, Add. MS 4220, fos 133v.-136v.; *Calendar of Patent Rolls 1340-3*, pp. 316-17.
[17] CUL, Add. MS 4220, fo. 145v.
[18] J.F. Nichols, 'An early fourteenth-century petition from the tenants of Bocking to their manorial lord', *Econ. Hist. Rev.*, 2 (1929-30), pp. 300-7.

were active again in 1381, principally in helping to track down and kill the prior of Bury when he sought refuge in the area.[19]

If some Suffolk peasants were already objecting to the claims of their landlords in the 1320s and 1340s, they had ample reason to resent them after the mid-century epidemics. The economic trends of the post-plague era are clear. The labour shortage pushed up wages, and the reduced numbers of tenants and potential tenants increased their ability to bargain for better conditions with their lords. Landlords did make changes at this time. Some leased their demesnes, handing over the management of agricultural production to farmers in return for fixed cash rents. Leasehold tenures, which had begun to replace customary tenures on some manors before 1349, continued to spread, again providing lords with fixed rents in money, often at the substantial rate of one shilling per acre. Yet the institutions that governed social relationships remained obstinately unchanged by the new circumstances, because the interest of landlords lay in maintaining their control over tenants and serfs.

A series of small-scale incidents illustrates the constant frictions between lords and peasants. The most elementary duties of tenants were to pay rents and perform labour services; they failed to carry out these obligations collectively and persistently, suggesting some protest against the level or the form of rent or services. So at least twenty-four Felixstowe tenants failed to do their winter works in 1363, seventeen tenants of Chevington did not attend a harvest 'bedrip' in 1375, and seventy-three boon-works in one harvest season at Hundon were not performed by forty-nine tenants. In 1377 four tenants of Great Barton were found to have been in arrears with rents and services for periods as long as six and ten years.[20]

Customary tenancies, which provided many landlords with the bulk of their rent income, were necessarily governed by many rules and restrictions. All transfers of customary land were supposed to pass through the lord's courts; if serfs bought or inherited free land they were expected to surrender it to the lord or receive it back on customary tenure; the upkeep of a holding, and especially its buildings and standing timber, were supervised by the lord. Tenants behaved as if they had freeholds, buying and selling land as they pleased. With the decreased demand for land, it was often in a tenant's interest to amalgamate holdings and to demolish the redundant buildings. Lords were worried that they would lose track of tenancies and so not be able to collect rents, and that holdings without buildings would diminish in value.

[19] Powell, *Rising in East Anglia*, p.139; H.T. Riley (ed.), *T. Walsingham, Historia Anglicana* (Rolls Series, 1863-4), ii, p.2; W.M. Palmer and H.W. Saunders, *Documents Relating to Cambridgeshire Villages* (Cambridge, 1926), p.31.

[20] SROI, HA 119: 50/3/80; Suffolk Record Office, Bury St Edmunds Branch (henceforth SROB), E 3/15.3/1,18; PRO, SC 2 203/89; SROB E 18/151/1.

Two examples will indicate the flagrant nature of some tenants' behaviour. Walter Baker of Chevington was reported in 1371 to have cut down trees worth 10s. 0d. growing on his holding, and to have carried them off and sold them without the necessary permission. Instead of repairing a ruinous barn as ordered, he dismantled the timber and doors to build a new house on a free tenement that he also held. At Earl Soham a serf, John Hamond, had in 1377 obtained illicitly a servile holding of $12\frac{1}{2}$ acres, the buildings of which needed repair. When the court dealt with him two years later, he was asked if he would receive the holding in the normal way and agree to repair the buildings: 'he said, expressly, "no"'. He had other lands, notably a free tenement of 7 acres which he had bought illegally in 1369, and for which he used the device of enfeoffment to trustees, normally the preserve of free tenants, so that he could enjoy the profits of the land for ten years without technically holding it himself.[21] These cases indicate both the assertive spirit of tenants, and the ability of lords, albeit slowly and inefficiently, to discover indiscipline.

Serfs appear prominently in Suffolk records because they broke the rules that were intended to control them: they left the manor; they married without permission and evaded marriage fines (*merchet*); and they acquired free land illicitly. A radical response by serfs to their disadvantages was not to evade them but to assert their free status. A jury at Iken in 1364 had to deal with Richard de More's claim to be free, which revealed a history of a family's long struggle against servility. The lord of Gosbeck, probably either Richard or Ralph de Gosbeck,[22] had claimed Richard's grandfather, Alexander de More, as his serf, and he had fled the 16 miles to Iken, married there, and settled down. When the lord of Gosbeck learnt of this he went to Iken, but Alexander heard in time and escaped, so the raiding party had to be content with taking forty sheep that belonged to another serf, presumably in order to bring pressure on the lord of Iken, William de Sturmy. The two lords eventually reached a settlement whereby Sturmy received Alexander as his serf. As Richard was descended from Alexander, the 1364 jury had no choice but to declare that he was unfree. A marginal note in the court roll shows that the More family were still claiming to be free in the reign of Henry IV.[23] Lords were anxious to keep their serfs, and imposed heavy penalties on ill-disciplined serfs or their allies. In 1371 at Bredfield two servile tenants allowed a young relative, a ward, to leave the manor; they were threatened with an enormous amercement of 40s. 0d.[24]

[21] SROB, E 3/15.3/1.15; SROI V 5/18/1.3.
[22] Copinger, *Manors of Suffolk*, ii, p.302.
[23] SROI, HD 32: 293/390.
[24] SROI, HA 91/1.

The records of manorial courts contain, as well as occasional major disputes of the Baker, Hamond and de More type, a constant succession of petty breaches of manorial discipline, such as the theft of the lord's corn at harvest time, or large-scale and persistent trespasses by tenants' animals in the lord's crops. Game and fish were poached, officials assaulted, and goods taken in distraint 'rescued'. The two-way nature of the conflicts must be emphasised. Peasants sought every possible loophole, while lords used all of their powers to protect their interests. The factor which gave an ancient struggle a new intensity was the growing self-confidence of the peasants, who were actually improving their material conditions at this time, for example by increasing the size of their flocks and herds.

The long campaigns of attrition waged by lords and peasants imposed strains on the administrative machinery. The officials of the manor and its courts were recruited from among the peasants. This gave the lord the advantage of unpaid administration by local people; undoubtedly they blunted the sharp edge of their lord's authority, and this helped to contain conflict within the system. The officials were put into an ambiguous position in which they had to compromise between their duty to the lord and their loyalty to their neighbours. The period of post-plague tension must have imposed uncomfortable strains on the officials, in which the lord punished them (see Appendix, v) and neighbours withdrew their co-operation, like Thomas Wynke of Framlingham who 'would not inform the chief pledges of various trespasses and articles touching the leet'.[25] It is not surprising that election to office was sometimes refused, notably by a future 1381 rebel, Thomas Gardiner (see Appendix, v). At Brandon in 1370 the whole body of officials boycotted a court session at a time of unusual agitation in which the lord's property had been stolen and the reeve seriously assaulted; 'the whole homage', when summoned by the steward 'to be here... for various articles touching the lord', were amerced 20s. 0d. for their failure to attend.[26]

Another essential ingredient in the troubles leading up to the 1381 rising was the antagonism aroused by the royal government. In the post-plague period landlords turned to the state for support, and the Statute of Labourers was designed to prevent increases in wages and to force workers to accept employment at the legal rates. Occasionally lords enforced the law in their own courts, for example at Redlingfield in 1378 John le Mowere, a 'common labourer', refused to work for the lady of the manor when ordered by the constable of the vill and the bailiff. He was 'attached by his body' to serve under a penalty of 20s. 0d.[27] The main task of enforcement fell on the royal courts, especially those of the justices of peace. The court

[25] Pembroke College, Cambridge, Framlingham court rolls, B.
[26] SROB, J 529/1.
[27] SROI, HA 12/C10/2.

of King's Bench itself held sessions in 1379 at Bury and Thetford, and dealt with many cases under the statute, including one involving Thomas Sampson (see Appendix, xi). We can be sure that the labour laws were much resented, not because they held earnings down, but because of the unfairness of the almost random selection of a small proportion of wage-earners for prosecution. It was probably hostility to the statute that led the constables of Lakenheath in 1379, John Carter and John Mayheu, to refuse 'to answer for certain articles' to King's Bench.[28]

The central government also provoked hostility with its demands for taxation. The experiment with a parish tax in 1371 was an example of administrative bungling that hit Suffolk hard because its assessment was doubled when the yield of the tax was found to be much lower than expected.[29] A riot broke out at Lakenheath, a large fen-edge manor not unlike Mildenhall in its social structure, when before January 1371 John, Earl of Pembroke, the steward-in-fee of the Abbey of Bury, sent three officials to collect cash on behalf of the king in the Liberty of St Edmunds. Money from Lakenheath had not been paid, so they took chattels in distraint. Twenty-six named people, 'and others', responded by assaulting the officials, breaking one's wand of office, taking back the chattels, and keeping the unpopular visitors out of the village with threats and force. The Crown sent four commissioners to deal with this rising, among them John Cavendish, later to become chief justice of the King's Bench.[30] Nine of the rioters appear on Lakenheath lists of chief pledges and jurors for 1361 and 1376 (no court rolls survive at the exact time of the disturbance), so it appears that, as in 1381, the village élite adopted a leading role, among them the two constables who in 1379 refused to co-operate with the King's Bench.[31] In 1381 Cavendish was to have another last contact with Lakenheath, when he arrived there as a fugitive from the rebels. The villagers assisted in his capture, notably when Katherine Gamen pushed a boat out of reach to prevent his escape. Their hostility to him was presumably not just because of his supposed corrupt alliance with Bury, or his general reputation, but because they had direct experience of his enforcement of the law.

The essential pre-requisite for the events of 1381 was provided by the combination of actions by landlords and by the royal government to create a universal sense of grievance among all sections of Suffolk's rural society including bailiffs, chief pledges and other members of the village élites, and even a few gentry and clergy. The interweaving of social and political

[28] PRO, KB 29/32; KB 27/475.

[29] E.B. Fryde, *The Great Revolt of 1381* (Historical Association pamphlet no. 100, 1981), pp.10-11.

[30] *Calendar of Patent Rolls 1370-4*, pp.100-1.

[31] CUL, EDC/7/15/II/2.

grievances can be observed in a petition of 1378 from the men of Bawdsey, a coastal village that had been given the task of contributing to the royal navy by building a *balinger*, along with Hadleigh, Ipswich and Sudbury. These were all market towns, the latter two being boroughs, and the men of Bawdsey resented their inclusion in such wealthy company. They objected that the combination of the four places was not customary; they emphasised that they were serfs by blood of the earl of Suffolk, and complained that they lacked the 'liberties and franchises whereby they might become rich'.[32] The views that they expressed – hostility to serfdom, resentment of the privileges of boroughs, and annoyance at royal fiscal pressures – were all to emerge in the demands and actions of the 1381 rebels, and it is not surprising to find that Bawdsey was involved in the rising.[33]

A final factor in explaining the outlook of the 1381 rebels must be their upbringing in a popular culture containing elements hostile towards established authority. A hint is provided by a clerk writing a court roll of the Bury manor of Chevington in 1380 who identified a brewer by a nickname, 'John called "Littlejohn" '.[34] A plausible explanation is that the Robin Hood stories were known in Suffolk within a few years of the first direct reference in the B text of Langland's *Piers Plowman*. Modern commentators disagree as to the social significance of the legends. Langland certainly thought that they were disreputable, but did they express lower-class antagonisms towards those in authority?[35] It is likely that their meaning varied, depending on the audience and the time and place at which they were told. In 1380 at Chevington, which was no doubt full of rumours about the collusion between the monks of Bury and Sir John Cavendish, the *Gest of Robyn Hode* with its story of the outlaws defeating an alliance between a grasping abbot and a corrupt judge would have had a very specific relevance![36]

Later in the Middle Ages the Robin Hood legend became associated with the popular festivities called 'summer games', in which social roles were reversed and 'lords' and 'ladies' were elected. It is usually thought that these rituals helped to release social tensions and to make real-life inequalities more acceptable. That such occasions could have the opposite effect is shown by an incident at Polstead in 1363, when John atte Forth was amerced 40d. (an unusually large sum) because he 'entered the lord's close and together with others played in the lord's hall a game called a

---

[32] *Calendar of Inquisitions Miscellaneous*, iv, p.38.

[33] Réville, *Soulèvement des travailleurs*, p.122.

[34] SROB, E 3/15.3/1/19.

[35] R.H. Hilton, 'The origins of Robin Hood', in idem (ed.), *Peasants, Knights and Heretics* (Cambridge, 1976), pp. 221-72; R.B. Dobson and J. Taylor (eds), *Rymes of Robyn Hood* (London, 1976), pp. 17-36; J.C. Holt, *Robin Hood* (London, 1982), pp. 109-58.

[36] J R Maddicott, *Law and Lordship: Royal Justices as Retainers in Thirteenth and Fourteenth-Century England* (Past and Present Supplement no. 4, 1978), pp. 63-4, 85.

somergamen'.[37] Perhaps the players overstepped the accepted limits; perhaps the lord had lost patience with the traditional customs. Either or both would have been characteristic tendencies in the harsh social climate of the late fourteenth century. Customs of the type recorded in Polstead are directly relevant to the 1381 revolt because the first outbreaks in Essex and Kent took place in Whit week, 1–8 June, the normal time for summer games. Court leet sessions were also held in that week.[38] The rebellion spread to Suffolk in the following week, one of the most active days being 13 June, which was also the feast of Corpus Christi when parish guilds often held their annual processions. Such guilds were especially common in Suffolk, and at least three of the eight parishes which produced rebels in our small sample had them.[39] Neither the summer games nor the processions of the parish guilds were in themselves rebellious, but they did express the sociability and solidarity of rural communities. They also caused large assemblies of people to gather in a holiday spirit, which we know from later disturbances could, in the right circumstances, become channelled into actions against authority.[40]

To sum up, then, the revolt of 1381 becomes more easily explicable if its many-stranded origins are accepted. First, the essential precondition lay in the tensions between lords and their subordinates, so well documented at Mildenhall, but evident at a petty level in any series of manorial court records. These tensions were more acute in Suffolk because of its heterogeneous society and dynamic economy whereby seigneurial restrictions seemed all the more irksome to self-confident and potentially independent peasants and artisans. The late fourteenth-century changes held out the promise of improvement, without seriously diminishing the powers of lords. At the same time the state played a more prominent role in the lives of ordinary people. There had always been a belief (however naïve) in the impartiality of the law, hence Roger Hervy's case against his lord; now the labour laws exposed the bias of the courts, and encouraged belief in the corruption of the justices. The new wave of taxation that began in 1371 and culminated in the poll tax seemed to prove the social bias and venal mismanagement of those in government. When the moment of uprising came, the local communities under their natural leaders could draw on traditions of organisation intended for more legitimate purposes, and a sub-culture that could be hostile to those wielding power.

---

[37] British Library, Add. Roll 27685; C. Phythian-Adams, *Local History and Folklore* (London, 1975), pp.23, 26-7; D. Wiles, *The Early Plays of Robin Hood* (Cambridge, 1981), pp.1-30.

[38] See above, Chapter 10, p. 195.

[39] H.F. Westlake, *The Parish Gilds of Medieval England* (London, 1919), pp.225, 229; SROB, J 529/2.

[40] B. Bushaway, *By Rite: Custom, Ceremony and the Community in England* (London, 1982), pp.190-202.

Appendix 11.1

Biographical details of some Suffolk rebels of 1381

Note: Various qualifications should be made about these biographies. The identification of rebels by name depends on the existence of juries making presentments, or the accused obtaining pardons. Jurors may have accused their enemies maliciously, or people may have taken advantage of pardons as an insurance against malicious accusations.

The reconstruction of the lives of relatively obscure medieval people is notoriously hazardous. In particular sons and fathers with the same names can be confused. Every effort has been made to avoid errors of identification, but the fragmentary nature of the records means that uncertainties will always remain.

The sources for the biographies are given in brackets at the end of each entry.

(i) Robert Brightwold of South Elmham

In 1356 Juliana Brightwold died and her holding of a garden and three roods of land was inherited by Robert Brightwold, Juliana's great nephew, on payment of a relief of $1\frac{1}{2}$ d. The lack of more direct heirs, and the presumed death of Robert's father and grandfather by the date of the inheritance may well have been due to the 1349 plague epidemic. Robert would have been quite young when he acquired this land, perhaps in his twenties. In 1364 and 1368 he came before the courts of his lord, the bishop of Norwich, in routine cases – for blocking a water-course, as the victim of an 'unjust' raising of the hue and cry; and in litigation with another tenant. From 1372 Robert served regularly in positions of responsibility in the administration of the manorial courts and courts leet of South Elmham, as juror and chief pledge. We may assume that he had acquired a substantial holding of land, for in 1380 he was employing a servant (the victim of an assault). Some degree of wealth was perhaps a necessary qualification to be one of the South Elmham chief pledges, since they were fined collectively 40s. each year, 'for concealment'.

He obtained a pardon in May 1382, but his participation does not seem to have affected his position in the administration of the courts of his lord, bishop Henry Despencer, who had played a major part in the suppression of the rising. In September and October of 1381 Brightwold served as juror, affeerer and chief pledge, and was still acting in the latter office in 1385 and 1388. (SROI, HA 12/C2/14-19; PRO, C 67/29.)

(ii) John Brown of South Elmham

John Broun makes his first appearance in the records of South Elmham in 1373, when he failed to attend a court, showing that he was already a tenant. He was then impleaded for trespass by John, the parson of the parish of St James. Also in 1373 he was the victim of a '*hamsoken*' (house breaking), and a 'rescue' (recovery of impounded or distrained goods). In 1380 he was involved with Margery Wodecock in pleas of debt and trespass, evidently arising out of some earlier dispute with her dead husband, William Wodecock. This litigation was still continuing in 1382. In the early 1380s a Margery Broun, perhaps John's wife, appears among those brewing ale for sale and on one occasion also selling bread. Like Robert Brightwold, he obtained a pardon in 1382, and seems to have continued to live in South Elmham for some years after the revolt; he is mentioned in the court rolls in 1386. (SROI, HA 12/C2/14-19; PRO, C 67/29.)

(iii) William Draper and Thomas Draper of South Elmham

William Draper, the son of another William Draper, is likely to have been born in the 1330s. In 1358 he was involved, together with his father, in a dispute over a holding called Erl's: they were accused of causing damage worth 40d. This may well have been the beginning of a dispute with the Erl family, though the earliest feuding is not known until the early 1370s. By 1372 William had a mature son, Thomas, and in that and the following year they were both involved in litigation over trespass with Henry Erl, and are mentioned in presentments of incidents of assault and '*hamsoken*' against other members of the Erl family. The fierceness of the conflict may be judged by the severity of the amercements taken in the court leet, 2s. from William and 1s. 3d. from Thomas in one session. The Drapers' position in the dispute may well have been aided by William becoming chief pledge in 1372, an office that he occupied regularly until 1388.

That William had resources is suggested by his appointment as chief pledge (see (i) above). In 1385 he was sharing with two other tenants a customary 30-acre holding called Wolsy's, and in 1386 he acquired a total of $25\frac{1}{2}$ acres of land in seven parcels at a total rent of 20s., which would place him among the wealthiest Elmham peasants.

William Draper's tendency to be quarrelsome continued in later life. In 1388 he was amerced 18d. for '*hamsoken*' on the parson of St James, and for assaulting the parson's servant seriously enough to draw blood. Some of his aggression was also directed against his lord. His lopping of the lord's wood in 1368 was a routine infringement of the rules; more unusual was the action of William's son Thomas in 1373 of 'making an unjust road' through the lord's new park. By 1385 William evidently owed a substantial amount of money to the lord, probably in unpaid rents, and the lord's officials took an ox and three cows from him in distraint, but William broke the pound and took the animals back. Both William and Thomas were pardoned after the 1381 revolt. (SROI, HA 12/C2/14-19; PRO, C 67/29.)

(iv) John Cole of Felixstowe

In 1363 a John Cole and a William Cole were among many customary tenants of Felixstowe amerced for failing to perform winter works for their lord the prior of Felixstowe. Other information on the Cole family before 1381 is lacking because of the destruction of the records of both Felixstowe and the parent manor of Walton by the rebels. John Cole junior was evidently a leading figure in this incident, since in May 1384 he was said to have come to an agreement to pay an amercement of 8s. 'in open court', 'for all forfeitures, damages, or trespasses...within the village of Walton in the time when the commons [*populares*] rose against the King and the magnates', which had involved burning 'the muniments of the said cell'. John Cole was a serf by blood [*nativus de sanguine*]. John Cole and his wife Joan are recorded in the 'first court after the burning of the books' in October 1381 as having acquired from another tenant a rood and a perch of servile land for a fine of 1s., and John Cole, son of William Cole, serf, some time before 1384 bought illicitly 30 perches of free land by charter, the seizure of which was ordered in line with the convention that serfs could not hold free land without permission.

John Cole did not accept the settlement of May 1384. In November 1385 he was amerced a total of 6s. 8d. for trespassing against another serf of the manor, John Smyth, and assaulting him on his own holding; Cole left the manor without licence and was described as a 'rebel'. He was ordered to be arrested 'by his body and by his chattels'. William Cole remained on the manor at this time. (SROI, HA 119: 50/3/17; HA 119: 50/3/80.)

(v) Thomas Gardiner of Little Barton

The many appearances of Thomas Gardiner in the court rolls of Little Barton between 1377 and 1385 show him pursuing normal agricultural activities and in so doing (along with many others) infringing some of the rules – ploughing so as to encroach on the common; allowing his animals (sheep and horses) to stray on the lord's pasture and crops; mowing rushes in the marsh in the season prohibited by a by-law; driving his cart over the lord's arable. The frequency with which he committed such offences, and particularly the revelation in 1380 that he had kept as many as 30 sheep out of the lord's fold, suggests that Gardiner was a peasant of above-average prosperity. He occupied a number of positions of responsibility, as juror in the 'general courts' and as chief pledge at the court leet. He also acted as a personal pledge.

His conventional round of activities as an official was interrupted in 1380. At a general court held in February of that year he refused to serve as a juror: 'he did not come when summoned twice, three times and four times to swear the oath with the other jurors'. In the following July he was back on duty, serving on the jury and as chief pledge, but there were hints of trouble at that court, with the affeerers failing to attend, and the jurors being fined 3s. 4d. for concealing the waste done to a customary holding by felling trees. Gardiner's involvement in the 1381 revolt, for which he obtained a pardon, is reflected in his absence from the jury at the court session held in September 1381, and in October he defaulted from suit of court and again failed to join the jury even after four summonses. He seems to have been absent from the jury in 1382, but acted as chief pledge, and still filled that office in 1385. (SROB, E 7/24/1.3; PRO, C 67/29.)

(vi) Edmund Gerneys of Little Barton

A presumed relative of Edmund, John Gerneys, had been involved in 1357 with a number of prominent local people, including Sir John de Shardelowe and the parson of Barton church, in resisting an attempt by Elizabeth de Burgh, Lady of Clare and a powerful magnate, to make distraint for customs and services owed to her. Edmund himself (who was pardoned for his part in the 1381 revolt) is revealed in the court proceedings of 1377-85 as a man of some substance who had a flock of 80 sheep in 1379, and horses and cattle which were occasionally found to have trespassed on the lord's land.
(*CPR, 1354-58*, p. 655; SROB, E 7/24/1.3; PRO, C67/29.)

(vii) John Haras of Herringswell

In January 1371 John Haras served as a juror in a general court held at Herringswell. He was a customary tenant, since he was presented for making waste on his holding. In a court held six months later there is a reference to a younger John Haras, the son of Matthew Haras, who raised a hue 'unjustly'. John Haras rebelled on 14 June 1381 and attacked the nearby Hospitallers' manor of Chippenham (Cambs.). He obtained a pardon in 1383.
(BL, Add. Charter 54072; Réville, *Soulèvement des travailleurs*, p. 241.)

(viii) William Metefeld, senior and junior of Brandon

William Metefeld senior was a leading free tenant of Brandon who appears regularly in the court rolls of the period 1365-89. He held a demesne meadow of $19\frac{1}{4}$ acres on lease in the 1370s and early 1380s. The elder Metefeld was a seller of bread and ale, especially active in this trade from 1377 to 1383. He also served as chief pledge between 1369 and 1382. He was pardoned after the revolt. William Metefeld junior first appears in 1369, when he drew blood from Alice Godhewe. In 1378 he was involved together with his father in a plea of trespass, but a year earlier he had evidently established his independence as a brewer, paying a fine of 2s. for breaking the assize of ale. He led a band of rebels in 1381 in south-west Norfolk, extorting money, stealing, 'assuming to themselves the royal power', and attacking the duke of Lancaster's manor of Methwold. He does not appear in the Brandon court rolls after the revolt, and when William Metefeld senior died in 1394 his land came into the hands of two feoffees, suggesting that his son was already dead.
(SROB, J 529/1-2; PRO, SC 6 1304/23-36; Powell, *Rising in East Anglia*, p.28; Réville, *Soulèvement des travailleurs*, pp.87,90.)

(ix) John Philip of Brandon

John Philip was appointed warrener of the bishopric of Ely's manor of Brandon on 15 April 1368, with wages of £4 0s. 8d. per annum. In the same year he was called a granger. In 1369 a thief broke into his chamber and took his keys in order to steal corn and 'utensils' from the lord of the manor. By 1374 he had been promoted to bailiff, and as he seems to have retained his position of warrener, his annual wages must have totalled £7 1s. 4d. His considerable income was augmented from landholdings. In 1369-70 he was renting 7 acres of the demesne and other lands for a total of 8s. 8d. He added the leasehold of two other customary holdings in 1371, so that in 1371-72 he was paying rents totalling 23s. 8d. – the area of land must have been in excess of 20 acres. In 1374 he did fealty as a free tenant to the new bishop of Ely, Thomas Arundel, and he took more land on lease, some on ten-year terms. The court roll of that year records that he also acquired land with a rental of 52s. 8d., but this does not appear on the accounts of the manor. Like any landholder he was involved in the usual manorial offences, trespassing with sheep and pigs, and being ordered (in 1381) to repair buildings on his customary holdings. He must have married before or soon after his first appearance in the records, since he had a twelve-year-old son in 1384. He served as affeerer in 1370, and later in life as chief pledge. In 1381, when he was still acting as bailiff, he joined the band of rebels led by William Metefeld junior (see (viii) above). He reappears as a Brandon tenant after the revolt, in the court of neighbouring Lakenheath. He died at some time between November 1392 and September 1393; at the latter date Christiana Philip and Thomas her son took over his lease on 4 acres of land. (SROB, J 529/1-2; PRO, SC 6 1304/23-36; Réville, *Soulèvement des travailleurs*, p. 87; CUL, EDC/7/15/II/2.)

(x) Adam Rogge of Aldham

John Rogge, a serf (*nativus*) of Aldham, died in 1359 leaving his widow Matilda with his villein holding as her free bench; it was a substantial tenement of a messuage and 8 war acres. Matilda's children were already grown up. Her daughter Elena married in 1359, and Adam first appears in the records a year later, when he 'unjustly and against the peace raised the hue on Matilda his mother', a very unusual presentment indicating a serious family quarrel. In 1365 Adam was again in trouble, beating Thomas Elenesfenne so that he raised the hue. In 1371 Adam was involved in litigation over debt with another Aldham man, and in the same year was amerced 1s. for allowing cows belonging to four different people to stray on to the demesne; the most likely explanation of this last incident would be that he was employed as a common herdsman. The records cease here, but it is likely that Adam succeeded to his father's holding; he would also have inherited his servile status. By 1381 he had become a figure of some importance, bailiff of the manor of his lord, Robert de Vere, earl of Oxford. On 14 June 1381 he attacked the house of William Gerard of 'Watlesfield' (? Whatfield) and on the next day went to Roger Usshefeld's house and stole goods worth 100 marks. (SROI, HA 68: 484/135; Powell, *Rising in East Anglia*, p.21; Réville, *Soulèvement des travailleurs*, p.81.)

(xi) Thomas Sampson of Kersey

A John Sampson was active in the Kersey area in the second quarter of the fourteenth century. By 1364 Thomas was involved in agriculture on a large scale, judging from a complaint in that year that he was pasturing 180 sheep on the common pasture of Polstead, and a report to Polstead manor court that a serf had gone to live with him, presumably as a servant. An indication of his relatively high status in the locality is his appearance as the first witness to a deed conveying property in Hadleigh in 1369. By the time of the revolt he must be counted as a member of the lesser gentry, with land in at least three vills - Kersey, Harkstead and Friston, and goods worth £65 12s. 8d., including 161 acres under crops, 72 horses and cattle, and an eighth share in a ship at Harwich. In 1380 he was employing two servants who were accused before the King's Bench of taking excessive wages; the fact that he acted as their pledge might suggest that he sympathised with them.

In 1379 and March 1381 he served as collector of poll taxes in Suffolk. The list of collectors, like the witness list of a deed of 1379, show Sampson well down in the order of precedence, below knights like John Shardelowe or Richard Waldegrave.

In the 1381 revolt Sampson led rebels in the south-east of the county, proclaiming rebellion at Ipswich on 15 June, and on the next day going to Melton, after which he moved north as far as Bramfield. He was captured and condemned to death, but in spite of an initial exclusion from pardon, was pardoned in 1383. The Sampson family rose to become lords of the manor of Sampson Hall, and a later Thomas was knighted and served as knight of the shire.

(Hervey (ed.), *Suffolk in 1327*, p.157; *Calendar of Ancient Deeds*, i, p.540; British Library, Add. Rolls 27683, 27685; *Calendar of Close Rolls 1377-81*, p.329; ibid., *1381-5*, p.121; Powell, *Rising in East Anglia*, pp.22, 23, 127, 143-5; Réville, *Soulèvement des Travailleurs*, pp.79, 80; PRO, KB 27/479; *Calendar of Patent Rolls*, *1381-5*, p.226; *Calendar of Fine Rolls 1377-83*, ix, pp.145, 237; Copinger, *Manors of Suffolk*, iii, pp.181-2; J.C. Wedgwood, *History of Parliament, 1439-1509: Biographies* (London, 1936), p.739.)

(xii) Margaret Wrighte of Lakenheath

One of the relatively few known women rebels, Margaret Wrighte twice appears among those amerced for breaking the assize of ale in 1379. She was presumably a relative of the various members of the Wrighte family mentioned in the court rolls of Lakenheath, for example in 1360-67 a John, Nicholas and Walter le Wrighte are all mentioned. In 1381 she was accused with other Lakenheath people, including Katherine Gamen, of involvement in the death of Sir John Cavendish, chief justice of the King's Bench. Margaret Wrighte's name is absent from the court rolls of October 1381 and does not re-appear.

(CUL, EDC/7/15/II/2; Réville, *Soulèvement des travailleurs*, p.69.)

12

Towns and Cottages in Eleventh-Century England

Domesday Book provides us with a marvellous opportunity to explore the early history of towns. As Domesday describes both town and country, we ought to be able to investigate the proportion of town dwellers, and the interactions between urban and rural society. The source can also throw light on the extent to which the *burhs* set up by pre-Conquest rulers had become by the eleventh century true towns, that is settlements which contained concentrations of population and which had a wide range of non-agricultural occupations, especially those deriving from participation in trade and industry.[1]

The potential of Domesday has not been fully realised because of its many inadequacies as a source for the history of towns. It omits London and Winchester. Bristol's great wealth is indicated, but no hint is given of its size.[2] Coventry, as Professor Davis has shown in a characteristically lucid argument, counted as an important town in 1102 when it was chosen to be an episcopal city, and is likely to have had urban characteristics sixteen years earlier, yet Domesday describes it as a rural manor.[3] When Domesday does provide us with more detail, for example in its accounts of Gloucester and Winchcomb, almost contemporary surveys compiled independently show that it grossly understates the number of houses and burgesses.[4] Domesday's inconsistent terminology baffles modern interpretation; in

---

[1]   This definition resolutely avoids institutional criteria, as in S. Reynolds, *An Introduction to the History of English Medieval Towns* (Oxford, 1977), pp. ix-x; R.H. Hilton, 'Towns in English feudal society', *Review (Journal of the Fernard Braudel Center for the Study of Economies, Historical Systems and Civilizations)*, 3 (1979), pp. 4-5. Cf. M. Biddle, 'Towns', in D.M. Wilson (ed.), *The Archaeology of Anglo-Saxon England* (London, 1976), p. 100; E. Ennen, *The Medieval Town* (Amsterdam, 1979), pp. 1-3.

I am grateful to Mr R. Meeson, who commented on the place-name Coton in a seminar discussion and began the train of thought that led to this essay. References to Domesday Book are to the Farley edition of 1783. *P.N. Berks.* etc. refers to the appropriate volume published by the English Place-Name Society.

[2]   *Bristol Charters, 1378-1499*, ed. H.A. Cronne, *Bristol Record Society*, 11 (1946), pp. 20-2.

[3]   R.H.C. Davis, *The Early History of Coventry* (Dugdale Society Occasional Paper, 24, 1976), pp. 16-19.

[4]   H.B. Clarke, 'Domesday slavery (adjusted for slaves)', *Midland History*, 1 (1972), pp. 38-9.

one place we are told of houses, in another burgesses, in a third, 'men', in a fourth 'enclosures' (*hagae*). Often the terms are mingled. There are good administrative explanations for these problems: the commissioners were not issued with instructions for dealing with towns. The main purposes of the *descriptio*, to investigate the resources of tenants-in-chief, and to provide for reassessment of geld, both led to a focus on rural manors, hides and ploughlands. The king's resources, which included many of the boroughs, received unsystematic coverage.[5]

We must not be demoralised by its omissions and confusions, because Domesday can be made to yield much useful information. One obvious question concerns the proportion of the population who lived in towns. Inevitably we must make the rather hazardous assumption that places described by Domesday as 'boroughs' (an institutional term) had urban characteristics. Less than 3 per cent of the people recorded were described as burgesses, but if we calculate the total of burgesses, houses, *hagae* and 'men' in the 112 boroughs, we arrive at a total of a little more than 20,000. As the recorded rural population was 269,000, the proportion of families or households living in towns can be estimated at 7 per cent of the total.[6] The inclusion of conservative estimates for the obvious omissions (London, Winchester and Bristol) would raise the number of urban households to more than 23,000, or 8 per cent of the total.[7] Already these calculations have entered dangerous waters: for example, should the slaves (*servi*) be counted as being the heads of households on a par with villeins (*villani*) or burgesses? Surely they should not because slaves were treated as individuals, so the rural total is an overstatement. Allowance could be made for further omissions, like those already mentioned for the Gloucestershire boroughs, but the calculation would require more guesswork. We would need to estimate also the omitted households in rural society, and we cannot be certain (though we may suspect it) that the surveys of the boroughs were more prone to underassessment than those of the manors. So, although greater precision is impossible, we have good cause to assume that about one in every twelve Englishmen in 1086 lived in a town, making a total urban population (allowing 4.5 to each household) in excess of 100,000.

Domesday contains a great deal of evidence for an association between towns and people called bordars (*bordarii*), cottars (*cotarii*) and coscets

[5]   V.H. Galbraith, *Domesday Book: Its Place in Administrative History* (Oxford, 1974), pp. 147-60; S.P.J. Harvey. 'Domesday Book and Anglo-Norman governance', *Transactions of the Royal Historical Society*, fifth ser., 25 (1975), pp. 175-93; Davis, *Early History of Coventry*, pp. 17-18.

[6]   These calculations are based on figures given in H.C. Darby, *Domesday England* (Cambridge, 1977), pp. 337, 364-8; for a calculation using different methods but arriving at a similar conclusion see J.C. Russell, *British Medieval Population* (Albuquerque, 1948), pp. 45-54.

[7]   M. Biddle (ed.), *Winchester in the Early Middle Ages* (Oxford, 1976), p. 440 suggests 1,100 houses for Winchester in 1148. London and Bristol must have had well in excess of 2,000 between them.

(*coscez*), all terms implying tenants with only small holdings of land. In some counties the bordars were much superior to the cottars in the size of their holdings, even having as much as 15 acres (a half-virgate), but often the two terms seem to have been interchangeable. At the lower end of the social and economic ladder, such tenants had no more than a house and garden.[8] These smallholders occur everywhere in Domesday. They account for about a third of the recorded rural population, and in one county, Essex, half of the people were called bordars. There has been much discussion of their origin and function. No doubt some of them were colonisers, who had brought a relatively small amount of land under the plough, and relied for much of their living on the pastures and other resources of the woodlands and wastes.[9] Others originated as *servi casati*, slaves settled on holdings by lords who expected to call on their labour on the demesne.[10] Many of the smallholders must have earned wages by working either on the demesne or on the larger peasant holdings; the latter assumption is supported by the fact that the great majority of manors and vills contained a mixture of villeins and smallholders.[11] Some may have made a living as craftsmen. Here we are concerned with that small section of this large and disparate social group who lived in or near boroughs.

Some smallholders are simply listed in Domesday as part of a borough's population. The small borough of Ashwell (Hertfordshire) is said to have had fourteen burgesses and nine cottars, described in a way that clearly distinguishes them from the tenants of Westminster Abbey's manor there (i, fo. 135b). At St Albans (Hertfordshire) twelve cottars are said to be 'in the same vill', which probably means the borough with its forty-six burgesses (i, fo. 135b). The Yorkshire borough of Tanshelf was populated with sixty 'small burgesses' and sixteen *coteros* (i, fo. 316b). Much larger places than these counted cottars and bordars among their inhabitants. A hundred bordars made up almost a third of Huntingdon's recorded population, though they are said to be 'under' the burgesses (i, fo. 203). At Norwich also 480 out of a total of at least 1300 recorded people were called bordars (ii, fos. 116–18). There were eight bordars at Nottingham, and fourteen at Hastings (Sussex), linked with four burgesses of the abbot of Fécamp (i, fo. 280, 17). In the very confusing entry for Bury St Edmunds (Suffolk),

[8]   R. Lennard, *Rural England, 1086-1135* (Oxford, 1959), pp. 340-64; idem, 'The economic position of the bordars and cottars of Domesday Book', *Economic Journal*, 61 (1951), pp. 342-71.

[9]   S.P.J. Harvey, 'Evidence for settlement study: Domesday Book', in P.H., Sawyer (ed.), *Medieval Settlement* (London, 1976), pp. 197-9.

[10]   M.M. Postan, *The Famulus* (Economic Hist. Review Supplement, no. 2, 1954), pp. 5-14; this seems to be implicit in J.D. Hamshere, 'A computer-assisted study of Domesday Worcestershire', in T.R. Slater and P.J. Jarvis (eds), *Field and Forest: An Historical Geography of Warwickshire and Worcestershire* (Norwich, 1982), p. 108.

[11]   R H Hilton, 'Reasons for inequality among medieval peasants', *Journal of Peasant Studies*, 5 (1978), pp. 271-84; Lennard, *Rural England*, pp. 362-3.

fifty-two bordars and probably another forty-three were listed among the population at the time of King Edward, apparently in a subordinate position 'under' other tenants. In 1086 twenty-seven bordars were said to be 'now' living at Bury, again 'under' reeves and knights (ii, fo. 372).

The existence of such people and tenements in towns later in the Middle Ages is well recorded. The Winchester survey of c. 1110 shows groups of *bordelli* (a word translated as 'shacks' by the editor), which presumably were inhabited by bordars, in the western suburbs of the city. Cottages are known at Winchester in the later Middle Ages, both from documents and excavations.[12] A glance at the surveys in the 1280 Hundred Rolls reveals the presence of numerous cottages in towns as diverse as Coventry (Warwickshire) and Woodstock (Oxfordshire). In the rental of Gloucester of 1455 a tenth of the properties were called cottages, and they were also prominent in the 1454 terrier of Southampton.[13] Late medieval urban cottages were smaller than full burgages, and carried a lower rent charge. The buildings themselves could be very small, having a floor area in some cases of 5 metres by 5 metres. Their tenants naturally came from the lower ranks of urban society, which would include widows, journeymen, labourers and other wage-earners, and they often held their cottages as subtenancies of burgages. They are found most commonly in the poorer districts of the towns, and especially in the suburbs. Domesday's brief and enigmatic entries do not allow us to make generalisations about urban cottars and bordars in the eleventh century with the same certainty, but it is possible to see some similarities. The Domesday bordars were inferior in status and wealth to the burgesses, as the reference to their poverty at Norwich suggests. The entries for Bury and Huntingdon imply that they were either sub-tenants or servants, or indeed both. As will appear, cottars and bordars were often located in suburbs.

If we turn from the boroughs themselves to the manors and vills in their vicinity, we discover large numbers of cottars and bordars. Occasionally Domesday describes extra-mural smallholders in the main borough entry, giving an impression of a suburb that is part of the borough in terms of tenure. At Lincoln, for example, in 1066, there were twelve tofts and four crofts, terms implying minor tenements, 'outside the city', belonging to the church of All Saints, and therefore probably lying outside the walls of the upper town where the church stood (i, fo. 336). The burgesses of Nottingham themselves had agricultural land outside the borough, and twenty bordars

---

[12] Biddle (ed.), pp. 48-9, 381, 441; M. Biddle, 'Excavations at Winchester, 1967: Sixth interim report', *Antiquaries Journal*, 48 (1968), pp. 261, 265-6.

[13] *Rotuli Hundredorum* (Record Commission, 1812-18), ii pp. 839-42; R.H. Hilton, *A Medieval Society* (2nd edn, Cambridge, 1983), p. 185; J. Langton, 'Late medieval Gloucester: some data from a rental of 1455', *Transactions of the Institute of British Geographers*, new ser., 2 (1977), pp. 259-77; C. Platt, *Medieval Southampton* (London, 1973), pp. 265-6.

as tenants (i, fo. 280). The location of the seventy-two bordars of Grantham (Lincolnshire) is not clear. They are not mentioned alongside the burgesses, and they are linked with a plough-team suggesting that they were tenants of the manor rather than the borough (i, fo. 337b). More often Domesday makes plain that there were manors closely linked to boroughs, whose tenants were mainly bordars and cottars. The bishop of Lincoln's manor at Leicester consisted of property both inside and outside the borough.[14] Within the walls were seventeen burgesses; outside there were three villeins and twelve bordars (i, fo. 230b). An analagous manor at Thetford (Norfolk) belonged to Roger Bigot, with thirty-three men in the borough, and a manor outside, which appears to have been normal in its possession of a demesne, a mill and two slaves, but unusual in its population of twenty bordars and no other type of tenants (ii, fo. 173). Beccles in Suffolk is described as a complex estate combining borough and manor. Twenty-six burgesses formed the borough tenants, and the manor contained a predominance of smallholders, including forty-six bordars, and thirty sokemen who had insufficient land – one-and-a-half ploughlands – for us to assign to each of them more than a few acres (ii, fos. 369b, 370). The royal demesne of Colchester (Essex) had a tenant population of ten bordars only, and there were four bordars and two slaves on another small manor held by the church of St Peter of Colchester (ii, fos 107, 107b). A comparable pair of manors at Ipswich (Suffolk) held by the Queen and Count Alan contained in the first case twelve freemen sharing eighty acres, and ten bordars with 'no land of their own', but living on eighty-six acres; and in the second simply seven bordars (ii, fos. 290, 294).[15] Perhaps the largest concentration of suburban smallholders lay around the city of Canterbury, where St Augustine's Abbey, the archbishop and other lords held manors called Northgate, *Estursete* and St Martins which contained a total of 194 bordars, compared with only thirty-seven villeins, so that smallholders amounted to 84 per cent of the tenant population, whereas in Kent as a whole they were in a minority of 29 per cent (i, fos. 3b, 4, 5, 12).[16]

As we learn more about urban topography, it may be possible to demonstrate that some of the smallholders in manors called 'Grantham' or 'Colchester' in fact lived in separate settlements. Usually it is only possible to show this conclusively from Domesday when a village or hamlet lay in a manor distinct in its lordship and location from the borough. So Roger of Iveri's manor of Walton just to the north of Oxford, with its one slave and

[14] *VCH Leicestershire*, iv, pp. 350-61.

[15] L.J. Redstone, *Ipswich Through the Ages* (Ipswich, 1948), p. 28 identifies these manors with the later Wicks Ufford and Wicks Bishop.

[16] T. Tatton-Brown, 'The towns of Kent', in J. Haslam (ed.), *Anglo-Saxon Towns in Southern England* (Chichester, 1984), pp. 10-11; H.C. Darby and E.M.J. Campbell, *Domesday Geography of South-East England* (Cambridge, 1962), p. 617.

thirteen bordars, must be regarded as containing a village separate from Oxford, but in its social and economic life overshadowed by that large town (i, fo. 159). In the vicinity of London lay the manor of Bishopsgate, where ten cottars were recorded, and among nearby Stepney's large and varied peasant population were forty-six cottars, crowded into a compact hamlet if we are to accept literally the statement that they together occupied one hide. The mysterious royal manor of 'No man's land' (Middlesex) which probably also lay near London had thirty cottar tenants (i, fos. 127, 128). Other examples from relatively small western boroughs are Allington, next to Bridport (Dorset), where the only recorded tenants were twelve bordars and nine rent-paying tenants (*censores*), and the manor with eighteen cottars as its sole tenants at Ditchampton near Wilton (Wiltshire) (i, fos. 80b, 66).

The peculiar social structure and economy of these bordar/cottar settlements are brought home to us most forcefully when the compilers of Domesday, perhaps themselves aware of the distinctive character of some of the places they were describing, sometimes relaxed their usual reticence and revealed the nature of the tenant holdings. A vill on the northern edge of Warwick, *Cotes*, contained a hundred bordars 'with their gardens' (i, fo. 238). Such garden plots (in Latin *horti* or *hortuli*) are mentioned as the tenements of forty-one cottars at Westminster, eight cottars at nearby Fulham, and twenty-three men of Holywell, just to the east of Oxford (i, fo. 128, 127b, 158b). Seven gardens are also mentioned at Grantham, under the jurisdiction of Grantham, but belonging tenurially to the manor of Gonerby, which might point to a suburban location (i, fo. 377).

The Westminster gardens hint at another urban context for smallholders. While the cottars may have been living in a western suburb of London, they are more likely to represent the beginnings of the town of Westminster. This identification is strengthened by the appearance of communities of bordars at a number of nascent or newly-founded towns. The 'small borough named Seasalter' that appears to have been a relatively recent growth on the lands of the church of Canterbury on the north Kent coast had a recorded population of forty-eight bordars, without any other tenant being mentioned (i, fo. 5). Evesham (Worcestershire), which had acquired market rights by 1055, and was developing urban characteristics in the late eleventh century, was said to have a population of twenty-seven bordars (i, fo. 175b).[17] There were twenty-one bordars in the new borough outside the gates of Battle Abbey in Sussex (i, fo. 17b). Sixteen bordars lived 'around the hall' of Tewkesbury (Gloucestershire), physically separate from the thirteen burgesses of the apparently recently founded borough, but perhaps

[17] R.H. Hilton, 'The small town and urbanisation: Evesham in the Middle Ages', *Midland Hist.*, 7 (1982), pp. 1-2.

connected to them in their economic activities (i, fo. 163-163b).[18] Cookham (Berkshire) also looks like a newly developed borough, though it lay near to the ninth-century *burh* on Sashes island in the Thames. There was a new market, and two submanors held by clergy had as their tenants a total of ten cottars (i, fo. 56b).[19]

Finally, Domesday records bordar/cottar settlements which were not immediately adjacent to a borough, but which were still very near. There must be elements of uncertainty in the topographical interpretation of the written record. For example, the manor of Witton, south of Droitwich (Worcestershire) included parts of the main street and the salt-making heart of Droitwich within its complex boundaries, though it also contained presumed settlements as much as a mile from the town centre.[20] So we cannot know whether to count the twenty bordars of the manor as belonging to the town, its suburbs or some nearby separate settlement; they probably were spread over all three locations (i, fo. 177b). Chesterton, to the north of Cambridge, with its two villeins, sixteen bordars and six cottars included both the fringes of the north-western trans-pontine extension of Cambridge, and a more distant settlement to the east (i, fo. 189b). In other cases the settlement of bordars and cottars lay well apart from the town. Whitwell, $2\frac{1}{2}$ miles from Cambridge, had a very unusual social structure, as ten of its eleven tenants were bordars and cottars (i, fos 194b, 198b, 200b). Good examples of similar vills are Walditch, a mile east of Bridport, Whittington almost 2 miles south-east of Worcester, and Headbourne Worthy which lay nearly 2 miles north of Winchester (i, fos 85, 173b, 46b). Such villages seem to occur too frequently to be coincidences, but there are obvious dangers as we leave the immediate vicinity of towns that we are encountering places where the social and landholding structure had been influenced by such factors as seigneurial policy or colonisation. A scatter of manors of which the tenants were wholly or predominantly cottars or bordars can be found in a variety of locations, not just near boroughs.

Further evidence for the link between towns and smallholdings comes from place-names. *Cot* is one of the more common place-name elements, and refers to a cottage or cottages; *cot* names are found in a wide variety of locations, among which a noticeable minority are close to towns.[21] *Cotes* near

---

[18] For two possible sites of the hall, see *VCH Gloucestershire*, viii, p. 125; *Medieval Archaeology*, 20 (1976), p. 160.

[19] N. Brooks, 'The unidentified forts of the Burghal Hidage', *Medieval Archaeology*, 8 (1964), pp. 79-81; G. Astill, 'The towns of Berkshire', in Haslam (ed.), pp. 63-4; idem, *Historic Towns in Berkshire, an Archaeological Appraisal* (Reading, 1978), pp. 23-7.

[20] Information from S.R. Bassett.

[21] It might be alleged that cot is such a common place-name that a random distribution would result in a number of such names lying near towns. However, *cots* are not very numerous in Berkshire, for example, yet five of them lie near towns.

Table 12.1 Place-names incorporating *cot* near early boroughs.

County	Modern Name	Borough	Distance from borough centre	Earliest form; Domesday population	Reference
Berkshire	CALDECOTT	Abingdon*	½ mile	CALDECOTE EXTRA ABINGDON 1261-6	*PN Berks.*, ii, pp. 437-8
Berkshire	CLAPCOT	Wallingford	Adjacent	CLOPECOTE 1086 9 villeins, 8 cottars (i, fo. 6lb)	*PN Berks.*, ii, pp. 536-7
Berkshire	NORCOT	Reading	2 miles	NORTHCOT 1327	*PN Berks.*, ii. p. 177
Berkshire	NORTHCOURT	Abingdon*	1 mile	NORTHCOTE *c.* 1180	*PN Berks.*, ii, p. 438
Berkshire	SOUTHCOTE	Reading	1½ miles	SUDCOTE 1086 5 villeins, 8 bordars (i, fo. 61)	*PN Berks.*, i, p. 177
Buckinghamshire	CALDECOTE	Newport Pagnell	1 mile	CALDECOTE 1086 1 knight, 2 vavassors, 2 villeins, 7 bordars 1 slave, (i, fo. 146b, 148b, 153)	*PN Bucks.*, p. 21
Buckinghamshire	GAWCOTT	Buckingham	1½ miles	CHAUESCOTE 1086 2 bordars, 1 slave (i, fo. 144)	*PN Bucks.*, pp. 60-1
Buckinghamshire	FOSCOTT	Buckingham	1½ miles	FOXESCOTE 1086 1 villein, 2 bordars, 1 slave (i, fo. 144b)	*PN Bucks.*, p.43
Cambridgeshire	COTON	Cambridge	2½ miles	COTIS 1086 (In D.B. as Whitwell) 1 villein, 1 bordar, 9 cottars (i, fo. 194b, 198b, 200b)	*PN Cambs.*, pp. 74-5
Cumberland	CALDECOTES	Carlisle*	Adjacent	CALDECOTE 1253	*PN Cumb.*, i, p. 42
Gloucestershire	COATES	Winchcomb	Adjacent	CHOTES and COTA 12th C.	*PN Glos.*, ii, p. 32
Herefordshire	BURCOT	Hereford	1½ miles	BURCOTA before 1172	A.T. Bannister, *The Place-Names of Herefordshire* (Cambridge, 1916), p.34
Kent	CALDECOTE	Canterbury	1 mile	CALDICOT 1326 (in D.B. as *Estursele*), 25 villeins, 114 bordars, 1 slave (i, fo. 3b)	R.A.L. Smith, *Canterbury Cathedral Priory* (Cambridge, 1943), p. 46
Northamptonshire	COTTON END	Northampton	Adjacent	COTES 1199	*PN Northants.*, p. 147
Shropshire	COTON	Shrewsbury	½ mile	COTA *c.* 1160	M.O.H. Carver, 'Early Shrewsbury', *Trans. Shropshire Arch. Soc.*, 59 (1973-4), fig. 27, facing p. 237

Table 12.1 cont.

Somerset	WALCOT	Bath	Adjacent	WALECOT 1260	*Two Cartularies the Priory of…Bath,* Somerset Record Soc., 7 (1893), pt.2, no.249
Staffordshire	COTON	Stafford	Adjacent	COTE 1086 1 villein, 1 slave (i, fo. 248)	—
Staffordshire	COTON	Tamworth	1½ miles	COTON 1309	H.Wood, *Medieval Tamworth* (Tamworth, 1972), p. 101
Warwickshire	COTON END	Warwick	Adjacent	COTES 1086 100 bordars (i, fo. 238)	*P.N. Warw.*, p. 264
Warwickshire	GLASCOTE	Tamworth	1 mile	GLASCOTE t. Henry II	*P.N. Warw.*, p. 26
Wiltshire	CALCUTT	Cricklade	1 mile	COLECOTE 1086 1 villein, 4 bordars, 1 slave (i, fo. 73b)	*P.N. Wilts.*, pp. 42–3

*Not recorded as boroughs in 1086. Show urban characteristics in twelfth century.

Table 12.2   Money rents paid by bordars, cottars, etc.

County	Manor	Borough	Type of tenant	Number	Rent per annum	Rent per capita per annum	D.B. reference
Dorset	Allington	Bridport	*censores*	9	11s. 0d.	14.7d.	i, fo. 80b
Middlesex	'No man's land'	London	cottars	30	14s. 10½d.	6d.	i, fo. 127
Middlesex	Holborn	London	cottars	2	20d.	10d.	i, fo. 127
Middlesex	Stepney	London	cottars	46	30s. 0d.	7.8d.	i, fo. 127
Middlesex	Bishopsgate	London	cottaas	10	18s. 6d.	22.2d.	i, fo. 128
Middlesex	Westminster	London	cottars	41	40s. 0d.	11.7d.	i, fo. 128
Sussex	—	Hastings	bordars	14	63s. 0d.	(rent total includes payments by 4 burgesses)	i, fo. 17
Warwickshire	Coten	Warwick	bordars	100	50s. 0d.	6d.	i, fo. 238
Worcestershire	—	Evesham	bordars	27	20s. 0d.	8.9d.	i, fo. 175b

Warwick, now Coten End, has already been mentioned, as also has the Domesday manor of Whitwell near Cambridge, in which a settlement in 1086 was known as *Cotis*, which later became Coton. Table 1 gives twenty-one examples. Nine of the names are mentioned in Domesday or in a Domesday satellite, and seven of them show the predominance of smallholders that we would expect. Another twelve names are not recorded until the twelfth, thirteenth or early fourteenth centuries, though this should not be taken to mean that the settlements did not exist in 1086. As the example of Whitwell/Coton shows, the name by which a manor or village was known could vary, and two names could have co-existed at the same time. Many of these small places were not mentioned earlier than the twelfth century merely because they tended not to be the chief settlement of a manor and so would not appear in early charters or Domesday, and it is likely that all of them originated before the Conquest. Indeed, they may be much earlier, because although it was once believed that the formation of these names came in the late Anglo-Saxon period, it is now thought that some *cots* could belong to the period before 850. This means that the settlements, and the distinctive social structure which gave rise to their names, might belong to the formative stages of the boroughs near which they lay. The development of the manorial centre of Caldecote (Buckinghamshire) is likely to have pre-dated the later borough of Newport Pagnell.[22] The majority of the settlements with *cot* names look like small subsidiary places, notably the Northcots and Southcote in Berkshire which were named in relation to the boroughs of Abingdon and Reading, or at least with reference to the estates, settlements or churches that acted as 'pre-urban nuclei' at these places.[23]

Having established the existence of numerous cottars and bordars, and cottage settlements, in and around more than forty early boroughs, we can begin to examine their significance. Who were the bordars and cottars? How did they live? The size of the woodland smallholdings can be taken to reflect the relatively minor contribution of arable farming to their economies. The urban or suburban cottars and bordars also had holdings of arable land too small to feed themselves and their families. The better-off, such as those at Ipswich, had as much as 8.6 acres each, but the forty-six Stepney cottars who lived on one hide must have averaged only a few acres each, and the Bishopsgate cottars each had less than an acre. These smallholdings could have been cultivated intensively under stimulus of the demand from the nearby market. Like later urban gardens, they may have been planted with such saleable crops as vegetables and fruit, or with industrial crops like flax

[22] *PN Berks.*, iii, pp. 924-5; M. Gelling, 'On looking into Smith's Elements', *Nomina*, v (1981), pp. 42-3.
[23] Astill, *Towns of Berkshire*, pp. 57-61; M. Biddle et al., 'The early history of Abingdon, Berkshire, and its abbey', *Medieval Archaeology*, 12 (1968), pp. 26-69.

and hemp.[24] The tenants no doubt supplemented their income from agriculture or horticulture with wages or other profits gained from trading and industrial activity in the borough. That some of their income came in the form of cash is implied by the money rents recorded sporadically in Domesday (see Table 12.2). Others are known to have paid rents or taxes, but the exact amount is not recorded: nine coscets outside the borough of Malmesbury 'geld with the burgesses', and the origin of the name of Gawcott near Buckingham, which means 'gafol-cot', refers to the bordars' predecessors' obligation to pay rent, perhaps to the reeve of the borough of Buckingham (i, fols. 64b, 144).[25] The bordars on the Bigot manor near Thetford paid head-money (*scotum de suo capite*) to the king, again acknowledging their connections with the royal borough.

The smallholders were expected to produce sums of money in rent comparable with, or sometimes in excess of, those paid by the burgesses, which tended to be standard sums of between 6d. and 1s. 0d. per annum.[26] Indeed some of the rents listed in Table 12.2, such as those at Westminster and Evesham, may represent embryonic burgage rents. Evidently the lords of the bordars and cottars, observing the profits that they could make from the sale of produce, wage-earning and petty trading, fixed rents in cash that would enable them to reap a share of the benefits of urban growth. The exact nature of the smallholders' participation in the urban economy must remain hidden from us. In the case of a town with a prominent industry, like Droitwich, it seems reasonable to guess that the bordars of Witton cut and loaded firewood and manned the boiling houses of the salt works. Elsewhere they could have been involved in a wide range of crafts and trades, judging from later evidence, especially those regarded as too noxious or dangerous to be practised in the town centre, and perhaps even at this early date the suburbs contained the criminals and prostitutes who gave an unsavoury reputation to such late medieval extramural enclaves as Southwark in London or the Tithing at Worcester.[27] It is no accident that the word *bordellus* has two meanings, of a small cottage and a brothel.

The importance of the bordars and cottars for our understanding of towns is twofold. They help indicate the scale and intensity of urban

[24] On the viability of smallholdings, see e.g. J.Z. Titow, *English Rural Society* (London, 1969), pp. 89-90; on urban gardens in the fifteenth century, *Ministers' Accounts of the Collegiate Church of St Mary, Warwick, 1432-85*, ed. D. Styles, *Dugdale Society*, 26 (1969), pp. 125-7, and for earlier crops grown near towns, H.K. Kenward et al., 'The environment of Anglo-Scandinavian York', in R.A. Hall (ed.), *Viking Age York and the North* (CBA Research Report, 27, 1978), p. 61.

[25] *PN Bucks*, p. 60.

[26] A. Ballard, *The Domesday Boroughs* (Oxford, 1904), pp. 71-2; M. de W. Hemmeon, *Burgage Tenure in Mediaeval England* (Cambridge, Mass., 1914), pp. 61-77; on bordar rents in general, see Lennard, *Rural England*, pp. 359-60.

[27] D.J. Keene, 'Suburban growth', in M.W. Barley (ed.), *The Plans and Topography of Medieval Towns in England and Wales* (CBA Research Report, 14, 1975), pp. 71-82.

development by 1086; and they contribute to our knowledge of urban origins. The inclusion of the bordars and cottars in our view of eleventh-century society dispels any lingering doubts that the boroughs were really towns. A small place like St Albans looks more convincing as a significant concentration of population when the cottars are added to the burgesses, giving a total of more than 250 people (using a multiplier of 4.5). Middle-sized towns like Warwick gain in our estimation when the hundred bordars of *Cotes* (and their dependants and families) are added to the 244 burgesses and houses of the borough, to suggest a population of more than 1,500. The inclusion of the urban and suburban bordars and cottars with the burgesses and houses for the whole country would help to push the number of town-dwellers of Domesday nearer to 10 per cent of the total population. Their landholdings should present no obstacle to regarding the bordars and cottars as part of the urban economy, as burgesses often had some land, yet still gained their main income from non-agricultural pursuits.[28] The cottars could only have made a living if the boroughs were generating wealth and employment. Places like Buckingham, Grantham and Warwick, which were not to become very large or thriving towns in the later Middle Ages or in modern times, must have had relatively healthy economies in the eleventh century to maintain the large numbers of bordars and cottars settled on their peripheries. In this respect the towns of the eleventh century resemble those of the later Middle Ages, on whose outskirts concentrations of smallholdings are also found.[29]

Not all of these groups of smallholders can be regarded as part of the urban population. Those who lived in a separate settlement a mile or two from the town were still under its influence, judging from their ability to make a living in spite of the small size of their holdings. The interaction between town and country can be seen as falling within a series of zones, of which Domesday allows us to observe an outer and an inner. In a large outer area, up to a radius of 10 or 20 miles, lay manors which held burgesses or houses in the town, indicating long-distance connections with the urban market, where rural produce was sold, and manufactured or traded goods purchased.[30] In a much smaller zone lay the villages under more intense influence, where the town stimulated the countryside into fulfilling its needs for commodities and labour. The outlying villages had only occasional contact with the town; those in the inner ring would have participated frequently, even continuously, in the intercourse between town and country.

In the late eleventh century we can observe both well-established royal boroughs, mostly developed over the previous two centuries, and a recent

---

[28] J. Tait, *The Medieval English Borough* (Manchester, 1936), pp. 68-75.

[29] E.g. D. Greenblatt, 'The surburban manors of Coventry, 1279-1411' (unpublished University of Cornell Ph.D. thesis, 1967), pp. 27-30.

[30] Darby, *Domesday England*, pp. 309-13.

generation of small boroughs on the estates of churchmen and lay magnates. In the latter the bordars and cottars represented the new townsmen, who appear to have begun as servants and dependants, with the function of supplying goods and services to their lords. This is especially clear at Evesham, where the twenty-seven bordars were called 'servants of the court'. The inhabitants of Battle were described in Domesday as bordars, and a list compiled twenty years later shows the town containing abbey servants living alongside artisans and traders; a comparable case is Seasalter, where the bordars apparently belonged to the archbishop or the monks of Christ Church, Canterbury, to provide those lords with salt and fish.[31] Townsmen seem to have originated as servants or minor tenants at Tewkesbury, Bury St Edmunds and Westminster. Those who held manors on the edge of royal boroughs, like the pre-Conquest lords of Holywell and Walton near Oxford, could also have deliberately settled dependants in the suburbs in order to gain some profit from the town.

All of this might seem to strengthen the arguments of those who see pre-Conquest towns as deliberate and conscious creations by rulers.[32] This is not the whole story of urban development, and the presence of the bordars and cottars indicates the various paths that led to the emergence of towns. The gatherings of relatively poor people around centres of economic activity suggest the results of migration. A specific example of this might be Clare (Suffolk), a developing borough on an aristocratic estate, where the numbers of bordars on the manor between 1066 and 1086 increased threefold from ten to thirty, while the numbers of villeins dwindled (ii, fo. 389b).[33] Possible sources of newcomers would include the pedlars, settling in or near a town in accordance with the classic Pirenne model, but a more plausible recruiting ground would be the peasantry, especially their younger sons, gravitating towards the town from an already crowded countryside. Settlements near towns and suburbs could have served as staging posts for such migrants who could not immediately become burgesses. Another explanation of the role of smallholders in the growth of towns would be to link them with those theories of origin, as proposed for such places as Cambridge, Lincoln and Norwich, which portray the town emerging from the coalescence of a number of nuclei (some or all of which would have had a semi-rural character before the tenth century), or expanding to swallow

---

[31] *The Chronicle of Battle Abbey*, ed. E. Searle (Oxford, 1980), pp. 50-9; Tatton Brown, 'Towns of Kent', pp. 32-4.

[32] e.g. M. Biddle and D. Hill, 'Late Saxon planned towns', *Antiquaries Journal*, 51 (1971), pp. 70-85; R. Hodges, *Dark Age Economics* (London, 1982), pp. 153-98.

[33] G.A. Thornton, 'A study in the history of Clare, Suffolk, with special reference to its development as a borough', *Transactions of the Royal Historical Society*, 4th ser., 11 (1928), p. 87.

a nearby rural settlement.[34] In such a model the smallholders would represent an intermediate stage in the social mobility of people en route from the peasantry to full integration into urban society. Under the stimulus of the trade and industry of nearby growing towns large villein holdings would have been fragmented, because lords would have seen the advantages of increasing the number of tenants, and because the tenants would have been tempted to divide their inheritance in view of the chances of their heirs making a good living out of smaller holdings. Some holdings could have broken up under the pressures of the land market.[35] So even if the evidence from such places as Evesham points to the originating urban nucleus being organised by a higher authority (and this does not need to be true in every case), in their expansion towns took in peasants, whether because they happened to be living nearby, or because they were attracted as migrants. In other words, in seeking the origins of urban populations we must allow for evolutionary and spontaneous elements as well as direction from above.

In the same way the development of towns must have taken place in a favourable rural environment, one in which exchanges of goods and services were growing. The existence of large numbers of smallholders is in itself evidence of the penetration of small-scale exchange throughout English society by the eleventh century, because such people needed to buy foodstuffs to supplement the produce of their holdings, and they had surplus labour to sell. In such a context, especially when at a higher social level lords were anxious to sell demesne produce, and to squeeze more cash in rents from their tenants, towns in the tenth and eleventh centuries look more like natural growths and less like alien implants.[36]

Finally the urban and suburban bordars and cottars of Domesday draw attention to the role of the lower ranks of society in medieval towns. The written sources leave no doubt of the sharply differentiated social hierarchy, even in early towns, and the excavation of urban sites indicates great inequalities in housing conditions.[37] Various historians have attempted to assert the importance of craftsmen rather than merchants in the early

[34] M.D. Lobel, 'Cambridge', in *The Atlas of Historic Towns*, ii (London, 1975), pp. 3-5; D. Perring, *Early Medieval Occupation at Flaxengate, Lincoln* (The Archaeology of Lincoln, xi, pt. 1, CBA, London, 1981), pp. 44-5; A Carter, 'The Ango-Saxon origins of Norwich: the problems and approaches', in P. Clemoes (ed.), *Anglo-Saxon England*, 7 (1978), pp. 175–204.

[35] W.G. Runciman, 'Accelerating social mobility: the case of Anglo-Saxon England', *Past and Present*, 104 (1984), pp. 19-21.

[36] G. Duby, *Early Growth of the European Economy* (London, 1974), pp. 221-48; J. Merrington, 'Town and country in the transition of capitalism', in R.H. Hilton (ed.), *The Transition from Feudalism to Capitalism* (London, 1976), pp. 170-95.

[37] Russell, *British Medieval Population*, p. 46; B.K. Davison, 'The late Saxon town of Thetford', *Medieval Archaeology*, 11 (1967), pp. 189-208.

stages of urban growth.[38] Towns in Poland, for example, seem to have begun as small industrial communities established at the gates of aristocratic residences.[39] One of the achievements of recent archaeological research in England has been to show the wide range of industries practised both in an early emporium like *Hamwih* and in a city like York which flourished in the tenth and eleventh centuries.[40] A feature of the economic history of late Saxon England was the growing concentration of certain industries in towns, most easily demonstrated in the case of pottery manufacture, but also evidently in cloth-making.[41] No doubt the economy of the larger towns depended a good deal on long-distance and inter-regional trade, but they supported large populations within their walls, in their suburbs, and beyond, through the flourishing of labour-intensive industries and crafts. The urban economy, especially in the smaller towns, must have also provided many roles for the petty trader, like the one-eyed garlic (or onion) seller who appears in an Old English riddle. Small towns, when they are better documented in the thirteenth century, were full of people who traded on a small scale over short distances in cheap commodities, mostly food-stuffs.[42] This must have been the economic basis for eleventh-century towns like Ashwell and Evesham, and for the cottars and bordars who lived in such places.

The association between cottages and towns can be traced at all stages of medieval urban development. Cottager communities might form proto-urban settlements. Cottages could become part of the fabric of urban society, within the town centre and especially in its suburbs. Cottar settlements on the edge of the towns might be deliberately created by lords, or gather more spontaneously. Urban growth exerted an influence on the countryside, by engulfing peasant settlements, attracting migrants, and transforming the economy and landholding structures of nearby villages, in all cases providing an environment in which cottars could live. If we focus our attentions too narrowly on the burgesses and the town centres, we are in danger of minimising the extent and the influence of early medieval urbanisation.

---

[38] E.V. Gutnova, 'Levitsky's artisanal theory in England', in J.F. Benton (ed.), *Town Origins* (Boston, Mass., 1968), pp. 37-41; C. Verlinden, 'Marchands ou tisserands? A propos des origines urbaines', *Annales E.S.C.*, 27 (1972), pp. 396-406.

[39] P. Francastel (ed.), *Les origines des villes Polonaises* (Paris, 1960), pp. 20-4.

[40] P. Holdsworth, 'Saxon Southampton: a new review', *Medieval Archaeology*, 20 (1976), pp. 26-61; A. MacGregor, 'Industry and commerce in Anglo-Scandinavian York', in Hall (ed.), *Viking Age York*, pp. 37-57.

[41] J.G. Hurst, 'The pottery', in Wilson (ed.), *Archaeology in Anglo-Saxon England*, pp. 314, 323, 326-34; E. Crowfoot, 'Textiles', in M.O.H. Carver, 'Three Saxo-Norman tenements in Durham CIty', and J.W. Hedges, 'Textiles', in C.M. Heighway et al., 'Excavations at 1 Westgate Street, Gloucester, 1975', *Medieval Archaeology*, 23 (1979), pp. 36-9, 190-3.

[42] R.H. Hilton, 'Lords, burgesses and hucksters', *Past and Present*, 97 (1982), pp. 3-15.

13

The Consumer and the Market in the Later Middle Ages

Everyone accepts the importance of the market in the late medieval economy. Apart from the volume of international trade, which was worth more than £250,000 per annum for the whole of the period 1275-1500, England's internal trade may well have handled a quarter or more of GNP, the estimated proportion in the sixteenth and seventeenth centuries.[1] By the late thirteenth century all sections of society participated in a complex commercial network: the aristocracy drew most of their landed income in cash from rents and the sale of demesne produce; peasants needed to raise money both to pay rents and to buy goods and services; the urban population (one in seven of the total if the numerous small towns are included) depended for their incomes on the profits of trade and crafts; at least one in three of those living in both town and country earned wages, often paid in cash. We tend to have a one-sided view of the market, because our sources contain more information about selling: exports are better documented than imports, and manorial accounts record more sales than purchases. Historians have also concentrated their attention on the sellers, such as merchants and hucksters in the towns, or demesne managers and better-off peasants in the country. Consumption deserves more research, and a long-term aim must be to identify the buyers, to see what they bought, and from whom, and how purchases were organised.[2]

   This contribution to the subject is designed to answer questions about the location of purchases. The approach adopted here is based on recognition of the fact that consumers were ranged in a social hierarchy, and that commercial centres also formed a hierarchy. It is therefore necessary to establish the connections between the two. The behaviour of a range of consumers will be examined, beginning with the great lords – dukes, earls, bishops and wealthy religious institutions – and continuing through the

[1]   J.A. Chartres, *Internal Trade in England, 1500-1700* (London, 1977), p. 10.
[2]   For extended treatment of this approach, see C. Dyer, *Standards of Living in the Later Middle Ages* (Cambridge, 1989).

lords of the second rank, such as minor barons, rich knights and monasteries with middling incomes. Then as much as possible will be deduced about the spending of the lesser gentry, clergy and peasants. In each case the trading centres used by these social groups will be analysed, from London, through the regional capitals, major ports, provincial towns and smaller market towns, to the market villages and venues outside the system of chartered markets.

Geographers explain the marketing pattern in terms of a spatial distribution of towns, which differed in size and function. Above the local network of small towns, the 'higher order centres' sold a variety of specialised goods and services over a wide area, so that a customer requiring an unusual or expensive article would go to a large and distant centre. A farmer's wife in twentieth-century Iowa buys her groceries in a nearby small town, but travels to the regional capital, Omaha/Council Bluffs, for her winter coat.[3] The historian's contribution to the analysis is to add to the geographer's concern for size and space a long-term chronological view and an emphasis on social distinctions. Indeed, historians have already made assumptions about the role of towns in medieval society. Duby has linked the origin of medieval cities with the growth in demand for luxuries among the post-Carolingian aristocracy. It is widely accepted that declining aristocratic incomes in the early fourteenth century reduced the market for fine textiles and so helped to precipitate the crisis in the Flemish cloth towns. The recent wave of research on English small towns and rural markets in the late thirteenth century has led to the suggestion that these low-grade centres of exchange provided for the needs of the local peasant population.[4] This essay does not seek to overthrow such perceptions, but rather to define the interconnections between the social and commercial hierarchies in a systematic way, and to explore some of the implications for economic changes in the later Middle Ages.

Where Did Consumers Make their Purchases?

The main sources of information about aristocratic purchases are household accounts. They can only be used with difficulty, because the information they contain is often incomplete, and they identify the sources of purchases

[3]   B.J.L. Berry, *Geography of Market Centers and Retail Distribution* (Englewood Cliffs, N.J., 1967); C. Renfrew, 'Alternative models for exchange and spatial distribution', in idem, *Approaches to Social Archaeology* (Edinburgh, 1984), pp. 135-53.

[4]   G. Duby, *Early Growth of the European Economy* (London, 1974), pp. 162-80; R.H. Britnell, 'The proliferation of markets in England, 1200-1349', *Econ. Hist. Rev.*, 2nd ser., 34 (1981), pp. 209-21; R.H. Hilton, *The English Peasantry in the Later Middle Ages* (Oxford, 1975), pp. 76-94; T. Unwin, 'Rural marketing in medieval Nottinghamshire', *Journal of Historical Geography*, 7 (1981), pp. 231-51.

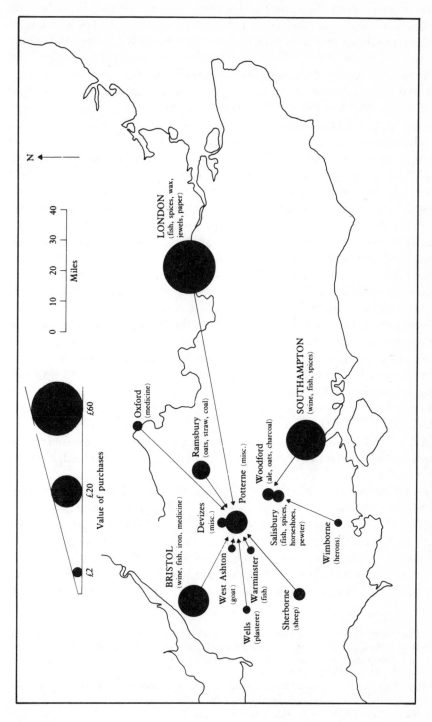

Fig. 13.1 Purchases (valued) of Richard Mitford, bishop of Salisbury, 1406–7.

without consistency.[5] The first accounts date from around 1200, but the documents become more detailed between 1280 and 1500. They survive in uneven quantities with a marked bunching in the early fourteenth century and in the decades around 1400. The greatest number of accounts, and the most detailed, derive from the wealthier households.

A characteristic magnate consumer, with an annual income in excess of £1,000, was Richard Mitford, bishop of Salisbury, whose accounts cover most of the last year of his life, in 1406/7.[6] He divided his time between his Wiltshire manor houses at Potterne and Woodford, which lay near two towns founded by earlier bishops, at Devizes and Salisbury (see Figure 13.1). Like many great lords at this time, Mitford obtained some grain and meat from his demesnes, but was otherwise dependent on the market for his supplies.[7] Much of his preserved fish, together with wax, jewellery and spices (including dried fruits and almonds) were bought in London. The large ports of Southampton and Bristol provided wine, together with fish, spices and imported iron. The bishop's household made much more limited use of places within his diocese. Fresh fish and horseshoes came from the largest town, Salisbury, and a succession of minor purchases was made at Devizes and villages on the estate, notably Potterne. These last transactions were on a small scale. By them the bishop acquired occasional animals, hay, rushes and minor unspecialised services such as those of a local washerwoman. To indicate the relative importance of the various sources of supply, out of a total recorded expenditure of £143, Mitford bought goods worth £59 (41 per cent of the total) from London. His purchases in the large towns of Bristol, Southampton and Salisbury amounted to £56 (39 per cent), of which Salisbury came a poor third with a total spending of less than £5. The remaining 20 per cent was used to buy goods locally, or in more remote specialist centres such as Oxford, a source of medicines.

A static household with a similar income, King's College, Cambridge, in 1466/7 made some of its most expensive purchases, such as bells, pewter and fish, from London merchants, both directly and through contacts at the Stourbridge Fair.[8] This major commercial event, held on the outskirts of Cambridge, was the source of much of the college's fish, supplied in many cases by traders from the Norfolk port of Lynn. Cloth was bought at some distance at Salisbury and Winchester. Foodstuffs, fuel and building materials

---

[5]   The best study of these documents is C. Woolgar, 'The development of accounts for private households in England to *c.* 1500 A.D.' (unpublished Ph.D. thesis, University of Durham, 1986). The point about their uneven distribution is in Dyer, *Standards of Living*, pp. 92-4.

[6]   British Library, Harley MS 3755.

[7]   Dr John Hare has told me of the continuation of direct management on some manors of the bishopric of Salisbury's estates at this period.

[8]   King's College, Cambridge, Mundum Book, iv, no.2.

came from the villages around Cambridge; the town itself figured less frequently as a source of purchases than might have been expected, though some grain, poultry, wax and cheap cloth were bought there.

These spending patterns are to be found repeated in the records of many of the grandest households. Agricultural produce came from demesne manors, if they were located nearby and were kept under direct management. Even in the late thirteenth century, in the heyday of demesne production, some lords preferred to sell their own produce and buy in supplies as they were needed, but most obtained at least a proportion of their grain and meat from their demesnes. After 1400 large-scale leasing of demesnes made lords more dependent on purchased foodstuffs and fodder. In the late fourteenth and the fifteenth century, the period to which the bulk of our information about the magnates relates, they bought a great deal from London, because in the capital they could obtain luxuries, and especially imports, in the quantity and quality they required. These included wine, spices and wax, together with manufactures such as Dutch, Flemish or German linen, silks from southern Europe, and the products of English industries such as pewter. London craftsmen, notably the goldsmiths and skinners, came to dominate the market in expensive goods. Less exotic manufactured articles were also purchased there: Thomas Arundel, bishop of Ely, in 1381 had his heavy carriage (chariot) made in London at a cost of £8.[9] Even quite cheap imports, such as onions and garlic, were bought in London by provincial magnates. Goods cost less if they were purchased in bulk from the importing merchant at the point of unloading. For example, Richard Mitford was able to obtain that essential ingredient of medieval cooking, liquorice, at 1d. per pound in London, compared with $1\frac{1}{2}$d. at Southampton and 2d. at Devizes.

Transport costs discouraged magnates living in the far north from making as much use of London suppliers as did their southern contemporaries, but London's tentacles in the fifteenth century spread over the whole kingdom, so that even the bishop of Carlisle and the cellarer of Durham Priory bought spices from merchants in the capital.[10] Magnates owned houses along the Strand, or in such suburbs as Holborn and Southwark, in which they stayed when attending parliament or the royal court. Their mansions could also serve as depots in which goods were stored for eventual consumption on the spot, or preparatory to their transport to provincial castles, manor houses and monasteries. The cost of carrying bulky goods such as barrels of herring, loads of wax, or tuns of wine over distances of 100 miles or more might be thought to have been

---

[9] Cambridge University Library, EDR D5/2.
[10] Cumbria RO, DRC 2/15; J.T. Fowler (ed.), *Extracts from the Account Rolls of the Abbey of Durham*, 3 vols (Surtees Soc., 99, 100, 103, 1898-1900), i, pp. 69-72.

prohibitive, especially by road which was substantially more expensive than water transport. Yet although the costs of both forms of carriage rose during the period as wages increased, magnates evidently judged that road transport could be afforded (see Table 13.1).

Table 13.1 Cost of transporting wine by water and road, per tun, per mile (pence).

Date	Water transport up the Severn	Road transport in the West Midlands
1308/9	0.4	2.5
1452/3	0.6	3.2

The figures in Table 13.1 have been calculated from accounts of two long-distance journeys. One was to bring wine from Bristol to Lichfield for the bishop of Coventry and Lichfield in 1308/9, which was achieved by a first leg on the Severn to Bridgnorth and then a trip overland. In the second example, wine for the first duke of Buckingham was transported from Bristol by boat to Bewdley, and transferred to carts for the journey to Maxstoke Castle in Warwickshire.[11] Consumers who bought at a distance incurred many other costs, such as sending a representative to make a choice and pay the merchant, and then the incidental expenses of repairing barrels and moving them from quay to boat and from boat to carts. In 1308/9, a guard had to be posted on the barrels while the carts were being assembled at the quay at Bridgnorth. Such items brought the total transport costs for Buckingham in 1452/3 to £16 13s. 10d. for 22 tuns. The wine itself had cost £117 6s. 8d. to buy in Bristol. Presumably the extra 14 per cent for transport was judged to be worthwhile, because the alternative local suppliers, the vintners of Coventry, would no doubt have incurred the same costs, and would have added their own mark-up of perhaps another 10 per cent.

For a whole cargo of wine many carts had to be hired, but for the occasional load of less bulky purchases, a lord would send his 'chariot' to London. These vehicles were kept for routine journeys, notably for carrying the ladies when the household was moving from one residence to another. As the building and main running costs of the chariot were paid already, the additional sums needed for repairs, horse bread and servants' accommodation on the journey to London did not make the trip impossibly

[11] J. Isaac, 'Two medieval accounts for the town of Lichfield', *Trans. South Staffs. Arch. and Hist. Soc.*, 18 (1977), p. 63: M. Harris (ed.), 'The account of the great household of Humphrey, first duke of Buckingham, for the year 1452-3', in *Camden Miscellany* (Camden Soc., 4th ser., 29, 1984), pp. 20, 26.

expensive. The long distances covered show that carriage by land posed no insuperable technical difficulties. Richard Mitford's chariot was able to take a heavy load of fish and spices 75 miles from London to Wiltshire in January 1407, and still more impressively, the duke of York's vehicle in December 1409 brought fish from London to Hanley Castle in Worcestershire. This journey of more than 100 miles included the negotiation of the escarpment of the Cotswolds in winter.[12] It shows yet again that the medieval road system, like that of the seventeenth century, provided a more than adequate means of transporting goods.[13]

Magnates made considerable use of the major fairs. A book of advice on household management in the mid-thirteenth century urged the advantages of patronising the fairs of Boston, Bristol, St Ives and Winchester. Later in the century the archbishop of York and Durham Priory spent large sums (more than £130 in the latter case) at St Ives and Boston on cloth, fish, furs and spices.[14] Less wealthy consumers, like Merton College, Oxford, in the 1290s bought cloth and horses at Aylesbury Fair.[15] The fairs declined in the later Middle Ages, much to the benefit of the London merchants as we have seen, but Stourbridge Fair remained an important occasion, where many great households in eastern England obtained their fish, wax, spices, timber, salt, cloth, iron goods and pewter ware. The fairs gave rich consumers the opportunity to make bargains with the major merchants, and to choose from a wide range of goods of the right quantity and quality, obtainable at 'wholesale' prices, because the fairs' main commercial function was to provide a point of contact between the large-scale importers and the provincial merchants who distributed the goods to retail outlets.

Purchases by the great households were also made at the ports and regional capitals – in geographical order, at Newcastle-on-Tyne, York, Hull, Boston, Lynn, Norwich, Ipswich, Canterbury, Southampton, Exeter, Bristol, Coventry and Chester. Often the magnates bought their wine or fish in the nearest large port, but sometimes the attraction of a special product was judged to be worth a long journey. So, King's College, Cambridge bought cloth at two regional centres, Salisbury and Winchester, presumably because textiles of appropriate quality were available in those

---

[12] Northamptonshire RO, Westmorland (Apethorpe), 4xx4, fo. 17.

[13] J.A. Chartres, 'Road carrying in England in the seventeenth century: myth and reality', *Econ. Hist. Rev.*, 2nd ser., 30 (1977), pp. 73-94; F.M. Stenton, 'The road system of medieval England', *Econ. Hist. Rev.*, 7 (1936-8), pp. 1-21; R.S. Lopez, 'The evolution of land transport in the Middle Ages', *Past and Present*, 9 (1956), pp. 17-29. The ratio of land to water transport costs of *c.* 6:1 seems a little less than in modern times: T.S. Willan, *The Inland Trade* (Manchester, 1976), pp. 6-8.

[14] D. Oschinsky (ed.), *Walter of Henley and Other Treatises on Estate Management and Accounting* (Oxford, 1971), pp. 398-9; E.W. Moore, *The Fairs of Medieval England* (Toronto, 1985), pp. 60-2, 204; Fowler (ed.), *Account Rolls of...Durham*, ii, p. 495.

[15] J.R.L. Highfield (ed.), *The Early Rolls of Merton College, Oxford* (Oxford Historical Society, new ser., 18, 1964), pp. 232-71.

towns. A fairly consistent link can be recognised between the wealthiest households and the towns that occupied the first twenty places in the urban hierarchy.

The larger towns and especially London furnished the higher aristocracy with another facility that deserves mention. The life of a great household was punctuated by special occasions when large numbers of guests had to be entertained. Such an event was the funeral of Richard Mitford, which was attended by 1,450 guests. At these times large quantities of high-quality foodstuffs needed to be bought, utensils hired, and specialised labour, such as cooks, engaged. These preparations were possible only through mobilising the resources of a sizeable city.

Smaller towns were used only sporadically for magnate purchases. Indeed, they were sometimes conspicuously ignored. At the time of Richard Mitford's sojourn in Wiltshire in 1406/7 that county contained no fewer than twenty-six boroughs, most of which had some urban characteristics, yet he is recorded as making purchases at only three of them. When the duchess of Buckingham was staying at Writtle in 1465/6 her household lay within easy reach of a dozen small towns, some of them on the Essex coast, yet her fresh sea fish came regularly from Winchelsea in Sussex, involving a journey of more than 60 miles.[16] Outside the gates of Battle Abbey lay the small town that the monastery had encouraged from the early days of its foundation, yet the cellarer obtained his main supplies of fish, spices and other goods from Hastings, Winchelsea, Canterbury and London.[17] A few small towns that were in the right place at the right time benefited from magnate patronage. Coleshill in Warwickshire and Chelmsford in Essex both had the good fortune to lie within easy carting distance of the two chief residences of the dukes of Buckingham in the mid-fifteenth century, at a time when the household had ceased to operate its own brewhouse. So the brewers of these small places who normally provided ale for a few hundred townsmen and travellers, not all of them wealthy, responded occasionally and temporarily to orders for thousands of gallons of ale for the servants and guests of the ducal entourage, and the local roads became busy with carts burdened with barrels covering the mile or two that separated the town and its largest customer.[18] Other small towns were chosen because of their specialities: for example, Warminster was evidently favoured by Richard Mitford as a source of fresh sea fish. Another reason for buying goods at a small town might have been its situation on the lord's estate, both for the sake of patronage, and because of the convenience

[16] British Library, Add. MS 34213.

[17] E. Searle and B. Ross (eds), *The Cellarers' Rolls of Battle Abbey, 1275-1513* (Sussex Record Society, 65, 1967), pp. 22-113.

[18] Harris (ed.), 'Account of the great household', pp. 37, 51; W.B.D.D. Turnbull (ed.), *Compota domestica familiarum de Bukingham et d'Angouleme* (Edinburgh, 1836), p. 5.

of using the local officials to pay for supplies from their rent receipts, and to arrange transport. So in 1385/6 the countess of Norfolk bought fresh salmon and lampreys at Chepstow, in Monmouthshire, part of her far-flung inheritance, for consumption at her permanent residence at Framlingham in Suffolk.[19]

For bulky and cheaper items, the wealthiest households often did not make use of towns or markets at all. Instead they negotiated directly with the rural producers, as did King's College, Cambridge, which obtained its grain, meat and sedge in such nearby villages at Coton, Knapwell and Bottisham. The duke of York bought much of his hay, grain, pigs and poultry *in patria*, that is, in the countryside of the Severn valley where the household resided, and the duke of Buckingham obtained most of his hay and grain in the north Warwickshire villages surrounding Maxstoke Castle. The suppliers were often the estate's own tenants, especially the demesne farmers or the more prosperous peasants who produced on a scale sufficient to meet the requirements of a large household.[20] They would oblige their lord by not demanding immediate payment, and might charge lower prices, out of deference and because the sum would be offset against rent payments. Such deals strengthened the links between lord and tenant, cut out middlemen's profits, and kept transport costs to a minimum.

In short, far from distributing their great wealth in careless displays of largesse, the magnates are seen to have been prudent consumers, whose transactions were intended to give them the advantage of both high quality and reasonable prices. They purchased with discrimination, and found that they could only procure the goods they needed at the largest urban centres. If the Paston women, belonging to the top rank of the gentry, could find so little to please them in the large provincial capital of Norwich – 'I can get none in this town'; 'there is no good in this town'; 'there is not enough of one cloth and colour to serve you' – how much more dissatisfied would have been the countesses, cellarers and stewards who made the purchasing decisions of households with double or treble the spending power of the Pastons?[21]

The second tier of consumers, to which the Pastons belonged, included superior knightly families with interests in administration or the law, such as the East Anglian de Norwich family, the Oxfordshire Stonors, and the Catesbys of Northamptonshire, and a knight active in war, Hugh Luttrell of Dunster (Somerset). Others comparable in wealth were the Warwickshire

[19] J. Ridgard (ed.), *Medieval Framlingham: Select Documents, 1270-1524* (Suffolk Record Soc., 27, 1985), p. 99.

[20] A. Watkins, 'Society and economy in the northern part of the Forest of Arden, Warwickshire, 1350-1540' (unpublished Ph. D. thesis, University of Birmingham, 1989), pp. 208-9, 230-1.

[21] N. Davis (ed.), *Paston Letters and Papers of the Fifteenth Century*, 2 vols (Oxford, 1971-6), i, pp. 227, 236, 247, 252, 263.

Mountfords, Alice de Bryene of Acton (Suffolk), the widow of a minor baron, and institutions of middling rank like Halesowen Abbey (Worcestershire), Merton College, Oxford, and Mettingham College in Suffolk. All received incomes in the range of £200 to £400 per annum.

They were more likely than the magnates after 1400 to retain at least one manor in direct management and so to victual the household directly. Some of them bought supplies from London, but the extent to which they did this depended on accessibility. The Stonors, whose house was situated in the Chilterns near to the Thames, bought a wide range of goods from London in the 1430s and 1470s which included, as well as the usual wine, fish, cloth and spices, such mundane rural produce as rushes; and the Pastons, with members of the family spending so much of their time on legal business in the capital, were able to make many purchases there also.[22] But the Luttrells, in the first quarter of the fifteenth century, and Sir William Mountford in 1433/4, both living more than 100 miles from London, bought very little there, apart from high-quality clothing.[23] The goods that the magnates obtained from London merchants – fish, wine, pewter and so on – were purchased by second-rank households in provincial towns, such as Bridgwater, Reading, Lichfield, Worcester and Beccles, and in regional capitals and ports such as Coventry, Bristol and Ipswich, if they were near enough. Households at this social level often owned houses in the regional capitals, like the de Norwichs' stone house in the Coslany suburb of Norwich, which they occupied in the early fourteenth century, and the house in Coventry where the Catesbys stayed, which they used as a base for buying and storing goods.[24] The longest journeys made by such purchasers took them to the coastal towns – for example from Halesowen to Boston – to obtain fish. Like the magnates, in the fifteenth century they patronised Stourbridge Fair, not just those who lived in East Anglia, such as Alice de Bryene, but also the Midland knight Sir William Mountford.[25]

These middle-ranking landlords made more use of the facilities of the smaller towns than did their social superiors. Some of these lay very near to their residences, like Dunster beneath the walls of the Luttrells' castle, or in the vicinity: Henley-on-Thames for the Stonors, Coleshill in the case of Mountford, and Dudley and Walsall for Halesowen.[26] These visits to small

[22] PRO, C47 37/2; C47/37/7, fo. 24; C.L. Kingsford (ed.), *The Stonor Letters and Papers, 1290-1483*, 2 vols (Camden Soc., 3rd ser., 29-30, 1919), ii, nos 164, 252.

[23] Somerset RO, DD/L P1 and P37; H. Maxwell-Lyte, *History of Dunster* (London, 1909), pp. 99-100; Shakespeare's Birthplace Trust RO (hereafter SBT), DR 37/73.

[24] British Library, Add. Roll 63207; F. Blomefield, *An Essay Towards a Topographical History of the County of Norfolk*, 11 vols (1805-10), iv, p. 485; PRO, E 101/511/15; E 101/512/5.

[25] V.B. Redstone (ed.), *The Household Book of Dame Alice de Bryene* (Suffolk Institute of Archaeology and Hist., 1931), pp. 120, 123, 135-6.

[26] For the Luttrells, Stonors, and Mountford, see notes 22 and 23 above; for Halesowen, see Society of Antiquaries' Library, London, MS 535.

towns reflect two characteristics of the domestic economy of such lords. Firstly, in the case of the laity, their relative lack of mobility meant that they built up a long-term commercial relationship with local traders, who could lay in supplies of goods suitable for the 'big house' down the road. Secondly, a higher proportion of their spending than was the case with the magnates went on baskets of miscellaneous shopping, with fresh meat or fish figuring prominently, which the small-scale retailers of the market towns could supply without difficulty. This is apparent from the jottings of expenditure made during Lent in 1473 by an official of the household of Henry Langley, a wealthy esquire from north-west Essex, who was constantly sending out to Saffron Walden and Bishop's Stortford. A typical day's purchases, for Saturday 3 April, consisted of 100 white herrings, 200 oysters, eels, a thornback and some pack thread for mending a carpet, all for 3s. 2d.[27]

In general the commercial patterns revealed by the accounts of the second-rank households show much local diversity. The Mountford household at Kingshurst was sited only 13 miles from Halesowen Abbey, yet the towns used by the two establishments were markedly different (see Fig. 13.2). This may simply reflect the different dates at which the purchases were recorded (1433/4 for the Mountford household, and 1365/7 for Halesowen), but is more likely to result from the location of the households in distinct commercial hinterlands. Both lay within the large marketing zone surrounding the regional centre of Coventry, and both bought goods from the important river port of Worcester, but Halesowen looked to the west for its other needs, to the towns and villages of Worcestershire and south Staffordshire; it had long-distance links with Bristol and Boston. The Kingshurst household faced more to the east and south-east, and sent to Stourbridge rather than Boston for its fish. Our other documented households are too widely scattered to observe such local variations in detail, though it is worth noting that the household of the Luttrells, near the Somerset/Devon border, was sited just within the area of influence of Bristol and its satellites such as Bridgwater, but households a little to the west would no doubt have looked more to Exeter.

We should not expect geography to determine rigidly the decision-making of individuals, whose tastes and preferences, as the Paston letters show so plainly, could influence the choice of shopping centres. Feudal relationships could have an effect on the choice of market, as when Hugh Luttrell bought much of his fish from the small port of Minehead, where as lord he had the right of preemption at very advantageous prices. Lords could be opportunists, again well illustrated by Luttrell, who went off to campaign against the rebellion of Glyn Dwr in 1405/6, and in Wales

[27] PRO, E 101/516/9, fo.1.

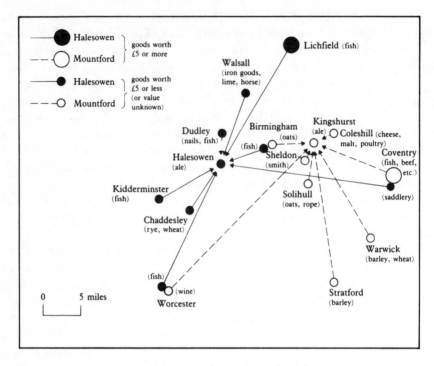

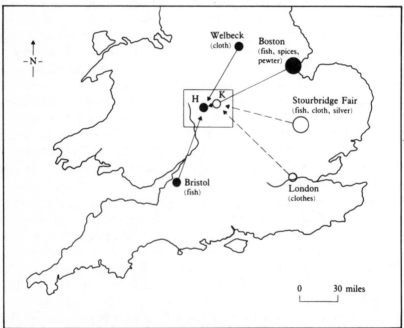

Fig. 13.2 Purchases by Halesowen Abbey, 1365–7,
and by Sir William Mountford, 1433–4.

evidently found that cattle could be obtained very cheaply, so he bought a herd of forty-one head and sent them back by boat across the Bristol Channel for consumption by his household. An accident of personal contact might result in an unexpected purchase from a small place; for example, Merton College bought cloth at Wantage in Berkshire in 1298/9, when John de Wantage was serving as subwarden.[28]

Investigating the spending patterns of the gentry and clergy who received incomes of £100 or less is by no means easy because of the shortage of good documents. Institutions situated in or very near to a large town naturally relied on local suppliers. This must be assumed from the accounts of Munden's chantry at Bridport in Dorset in the 1450s, because the price of foodstuffs, building materials, and other items is given but not the place where they were bought. The occasional reference to nearby villages as sources of straw and timber suggests that the usual venue for purchases was Bridport itself.[29] The accounts survive for St Radegund's Priory, a poor small nunnery on the outskirts of Cambridge, for the mid-fifteenth century. As befitted a house with an endowment worth £75 per annum, three or four times the income of the Bridport priests, the nuns of St Radegund's had wider commercial horizons.[30] They obtained some goods and services as far afield as Ely, Lynn and St Ives, but most of their dealings were with Cambridge traders, or with those attending fairs held in or near the town. This provides a considerable contrast with King's College, though there is some similarity between the two institutions in their sources of supply of turf, tiles and cheese from villages within 10 miles of Cambridge. The priory's situation on the eastern side of Cambridge led it to buy from villages in that direction, while King's College bought over the whole neighbourhood.

A north Derbyshire gentry family, the Eyres (the account books of the 1470s probably derive from the branch of the family living at Hassop), sent a horse regularly to the local market towns – Sheffield most often, then Chesterfield, followed by Rotherham and Chapel-en-le-Frith (see Fig. 13.3).[31] Small quantities of specialised products came from places as far away as Cheshire (salt), Burton-on-Trent (beer) and Lenton Fair near Nottingham. Equally dependent on local sources were the Giffards of Weston Subedge in Gloucestershire who in the 1440s bought their wine

[28] Highfield (ed.), *Early Rolls of Merton*, pp. 181, 184.
[29] K.L. Wood-Legh, *A Small Household of the Fifteenth Century* (Manchester, 1956), especially pp. 14, 78.
[30] A.G. Ray, *The Priory of St Radegund, Cambridge* (Cambridge Antiquarian Society, 1898), pp. 145-79.
[31] Bodleian Library, Oxford, MS DD Per Weld C 19/4/2-4. I have consulted these documents, but have relied mainly on a transcript made by Dr Ian Blanchard, for whose help I am most grateful. On the family, R. Meredith, 'The Eyres of Hassop, 1470-1640', *Derbyshire Archaeological Journal*, 84 (1964), pp. 1-51.

from Worcester, but seem to have made most use of the traders of Chipping Campden and Evesham, both small towns within 6 miles, as well as patronising surrounding villages.[32] Perhaps the least affluent of the gentry for whom we have records, Thomas Bozoun of Woodford (Northamptonshire), constantly sent out to the small borough of Higham Ferrers in 1348, though he may have had the opportunity to make purchases on his occasional visits to the county town to attend court sessions or to watch jousting.[33]

The Eyres found much of their cattle, grain, and dairy produce in the north Derbyshire countryside. A high proportion of their woollen cloth was woven and fulled by country craftsmen. For example, Jack Thomasson agreed to produce a total of 123 yards of cloth for them in 1472, though it is instructive to note the influence of the urban calendar on a contract made between a rural client and a rural weaver, because the job was to be completed by the Friday before Chesterfield Fair. The Eyres' accounts demonstrate conclusively a pattern that is discernible in other, more fragmentary gentry records. They shopped in market towns, but not in the smallest centres. They preferred places like Chesterfield or Sheffield, with populations of more than 1,000 and an appropriate range of goods and services, and made few visits to the lesser places with more limited facilities, such as Bakewell or Castleton.[34]

An extrapolation from the known to the unknown would lead us to predict that the small market towns (places with between 300 and 1,000 inhabitants, which account for the bulk of the 600 known boroughs) and the 1,500 or so market villages served the needs of groups who have left us no household accounts, such as the minor gentry, clergy, peasants and artisans.[35] In fact a good deal about the market contacts of such people can be learned from records of their debts.

Two examples of individuals for whom a number of debts are recorded are Thomas Hobbyn of Norton Subedge (Gloucestershire), and William Gibbes of Blockley in the same county (see Fig. 13.4).[36] Hobbyn died in 1447, and Gibbes made his will in 1529. Hobbyn's debts suit well the purposes of this enquiry because they were owed by him, and therefore probably related to his purchases of goods or services. Most of his creditors lived in villages within a 6-mile radius, but two of them lived 8 miles away,

[32] Dorset RO, D 10/M231.

[33] G.H. Fowler, 'A household expense roll, 1328', *Eng. Hist. Rev.*, 55 (1940), pp. 630-4. Woolgar (see note 5 above), dates this document to 1348.

[34] J.M. Bestall, *History of Chesterfield, i: Early and Medieval Chesterfield* (Chesterfield, 1974), pp. 71-96; S.I. Tucker, *The Descent of the Manor of Sheffield* (London, 1894), pp. 12-15 for the two towns.

[35] R.H. Hilton, 'Medieval market towns and simple commodity production', *Past and Present*, 109 (1985), pp. 3-23; M.W. Beresford and H.P.R. Finberg, *English Medieval Boroughs* (Newton Abbot, 1973), pp. 21-57; Britnell, 'Proliferation of markets', p. 210.

[36] Dorset RO, D 10/M233; Hereford and Worcester RO, ref. 008:7 BA 3590 fo. 104.

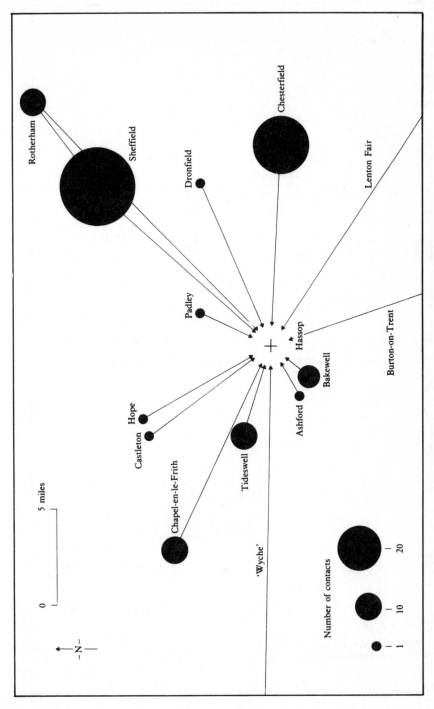

Fig. 13.3 Purchases of the Eyres of Hassop, Derbyshire, 1472–6.

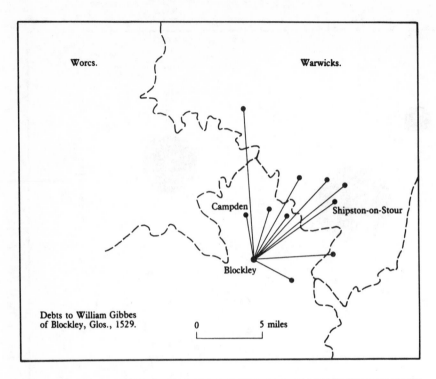

Debts to William Gibbes
of Blockley, Glos., 1529.

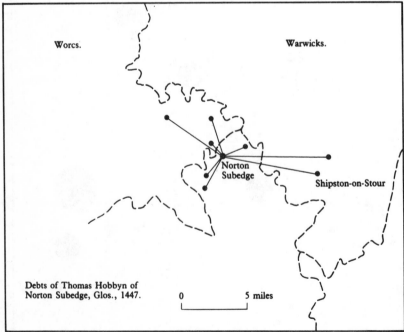

Debts of Thomas Hobbyn of
Norton Subedge, Glos., 1447.

Fig. 13.4 Peasant debts.

one in the very small town of Shipston-on-Stour. Gibbes's will records debts owed to him, perhaps resulting from the sale of sheep; certainly they show a strong directional pattern towards the valley below the Cotswolds, and like Hobbyn's contacts were mostly confined within a distance of 8 miles. The debtors were mainly villagers; one of the two townsmen lived at the quite important local market town of Chipping Campden, and the other again came from the very modest centre at Shipston. In neither of these examples can we be sure how the debts had originated, but in pleas pursued through manorial courts more details are given. Debt cases from Stoneleigh in Warwickshire show that its inhabitants were naturally drawn into the commercial life of the neighbouring great city of Coventry. In 1433 John Couper of Coventry brought a case against Robert Lewys of Ashow alleging that he owed him 3s. $11\frac{1}{2}$d. for nineteen barrel hoops. Another case reveals that either an urban craftsman, or a chapman, had come into the country to sell, because in 1490 John Stanlowe of Coventry claimed that he had not been paid 2s. 11d. for three pairs of hose that John Hall of Finham (a hamlet of Stoneleigh) had bought from him in 1482 at Stoneleigh.[37] Such debts also arose in other places from purchases made in small market towns. Shipston-on-Stour figures once more in the records of Thornton in Ettington (Warwickshire) in 1376, when William Webbe of Shipston sued Richard Stele for a debt, the cause of which is not given, but in view of Webbe's name could well have originated in a contract to weave cloth.[38]

In the great majority of debt pleas both parties lived in rural settlements. Disputes coming before the court of Kirton-in-Lindsey in Lincolnshire in 1319/20 arose from separate sales of an ox for 10s., 2 quarters of barley for 11s. and 4 stones of hemp for an unstated price.[39] In the same county at Toynton All Saints in 1428-30 pleas between villagers concerned the sale of a boat on one occasion, a contract to repair a boat on another, and the sale of a pair of cart wheels on a third.[40] Similar transactions could be cited in their hundreds, and demonstrate that a wide range of consumers' requirements, not just for agricultural products and equipment, but also for many types of manufactured goods and specialised services, could be satisfied by dealing with peasant neighbours and rural craftsmen and traders. This was true in particular of those regions, such as East Anglia or the wood-pasture districts of the Midlands, where country-dwellers followed an especially wide variety of occupations. And everywhere villages had their sellers of food and drink, notably of ale.

The peasants' commercial range was shorter than that of the aristocrats, but their transactions often took them outside their immediate

---

[37] PRO, SC 2 207/79; SBT, DR18/25.
[38] Warwickshire RO, CR 1911/1.
[39] Lincolnshire RO, KR 96, 97, 98.
[40] Lincolnshire RO, Anc 3/18/55/1-3; 3/18/56/3.

neighbourhood. If we assume that contacts beyond their home villages would reflect peasants' journeys made for commercial reasons, then it is worth noting that the patterns of migration into small towns in the thirteenth century often fell within a limit of 16 miles, and that the majority of emigrating serfs in the late fourteenth and fifteenth centuries moved no more than 10 miles.[41] Another indirect guide to the marketing horizons of country dwellers can be gained from the places mentioned in their wills, using in this case a sample of fifty west Suffolk wills of the fifteenth century.[42] Places were often cited by the testators for pious or personal reasons. They bequeathed money or goods to friends, relatives and churches out of affection and respect; they may well have become familiar with a place outside their parish through their own migration or that of a close relative, or because of a link established by marriage. Whatever the occasion for the contacts, they are likely to have occurred within a territory made familiar to individuals by their economic activity, predominantly through buying and selling. The places mentioned lay within a relatively short distance of the will-makers' homes, in 86 per cent of cases within 12 miles. Urban places accounted for 40 per cent of those mentioned, a proportion which was given a considerable lift by the fashion for leaving small sums to the friars, whose houses always lay in towns. Large urban centres such as Bury St Edmunds and Ipswich were mentioned, and also very small places like Newmarket, the East Anglian equivalent of Shipston-on-Stour. To sum up, it seems reasonable to conclude that groups below the gentry bought goods in towns of all sizes, depending on their proximity, and that they made proportionately greater use of the very small market towns which appear infrequently in the household accounts. Peasantry and aristocracy had a common characteristic in their consumption patterns: their habitual purchase of goods and services in the countryside.

How Did Consumers Make their Purchases?

The organisation and mechanics of purchase varied with the wealth and status of the consumer. For their major acquisitions of bulky and expensive goods the magnates would either travel in person, or more often send high-ranking officials, to a fair or to London to negotiate with the merchants. They would arrange the transport themselves, either in vehicles or boats belonging to the household, or by hiring them, as in the complicated journey by both water and land between Boston and Durham Priory for a

[41] E.M. Carus-Wilson, 'The first half-century of the borough of Stratford-upon-Avon', *Econ. Hist. Rev.*, 2nd ser., 18 (1965), p. 53; C. Dyer, *Lords and Peasants in a Changing Society: The Estates of the Bishopric of Worcester, 680-1540* (Cambridge, 1980), pp. 366-7.
[42] Suffolk RO (Bury St Edmunds Branch), 1C 500/2/9, Baldwyne.

load of cloth, furs and spices in 1299.[43] Households could not live solely on these bulk purchases, because of their desire for regular supplies of fresh food, and of their need to replenish stocks on a small scale as they ran out. So regular journeys to town were made by a servant with a pack horse. This beast was called a 'fish horse' in larger households. Such an activity can be described as 'shopping' rather than 'going to market', because although these journeys often occurred on market days, they might also involve travel on days convenient for the household, to retailers who maintained a regular daily service. Henry Langley of Essex, for example, was able to buy fish at Saffron Walden on both Wednesdays and Saturdays; the latter was probably the town's official market day, but there is no evidence that markets were held there on Wednesdays.[44] Large households would employ an agent – an *emptor* or *provisor* – to make purchases; Durham Priory had a representative who stayed at ports like Hartlepool and sent the fish on to the monastery.

Sellers sometimes took the initiative and sought out aristocratic customers. Household accounts refer to visits by tinkers or traders. A 'merchant' called on the bishop of Salisbury at Potterne in 1407 to sell a gold rosary; it seems highly likely that this was no chance encounter, but that the tradesman had made a special journey. Alice de Bryene's Suffolk household occasionally paid for 'bread for the merchant's horse', implying that the routine loads of fresh provisions originated in the town, perhaps in response to some regular order from the household, an arrangement that could easily develop in the case of this unusually static establishment. For the purchase of agricultural produce vendors and buyers sometimes met in the market place; but in estate accounts which specify whether deals were done *in foro* (in the market) or *in patria* (in the country), the latter often predominated.[45] Some household accounts give the names and place of origin of the sellers of grain or cattle, again implying that a private treaty had been made. The unusually detailed records of King's Hall, Cambridge (1337-1544), show that the college made regular contracts in advance of delivery with farmers and other rural suppliers in the villages near Cambridge, to secure supplies of wheat, malt, turf and sedge.[46] When low grain prices set in after 1375, the buyers' market must surely have brought the large-scale producers, such as the demesne farmers or the lessees of tithes, queuing at the door of a manor house when a large household arrived.

[43] Fowler (ed.), *Account Rolls of Durham*, ii, p. 495.

[44] H.A. Cronne and R.H.C. Davis (eds), *Regesta regum Anglo-Normannorum*, iii (Oxford, 1968), no. 274; *Royal Commission on Market Rights and Tolls* (P.P. 1889), iii, p. 134.

[45] PRO SC 6/988/12 shows at Stafford in 1437/8 205 qrs 2bs grain were sold *in patria*, and 1qr 2bs *in foro*; according to Gloucestershire RO, D 1099 M30/22, of 191 sheep sold by the Todenham and Bourton-on-the-Hill sheep-reeve of Westminster Abbey in 1396/7, only 30 were sold *in foro*.

[46] A.B. Cobban, *The King's Hall within the University of Cambridge in the Later Middle Ages* (Cambridge, 1969), pp. 212-15.

The better-off peasants – those with a half-yardland (15 acres of arable) or more – owned a cart or wain capable of taking a load of produce to a town, and of returning with any purchases.[47] Lower down in village society many cottagers kept a horse, especially in the fifteenth century, and women were accustomed to going to town on foot with baskets of dairy produce and other light goods for sale, and again would have had the opportunity to buy as well as to sell. The town traders themselves visited villages, leading to references in court proceedings to bakers and butchers from towns breaking the assize of bread or selling at excessive profit.[48] Chapmen and peddlars make only a shadowy appearance in the records, yet have probably left durable traces of their rural wanderings in the small copper alloy brooches, buckles and ornaments that are found in such number in archaeological excavations of rural sites. These objects are very likely to have come from their packs along with perishable goods such as small articles of clothing and items of haberdashery.[49] It should be emphasised, however, that in addition to the ubiquitous ale sellers, resident retailers of bread, meat, candles, fish and cheese plied their trades in many villages.

Sales need not have involved an immediate payment of cash. Magnates were given credit, and some of them took maximum advantage, like the first duke of Buckingham who kept some of those supplying his household without payment for thirteen years. Less prestigious aristocrats who were treating with merchants at a distance, like the Pastons buying in London, expected to pay directly, as we find when the womenfolk in Norfolk sent cash with their letters requesting the purchase of textiles or spices. All kinds of consumers were given credit when dealing with their neighbours in their own countries. The Eyres of Derbyshire maintained an elaborate set of 'counters' by which those who supplied goods or services received in exchange remission of rent, allowances in kind, and other benefits which in the end might cancel out the debt without any money changing hands. St Radegund's Priory practised simple barter when it exchanged malt for reeds. Even an ecclesiastical magnate like Fountains Abbey in the early 1450s was dealing with a carpenter called Richard Bollton, who was owed £4 3s. $10\frac{1}{2}$ d. for various jobs, by giving him a cow worth 9s., two stones of wool worth 3s., meals valued at 10s. 10d., and cash payments that brought the total to £3 9s. 4d., so that he was still out of pocket by 14s. $6\frac{1}{2}$ d. at the time of the account.[50] Such arrangements must have been even more

[47] J. Langdon, 'Horse hauling: a revolution in vehicle transport in twelfth and thirteenth century England', in T.H. Aston (ed.), *Landlords, Peasants and Politics in Medieval England* (Cambridge, 1987), pp. 51-62.

[48] Dyer, *Lords and Peasants*, p. 349.

[49] M.W. Beresford and J.G. Hurst, *Deserted Medieval Villages* (London, 1971), p. 143.

[50] J.T. Fowler (ed.), *Memorials of the Abbey of St Mary of Fountains*, iii (Surtees Soc., 130, 1918), pp. 213-14.

common in the peasant economy, as is revealed by the debt litigation of Havering atte Bower (Essex).[51] Money was always in short supply in the Middle Ages, and systems of credit and barter became even more necessary during the fifteenth-century 'bullion famine'.[52] Throughout the period, in a pattern of behaviour with ancient roots, the aristocracy practised gift exchange, by which goods of all kinds (but especially prestigious game, wine and freshwater fish) were sent to other households as expressions of mutual esteem, deference, or patronage.

Finally, the relationship between consumers and craftsmen deserves some examination. It is well known that in large-scale building projects either the patron could make a bargain with a mason or carpenter, who would act as a contractor, buying materials and obtaining labour to carry out the work, or alternatively the lord could put the detailed organisation in the hands of an administrator, who would hire workers and account for all of the costs incurred. It is often assumed in relation to cloth-making, in which the main manufacture involved a succession of separate processes, that clothiers took control of production, and that consumers would usually buy the completed cloth from the entrepreneur. In fact it was a common practice, recorded mainly but not exclusively among the middle and lower ranks of the aristocracy, to employ the craftsmen directly, and so to dispense with intermediaries. The craftsmen were paid by the yard or the ell for their work. In 1392/3, for example, John Catesby of Ashby St Ledgers (Northamptonshire) had a piece of blanket woven and fulled for 2s. 6d.; weaving and fulling a piece of russett cost 3s. 6d., with shearing 6d. extra; and an evidently superior piece of 'white russett' was woven for 3s. 8d. and fulled and sheared for 4s. 6d.[53] The thinking behind direct employment of craftsmen, both in building and in clothmaking, as in the purchase of luxuries in London, was that the exclusion of the middlemen would allow a reduction in cost and give the consumer more choice. Aristocrats preferred to buy goods as near as possible to their point of origin. Nor were such arrangements confined to the aristocratic consumers. In a countryside permeated by craftsmen of all kinds, like that of central Essex, peasants could make direct bargains with artisans, as was revealed when an uncompleted contract resulted in litigation in a manorial court. For example, John Geffrey of East Hanningfield sent 18 pounds of wool to be dyed, intended ultimately for weaving into cloth for a bed, but he was

[51] M.K. McIntosh, *Autonomy and Community: The Royal Manor of Havering, 1200-1500* (Cambridge, 1986), pp. 166-170. See also, N.J. Mayhew, 'Money and prices in England from Henry II to Edward III', *Agricultural History Review*, 35 (1987), p. 121.

[52] J. Day, 'The great bullion famine of the fifteenth century', in idem, *The Medieval Market Economy* (Oxford, 1987), pp. 1-54.

[53] PRO, E 101/511/15.

executed for his part in the rebellion of 1381 before the job was done, leaving his widow to bring a law suit against the artisan, John Rybode.[54]

Conclusions

These observations of the varying patterns of consumers' behaviour in the market suggest a number of general conclusions about the late medieval economy and its changing character.

First, a striking feature of the consumption evidence is the large number of transactions that were made outside a town or formal market. Private treaty sales of grain in which bargains were struck in the fields, or in an inn over a small sample of the crop are often thought to have been a modern development. Clearly such methods had a long medieval ancestry. In 1293/4, Worcester Priory, situated a few minutes' walk from a major corn market, obtained only $7\frac{1}{2}$ quarters of wheat in the market out of a total of 228 quarters purchased.[55] It is true that markets at their height in the late thirteenth and early fourteenth centuries could be very busy places, as their annual toll income shows. The £15 6s. 8d. per annum for which Oakham market in Rutland was farmed in the 1290s must represent payments on thousands of sales, at such rates of toll as a penny on a horse or cow, or a penny on a cartload.[56] Who then was using these institutions? They were designed to bring together the largest possible numbers of sellers and buyers who were unknown to one other. They were ideally suited for traders from a distance (like the drovers who brought northern and Welsh cattle into the beast markets of the Midlands), and for small-scale traders wishing to pick up commodities for eventual resale. They were also useful for those buying small quantities of goods: gentry households could obtain a joint of meat or a pound of spices, and poorer households a bushel of grain or a loaf of bread. The weekly rhythm of the market fitted the shopping patterns of people who were paid by the week, as seems to have been the case with many urban journeymen. The market also provided the most convenient opportunity for country people to gather at a local centre, confident of the presence of buyers for their produce, and where goods such as textiles, clothes, shoes, metal goods and agricultural equipment would be offered for sale in affordable quantities – a few yards of cloth, a pair of boots, a set of horseshoes, and so on.

---

[54] Essex RO, D/DP M833.

[55] J.M. Wilson and C. Gordon (eds), *Early Compotus Rolls of the Priory of Worcester* (Worcs. Hist. Soc., 1908), pp. 22-3.

[56] L.M. Midgley (ed.), *Ministers' Accounts of the Earldom of Cornwall, 1296-1297* (Camden Soc., 3rd ser., 66, 67, 1942, 1945), ii, p. 160; *Royal Commission on Market Rights*, i, pp. 69-70.

Yet even the peasantry made many purchases outside the chartered markets. Presumably they attended the more informal trading places that dotted the medieval countryside – the *congregationes* in village streets and in remote places that make a fleeting appearance in our documents; or they patronised the concentrations of retailers in villages which were acquiring a semi-urban character without the aid either of borough status or of a formal market.[57] They bought from the 'village shops', or they made arrangements with rural craftsmen for their more specialised needs.

These patterns of behaviour made the town markets very vulnerable to competition. Slumps in toll revenues, much sharper than the fall in population or in the general volume of trade, give ample testimony to the decline of small markets in the fifteenth century. There was much buying and selling, but such was the commercial vitality of the countryside that many transactions bypassed the market places entirely. Rural trade, as well as rural industry, could be a formidable rival for the towns.

Secondly, the revelation of the limited importance of the towns as the locations for commercial contacts between traders and consumers should lead us to re-examine the interaction between town and country. The urban market place and the retailer's house did provide meeting places and points of sale for rural customers, but we should never underestimate the internal exchanges that went on between townspeople, which must account for a great deal of urban commercial activity. Many of those in service occupations or the food trades relied for their living mainly on satisfying urban demand. A town's fortunes were not necessarily bound up entirely with those of its immediate hinterland, as has been shown in the case of Colchester, which drew some of its food supplies from Norfolk, and sold much of its cloth in European markets.[58]

Thirdly, we can learn about the changes in the larger towns from the evidence of upper-class spending. The common assertion that the trade taking place in fairs during the thirteenth century later shifted to the towns and especially to London is confirmed by the evidence of consumption. Yet the vitality of Stourbridge throughout the fifteenth century shows that the fairs should not be dismissed as commercial centres, nor should we forget that the merchants who traded at the fairs came from the major towns, and took their profits back to such places as Lincoln, York and London. It is well known from studies of such trades as the skinners and grocers that the

[57] P.H. Sawyer, 'Early markets and fairs in England and Scandinavia', in B.L. Anderson and A.J.H. Latham (eds), *The Market and History* (London, 1986), pp. 64-5.
[58] R.H. Britnell, *Growth and Decline in Colchester, 1300-1525* (Cambridge, 1986), pp. 163-80, 246-53.

luxury trades became increasingly concentrated in London, to the detriment of provincial centres such as Winchester and Southampton. This partly reflects London's position as a capital to which aristocratic households were drawn for political and social reasons, and partly the preference of the consumers for buying at the quayside. The larger towns did not lose all their wealthy customers at this time, but as the spending power of the landed aristocracy slipped, the provincial merchants found themselves serving a smaller share of a declining market.[59]

Fourthly, records of actual spending suggest that we should be wary of linking towns too readily with the great lords who founded them or who lived in their vicinity. We see urban communities now lying outside the gates of a monastery or castle, and assume that they prospered in the Middle Ages from provisioning their rich neighbour. It is true that a place like Chelmsford benefited from a boom when nearby Writtle was sheltering a ducal household demanding vast deliveries of ale. But a duke led a wandering life, his movements were unpredictable, and his intermittent purchases provided a slender basis for a permanent urban economy. Many households brewed for themselves, and there were few other commodities in a small town's repertoire of goods that a grand lord wished to buy. The records of a static household, such as that of Battle Abbey, show that many of the monks' needs were satisfied by remote towns, and the people of Battle must have gained at least as much trade from the abbey's servants and tenants as from the wealthy lord. This is confirmed by the survival, and indeed the continued prosperity, of many monastic boroughs after the dissolution. Secular lords of middle rank, like the Shropshire Talbots in the early fifteenth century, stayed for long periods in one place, and their presence benefited the local town, in their case Whitchurch, from which they bought much ale.[60] However, in order to flourish, the town would need to attract many other customers.

Lastly, the economy of many small towns seems to have been bound up with the spending of consumers of modest means, above all the peasantry. Despite their small surpluses, these quite poor people cumulatively generated a huge demand. If each household in *c.* 1300 bought 4 yards of cloth each year, total consumption would have exceeded 2,000 miles. Every adult's requirement of a pair of shoes each year gave employment to thousands of cordwainers. Some small towns eked out a living at that time by servicing a poor local clientele. As population declined in the fourteenth and fifteenth centuries, and the survivors gained higher wages and cultivated larger areas of land, some small towns declined or even lost their urban

[59] R.B. Dobson, 'Urban decline in late medieval England', *Transactions of the Royal Historical Society*, 5th ser., 27 (1977), pp. 1-22.

[60] B. Ross, 'The accounts of the Talbot household at Blakemere in the county of Shropshire, 1394-1425' (unpublished M.A. thesis, Australian National University, 1970), pp. 89-127.

functions. Many markets located in villages ceased to exist. Their former customers could now afford the time and the transport to travel a little further to larger towns which offered a wider choice. Among the success stories of the period of late medieval urban decline were market towns with populations of 1,000 or so which could cater for a large hinterland of rural customers, and those which developed specialities, like Walden's saffron, or Walsall's horse-bits, allowing them to trade beyond their traditionally restricted commercial territory.[61]

---

[61] R.H. Hilton, *Class Conflict and the Crisis of Feudalism* (London, 1985), pp. 190, 259; *VCH Essex*, ii, pp. 360-1; *VCH Staffs.*, xvii, pp. 194-5.

14

The Hidden Trade of the Middle Ages: Evidence from the West Midlands

Modern interpretations of the medieval economy are assigning an increased importance to trade. Commerce both fuelled the great expansion of the long thirteenth century (*c.* 1180-1330), and influenced economic developments after the Black Death of 1348-9, for example by encouraging agricultural specialisation.[1] Such views have found scant support in historical writings of the recent past. Postan preferred to see changes in population and the availability of land as the main influence on the cycle of expansion and subsequent contraction, and in his textbook he relegated towns and trade to the last chapters;[2] even Postan's most radical critic, Brenner, agrees with him that trade played a secondary role.[3] These opinions, especially in relation to the English economy, receive statistical support from Bairoch's team's work on urban population. They calculate that in *c.* 1300 about 14 per cent of Europe's inhabitants lived in towns (which they call 'cities') with populations in excess of 2,000, rising to about 18 per cent in 1400. The contributions made by the 'United Kingdom' (modern political units are used) to this overall total seems slight. In 1300, while a fifth or more of the inhabitants of 'Belgium', Italy, and Spain lived in towns with more than 5,000 people, 'cities' in the 'U.K.' could account for less than one in twenty of the population, 4.4 per cent to be precise.[4]

New research suggests that we should not write off the medieval English urban sector so readily. Demographic calculations for the larger towns,

---

[1] P. Spufford, *Money and its Use in Medieval Europe* (Cambridge, 1988), pp. 240-63; B.M.S. Campbell, 'Towards an agricultural geography of medieval England', *Agricultural History Review*, 36 (1988), pp. 87-98; J. Langdon, *Horses, Oxen and Technological Innovation* (Cambridge, 1986), pp. 287-8.

[2] M.M. Postan, *The Medieval Economy and Society* (London, 1972), especially pp. 183-206.

[3] R. Brenner, 'Agrarian class structure and economic development in pre-industrial Europe', in T.H. Aston and C.H.E. Philpin (eds), *The Brenner Debate* (Cambridge, 1985), especially pp. 25-9.

[4] P. Bairoch, J. Baton and P. Chèvre, *The Population of European Cities from 800-1850* (Geneva, 1988), pp. 253-61.

unfortunately carried out after Bairoch's group gathered their figures, indicate that they contained more people than was previously thought. London, once believed to have had a population of about 50,000 in *c.* 1300 could, according to recent revisions, have accommodated 80,000 or more.[5] The estimated population of Norwich in the early fourteenth century has been revised upward from about 10,000 to 20,000 and for Winchester the figures have risen from 4,000 to 10,000 or 12,000.[6] If these figures, based partly on close topographical analysis and sources not previously used, were to be applied generally to the larger towns, then Bairoch's figure for the 'U.K.' could well be doubled. Neither do Bairoch's figures tally with our enhanced appreciation of the deep roots of English urban life resulting from archaeological research. The more important towns of the thirteenth century can often be shown to have been large and well-established in the tenth, and in the case of Canterbury, Ipswich, London, Norwich, Southampton and York (allowing for some shifts in site) their commercial and industrial past can be taken back to the seventh and eighth centuries.[7] Recent work on Domesday suggests that J.C. Russell was by no means mistaken in thinking that a tenth of the population in 1086 lived in towns, and we can scarcely believe that the urban proportion had diminished in the twelfth and thirteenth centuries.[8]

Of course the problem hinges on definitions of 'towns' and our assessment of the urban hierarchy. Terms such as 'city' which derive from administration and law cannot be used to define urbanism, which is an economic and social concept. A town is best characterised as 'a relatively dense and permanent concentration of residents engaged in a multiplicity of activities, a substantial proportion of which are non-agrarian'.[9] Population thresholds such as 2,000 cannot be used to isolate the urban communities, because many places which have all of the required features are found to have contained only a few hundred inhabitants – perhaps as few as 300.[10]

[5]   D. Keene, 'A new study of London before the Great Fire', *Urban History Yearbook* (1984), pp. 11-21.

[6]   E. Rutledge, 'Immigration and population growth in early fourteenth-century Norwich: evidence from the tithing roll', *Urban History Yearbook* (1988), pp. 15-30; D. Keene, *Survey of Medieval Winchester* (Winchester Studies 2, Oxford, 1985), part 1, pp. 366-8.

[7]   R. Hodges and B. Hobley (eds), *The Rebirth of Towns in the West* (Council for British Archaeology Research Report 68, 1988), pp. 69-108, 125-32; T. Tatton-Brown and N. Macpherson-Grant, 'Anglo-Saxon Canterbury', *Current Archaeology*, 98 (1985), pp. 89-93; A. Carter, 'The Anglo-Saxon origins of Norwich: the problem and approaches', *Anglo-Saxon England*, 7 (1978), pp. 175-204.

[8]   J.C. Russell, *British Medieval Population* (Albuquerque, 1948), pp. 45-54; H.C. Darby, *Domesday England* (Cambridge, 1977), pp. 88-9.

[9]   R. Holt and G. Rosser, 'Introduction: the English town in the Middle Ages', in R. Holt and A.G. Rosser (eds), *The Medieval Town* (London, 1990), p. 4. A similar definition is given in S. Reynolds, *An Introduction to the History of English Medieval Towns* (Oxford, 1977), pp. ix-x.

[10]   R.H. Hilton, *The English Peasantry in the Later Middle Ages* (Oxford, 1975), pp. 77-80.

Inclusion of the numerous small towns will make a considerable difference to our estimates of the size of the urban sector. Using Beresford and Finberg's convenient list we can estimate that in 1300 there were 450 small boroughs with a combined population well in excess of 250,000, or 5 per cent of the inhabitants of England.[11] But this involves taking too easy a short cut, because 'borough' is as dangerously misleading a term as 'city': it is a constitutional, not an economic category.

The number and size of towns help us to appreciate not just the importance of the commercial sector, but also to make an assessment of the productivity of agriculture.[12] We have learned to recognise that the countryside had become deeply involved in trade by the late thirteenth century. Lords sent much demesne grain, wool and animals for sale. Peasants went to market to sell their produce partly to pay rents and taxes, and partly to buy goods. Many peasant households, contrary to legend, were not self-sufficient, but regularly bought clothing, tools and foodstuffs. Almost half of peasants lacked enough land to feed their own households, and those with larger holdings found it convenient to buy their bread, ale, joints of meat, pies and puddings from neighbours or from local markets.[13] Throughout the country a sprinkling of rural craftsmen, and in some regions denser concentrations of industrial workers, required markets for the goods that they made, and the opportunity to buy food. We now realise that the peasant land market revealed in the court rolls of the thirteenth century was a real market and not an exchange of parcels between families, depending on their subsistence needs.[14] The markets for land and produce were closely connected, and successful peasants used their profits to expand their acreage. More than a thousand village markets were founded by 1349, indicating the close network of rural trade; as with the boroughs, however, we must beware of using a legal institution as the sole basis for identifying trading places.[15]

[11] M.W. Beresford and H.P.R. Finberg, *English Medieval Boroughs: A Handlist* (Newton Abbot, 1973); M.W. Beresford, 'English medieval boroughs: a handlist: revisions 1973-81', *Urban History Yearbook* (1981), pp. 59-65.

[12] E.A. Wrigley, 'Urban growth and agricultural change: England and the continent in the early modern period', *Journal of Interdisciplinary History*, 15 (1985), pp. 683-728.

[13] C. Dyer, *Standards of Living in the Later Middle Ages* (Cambridge, 1989), pp. 110-18, 151-60.

[14] P.D.A. Harvey (ed.), *The Peasant Land Market in Medieval England* (Oxford, 1984), pp. 19-28; R.M. Smith (ed.), *Land, Kinship and Life-cycle* (Cambridge, 1984), pp. 6-21.

[15] R.H. Britnell, 'The proliferation of markets in England, 1200-1349', *Economic History Review*, 2nd series, 34 (1981), pp. 209-21.

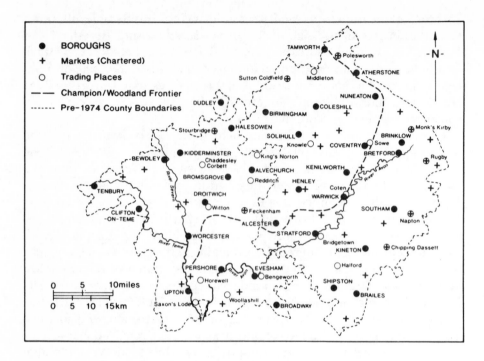

Fig. 14.1 Warwickshire and Worcestershire (pre-1974 modern boundaries), showing boroughs and markets pre-1500 and the trading places mentioned

The Trading System of the West Midland Region

The pattern of medieval trade is best understood on a regional basis, and the bulk of this paper will be concerned with identifying the full range of towns and commercial centres in the English West Midlands. This will involve investigating both the officially recognised boroughs and markets, and some places which are normally hidden from view. The counties of Warwick and Worcester contained contrasting rural landscapes. In the woodlands of the west and north (including the Warwickshire Arden), were dispersed settlements, irregular field systems and mixed land use. The feldon landscapes in the south and east of both counties were characterised by nucleated villages, open fields and extensive cereal cultivation.[16] (Fig. 14.1).

[16] R.H. Hilton, *Social Structure of Rural Warwickshire in the Middle Ages* (Dugdale Society Occasional Paper, 9, 1950); J.B. Harley, 'Population trends and agricultural developments from the Warwickshire Hundred Rolls of 1279', *Economic History Review*, 2nd series, 11 (1958–9), pp. 8-18; J.B. Harley, 'The settlement geography of early medieval Warwickshire', *Transactions of the Institute of British Geographers*, 34 (1964), pp. 115-30; B.K. Roberts, 'Field systems of the West Midlands', in A.H.R. Baker and R.A. Butlin (eds), *Studies of Field Systems in the British Isles* (Cambridge, 1973), pp. 188-231; C. Dyer, *Warwickshire Farming 1349-c. 1520* (Dugdale Society Occasional Paper, 27, 1981).

Water transport along the Severn connected the region with the Bristol Channel. A network of roads was focused on the towns. These included Worcester (a cathedral city in the seventh century, a fortified *burh* in the ninth, and shire capital in the tenth), Droitwich, an important salt-making centre, and Coventry which was made a see of a bishopric by 1102, and by the late thirteenth century had become the largest town in the region. Tamworth, and probably Warwick, were important in the administration of the Mercian kingdom, and were strongly fortified in the tenth century. The latter became the head of a new shire.[17] Besides these five towns, twenty-seven places with the status of borough (fifteen in Warwickshire, twelve in Worcestershire) appear in the records between the eleventh and fourteenth century, and especially in the period 1190-1270.[18] These were privileged institutions, where the burgesses held plots of land by burgage tenure, which varied from place to place, but normally included a fixed annual cash rent such as 8d., 12d. or 16d., and the freedom to buy, sell and bequeath land. The burgesses could trade without payment of market tolls. Boroughs were usually founded within a manor, and afterwards became jurisdictionally distinct from the rural 'foreign'.[19] They were commonly laid out as a planned pattern of streets, with measured plots of a standard size and shape.[20]

Every borough had a market, but in addition many markets were held in villages with no claim to borough status. Accordingly chartered markets far exceeded the number of boroughs – forty-two in Warwickshire, and twenty-five in Worcestershire, making a total of sixty-seven.[21] Again we are dealing with an institution, a royal franchise granted to a lord, which conferred on him the right to take tolls and which gave him protection from rival markets in the vicinity.

[17] Worcester: P.A. Barker (ed.), *The Origins of Worcester* (being the *Transactions of the Worcestershire Archaeological Society*, 3rd series, 2, 1968-9), especially pp. 7-33; M.O.H. Carver (ed.), *Medieval Worcester* (being the *Transactions of the Worcestershire Archaeological Society*, 3rd series, 7, 1980), especially pp. 1-64; Droitwich: D. Freezer, *From Saltings to Spa Town* (Droitwich, 1977); Coventry: P.R. Coss (ed.), *The Early Records of Medieval Coventry* (British Academy Records of Social and Economic History, new series, 11, 1986), pp. xv-xlii; Tamworth: P.A. Rahtz, 'The archaeology of west Mercian towns', in A. Dornier (ed.), *Mercian Studies* (Leicester, 1977), pp. 107-29; Warwick: T.R. Slater, 'The origins of Warwick', *Midland History*, 8 (1983), pp. 1-13.

[18] Beresford and Finberg, *English Medieval Boroughs*; Beresford, 'English medieval boroughs'.

[19] Reynolds, *Introduction to the History of English Medieval Towns*, p. 93; M. de W. Hemmeon, *Burgage Tenure in Medieval England* (Cambridge, Mass. 1914), pp. 107-53.

[20] T.R. Slater, 'Urban genesis and medieval town plans in Warwickshire and Worcestershire', in T.R. Slater and P.J. Jarvis (eds), *Field and Forest, An Historical Geography of Warwickshire and Worcestershire* (Norwich, 1982), pp. 173-202; T.R. Slater, *The Analysis of Burgages in Medieval Towns* (Dept. of Geography University of Birmingham Working Paper, 4, 1980).

[21] R.H. Hilton, *A Medieval Society* (2nd edition, Cambridge, 1983), pp. 172-3; W. Barker, 'Warwickshire markets', *Warwickshire History*, 6 (1986), pp. 161-75.

Geographers and historians have rightly listed, plotted and analysed boroughs and markets as the basis for studies of the trading system in a number of English counties. They point to the dense distribution of markets which gave country dwellers a choice often of two, three or four places in which to buy and sell.[22] The pattern of market days has been noted, which allowed traders to proceed along a chain of venues from day to day until they arrived at a large centre towards the end of a week.[23] Thus a middleman could buy small quantities of goods at a succession of minor markets, and then sell them at a profit at a large town. A hierarchy of markets is apparent, ranging from those visited mainly by peasants and other relatively poor consumers, to those in larger towns catering for the needs of the aristocracy.[24] A market might enjoy the advantage of lying on a major route such as a navigable river; another might be sited on a frontier between landscape types and serve as a point of exchange for the produce of the contrasting regions.[25] Researchers are justified in using the known boroughs and markets for these analyses, because our dependence on administrative documents makes the study of institutions a necessary and useful starting point. There was undoubtedly a strong correlation between boroughs and towns. A borough was founded to provide an institutional and physical environment for urban growth. The privileges of burgage tenure freed the traders and craftsmen from restrictive labour services and the lord's power to take away their savings by levying heriots and entry fines. Free disposal of their burgages allowed them to use the land to raise capital or to sublet in order to obtain a rent income. The orderly town plan gave the tenants access to market places and street frontages where goods could be sold. The distinctive pattern of streets and the wide market place signalled to everyone that this was a settlement with a specific urban function.[26]

In the two West Midland counties urban characteristics are discernible in twenty-three of the thirty-two boroughs. The rest often lack documents which might contain such evidence. Borough court rolls, the lay subsidies and the poll taxes allow us to recognise in the period 1275-1525 a distinct urban hierarchy, dominated by the two large towns of Coventry and

---

[22] B.E. Coates, 'The origin and distribution of markets and fairs in medieval Derbyshire', *Derbyshire Archaeological Journal*, 85 (1965), pp. 92-111; D.M. Palliser and A.C. Pinnock, 'The markets of medieval Staffordshire', *North Staffordshire Journal of Field Studies*, 11 (1971), pp. 49-63.

[23] T. Unwin, 'Rural marketing in medieval Nottinghamshire', *Journal of Historical Geography*, 7 (1981), pp. 231-51.

[24] See above, Chapter 13, pp. 257-81.

[25] D. Postles, 'Markets for rural produce in Oxfordshire, 1086-1350', *Midland History*, 12 (1987), pp. 14-26.

[26] T.R. Slater, 'Ideal and reality in English episcopal medieval town planning', *Transactions of the Institute of British Geographers*, new series, 12 (1987), pp. 191-203 for the element of display in town plans.

Worcester (with populations varying between 5,000 and 10,000 in the first case, and from 2,500 to 4,000 in the second). A group of middling centres contained perhaps a thousand or two (Birmingham, Droitwich, Evesham, Stratford, Tamworth and Warwick), and then came the smaller towns with 300 to 1,000 people, such as Alcester, Atherstone, Coleshill, Halesowen, Nuneaton, Pershore and Shipston.[27] The urban places varied in size and function, from minor market towns with no important industry, and much involvement in the food trades, to the specialised cloth-making centres of Coventry and Worcester, whose merchants dealt in luxury, manufactured and long-distance traded goods in large quantities. Yet all of the towns had much in common, notably in their varied occupations – fifteen or twenty are recorded for some of the lesser towns, rising to fifty in the case of Worcester.[28] Even the smallest places had food traders (bakers, butchers, fishmongers), craftsmen in textiles, clothing, leather and metal, building workers, and those providing services such as inn-keepers and musicians. The bigger towns gave opportunities for a wider range of specialists, as well as for traders on a large scale – merchants, mercers, drapers and vintners. Records of the places from which buyers and sellers came, mainly from pleas of debt, allow us to see the small towns dominating hinterlands within a radius of 8-16 km, while the trade links of Worcester and Coventry spread over the whole region and beyond.[29]

Contemporary records, and the evidence of modern topography and architecture, shows in the West Midland towns the subdivision of burgages,

[27] Hilton, *Medieval Society*, pp. 168-207; C. Phythian-Adams, *Desolation of a City: Coventry and the Urban Crisis of the Late Middle Ages* (Cambridge, 1979), pp. 7-30; A. Dyer, *The City of Worcester in the Sixteenth Century* (Leicester, 1973); C.M. Barron, 'The fourteenth-century poll tax returns for Worcester', *Midland History*, 14 (1989), pp. 1-29; R. Holt, *The Early History of the Town of Birmingham* (Dugdale Society Occasional Paper, 30, 1985); R.H. Hilton, 'The small town and urbanisation: Evesham in the Middle Ages', *Midland History*, 7 (1982), pp. 1-8; T.R. Slater, 'The urban hierarchy in medieval Staffordshire', *Journal of Historical Geography*, 11 (1985), pp. 115-37; *Victoria County History* (hereafter *VCH*) *of Warwickshire*, 8, pp. 417-18; A Watkins, 'Society and economy in the northern part of the Forest of Arden, Warwickshire, 1350-1540' (unpublished Ph.D. thesis, University of Birmingham, 1989), pp. 301-24; A. Watkins, 'The development of Coleshill in the Middle Ages', *Warwickshire History*, 5 (1983-4), pp. 167-84; R.H. Hilton, 'Lords, burgesses and huxters, *Past and Present*, 97 (1982), pp. 3-15; idem, 'Small town society in England before the Black Death', *Past and Present*, 105 (1984), pp. 53-78; idem, 'Medieval market towns and simple commodity production', *Past and Present*, 109 (1985), pp. 3-23; idem, *English Peasantry in the Later Middle Ages*, pp. 76-94.

[28] Hilton, *English Peasantry in the Later Middle Ages*, pp. 78-9; Barron, 'The fourteenth-century poll tax', pp. 24-9.

[29] For debts in Atherstone and Nuneaton: Watkins, 'Society and economy in the northern part of the Forest of Arden', pp. 362-3; Stratford: Shakespeare's Birthplace Trust Record Office (hereafter SBT), DR75/4, 7, 8, Stratford borough court rolls, 1499-1509; Shipston-on-Stour: Worcester Cathedral Library (WCL), E1-E70, Worcester Cathedral Priory court rolls, 1314-1465; Alcester: Warwickshire County Record Office, CR1886/141-158, Alcester borough court rolls 1424-62. For Coventry and Worcester, see Phythian-Adams, *Desolation*, and A. Dyer, *City of Worcester*.

infilling of market places, encroachments on main streets, and high densities of two-storey buildings, which were characteristic of towns, pointing to an intensity in the use of space and high property values.[30] Less precise and tangible are the hints of a lively and even heated social atmosphere, in which quarrels broke out and complaints of nuisance were often voiced, and in which the busy market led to illegal trading practices such as forestalling and regrating. A characteristic of urban society is that women played an active economic role, or at least their work is more visible than in the country.[31] Townspeople were more likely than country dwellers to belong to a fraternity which acted as the religious and social focus for the community. These guilds also gave the leading figures of the town the means to meet to discuss matters of common interest, and then to bring their influence to bear on the seigneurial officials who, through such institutions as borough courts, governed most towns.[32]

The discovery that many of the boroughs functioned as real towns at some time in the period 1270-1540 does not mean that places possessing burghal privileges and those that were urbanised exactly coincided. In the pre-Conquest period, administrative centres of large estates, or meeting places of hundred courts, or minster churches, could provide convenient places for exchange.[33] An assembly of people who gathered for a court or church ceremony could buy and sell afterwards. At Coleshill a hilltop settlement with a church, that lay at the centre of a royal estate, was evidently the site of such an early market, held on a Sunday. Coleshill only appears in the records as a borough in the thirteenth century, but could well have enjoyed an active commercial life for hundreds of years.[34] Other boroughs with similar origins included Bromsgrove, Kidderminster and Kineton, all royal estates, and Stratford-upon-Avon, which belonged to the church of Worcester. Lords who were planning town foundations in the twelfth or thirteenth century would have observed the informal marketing already going on at favoured places, and sited their new boroughs accordingly. This hidden trading network must have been well-established

---

[30] E.g. E.M. Carus-Wilson, 'The first half-century of the borough of Stratford-upon-Avon', *Economic History Review*, 2nd series, 18 (1965), pp. 46-63; N.W. Alcock, 'The Catesbys in Coventry: a medieval estate and its archives', *Midland History*, 15 (1990), pp. 1-31; S.R. Jones and J.T. Smith, 'The wealden houses of Warwickshire and their significance', *Transactions of the Birmingham Archaeological Society*, 79 (1960-1), pp. 24-35; F.W.B. Charles, 'Timber-framed houses in Spon Street, Coventry', *Transactions of the Birmingham Archaeological Society*, 89 (1978-9), pp. 91-122.

[31] Hilton, *English Peasantry in the Later Middle Ages*, p. 91; idem, 'Small town society', pp. 65-73.

[32] Hilton, *English Peasantry in the Later Middle Ages*, pp. 91-4; idem, 'Medieval market towns', pp. 18-19.

[33] J. Blair, 'Minster churches in the landscape', in D. Hooke (ed.), *Anglo-Saxon Settlements* (Oxford, 1988), pp. 40-50; R.H. Britnell, 'English markets and royal administration before 1200', *Economic History Review*, 2nd series, 31 (1978), pp. 183-96; A. Everitt, 'The primary towns of England', in A. Everitt (ed.), *Landscape and Community in England* (London, 1985), pp. 93-107.

[34] Watkins, 'Development of Coleshill', p. 170.

by the eleventh century, when we are aware of frequent levies of royal geld, and payments of money rents; Domesday insists that every manor, no matter how small and remote, had a value that could be expressed in terms of cash. Every peasant must have been able to raise money from sales of produce, but it is difficult to believe that those in Warwickshire, for example, travelled to the only two trading centres mentioned in 1086, Warwick and Tamworth. There is good reason to believe that Coventry, recorded as a rural manor in 1086, had already developed a trading function, because by 1102 it was judged to be sufficiently urban to become the see of a bishopric.[35] Other places which were entirely omitted from Domesday, such as Alcester, may also have had an urban character at the time, but Domesday is a notoriously unreliable record of non-rural places.[36]

Towards the end of the Middle Ages some boroughs, if they had ever been towns, had ceased to perform that function – Brailes, Bretford and Broadway for example. Similarly a number of chartered markets no longer attracted traders – in Warwickshire by 1600 less than twenty of the forty-two markets were still in operation.[37]

In addition to the evidence that towns preceded boroughs, and that some boroughs failed as towns, we must ask if borough status was an essential attribute of an urban place. The small borough of Halesowen founded near Halesowen Abbey enjoyed a modest prosperity in spite of the limited privileges that its monastic lord was prepared to allow.[38] An even more conservative lord, Worcester Cathedral Priory, established a borough in about 1268 on its manor of Shipston-on-Stour, but showed reluctance to grant the tenants the basic rights of burgage tenure. After a rebellion in 1395-1406 the priory ceased to use the terms 'burgage' and 'borough' in its dealings with Shipston. Nonetheless the town grew in the late thirteenth and fourteenth centuries, and indeed survived through the fifteenth-century depression.[39] Evidently commercial success did not depend on the possession of full burghal privileges.

Lords wished to canalise trade for their own profit, but they lacked the comprehensive coercive power that enabled them to dominate the market. Trade had a life of its own; the subtleties of supply and demand could not be comprehensively managed by even the most powerful lord. If the argument that has been presented is correct, it ought to be possible to find

[35] R.H.C. Davis, *The Early History of Coventry* (Dugdale Society Occasional Paper, 24, 1976), pp. 16-18.

[36] Alcester may have been an appendage of Bidford, or an independent place.

[37] Brailes: Birmingham Reference Library, 167901, 167902, 167903, 168025, 168115, 168198, court rolls of Brailes 1410-20; Bretford and Broadway: Hilton, *A Medieval Society*, pp. 192-3. The decline in the number of markets: Barker, 'Warwickshire markets'.

[38] Hilton, 'Lords, burgesses and huxters', pp. 11-12.

[39] C. Dyer, 'Small-town conflict in the later Middle Ages: events at Shipston-on-Stour', *Urban History*, 19 (1992), pp. 183-210.

towns which were not boroughs, and trading places which did not enjoy the privilege of chartered markets. There are indeed a number of places in the region, which are hidden in the sense that they can only be discovered by sifting through dozens of different sources, and by taking note of archaeological, architectural and topographical evidence. Seven types of 'hidden' commercial centres will be described here: 1. towns and potential towns which lacked burgage tenure; 2. trading places on sites marginal to centres of administration; 3. trading places at administrative centres; 4. suburban villages; 5. country inns; 6. ports and landing places; 7. country fairs.

1. Town and potential towns lacking burgage tenure

Some towns developed with a degree of encouragement from their lord, but without the benefit of borough status. Rugby in north-east Warwickshire, well sited on a major road out of Coventry, grew after a market grant of 1255.[40] Its tenants held 'messuages' without lands attached, implying their non-agricultural occupations, but there is no mention of burgage tenure.[41] And yet the place had all the attributes of a town. It looked like a town, with its triangular market place between Sheep Street and High Street, infilled with permanent stalls, and its 'cottages' partly of two storeys which resembled the 'Wealden' houses of Coventry.[42] It worked like a town, according to the shops, stalls, shambles, toll-booth, drapery and 'tenter barn' that stood there in the fifteenth century, and judging from the dozen occupations recorded in the poll tax and court rolls of the 1370s. At that time its population exceeded 400.[43] In the early sixteenth century John Leland called Rugby a market town and it seems to have had an urban character for at least two centuries before his visit.[44]

In other cases there is more doubt as to whether a settlement can be correctly described as urban. Southend, one of the five villages in the south-east Warwickshire parish of Great Dassett, became known as Chipping Dassett after it had been granted a market in 1267, and its lord, John de

[40] *VCH Warwicks.*, 6, pp. 202-10.

[41] E. Stokes and L. Drucker (eds), *Warwickshire Feet of Fines* (Dugdale Society, 15, 1939), pp. 2, 30, 36; L. Drucker (ed.), *Warwickshire Feet of Fines* (Dugdale Society, 18, 1943), p. 78; SBT DR98/775, deed conveying a 'plot' located between plots, 1301.

[42] Staffordshire County Record Office, D 641/1/2/269, 274, 275, Rugby bailiffs' accounts 1437-66; W.B. Bickley (ed.), *Abstract of the Bailiffs' Accounts of Monastic and Other Estates in the County of Warwick* (Dugdale Society, 2, 1923), pp. 107-8, all mention cottages and the bailiffs' accounts give details of construction; Jones and Smith, 'The wealden houses'; I am grateful to the local studies department of Rugby Public Library who showed me nineteenth-century maps and plans.

[43] PRO, E 179/192/23, poll tax of 1379; Staffordshire County Record Office, D 641/1/4V1, Rugby court roll of 1370.

[44] L. Toulmin Smith (ed.), *The Itinerary of John Leland in or About the Years 1535-1543* (2nd edn., London, 1964), 4, p. 118. Leland of course did not use the word 'town' to imply urban functions.

Sudeley, in the 1280s and 1290s laid out a row of free tenements along a street appropriately called Newland.[45] The new development attracted immigrants, and the tenants practised a variety of trades indicated by such surnames as Cobbler, Cook, Skinner and Smith. Excavations on the site show that they used pottery, coal and slates from the vicinity of Nuneaton, suggesting an exchange of goods between the woodlands of north Warwickshire and the grain-growing feldon around Dassett. The houses along Newland were built in an urban style, of two storeys, some in a terraced row, others closely packed near the wide main street which presumably served as a market place.[46]

There are hints of an urban culture among the people of Chipping Dassett; they may have expressed their sense of common identity through their attendance at the chapel built at the end of the main street. An inscription recording the name of a tenant on the stone door jamb of a house implies among inhabitants or visitors a practical literacy appropriate to a trading community.[47] Contemporaries recognised that the settlement had some claim to a position in the urban hierarchy of its county. In 1300 when the townsmen of Leicester were paying money to juries (perhaps as a bribe for some unknown purpose), they listed the Warwickshire towns in approximate ranking order, beginning with Coventry and Warwick, and placing Dassett between the two small boroughs of Alcester and Brailes.[48] And yet it is difficult to accept that this settlement became fully urbanised. It formed part of the peasant village of Southend, and although it retained its market booth hall and a shop as late as 1480 it succumbed when the village was depopulated in 1497.[49]

2. Trading centres on marginal sites

Boroughs were not infrequently founded on the fringes of estates or parishes – Bewdley and Henley-in-Arden are two West Midland examples. More informal trading centres grew in similar locations, like Redditch, a

[45] *VCH Warwicks.*, 5, p. 70; PRO, E 164/15, fos lxxxiv-lxxxv, Hundred Rolls of 1280; PRO, Ancient Deeds A10890; SBT, DR37/2086, deeds of the late thirteenth century. These two series of deeds throw much light on the topography, society and economy of Southend. More details will be given in the historical essay by the author and N.W. Alcock which will appear in the report on the Burton Dassett excavations by N. Palmer.

[46] Information from N. Palmer. Interim reports in *Annual Report of the Medieval Settlement Research Group*, 2 (1987), pp. 24-5 and 3 (1988), pp. 24-5. The link with the Nuneaton area began because the Sudeleys held the manor of Griff near Nuneaton.

[47] N. Palmer and C. Dyer, 'An inscribed stone from Burton Dassett, Warwickshire', *Medieval Archaeology*, 32 (1988), pp. 216-19.

[48] M. Bateson (ed.), *Records of the Borough of Leicester* (Cambridge, 1899), 1, p. 233.

[49] Northamptonshire County Record Office, TS Box 6/2, bailiff's account of Burton Dassett 1480-1; N. Alcock (ed.), *Warwickshire Grazier and London Skinner, 1532-1555* (British Academy Records of Social and Economic History, new series, 4, 1981), pp. 27-38.

settlement in the large parish of Tardebigge (Worcestershire). It lay 4.5 km from the parish church and 1.5 km from the Cistercian abbey of Bordesley which had become the lord of the manor in the twelfth century.[50] Many of the tenements in Redditch consisted of messuages and cottages with only small plots of land, reflecting the commercial and industrial character of the community. Surnames in the period 1274-1341 derive from nine different non-agricultural occupations, and cloth-making in the district justified the building of a fulling mill, first recorded in 1339. Chance references show that a turner and tanners were active in the fifteenth century.[51] The concentration of food traders – brewers, regraters of ale, bakers, butchers, and a fishmonger – provided for the needs of the local population, but were also well placed to serve travellers on the two important roads that met at Redditch, one linking Warwick and Kidderminster, and the other running south from Staffordshire to Evesham. In 1408-9, when a party of prominent officials of the earl of Warwick were touring estates from Sutton Coldfield to Pattingham (Staffordshire) and back, they broke their journey at towns like Kidderminster, Wolverhampton, Walsall and Birmingham, but their first stop for lunch was at Redditch.[52]

A rather later development in Warwickshire is found at Knowle, an outlying hamlet of the large woodland parish of Hampton-in-Arden. Like Redditch it lay on an important junction of roads which led to Birmingham, Solihull, Coventry and Warwick. Knowle was however given a considerable boost between 1396 and 1413 by Walter Cook, a pluralist churchman of local origins, who rebuilt the chapel, and then founded a college of chantry priests and a religious fraternity.[53] These institutions gave Knowle a resident population of moderately prosperous clergy, but more important made it a famous place in the region: hundreds of people, mostly from Warwickshire and Worcestershire, joined the fraternity and attended its ceremonies.[54] We cannot be sure if Knowle had developed a commercial role before Cook's intervention, but it seems unlikely in view of the paucity of references to non-agricultural occupations there in the thirteenth and fourteenth centuries. The new chapel may have represented a turning point in the history of the settlement. Certainly new building plots near the chapel were rented out to tenants in 1396, rather in the fashion of a

[50] *VCH Worcestershire*, iii, pp. 223-30.

[51] Hereford and Worcester County Record Office (Worcester branch), ref. b 705: 128 BA 1188/ 12, Tardebigge court rolls; Hilton, *A Medieval Society*, p. 212. The occupational names include Baxter, Cooper, Glazier, Hostler, Plumber, Smith, Tailor, Tiler and Wheeler.

[52] British Library, Egerton roll 8772, receiver's account of Richard Beauchamp, earl of Warwick, 1408-9.

[53] *VCH Warwickshire*, iv, pp. 81-2, 91-8.

[54] W.B. Bickley (ed.), *The Register of the Guild of Knowle* (Walsall, 1894).

thirteenth-century new town.[55] By the 1470s and 1480s Knowle had a busy group of food traders – brewers, bakers of bread for both humans and horses, butchers, a fishmonger, as well as a tallow chandler, tailor and tanner. 'Foreign' bakers were attracted into Knowle by the trade that it offered, and its butchers were buying cattle as far afield as Bosworth in Leicestershire. Knowle's achievement of commercial vitality after very humble beginnings is suggested by its description in 1535 as both a hamlet and a market town.[56]

Two further examples from north-east Worcestershire, King's Norton and Stourbridge, help to emphasise the location of these outlying trading settlements in woodland landscapes. King's Norton lay in a subdivision of the great royal manor of Bromsgrove called Moundsley yield. Here lived a wide range of craftsmen and the usual concentration of food retailers. At its centre lay the chapel of King's Norton, rebuilt on an imposing scale in the thirteenth, fourteenth and fifteenth centuries, and to the south a green which probably served as an informal market place. When Leland visited he was told that the impressive houses that stood around the green had belonged to wool staplers, but in his day were probably occupied by drapers, a mercer and innkeepers, like Richard Benton who in 1503 bought more than 100 gallons of wine from a Coventry trader.[57] Stourbridge's history is more obscure, as little survives of the records of its parent manor of Old Swinford. A charter at the unusually late date of 1482 probably formalised an existing market. The vill had not merited a mention in the lay subsidies of 1275-1334, but appears in the 1522 muster with 122 names, implying a population of at least 500.[58] Needless to say, both King's Norton and Stourbridge lay on roads of more than local importance.

3. Trading places at administrative centres

Some of the estate headquarters, already noted as pre-Conquest centres of exchange, did not become boroughs, but continued to act as places of local trade. Chaddesley Corbett was one of those old estates which persisted as

[55] T.W. Downing (ed.), *Records of Knowle* (London, 1914), pp. 349-53; Westminster Abbey Muniments, pp. 27692-5, 27700-5, 27737, Knowle reeves' and bailiffs' accounts; PRO, E 179/192/23; John Rylands Library, Manchester, Bromley Davenport deeds, Knowle deeds.

[56] British Library, Add. Roll 72115; Warwickshire County Record Office, CR1886/297-302, Knowle court rolls 1470-85; Downing, *Records of Knowle*, p. 399.

[57] *VCH Worcestershire*, iii, pp. 19-20, 179-91; Toulmin Smith, *Itinerary of John Leland*, 2, p. 96; Hereford and Worcester County Record Office (Worcester branch), ref f 970.5:7 BA 1101/1, estate map of 1731/2 showing the green; A.F.C. Baber (ed.), *The Court Rolls of the Manor of Bromsgrove and King's Norton* (Worcestershire Historical Society, 1963), pp. 59, 105-34; PRO, E 36/35 fos 52v-54v, muster of 1522; WCL, E58, E69, court rolls of King's Norton rectory manor, 1443, 1464; Birmingham Reference Library, 428428, deed 1480. Recorded occupations include carpenter, cook, fuller, glover, hosier, shoemaker, tailor, tile maker and weaver.

[58] *VCH Worcs.*, 3, pp. 213-16; PRO, E 36/36, fos 29r-32r, muster of 1522.

a large manor and parish in the later Middle Ages, exceeding 2,000 ha in area and containing eight hamlets and many scattered farms. The main village of Over Chaddesley had no market charter, yet its layout, with its wide main street, is reminiscent of a market place; here in the late fourteenth and early fifteenth century stood a shop; fish was sold, and a group of ale houses plied a steady trade.[59] Elsewhere the chief village of a large manor was chosen as the site of a chartered market, for example at Feckenham (Worcestershire) and Monk's Kirby (Warwickshire), where the retailers of food and drink congregated near the market place, selling to the people of the outlying hamlets.[60] Although such commerce was often of a transient nature, conducted mainly on market day, some traders or craftsmen might be attracted to live in the village, like the ironmonger recorded at Monk's Kirby.[61] Napton-on-the Hill, another of Warwickshire's chartered markets, came to resemble around 1400 what in a later period would be called an 'open village' with its resident draper, a butcher dealing in cattle over long distances, and a woman called Susanna Stevenes who claimed that she was prevented from trading (*facere mercandizare*) by criminal threats.[62]

Some settlements were eventually elevated in status after informal commercial development, like Sutton Coldfield, already the scene of a busy trade in food in the 1420s and 1430s, much of it at Great Sutton for travellers on the Birmingham-Lichfield road. After exhibiting this urban potential, it was granted the privileges of a borough in 1528.[63] Polesworth also in north Warwickshire shows at a late date the ability of a monastery to attract to its gates a settlement of a potentially urban character. At the time of the Dissolution it was said that 'the town of Polesworth has 44 tenements and never a plough but one, the residents be artificers, labourers and victuallers'.[64]

[59] *VCH Worcs.*, 3, p. 35; SBT DR5/2742, 2790, 2792, 2798, Chaddesley Corbett court rolls, 1397-1441.

[60] PRO, SC 2/210/42, Feckenham court roll 1504; SC 2/207/45, 46, Monk's Kirby court rolls 1380, 1483-4.

[61] PRO, E 179/192/23, poll tax of 1379.

[62] A. Beardwood (ed.), *Statute Merchant Roll of Coventry, 1392-1416* (Dugdale Society, 17, 1939), p. 3; *VCH Warwickshire*, vi, p. 184; Warwickshire County Record Office, CR 1886/488, Wedgnock bailiff's account 1430-1; E.G. Kimball (ed.), *Rolls of the Warwickshire and Coventry Sessions of the Peace, 1377-1397* (Dugdale Society, 16, 1939), p. 160.

[63] Nottingham University Library, MiM 134/5, 134/13, Sutton Coldfield court rolls 1422-34; *VCH Warwickshire*, iv, pp. 230-5.

[64] Watkins, 'Society and economy', p. 313; in 1406 a Polesworth tanner was accused of felony, PRO, KB 27/580 m. vi, King's Bench plea roll.

4. Suburban villages

Settlements on the fringes of towns appear in Domesday as communities of smallholders who participated in the urban economy. The 100 bordars of Coten End near Warwick held no more than small gardens, and must have lived from the sale of fruit and vegetables in the town, or from employment by the townsmen, or indeed directly as traders and craftsmen. They paid their rents in cash. There were similar concentrations of bordars at Witton near Droitwich. The existence of place-names such as Coten End suggests well-established settlements of cottagers which may date back to an early stage of urbanisation.[65] These suburban appendages proliferated in the later Middle Ages, not just around the largest towns of the region such as Coventry (where the manors of Coventry Priory, like Sowe, contained many smallholders)[66] and Worcester, but also in the vicinity of smaller towns. Bridge-head settlements fall into this category, for example Bengeworth across the river Avon from Evesham which contained by the late twelfth century twenty-seven bordars mostly paying a town-like 12d. annual rent, two of whom were smiths. By 1394 a dyer was working there on a sufficient scale to owe £16 to a Coventry merchant.[67] On the same river at the end of the bridge at Stratford-upon-Avon a small colony of cottagers lived in a separate hamlet of the manor of Alveston, called Bridgetown. They included in 1240 a fuller, and the inhabitants were well placed to profit from the traffic to and from the borough of Stratford.[68]

5. Country inns

Inns, as distinct from taverns and ale-houses, deserve more attention from historians. They provided food and water for horses, and refreshment and accommodation for long-distance travellers. They were patronised by a varied clientele, including aristocratic households, lawyers and adminis-trators on business trips, and probably also carters. Journeys could not be arranged to arrive at a town at every stage, and this gave the opportunity for rural inns to develop. At Middleton on the road between Coventry and Lichfield a well-connected landowner, William de Kellingworth, bought a croft in *c*. 1400 and built on it an inn called the George. He appears in the court rolls of Middleton as a brewer and hostler, and a seller of white bread, horse bread, beans and oats, typical food and fodder for the travelling trade.[69] Provisions for horses were consumed in considerable quantity at

---

[65] See above, Chapter 12, pp. 241-55.

[66] D. Greenblatt, 'The suburban manors of Coventry, 1279-1411' (unpublished Ph.D. thesis, Cornell University, 1967), pp. 29-30.

[67] Hilton, 'Small town and urbanisation', p. 31; Beardwood, *Statute Merchant Roll*, p. 11.

[68] W.H. Hale (ed.), *Registrum Prioratus Beatae Mariae Wigorniensis* (Camden Society, 1865), p. 83a; WCL, C525, Alveston rental of 1385.

Halford, on the Fosse Way in south Warwickshire, where a hostler in a three-month period in 1385 sold 44 qrs. of peas and oats, so that he could have had an annual turnover in excess of £20.[70] Inns became centres of other types of trade. In 1408 Kellingworth of the George at Middleton was owed £40 by Henry Corviser from the nearby borough of Solihull, presumably for goods sold.[71] In later centuries inns provided the ideal meeting places for traders to haggle and strike bargains, and it would surely be plausible to imagine that the many sales of grain which took place outside market places were negotiated over cups of ale in inns like the George.

6. Ports and landing places

Along the Severn with its busy boat traffic stood a series of towns, with quays at which goods were loaded, and also bought and sold. Some had the additional commercial advantage of a bridge. These ranged from the larger towns of Gloucester and Worcester, middling places such as Tewkesbury and Bridgnorth, and small towns like Upton-on-Severn and Bewdley. There were however rural quays at intermediate points, often combined with ferries. One of these was sited at Saxon's Lode in the parish of Ripple, which seems to have been equipped with a building, where lime, having been brought by boat, was stored for the construction of the earl of Warwick's Elmley Castle in 1345-6.[72] A few miles down the river, people from the hamlet of Haw in the parish of Tirley (Gloucestershire) were trading in Gloucester at the end of the fourteenth century, and accusations of malpractice suggest that it was the centre of a flourishing commerce in grain.[73]

7. Country fairs

Many charters granting the right to hold a weekly market also provided for an annual fair. Chance references show that fairs were held in remote places in south-west Worcestershire without benefit of royal charters. One was being held at Horewell between Earl's Croome and Defford in 1401, and another is recorded as a traditional event at Woollashill in Eckington

---

[69] A. Watkins, 'William de Kellingworth and the George: an early reference to a Warwickshire rural inn', *Warwickshire History*, 17 (1989), pp. 130-5.

[70] Kimball, *Rolls of the Warwickshire and Coventry Sessions*, pp. 159, 169. The hostler was accused of selling grain worth £6 13s. 4d. in 75 days, which could be taken to imply a £30 turnover.

[71] Beardwood, *Statute Merchant Roll*, p. 56. On inns and commerce, J.A. Chartres, 'Les hôtelleries en Angleterre à la fin du moyen age et aux temps modernes', in *L'homme et la route en Europe occidentale au moyen age et aux temps modernes* (Auch, Centre culturel de l'Abbaye de Flaran, 1982), pp. 207-28.

[72] R.H. Hilton, 'Building accounts of Elmley Castle, Worcestershire, 1345-6', *University of Birmingham Historical Journal*, 10 (1965), pp. 84-5.

[73] R. Holt, 'Gloucester in the century after the Black Death', *Transactions of the Bristol and Gloucestershire Archaeological Society*, 103 (1985), p. 151; *VCH Gloucestershire*, iv, pp. 46-7.

in the sixteenth century.[74] By their very nature, we cannot know the type or volume of trade on these occasions, nor the extent to which similar unofficial fairs happened elsewhere.

Trading Places in Other Regions

This survey of two counties has established the existence of a wide range of trading places outside the formal framework of boroughs and markets. These alternative commercial centres are to be found in every English region, though their number and type varied. The West Midlands contained a notably high density of boroughs, so there were relatively few towns without borough privileges. In eastern England numerous towns lacked burghal status. No less than thirty-nine of the places with chartered markets in Essex appear in land transfers as having messuages without land, indicative of a non-agricultural population.[75] In Suffolk only eleven boroughs are known, yet at least twenty places appear to have had the necessary variety of non-agricultural occupations.[76] Norfolk, because of its total of only six boroughs, has been described as 'lightly urbanised', yet this is to ignore such clearly urban places as Downham Market, East Dereham, Fakenham and Wymondham, to which detailed studies of the county could no doubt add many more.[77] Perhaps the most celebrated of all of these urban settlements which were not boroughs is Westminster, a successful town which attracted traders of all kinds; in *c.* 1400 it had a population of 2,000.[78] One might almost associate those regions with high densities of boroughs, such as the south-west and the Welsh marches, with an insecure urban life, in which lords felt the need to give nascent towns an institutional encouragement, while the more market-oriented east had less need of such artificial stimuli.

The West Midland counties have provided only a few examples of minor ports, but the coast is dotted with small harbours which also served as places of exchange. Examples which have recently been the subject of research

---

[74] Hereford and Worcester County Record Office (Worcester branch), ref 705: 53 BA 111/1, bailiff's account for Earl's Croome 1401-2; ref 705: 85 BA 950/1/29, note on an agreement between Pershore Abbey and Sir Thomas Vampage.

[75] R.H. Britnell, 'Burghal characteristics of market towns in medieval England', *Durham University Journal*, 73 (1981), pp. 147-51; only 11 of the 24 'historic towns' recently listed for Essex were boroughs: M.R. Eddy and M.R. Petchey, *Historic Towns in Essex* (Chelmsford, 1983).

[76] M. Duddridge, 'Towns in Suffolk and the urban crisis of the later Middle Ages' (unpublished B.A. dissertation, University of Birmingham, School of History, 1983), pp. 10-35.

[77] M.W. Beresford, *New Towns of the Middle Ages* (London, 1967), p. 467; D. Dymond, *The Norfolk Landscape* (London, 1985), chapter 12.

[78] G. Rosser, *Medieval Westminster 1200-1540* (Oxford, 1989), pp. 167-82, 226-48.

include Exmouth in Devon and Saltfleethaven in Lincolnshire.[79] Minor administrative centres and open villages containing groups of craftsmen and small-scale retailers are found all over England, like the wide range of villages in Somerset and Wiltshire with which the officials of Glastonbury Abbey's manors of Longbridge and Monkton Deverill traded.[80] A striking early example comes from Ramsbury in Wiltshire, the centre of a large pre-Conquest estate, which served as a focus of iron-working in the eighth and ninth centuries, and which later acquired a market, and supported a variety of crafts and trades in 1379.[81] Rural inns were likewise widespread and many accounts for journeys record the expenses of stopping at country places like Wansford (Northamptonshire), where a warden of Merton College, Oxford in 1299 paid for bread, ale, fodder, beds and the services of a barber.[82] The two West Midland counties lack examples of industrial villages, that is, settlements whose people pursued non-agricultural occupations, but which were too specialised to be regarded as urban. These could acquire enough services and varied crafts to resemble towns, like the cloth-making villages of Castle Combe (Wiltshire) and Nayland (Suffolk), or Rugeley in Staffordshire which in 1381 contained people with sixteen non-agricultural occupations as well as twelve cutlers.[83]

Clearly throughout the country a great variety of places offered commercial opportunities. We do not need to shift or blur the boundary between 'urban' and 'rural', except to reiterate to any diehards that attempts to define a town as a place with a population above 2,000 or even 1,000 must be abandoned. We need to recognise also that although much trading activity was concentrated on market days in towns, not all of those towns enjoyed the privilege of borough status, and in addition people bought and sold in many different circumstances, in villages, inns and other non-urban places. There can be no doubt in view of the location of official and unofficial trading venues alike of the importance of road transport in the Middle Ages.

---

[79] P.J. Weddall, 'The excavation of medieval and later houses and St. Margaret's chapel at Exmouth, 1982-1984', *Proceedings of the Devonshire Archaeological Society*, 44 (1986), pp. 39-57; S. Pawley, 'Lincolnshire coastal villages and the sea' (unpublished Ph.D. thesis, University of Leicester, 1984), pp. 198-243.

[80] D. Farmer, 'Two Wiltshire manors and their markets', *Agricultural History Review*, 37 (1989), pp. 1-11.

[81] J. Haslam, 'A middle Saxon iron smelting site at Ramsbury, Wiltshire', *Medieval Archaeology*, 24 (1980), pp. 1-68; *VCH Wiltshire*, xii, pp. 40-1; J. Hare, 'Lords and tenants in Wiltshire, 1380-1520' (unpublished Ph.D. thesis, University of London, 1976), p. 87.

[82] J.R.L. Highfield (ed.), *The Early Rolls of Merton College Oxford* (Oxford Historical Society, 18, 1964), p. 177.

[83] G.P. Scrope, *History of the Manor and Ancient Barony of Castle Combe* (London, 1852), pp. 233-47; Hare, 'Lords and tenants', pp. 81, 89-90; J. Patten, 'Village and town: an occupational study', *Agricultural History Review*, 20 (1972), pp. 1-16; G. Wrottesley (ed.), 'The poll tax of 2-4 Richard II, AD 1379-81', *Collections for a History of Staffordshire*, 17 (1896), pp. 186-8.

Conclusions

Our first general conclusion must be that lords and the state may have attempted to channel trade through the institutions which they created, but that their efforts did not meet with universal success. Those who credit pre-Conquest rulers with the conscious planning of the urban network are attributing to them almost super-human powers. When the documents are sufficiently detailed to allow us to observe lordship at work after 1200 it is seen to have been inefficient, without proper means of enforcement, and constantly frustrated by the rivalry of other lords or the state. Lords were not so much seeking to expand commerce as to control it and profit from it, but the traders had their own ideas. Sometimes lords were able to found towns and markets where none had existed before – in our examples this could well be true of Chipping Dassett. But there are others, notably Sutton Coldfield, where the foundation of a borough followed signs of incipient urbanisation. In many cases the traders found their own venues, as happened at Redditch, and the lord could observe but not take much in the way of rents and tolls. The problem for the historian is that documents were produced for lords, and consequently activities from which lords did not profit went largely unnoticed.

Secondly, despite our realisation that so much medieval buying and selling is hidden from view, we can still make some judgement of its importance? In 1086 the urban population can be calculated as near to a tenth of the overall total. The lay subsidies of the early fourteenth century ought to show a substantial increase after 250 years of urban growth, yet in our two counties the figure seems to lie in the region of 14-15 per cent, basing the calculation on the tax payers in the boroughs.[84] The figure cannot be trusted, because comparisons with surveys show that a high proportion of urban households were exempted from tax, and we cannot allow for the inhabitants of the rural 'foreigns' who were often taxed with the boroughs.

The poll taxes of 1377 give more reliable figures because there was less exemption, though the problem of the 'foreigns' often remains. They suggest higher figures – 21 per cent of the population of Staffordshire lived in the ten largest boroughs for example.[85] Admittedly some of these had 'foreigns', but the smaller boroughs and the people of the non-burghal town of Rugeley could cancel out this non-urban element. In Warwickshire

---

[84] W.B. Bickley (ed.), 'Lay subsidy roll, Warwickshire, 1327', *Transactions of the Midland Record Society*, 6 (1902), pp. 1-44; F.J. Eld (ed.), *Lay Subsidy Roll for the County of Worcester* (Worcestershire Historical Society, 1895).

[85] L.M. Midgley, 'Some Staffordshire poll tax returns', *Staffordshire Historical Collections*, 4th series, 6 (1954), pp. 1-25.

in 1377 16 per cent of the taxed population lived in Coventry alone.[86] The situation in eastern England is more difficult to calculate because of the many towns which will not appear in any list of boroughs, but the percentages are unlikely to have been lower than 15 per cent. We should consider it probable that in the fourteenth century at least 15 per cent of the population of England, and more likely 20 per cent, were located in towns. This is of legitimate interest to urban historians, but what of the wider question of the proportion of people who lived from commerce and industry? The answer must be that the figure exceeded 15 per cent. One thinks of the 34 per cent of people listed in non-agricultural occupations in an industrialised Suffolk hundred in 1522 – but how can we allow for the part-time nature of occupations, so that many husbandmen had a hand in industry, and many cloth workers kept animals and cultivated at least a few acres?[87] And what of the labourers and servants, listed without further description, who could have been employed in farming or domestic work, or industry, or all three, depending on the season or the state of the economy?

Thirdly, what do these investigations contribute to our knowledge of the chronology of the rise and fall of the market? The history of institutions certainly suggests that the thirteenth century saw a surge in commerce of almost explosive force. A veritable 'big bang' increased the number of English boroughs from 217 to 495, and the number of markets doubled and trebled between 1200 and 1300. The revolutionary character of the thirteenth century might be doubted if we regard some of these apparent innovations as institutionalising existing urban settlements and informal markets. They also seem less impressive if we take into account those new boroughs and markets which never succeeded, or fizzled out after a brief episode of activity. The new foundations tell us as much about the anxiety of lords and the crown to milk every opportunity for profit in an inflationary age, and (in the case of markets) the growth in the licensing power of the crown. On the other hand, many of our 'hidden' centres of trade also seem to have emerged in the thirteenth century – Rugby, Chipping Dassett and Redditch for example.

The great discrepancy between the history of institutions and the real commercial world is surely found in the period 1350-1500, when the foundation of new boroughs and chartered markets almost came to a halt, market tolls and the income from boroughs declined, some boroughs were depopulated, and many markets were discontinued. Those who rely on institutions as a guide to trading activity would conclude that the economy

---

[86] R.B. Dobson, *The Peasants' Revolt of 1381* (2nd edn, London, 1983), p. 57.

[87] J. Pound (ed.), *The Military Survey of 1522 for Babergh Hundred* (Suffolk Record Society, 28, 1986). Wrigley, 'Urban growth', estimates the non-agrarian population in 1520 at 24%.

was gripped by a crippling recession. However, other indices, such as *per caput* incomes and expenditure, the growth of more specialised and market-oriented production in agriculture, and the amount of building activity, all point to a lively trading system. In fact the boroughs and chartered markets were not all in decline, and many small towns seem to have retained their prosperity and occasionally expanded. The market tolls suffered, one suspects, from evasion which eroded seigneurial dues of all kinds, and do not accurately reflect the changing volume of trade. Some of the hidden trading places, such as Knowle, King's Norton and Stourbridge, seem to have developed at this time. The woodland landscapes, which had encouraged by their industries and pastoral farming the growth of boroughs and commercial centres in the thirteenth century, fared relatively well in the period after 1350, and so continued to stimulate exchange.[88] The hidden trade was growing to serve new economic needs.

---

[88] E. Miller (ed.), *Agrarian History of England and Wales*, 3 (Cambridge, 1991), pp. 642-3.

15

Were there any Capitalists in Fifteenth-Century England?

The intellectual gap that separates historians and social scientists is regrettably wide. Most historians of the fifteenth century are not fully aware of the interest taken in their period by sociologists, political scientists and economists who devise theories of historical change. On the other side the social scientists clearly do not read more than a few general historical works, and so their information is often out of date and inaccurate. The social scientists have the excuse that their surveys of history range over many centuries and even millennia, and often seek to compare the development of two or three continents, so that they cannot make themselves familiar with recent research on the details of the history of England or western Europe in a single century. But the barrier between the disciplines is much greater than a mere mutual lack of knowledge. All historians, and especially those educated in the British empirical school, are suspicious of theories that seem to have been plucked out of the air. To them the grand hypotheses launched by some of the sociologists seem both pretentious and ill-founded. The social scientists are bemused by the historians' refusal to generalise, and by their seemingly petty and narrow obsession with the minutiae of their data. This essay is aimed at bridging the gulf between the different academic traditions, in the belief that the practitioners of the social sciences are posing large and important questions about long-term change and the origins of our own society, and that historians should play a larger part in defining the problems. It is important that historians should help to frame the questions, because of course they alone are in a position to gather the evidence that provides the answers. In a short essay it will be impossible to do more than refine the questions into answerable form, and to suggest some avenues for research.

Defining capitalism causes much difficulty for historians and social scientists alike. The word 'capital' was used in Italy in the thirteenth century to mean the money and goods used by a merchant in his trade,[1] but the idea

[1] R. de Roover, *Business, Banking and Economic Thought in Late Medieval and Early Modern Europe* (Chicago, 1974), pp. 28-9 (introductory chapter by J. Kirshner).

of capitalism as a term embracing a whole social and economic system is an invention of the nineteenth century. The possible definitions are legion, but can be summarised under three headings. One emphasises capitalism as a system of exchange relations, meaning an economic system dominated by the market, in which entrepreneurs are involved in specialised production and competition. Those who own capital use it to earn profits in the market place. Everything of utility – labour, land, credit – can be bought and sold. Secondly there is the more idealistic interpretation, originating in the work of Weber and Sombart, which stresses the mentality of capitalism. Economic activity is conducted in a rational spirit, by which producers and traders learn to appreciate the disciplines of the market, and develop habits of thought that will help them to maximise profit. Capitalism is therefore characterised by individualistic, acquisitive and thrifty attitudes. Thirdly, capitalism can be seen in the classic Marxist definition as a system of relationships in production, in which the ownership of the means of production is concentrated in the hands of entrepreneurs. They are able to employ a free labour force, who have themselves become separated from the means of production. Capitalists buy the labour of the workers, and sell the goods at a profit.[2]

The third definition has the great virtue of precision, and concentrates attention on specific economic enterprises which can only be found in particular places at particular times. The term 'capitalist system' could only be used to describe the western world in the last 200 years, and if strictly applied, even, say, to nineteenth-century Britain, large areas of economic life would have to be regarded as falling outside the system. The problem with the definitions emphasising exchange and mentality is that both trade and acquisitiveness have such a long ancestry that almost any age can be said to have had some capitalist characteristics. The search for a 'spirit' is especially difficult because of the vagueness of the concept. We might expect in any case that the mental climate of capitalism would follow from the establishment of the economic reality. Most social scientists would eliminate the second definition, and therefore ponder the dilemma of emphasising either the broad notion of exchange or the narrower focus on production. Some have tried new formulations, like K. Tribe, who suggests that they key elements in a definition should be the separation of consumption and production, the competition between enterprises, and a national economy 'co-ordinated according to the profitability of the commodities sold by enterprises'.[3] This puts exchange in a prominent place, but aims to

    [2] M. Dobb, *Studies in the Development of Capitalism* (rev. edn., London, 1963), pp. 4-8; R.H. Hilton, 'Capitalism - what's in a name?', in idem, *Class Conflict and the Crisis of Feudalism* (London, 1985), pp. 268-77; R.J. Holton, *The Transition from Feudalism to Capitalism* (London, 1985), pp. 11-18; J. Baechler, *The Origins of Capitalism* (Oxford, 1975), pp. 29-50.
    [3] K. Tribe, *Genealogies of Capitalism* (London, 1981), p. 38.

give it more precision. Some writers, including economic historians, have attempted to resolve the problem by defining different varieties of capitalism – agricultural, mercantile and industrial. Marxists can then regard the sixteenth and seventeenth centuries as an age of merchant capitalism, eventually to be succeeded by industrial capitalism.

In arriving at a definition we do not receive much help by turning to feudalism, often regarded as the preceding social system. If we characterise feudal society in the narrow traditional way, by the presence of peasant labour services, general self-sufficiency, and military service in return for the tenure of land, we find that its existence was confined to a short period in the early Middle Ages. Modern Marxist analysis stresses the more enduring features, such as the relationship between lords and peasants, based on the non-economic powers of compulsion exercised by the lords, which allowed them to extract rents and services from their tenants. Power is emphasised, because the peasants were economically autonomous – they did not need the lords, but the lords relied for their wealth on their share of the surplus product of the peasant. The level of rent was accordingly not fixed primarily by market forces, and land was possessed rather than owned. The basic unit of agricultural production was the peasant household, peasants being defined as small-scale cultivators. Production and consumption were mingled, and goods were often made or grown for use rather than exchange. A market existed, but its needs were satisfied by craft production in artisan workshops, and by a relatively minor urban sector.[4]

There are those who doubt the utility of the term 'feudalism' because its characteristics are so nebulous.[5] Many of the features detailed above would apply to any pre-industrial or peasant society, and derive from technical backwardness rather than a specific relationship between social classes. It would perhaps be most valuable to stress the landed hierarchy with its basis in political power, though of course this type of social organisation stems from the weak market and self-sufficiency of the peasant household, which could only be controlled and milked by some form of compulsion. If the term 'feudalism' (itself a late coinage) had not existed, it would have been necessary to invent it. Like 'capitalism', it came into the language because of the need for a vocabulary to describe general types of human society. The occasional attempts to produce alternative terms ('pre-industrial', for example) have some value, but likewise are very imprecise.

In the period between the crises of the fourteenth century and the Industrial Revolution, say between 1350 and 1750, English society and economy cannot easily be described by means of the general labels available

---

[4]   R.H. Hilton (ed.), *The Transition from Feudalism to Capitalism* (London, 1976), pp. 9-30.

[5]   E.A.R. Brown, 'The tyranny of a construct: feudalism and historians of medieval Europe', *American Historical Review*, 37 (1974), pp. 1063-88; M.M. Postan, 'Feudalism and its decline: a semantic exercise', in T.H. Aston et al. (ed.), *Social Relations and Ideas* (Cambridge, 1983), pp. 73-87.

to us, hence the cliché that it was 'an age of transition'. It is generally recognised that this was a period of important changes – in the tenancy and ownership of land, in the size and intensity of the market, in the productivity of agriculture, in the scale of industry, in the transport network, in the size and composition of the wage-earning sector, in attitudes to economic life (the treatment of poverty, for example), and in the economic role of the state. These enabled a society in which units of large scale agricultural and industrial production, based on the ownership of land, machinery and buildings by entrepreneurs, employing a numerous workforce of wage earners, and selling their products through a complex and all pervasive commercial system, succeeded a mainly agrarian economy with much small-scale peasant and artisan production, and dominated by a landed aristocracy. The nature of the transition is a cause of debate. Some emphasise the evolutionary process by which capitalists emerged out of the interstices of traditional landed society; others see the birth of a new economic order as possible only with sharp conflicts, notably the subversion of the authority of the aristocracy, and the expropriation of the peasantry to create the new class of wage earners.

The proponents of the different theoretical schemes give the fifteenth century a varying degree of significance. The fashionable neo-classical approach accords primary importance to commercial growth, from which developments in agriculture and industry followed. In this view the fifteenth century was a period of limited significance, because the really creative episodes in European history lie in the much earlier birth of commerce and towns in the ninth, tenth and eleventh centuries. In a characteristic hyperbolic flourish, Hodges advances the belief that the ninth century saw the origin of the 'modern world economy' – he means a system of commercial exchange linked to the early emergence of state power.[6] Others, again following the logic that trade lay at the roots of all other changes, argue that the 'commercial revolution' of the thirteenth century (actually, 1160-1320) marks a breakthrough, and that it was then, not at any later period, that Europe established its economic supremacy over other continents, measuring their performance in terms of technology and living standards.[7] Such schemes will give the fifteenth century scant attention because it was well before 1400 that the course was set for commercial and colonial expansion, and ultimately industrialisation. Indeed the depression in international trade of the fifteenth century seems to mark a setback, or at the very least a 'blip', in the progressive expansion of exchange from the early Middle Ages until modern times.

[6]   R. Hodges, 'Anglo-Saxon England and the origins of the modern world economy', in D. Hooke (ed.), *Anglo-Saxon Settlements* (Oxford, 1988), pp. 291-304.

[7]   J. Abu-Lughod, 'The shape of the world system in the thirteenth century', *Studies in Comparative International Development*, 22 (1987-8), pp. 3-25.

Another view of capitalist origins is even more dismissive of the fifteenth century. Followers of Adam Smith look for the 'take off', that is the upward spiral of production and consumption that lifts society out of rural drudgery on to a higher plane of intense economic activity. If such a transforming surge, associated with rapid technological innovations, is thought to be necessary for the advent of true capitalism, then not only the fifteenth century but also the seventeenth and a good part of the eighteenth would be regarded as pre-capitalist.[8]

While the Middle Ages might be treated as irrelevant by those who focus on the decisive phase of industrialisation after 1750, there is some interest in the underlying structures which made society in Europe (or just in England) especially receptive to economic development.[9] Geographers point to the natural advantages of a continent with many opportunities for water transport, to a variety of regions that needed to trade their products with one another, or to the absence of natural disasters, such as earthquakes and floods, which regularly destroyed the investments of Asian societies. A prevalent interpretation of the history of the family identifies the simple household structure of Europeans (or north-west Europeans, or only the English) as predisposing the individual towards self-reliance, enterprise and profit. In other parts of the world large, extended families acted, it is said, as a drag on economic activity because, in protecting their members, they also stifled individual initiative. The nuclear family, far from cocooning its children, sent them out into the world to make their own living, and, together with systems of poor relief that depended on community rather than family charity, provided some of the preconditions of capitalism. Western families also practised prudential marriage, by which legitimate procreation was delayed until a couple could afford to set up an independent household. Thus the birth rate was limited to the numbers that the economy could support, and every advance in production or living standards was not immediately dissipated by another increase in population. This family system was firmly established by the sixteenth century, and it may be possible to trace it back to the fifteenth, or the thirteenth, or even earlier. In which case the medieval period gave rise to, or at least nurtured, social institutions that paved the way for the eventual emergence of the capitalist economy.[10]

In searching for the environment in which capitalism grew, much interest has recently been focused on the role of the state.[11] Did the western

---

[8]   W.W. Rostow, *How it All Began: Origins of the Modern Economy* (London, 1975), pp. 1-32.

[9]   E.L. Jones, *The European Miracle* (Cambridge, 1981), especially pp. 3-41; J.A. Hall, *Powers and Liberties: The Causes and Consequences of the Rise of the West* (Oxford, 1985), pp. 111-44; M. Mann, *The Sources of Social Power* (Cambridge, 1986), pp. 373-517.

[10]   E.A. Wrigley, *People, Cities and Wealth* (Oxford, 1987), pp. 4-13.

[11]   E.R. Wolf, *Europe and the People without History* (Berkeley and Los Angeles, 1982), pp. 101-25; Holton, *Transition from Feudalism to Capitalism*, pp. 169-87; Mann, *Social Power*, pp. 430-7.

European states, which were varied, competing and relatively weak, give commerce and entrepreneurs the right circumstances in which they could flourish, while the monolithic despotisms of the east discouraged individual profit-making? Or did strong states help the growth of commerce, by protecting merchants, and by suppressing the excesses of aristocratic power? The emergence of a more centralised state in western Europe in the late fifteenth century seems to have aided recovery from the mid-century depression, as the renewed French monarchy put an end to the Hundred Years War, and a number of countries' governments pursued policies designed to foster trade and manufacture. Some of these measures, however, could act as a drag on efficient production, like actions to protect the peasantry, who were judged to be of fiscal and military value. In any case the power and resources of governments, however much they might seem to have expanded in the age of the new monarchy, were puny beside the bureaucracies and budgets wielded by their absolutist successors in the seventeenth and eighteenth centuries.

Why did economies change? The question can apply both to the fluctuations of any pre-industrial period, and to the great transformation of the Industrial Revolution. For some analysts, movement was generated internally, primarily by the slow and cumulative growth of the market. Others, who suppose that systems tend to reproduce themselves without much change, look to shocks from outside, like plagues or the climate. Recourse to such mechanical explanations as the weather are greeted with general scepticism, but the effects of demographic fluctuations are given a more prominent place in analysing social and economic change. Both the Industrial Revolution proper, and the commercial expansion of the high Middle Ages, coincided with population growth, which stimulated demand, and which in turn encouraged further increases in numbers of people. On the face of it, the later Middle Ages looks like a poor candidate for a period of economic development, because population declined and stagnated. Those who survived the epidemics may have enjoyed individual prosperity, but their collective purchasing power was below that of the more numerous thirteenth- or sixteenth-century population. As Postan put it, the fifteenth century was at the same time 'the golden age of the peasantry', and 'a time of economic decline'.[12] However, there is no need to discount the possibility that structural changes could occur in demographic troughs. One only has to think of the 'disappearance of the small landowner' in the late seventeenth century. Demographic fluctuations belong to a different order of historical change, being quantitative rather than qualitative, as is recognised by Le Roy Ladurie when he writes of the cyclical rise and fall of population (the

---

[12] M.M. Postan, *The Medieval Economy and Society* (London, 1972), p. 142.

'respirations of a great organism') happening at the same time as the 'unlinear drift' towards capitalism.[13]

Another group of theorists who have problems with the idea of the fifteenth century as a period of growth are the monetarists. The supply of money increased, and its use penetrated deeply into every sphere of life, in the 'long thirteenth century', which was also a period of burgeoning commercial exchange. Similarly the sixteenth century is famed for its discovery of vast new sources of silver, and for its lively market for goods. The intervening period looks bleak by comparison, as silver and gold stocks were exported or gradually used up, without compensatory growth in mining of new supplies; this culminated in the great bullion famine of the mid-fifteenth century. Commerce also fell away, and the only ray of hope lay in the revival, albeit on a modest scale, in both the amount of money in circulation and in trade, in the last third of the fifteenth century.[14]

Marxists have traditionally assigned more importance to the fifteenth century in their accounts of capitalist origins than any of the schools of thought mentioned so far. Two episodes have been claimed as marking a significant stage in the development of capitalism – the enclosure movement in England, and the voyages of discovery by Europeans to other continents. Marxists are bound to give prominence to the antecedents of the fully developed capitalist economy, because of their expectation that the roots of a new system would be found in preceding social and economic structures. They depict medieval or feudal Europe as having many social and economic flaws. The agricultural sector predominated; the peasant and artisan producers were only capable of achieving low levels of productivity; the social structure was destructive of investment and efficiency, because the nobility took the surplus from the peasants and consumed it.

However, while many non-Marxists are content to dismiss the medieval period, consigning it to a pre-industrial limbo of gloom and inertia, Marxists are more willing to see the feudal centuries as containing elements of movement and even dynamism. Firstly, they share with Smith, Pirenne and others an appreciation of the period as one of expanding trade. This had initially been generated by demand from the nobility for imported luxuries and high-quality manufactured goods. From an original division of labour between townsmen and country dwellers developed a further differentiation of function between merchants and artisans within urban

[13]   E. Le Roy Ladurie, 'L'histoire immobile', *Annales E.S.C.*, 29 (1974), pp. 673-92; idem, 'A reply to Robert Brenner', in T.H. Aston and C.H.E. Philpin (eds), *The Brenner Debate* (Cambridge, 1985), pp. 101-6.

[14]   J. Day, 'The great bullion famine of the fifteenth century', in *The Medieval Market Economy* (Oxford, 1987), pp. 1-54; P. Spufford, *Money and Its Use in Medieval Europe* (Cambridge, 1988), pp. 363-77 (the latter author writes with great authority on the history of money, but is not a monetarist).

society. Urban growth encouraged advances in the rural economy, because the demand for foodstuffs led to commodity production (cultivation for sale) and primitive accumulation (the build up of property and wealth in the hands of the producers), both being regarded as pre-conditions for the emergence of capitalism.

Ideas have changed over the second source of dynamism in feudal society, social relationships. It was once believed that the main division of interest lay between the feudal nobility and the urban bourgeoisie. Towns had to struggle for their liberties and against the restrictive forces of lordship, and continued to be antagonistic to feudal privilege, because the economic life of the towns set them apart from the prevailing mode of production. In the long run the greater use of money – for example, when labour services were replaced by cash rents – was thought to have acted as a solvent on the traditional bonds of feudal society. Now it is argued that the merchants of the towns allied themselves with the nobility; the profits of lordship were used by buy the goods that the merchants supplied. On their side the merchants identified with the rural lords, sharing many of their tastes and interests, intermarrying with them, and some were able to buy land and give their descendants noble status.[15] The urban artisans, who worked in their houses with the help of family labour, bear some resemblance to the rural peasantry.[16] Indeed in small towns and throughout the countryside work in crafts was often combined with small-scale agriculture. There was a division of interest, and consequent social friction, between merchants and artisans, because the merchants dealt in the raw materials of industry, and in the finished goods, and consequently sought to reduce the artisans' remuneration in order to maintain competitive prices and to maximise their own profits. But the sharpest conflict in the Middle Ages arose between lords and peasants. The lords lived on the surplus of the peasants, which they levied in the form of goods, labour and cash. The peasants, who were given a degree of self-confidence by the potential independence of their household economies, and derived some strength from their association in village communities, disputed their obligations and sought to keep as much of the surplus as possible. The class struggle was therefore centred on the issues of serfdom and rents.

These two sources of movement in feudal society acted together in the thirteenth century, when the growth of the market encouraged lords to step up their demands, and to use their powers over serfs to levy more cash. The peasants could pay more, the lords judged, because they could profit

[15] Dobb, *Development of Capitalism*, p. 120; R.H. Hilton, 'Towns in English feudal society', in *Class Conflict*, pp. 175-86.

[16] R.H. Hilton, 'Popular movements in England at the end of the fourteenth century', in *Class Conflict*, pp. 152-64, especially p. 157.

from the sale of corn, meat and wool. These demands met with a spirited but fragmented resistance. In the fourteenth century commercial growth suffered a check as markets became glutted. Partly because of the new economic and demographic situation after the Black Death of 1348/9, which improved the bargaining position and confidence of the peasants, and partly because the lords were increasingly allied with the state in the imposition of social discipline and extra taxation, social struggles reached a new stage of large-scale rebellion. They were unsuccessful in the short term, but the combination of peasant resistance and the realities of a shrinking market, especially the reduced demand for land, forced lords to make concessions. In the fifteenth century labour services were finally converted into cash payments, serfdom withered away, and rents declined. These changes had many consequences for the future structure of society. A liberated peasantry could form the basis of a force of 'free' wage workers. A peasant no longer fettered with burdens of servile dues and heavy rents had a better chance of producing effectively for the market and thereby accumulating capital. The loss of powers of private jurisdiction, and the reduction of rent incomes, weakened the traditional means of social domination by the lords.

One school of Marxists, led by Gunder Frank and Wallerstein, expresses limited interest in the Middle Ages, except in that the discoveries at the end of the fifteenth century mark the beginnings of the great age of European expansion.[17] They argue that in the global scene Europe and Asia were roughly equal in terms of social and economic development, until the colonial movement from the sixteenth century onwards gave Europeans world domination. The discoveries opened up new sources of raw materials and new markets, and made available to capitalists a more tractable workforce than had been available at home. In the new world economy or 'world system' the main inequalities lay not between the privileged and underprivileged classes within Europe, but between the European and non-European peoples. The first beneficiaries of the exploitation of the new system were the merchants who gained capital that was eventually invested in technological innovations and industrial production.

R. Brenner puts more emphasis on internal developments within Europe, and especially in England. He rejects demographic fluctuations and the growth of the market as the motive forces behind the changes of the later Middle Ages. Instead he lays stress on the struggle between lords and peasants, and the extent to which the peasants gained control of their holdings. According to Brenner, while the French peasantry were able to consolidate a degree of proprietorship that protected them from seigneurial

---

[17] A. Gunder Frank, *On Capitalist Underdevelopment* (Oxford, 1975); I. Wallerstein, *The Modern World System: Capitalist Agriculture and the Origins of the European World Economy in the Sixteenth Century* (New York, 1974), especially chapters 1 and 2.

power, their English counterparts were still vulnerable to eviction in the late fifteenth century.[18] The enclosure and engrossing movement marked an important stage in the expropriation of the peasantry. As a result the gentry were able to create large farms appropriate for commodity production. This was all preparatory to the emergence of capitalist industry, as the loss of their lands separated the workers from the means of production, and so created a free labour force, while the new, large and efficient farms could supply foodstuffs for the workers in towns and industry.

A problem that poses some difficulty for the two lines of thought outlined here is the long period of time that divides the fifteenth-century origins of overseas expansion or the enclosure movement from the rise of industrial capitalism in the late eighteenth and nineteenth centuries. There is some agreement that the widely separated events are connected, yet some explanation is needed for the long delays between phases. Possible reasons might lie in the continued hegemony of the aristocracy, or the advent (on the continent) of the absolutist state, or the depression of the economy and the political crises of the seventeenth century. Whatever the reason, orthodox Marxists have long had to wrestle with the problem of an appropriate terminology for the 'early modern' centuries which seem to have been neither feudal nor capitalist. A related problem is the use of the concept of stages of history and of the possibility of a system developing piecemeal. The point of a 'system' is that it forms a coherent whole – in the case of capitalism the large farm feeds the workers in the factory, and their products are sold on the world market. Can one part of the system function before the other parts have been put into place? Can a system be reduced to its separate elements, when it works only as a whole?[19] Should we look therefore, not for a series of new inventions or developments, but for a short period of rapid innovation?

Another area of debate which concerns Marxist and non-Marxist historians alike is the relationship between town and country. In the last century it was assumed that towns played the key role as centres of innovation, and that the origins of capitalism would be closely related to the process of urbanisation. Marx wrote of industrialisation 'ruralising' the countryside, and he was full of admiration for the urban bourgeoisie, who had, among other achievements, rescued mankind from the idiocy of rural life. Now that medieval towns are seen as deeply embedded in feudal society, and

---

[18] R. Brenner, 'Agrarian class structure and economic development in pre-industrial Europe', and 'The agrarian roots of European capitalism', in Aston and Philpin (eds), *Brenner Debate*, pp. 10-63, 213-327.

[19] Mann, *Social Power*, pp. 16-18; P. Glennie, 'In search of agrarian capitalism, manorial land markets and the acquisition of land in the Lea Valley, *c.* 1450 - *c.* 1560', *Continuity and Change*, 3 (1988), pp. 11-40.

there is widespread recognition of an age of proto-industrialisation in rural areas, we may begin to wonder whether, at least as far as industrial organisation is concerned, the urban landscape was a hostile environment for early capitalism.[20]

This survey of ideas has been necessarily brief and superficial. Views have been oversimplified, and others omitted. I have naturally selected for inclusion those writers who believe in the significance of terms such as 'capitalism'. Those who do not accept the concept have not been included, though it ought to be said that there is a widespread view that acquisitiveness is an innate human trait, and that as this is the essence of capitalism, capitalism has always existed. Such views are incompatible with a thoughtful analysis of the past – the social scientists' obsessions with categories and phases may make historians impatient, but change is the preoccupation of all scholars, and they must make sense and order of the fragmented events of the past by depicting them in general terms.

Out of the mass of conflicting views presented above, certain questions can be extracted which are capable of being answered from our evidence. Firstly, on the basis of the strict definition of capitalism as a system of productive relations, can anyone in fifteenth-century England be described as a capitalist?

To begin to answer this central question, and in order to demonstrate that this is not a purely abstract subject, let us examine an individual with a claim to be considered a capitalist. His name was Roger Heritage, and he lived at Burton Dassett in Warwickshire. We know that he was an adult, but probably unmarried, in 1466, so he could have been born in the 1440s.[21] He died in 1495, having held the demesne of Burton Dassett on lease since 1480, and probably earlier.[22] His farm consisted of about 500 acres of land, with a rabbit warren and a windmill, for which he paid a rent of £20 per annum to the lords of the manor, who for most of his period as a farmer were Sir John Norbury and William Belknap, the nephews of the previous lord, and William's nephew who in turn succeeded him, Edward Belknap.[23]

Burton Dassett lay in south-east Warwickshire, not far from the point where the eastern boundary of that county meets both Oxfordshire and Northamptonshire. It could be described as lying on the eastern edge of the Warwickshire feldon, a clay plain famous for its champion husbandry;

---

[20] J. Merrington, 'Town and country in the transition to capitalism', in Hilton (ed.), *Transition from Feudalism to Capitalism*, pp. 170-95.

[21] J.H. Bloom (ed.), *The Register of the Gild of the Holy Cross...of Stratford-upon-Avon* (London, 1907), p. 135.

[22] PRO, PROB 2/457 (inventory); PROB 11/10, fo. 231v. (will); Northamptonshire CRO, Temple Stow Box 6/2.

[23] Shakespeare's Birthplace Trust Record Office, ER 1/66/538; *Victoria County History of Warwickshire*, v, p. 70; N.W. Alcock (ed.), *Warwickshire Grazier and London Skinner 1532-1555* (British Academy Records of Social and Economic History, new series, 4, 1981), pp. 27-37.

others would say that the hills rising to 600 ft (on which stand Burton Dassett church and the likely site of Heritage's house) mark the western edge of the wolds which stretched over much of Northamptonshire and Leicestershire. These wolds consisted of relatively high ground with clay soils which had in the remote past supported woodland and grassland, but which had over the centuries developed a champion landscape. In the thirteenth century both feldon and wolds supported a high density of nucleated villages, full of tenants with yardland and half-yardland holdings (10-40 acres of arable), who practised extensive cereal cultivation in open fields. Their lords exercised considerable discipline over them, and the majority held in villeinage, though not for very high rents.[24] A network of village markets (one was held at Dassett Southend, part of Burton Dassett) and towns gave the peasants opportunities to sell their produce in order to pay rents in cash and to buy goods that they could not grow or make for themselves. The area lay within the hinterland of the large town of Coventry.[25]

This homeland of the classic medieval peasantry had been transformed in the century before Heritage's birth. Villages shrank in size, and many of them were deserted. The power of the lords was weakened, and villeinage gradually disappeared, to be replaced by copyhold tenure. Although the fields continued to produce much grain, peasants increased the size of their flocks and herds, and in a minority of cases whole fields and village territories were totally converted into specialist pasture farms.[26] As the numbers of producers and consumers shrank, some of the smaller market centres decayed, though a number of Warwickshire towns flourished, including Coventry until the 1430s; even in decline in Heritage's time it was larger than it had been before the Black Death.[27]

It was in this world that Roger Heritage made his living. There are five reasons for describing him as a capitalist. Firstly, unlike the peasantry of the thirteenth century, or indeed most of those of his own time, he produced on a very large scale, using his hundreds of acres of land. His inventory taken in 1495 reveals that he owned 2 teams of oxen, 2 ploughs, 2 carts, 40 cattle, 12 horses and 860 sheep suggesting that his farming operations were on a scale six, eight or even ten times greater than those of a normal peasant cultivator.

[24] R.H. Hilton, *Social Structure of Rural Warwickshire in the Middle Ages* (Dugdale Society Occasional Paper, no. 9, 1950); J.B. Harley, 'Population trends and agricultural developments from the Warwickshire Hundred Rolls of 1279', *Econ. Hist. Rev.*, 2nd series, 11 (1958/9), pp. 8-18; H.S.A. Fox, 'The people of the wolds in English settlement history', in M. Aston et al. (eds), *The Rural Settlements of Medieval England* (Oxford, 1989), pp. 77-101.

[25] R.H. Hilton, *A Medieval Society* (2nd edn., Cambridge, 1983), pp. 168-83.

[26] C. Dyer, *Warwickshire Farming 1349 - c. 1520* (Dugdale Society Occasional Papers, no. 27, 1981).

[27] C. Phythian-Adams, *Desolation of a City. Coventry and the Urban Crisis of the Late Middle Ages* (Cambridge, 1979), pp. 7-50.

Secondly, he employed a considerable labour force. He had six living-in servants, judging from the six sets of bedding (sheets, blankets and coverlets) in the servants' chamber, but his total number of employees, both for farm and household work, was considerably higher. At the time of his death (in the autumn of 1495) he owed his servants £11 for their wages for the previous year, which leads to the conclusion that he employed about a dozen full-time workers at the prevailing rate of pay. No doubt he also made use of the labour of part-timers for such tasks as haymaking and harvesting.

Thirdly, Heritage was inevitably drawn into production on a large scale for the market. He had to find £20 rent money each year, and a great deal beyond that to cover his production costs and to make a profit. His arable cultivation had at the time of his death brought him crops worth £8, both the yield of the harvest of 1495, and some 'old wheat and old peas' left over from previous years. The hangover of unsold grain from one year to the next, which is attested in other fifteenth-century sources, reflects the slackness of the grain market; in a move again typical of his times Heritage left in his will pious bequests in the form of grain rather than cash.[28] Most of his grain production is likely to have been intended for internal consumption, that is for feeding his household and animals, and for providing liveries to employees as part of their pay. So the bulk of Heritage's cash income must have come from the profits of pastoral farming. His sheep would have yielded wool worth £12, and a surplus of animals was available for sale each year for at least £4. The milk and calves from twenty cows could have been worth £5 to £8, and there were enough beef cattle being fattened for market at a profit of 3s. to 4s. each to make another £2 or £3.[29] Rabbits were being bred in a warren and should be regarded as another product of pastoral husbandry. A payment of £6 for rabbits still owing in 1495 could represent all, or only a part of the income from the sale of these valuable delicacies. Together these sums would give Heritage an income from his pastures of about £30, and this estimate is confirmed by his debt to the vicar of Burton of 50s. 3d., presumably for wool, lambs, calves, and other small tithes, suggesting total production worth about £25. Other sources of cash included the hiring out of his plough teams, as four people owed him 21s. for 'tilling'. Perhaps he sold hay, or rented out pasture, as did other managers of demesnes in this period.

[28] C. Dyer, 'A small landowner in the fifteenth century', *Midland History*, 1 (1972), p.6.

[29] Calculations are based on the figures in T.H. Lloyd, *The Movement of Wool Prices in Medieval England* (Econ. Hist. Rev. Supplement no. 6, 1977), pp. 38-44; Dyer, *Warwickshire Farming*, p. 20; C. Dyer, 'Farming techniques, the West Midlands', in E. Miller (ed.), *The Agrarian History of England and Wales*, iii (Cambridge, 1991), pp. 222-38.

Heritage was able to make only limited profits. After he had paid his rent, servants' wages, and repairs of buildings and equipment he would have been fortunate to have made as much as £10 in cash for himself. He was labouring under the problems that faced all large-scale agricultural producers at that time – his large bill for wages, with servants receiving three or four times the amount of cash that their pre-Black Death predecessors earned, was hard to support in a weak market for crops. Grain prices, as we have seen, were so low that it was sometimes not worth carrying it to market, and wool, which he could probably sell for 4s. per stone, was fetching a shilling or two less than it did in the late fourteenth century. In order to make a profit in these difficult circumstances, he had to manage his farm to suit the shifts in the market. He had scaled down his arable farming because of the high labour costs and poor returns. His predecessors had planted as much as 200 acres each year in the fourteenth century; Heritage was equipped with enough ploughs to cultivate at least 150 acres, but probably confined arable crops to little more than a hundred acres, and hired out his spare ploughing capacity. He, or a predecessor, had noted that rabbits gave a good return for little expense, and had set up a warren on an area previously used for more conventional agriculture. He had decided, unlike some of his Midland contemporaries, to favour sheep rather than beef cattle, though he evidently saw advantages in dairying. He sold goods locally, not just in the chief market of the Warwickshire feldon, Stratford-upon-Avon, where he had joined the Holy Cross Guild and thus aided his commercial contacts in the town, but also in Coventry, Warwick and Kineton which he mentioned in his will. His trading also took him further afield; he had evidently sold produce to Richard Gibbons of Aylesbury (Buckinghamshire), as this man owed him money at the time of his death, and one of his daughters married a merchant of Witney (Oxfordshire).

Fourthly, Heritage invested in the buildings and equipment of the farm. His landlord, by the terms of the usual leasehold contract, would not have contributed to the upkeep or reconstruction of manorial buildings except in unusual circumstances. The inventory refers to a new farm building – evidently one erected by Heritage – which contained timber for four hovels. These were shelters of some kind, either for crops or livestock. The inventory values implements such as ploughs and carts because these also would have been bought and maintained by Heritage. He could well have spent money on the farm, for fencing for example, but these improvements would have been to the long term benefit of the lord and his successor in the farm, and would not appear in the inventory. The changes that had occurred on the Burton Dassett demesne in the later Middle Ages did not happen easily and naturally. True, grass would have grown on the disused arable land without much need of human intervention, but every management decision needed some innovation and investment. A large sheep flock had to be provided with a sheepcote or two – and these could be large and expensive buildings. Even the rabbits would have to be helped in their burrowing with artificial mounds, and the warren would need secure fencing to exclude vermin and poachers.[30] Changes in land use on the demesne would have implications for the remaining villagers' rights of common, and whether the changes were carried out by negotiation or imposition, new demesne pastures might well need to be fenced off. Pastoral farming was advantageous for lessees like Heritage because of its reduced labour costs, but this saving was achieved only by considerable capital investment.

Fifthly, Roger Heritage falls outside the conventional hierarchy of medieval society. He would have been known as a yeoman. Certainly his material possessions and income would have raised him well above the other inhabitants of his village. Not many of his neighbours, even those who were known as yeomen, would have lived like him in a six-roomed house or owned 60 lbs of pewter. He hob-nobbed with merchants, like Thomas Temple of Witney who married his daughter, and two other daughters were thought to be acceptable matches by local minor gentry families, who were no doubt willing to overlook the Heritages' lack of gentility because they brought plenty of money with them. One of his sons rose in the clerical hierarchy to become a fellow of Oriel College, Oxford, and rector of the wealthy parish of Hackney in Middlesex.[31] So we can locate Roger Heritage above the peasantry and below the gentry. He was socially mobile, and in a future generation, had the family survived in the male line, they would presumably have been accepted as gentry, as happened to those better-known east Warwickshire graziers, the Spencers.[32]

Heritage's will contains the usual conventional expressions of piety. For example, he admired the friars, and left them bequests of grain. He wished to beautify Burton church with a rood loft and images, and he hoped that his soul would benefit from two years of masses sung by a priest. An unusual passage in his will concerns the division of a sum of £40 among his sons. If one of them died, the share was to go to the others only if they were well-behaved: 'provided always that my executors and overseers...have a due consideration of the condition of my said sons, so that if they be wasters or of evil condition or disposition, that God forbid, that then they be only content with their part of the £40'. It would be tempting to see in this

[30] M. Bailey, 'The rabbit and the medieval East Anglian Economy', *Agricultural History Review*, 36 (1988), pp. 1-20; D. Austin, 'Excavation and survey at Bryn Cysegrfan, Llanfair Clydogan, Dyfed, 1979', *Medieval Archaeology*, 32 (1988), pp. 130-65.

[31] Alcock (ed.), *Warwickshire Grazier*, pp. 11-17, 21-2.

[32] M.E. Finch, *The Wealth of Five Northamptonshire Families* (Northamptonshire Record Society, 19, 1956), pp. 38-9.

statement evidence of special concern for individual responsibility by a self-made man whose success depended on hard work and personal discipline, but such phrases can be found in other wills, and it would perhaps be dangerous to make too much of this insight into an early puritanism. Also the inventory of Heritage's possessions seems to reflect a modesty in his consumption of goods. The total valuation of the 'utensils' of his household such as furnishings and kitchen equipment amounted to a mere £15, compared with farm stock and equipment worth £109. A contemporary knight's goods and chattels would divide almost equally in value between domestic possessions and the grain, animals and implements of the demesne.[33] Heritage, unlike the gentry of his day, owned very little that could be called showy or luxurious. A hanging in the hall, the most prestigious item in the principal room of the house, was clearly an object of value, being worth 6s. 8d.; but eleven silver spoons seem to account for most of his plate. The bulk of his possessions were practical and utilitarian items necessary for accommodating and feeding a household swollen by living-in farm servants. The explanation of his frugality could be either in the low profit margins of the Burton Dassett demesne, or in some temporary misfortune such as illness immediately before Heritage's death. If the inventory reflects a short-term episode of adversity rather than a lifetime of sobriety and thrift, it is still worth remembering that in hard times household goods had been relinquished more readily than farm stock. It would well be that a farmer did not need to maintain appearances for status reasons as did members of the gentry, and this helps to define the characteristic lifestyle and mentality of a capitalist farmer.

In any case, we do not need to use the stilted formulae of a will, or speculate about the missing items in an inventory, to establish Heritage's business-like outlook. He could never have made a success of fifteen years and more as a demesne lessee without the mental equipment that enabled him to invest, employ labour, and sell at a profit. And he did this in a harsh world, in which he lacked the social advantages of gentility, and where he needed to live on his wits to make farming pay despite low prices and high labour costs.

The reader may feel that although Roger Heritage changed and adapted his life to his environment, he was not sufficiently adventurous or innovative to merit the description of 'capitalist'. A real entrepreneur, it could be said, should have moulded his circumstances to suit his interests. In particular, we might note his reluctance to specialise, almost as if he continued in the peasant tradition of avoiding risk by practising arable cultivation, dairying, fattening beef cattle, keeping sheep, and raising rabbits. I doubt if heroic risk-taking and a bold, pioneering spirit are necessary prerequisites for the

[33] C. Dyer, *Standards of Living in the Later Middle Ages* (Cambridge, 1989), p. 76.

identification of capitalists. If these are essential attributes, many nineteenth- and twentieth-century businessmen would be found wanting. And if they are felt to be at least desirable qualities, then they can be found in other fifteenth-century farmers, for example John Heritage, Roger's son, who two years after his father's death did a deal with Edward Belknap, then the sole lord of the manor, to enclose land in the open fields, to convert 360 acres of arable land to pasture, and to remove the inhabitants of twelve houses. Roger must have been farming in the midst of a decaying village, in which the old distinction between arable and pasture was disappearing, while the remaining tenants demanded right of access to open-field strips and the common pasture. This must have constantly frustrated the demesne farmers' aim to use the land efficiently and intensively.[34] Perhaps the initiative to enclose came from the landlord, but implementing the scheme needed a partnership between Belknap and the new young farmer. One can imagine John Heritage waiting impatiently, like many farmers' sons in later centuries, for the chance to take over and wield a new broom. But the likelihood that John was more enterprising, and less caring of the interests of his poorer neighbours, cannot deprive his father of the description of 'capitalist farmer'.

Finally, we might expect capital to reproduce itself, and indeed we find that Heritage's farm, improved by Belknap and John, flourished in the hands of Heritage's great nephew Peter Temple in the 1540s and 1550s. He was by then paying nearly £100 in rent, but that was for 655 acres of enclosed land, unencumbered with tenants or peasants exercising common rights. The inflation of the sixteenth century had also raised livestock prices, and depressed the value of real wages. Temple was keeping on the pasture in the late 1540s as many as 220 cattle and more than 2,000 sheep; farmers had entered into a brave new world.[35]

The Heritages were characteristic of a small but significant group in fifteenth-century society.[36] Most demesnes on large estates, even on the manors of the middling and upper gentry, together with such assets as tithes and rectorial glebes, had been leased out in the late fourteenth

[34] Alcock (ed.), *Warwickshire Grazier*, pp. 27-38; idem, 'Enclosure and depopulation in Burton Dassett: a sixteenth-century view', *Warwickshire History*, 3 (1977), pp. 180-4.

[35] Alcock (ed.), *Warwickshire Grazier*, pp. 37, 39-99. John Heritage had expanded his operations in the first decade of the sixteenth century, as he appears as a tenant of Moreton-in-Marsh (Gloucestershire) and had a share in a lease of a pasture at Upper Ditchford in the same county: Westminster Abbey Muniments 8362 and Hereford and Worcester County Record Office, ref. 009:1 BA 2636/37 (iii) 43806, fos 23-4.

[36] F.R.H. Du Boulay, 'Who were farming the English demesnes at the end of the Middle Ages?', *Econ. Hist. Rev.*, 2nd ser., 17 (1965), pp. 443-55; B. Harvey, 'The leasing of the abbot of Westminster's demesnes in the later Middle Ages', *Econ. Hist. Rev.*, 2nd ser., 22 (1969), pp. 17-27; eadem, *Westminster Abbey and its Estates in the Middle Ages* (Oxford, 1977), pp. 148-63; J.N. Hare, 'The demesne lessees of fifteenth-century Wiltshire', *Agricultural History Review*, 29 (1981), pp. 1-15.

century or in the decade or two after 1400. Some demesnes were let in fragments to a number of tenants, or *en bloc* to a village community, so that the land made modest additions to the relatively small resources of many peasant households. The same may have occurred, without our knowledge, in cases where there was apparently one farmer, who had decided that subletting was the best way of exploiting the resources of the demesne. Most demesnes seem to have been leased as single units, and occasional supplementary evidence, such as inventories, shows that the lessee exploited the land himself, or that cultivation was left in the hands of a bailiff or a single subtenant. The lessees included a good number of gentry, merchants and clergy, and they were most likely to have used indirect methods of management. The majority of lessees, and probably a near totality of subtenants, were of peasant origin. Usually we know no more about them than is written in the lease – their names, the assets conveyed, the length of the term and the rent, with clauses dividing responsibilities for the maintenance of buildings. When additional information can be gathered, it can sometimes tell us of agricultural improvements, such as enclosure or conversion to pasture, or of the market orientation of lessees who had interests in towns or contacts with the wool and cloth trades. The most innovatory of the farmers, the butcher graziers of the Midlands, used their lands as specialised pastures, often occupying large areas of former arable, including the whole of the field system of a deserted village. They fattened animals for the urban markets, which were expanding because of high per capita incomes which brought regular meat-eating to a greater proportion of households.[37]

Not every lessee changed the management or technology of his demesne, but the arrival of the farmer marks three important and enduring developments in late medieval England. Firstly, the management of agriculture slipped out of the hands of the landlords and their officials, to the advantage of a lower social stratum. The lords still creamed off the profits, but left the lessees with the chance to make something for themselves. Secondly, the character of the demesne was changed, because leasing detached them from the peasant holdings to which they had been closely linked for many centuries. The demesne, instead of forming an integral part of a manor, became simply an area of land. No longer would production be supported or cushioned by the rents and services of the peasantry. To underline the growing divorce between demesne and village, some Midland farmers began that migration out into their fields which by the nineteenth century was to place the majority of farm buildings away from other settlements. And thirdly the whole structure of estates was

[37] R.H. Hilton, 'A study in the pre-history of English enclosure in the fifteenth century', in *The English Peasantry in the Later Middle Ages* (Oxford, 1975), pp. 161-73; Dyer, *Warwickshire Farming*, pp. 17-22.

transformed. The old estates had been based on the need in a pre-marketing age for scattered manors in different regions to give lords a balance of resources. Many of the new lessees held only one demesne, and those who acquired a number took them from different lords and organised them on fresh principles, often seeking to hold farms in a compact group for ease of management, and acquiring lands of the same type so as to be able to specialise – for example, in pastoral farming.[38] There were at least 5,000 farmers like Heritage, we can estimate, and they held as much as a fifth of the land in lowland England towards the end of the fifteenth century.

The gentry are worth considering as a second distinct group of possible fifteenth-century capitalists. It was once thought that the magnates of the thirteenth century ran their estates on capitalist lines, but the revelation that they invested relatively little, and relied heavily on 'feudal' revenues even at the apex of their 'high farming' phase, combined with their readiness to abandon direct management during the fourteenth century, has led us to concentrate more on the smaller landowners. Gentry sometimes continued after 1400 with the direct management of their demesnes, or took the demesnes of other lords on lease, or ran both their own lands and leaseholds simultaneously. Notable examples are John Brome of Warwickshire, the Catesbys of Northamptonshire, Thomas Keble of Leicestershire, the Townshends of Norfolk, and the Vernons of Derbyshire.[39] In many ways their activities are comparable with Heritage and the other non-gentry farmers. They produced for the market, specialised in pastoral husbandry, employed wage labour, and could invest in technical changes such as enclosures. We must, however, make some important reservations. For the gentry, agricultural production formed only one part, and then often a minor part, of their incomes. They could, and did, drop out of direct management of their estates, and resume it again when circumstances made it advantageous. They were not as heavily committed to the sale of produce as the yeoman farmers, because they maintained well-fed households who ate a high proportion of the grain and stock from their manors. For the yeomen farmers agricultural production was a way of life; the gentleman farmers regarded agriculture as a sideline, and were much more concerned with the usual aristocratic preoccupations of marriage,

[38] H. Thorpe, 'The lord and the landscape', in *Volume jubilaire M.A. Lefèvre* (Louvain, 1964), pp. 97-101.
[39] Dyer, 'Small landowner', pp. 1-14; idem, *Warwickshire Farming*, pp. 18-21; E.W. Ives, *The Common Lawyers of pre-Reformation England* (Cambridge, 1983), pp. 345-53; K.J. Allison, 'Flock management in the sixteenth and seventeenth centuries', *Econ. Hist. Rev.*, 2nd ser., 11 (1958), pp. 98-112; S. Wright, *The Derbyshire Gentry in the Fifteenth Century* (Derbyshire Record Society, 8, 1983), pp. 19-21. For a general comment on the economic activities of gentry, see C. Carpenter, 'The fifteenth-century English gentry and their estates', M. Jones (ed.), *Gentry and Lesser Nobility in Late Medieval Europe* (Gloucester, 1986), pp. 36-58.

patronage, government and the law. Perhaps the main contribution that the gentry made to the development of capitalism lay in forming partnerships with yeoman farmers (like that between Belknap and the younger Heritage) in which the power of the lord was complemented by the entrepreneurial skills of the lessee to enhance profits for their mutual benefit. Such a co-operative alliance became the basis of many subsequent advances in English agriculture.

A third group to be considered are the peasants who accumulated larger holdings. They sometimes did this by taking all or part of a demesne on lease, but more commonly built up a complex holding by acquiring their neighbours' lands by marriage, purchase, or simply by taking on tenements that had been abandoned and 'lay in the lord's hands'. To take an example, successive members of the Cubbell family of Coleshill and Eastrop (Berkshire) gathered to themselves 3 or 4 yardlands (60-80 acres) of land, together with pieces of pasture and a mill.[40] They were able to run a hundred sheep, and employ three or four workers. They raised enough money by sales of produce both to pay rents, which for them and for most peasants by the middle of the fifteenth century were levied entirely in cash, and to spend on their own consumption. When the lord built houses for the Coleshill peasants his costs amounted to £7 or more on each building, which were equipped with stone walls and slate roofs. Presumably the peasants, who normally paid for their own buildings, also bought expensive materials and hired skilled labour. Some of the buildings, such as barns, represent considerable investments, and we know also of peasants who consolidated their holdings and enclosed their lands. As with the gentry, but for different reasons, there are difficulties in using the term 'capitalist' to describe the Cubbels and their like. Their large holdings were not always cultivated very effectively, and they often broke up after a short period. The Cubbells paid modest rents of 6d. per acre, and very low entry fines on acquiring new holdings; land could be obtained cheaply, and because of labour shortages and low prices, did not yield high profits. Wealthy peasants were inhibited in changing their techniques by the pressures of the community with whom they had to co-operate. They were unable to employ many workers because of the expense of wages. Their sources of labour were either the life-cycle servants (young people gaining work experience before going on to a more independent way of life) or smallholders earning wages part-time. We can recognise the capitalist potential of the Cubbells and the many thousands of comparable yeomen. It was from their ranks that the Heritages and their like emerged. And yet we must wonder, in view of the failure of many villages to polarise sharply between a few yeomen and numerous landless

[40] R. Faith, 'Berkshire: fourteenth and fifteenth centuries', in P.D.A. Harvey (ed.), *The Peasant Land Market in Medieval England* (Oxford, 1984), pp. 116-17, 146-9, 152-74.

labourers, how many of the peasant elite really broke out of the economic and mental restraints of their communities.[41]

Fourthly, there were the merchants. Of course they can be regarded as capitalists in the sense that they risked large sums of money in buying goods, in order to sell them at a profit. There was nothing new about this in the fifteenth century; the merchant class had an ancestry of at least five centuries, and it was in the fourteenth century that English merchants extended their role in foreign trade and government finance. Although their mercantile activity resulted in high profits from long-distance trade and money-lending, they were neither specialised nor adventurous, even if some of them called themselves merchant venturers. Their business techniques, for example, in accounting, lagged behind those of the continent, and especially the Italians. They traded in manufactured goods, but took little interest in industry. Their close social and cultural links with the landed gentry shows that they were not cut off from the aristocracy by a special mentality.[42]

One section of the merchant class deserves mention because they did emerge as a significant group for the first time in the late fourteenth and fifteenth centuries. These were the clothiers, the entrepreneurs who orchestrated the various cloth-making processes, and sold the finished products. They were often based in small towns or the rural areas in which woollen cloth was made. James Terumber, for example, rose from obscurity as a Bristol fuller to become a major figure in the 1460s in the Wiltshire industry from his base at Bradford-on-Avon, selling as many as 236 cloths in one year.[43] He was not untypical in his specialisation, not just in the trade in woollen cloth, but in particular types of cloth. Clothiers sometimes acquired sheep pastures and fulling mills, showing their aim of gaining an interest in all stages of the lengthy production process. Indeed some clothiers, especially in East Anglia, in parallel with continental entrepreneurs, took the first tentative steps towards an early form of industrial capitalism, because they owned spinning houses and dye pans, and were employing workers on their own premises rather than merely co-ordinating the separate activities of artisans working in a state of semi-independence at home.[44]

As is clear from the many qualifications needed in discussing the various groups of capitalists, proto-capitalists and those caught up in a capitalist

---

[41] Hilton, *English Peasantry*, pp. 37-53.

[42] S Thrupp, *The Merchant Class of Medieval London* (Ann Arbor, Michigan, 1948), pp. 234-87.

[43] E.M. Carus-Wilson, 'The woollen industry before 1550', *Victoria County History of Wiltshire*, iv, pp. 128-47.

[44] E. Power, *The Paycockes of Coggeshall* (London, 1920); D. Dymond and A. Betterton, *Lavenham: 700 years of Textile Making* (Woodbridge, 1982); A. Derville, 'L'héritage des draperies médiévales', *Revue du Nord*, 69 (1987), pp. 715-24.

tendency, on one could allege that England in the fifteenth century had a capitalist economy. The aristocracy still lived largely from rents that were fixed by custom, not by market forces, and their culture of chivalry and 'good lordship' influenced the thinking and behaviour of the rest of society. The middling peasantry survived in sufficient numbers to refute any notion of a generally polarised peasant society, or of wholesale removal of the peasants from the land. Wage labour seems not to have grown in use during the fifteenth century, and the preponderance of young servants and part-time smallholding labourers in the workforce prevents us from identifying a proletariat of any significant size. Although the fifteenth century saw much individual wealth, and industries such as iron and cloth expanded to satisfy the rising demand, there was no upward spiral of consumption and production. The generation of new industries and a decisive extension of home comforts for the middling sort came in the sixteenth century. Social attitudes were shifting – for example, a more corrective attitude to poverty was gaining ground, but this was still not enough to shatter the old community cohesion, even in the most commercially-minded districts.[45]

The pace of change was slow. We cannot sum up a complex society like that of fifteenth-century England in a single phrase. It retained many traditional characteristics, but society was open and varied enough to contain the likes of Heritage, the Cubbells and Terumber.

In conclusion, two supplementary questions require at least brief discussion. Was the fifteenth century an important period for the emergence of capitalists? And what were the mechanisms of social change?

On chronology it is of course true that the urban and commercial growth of the ninth to thirteenth centuries provided the preconditions for a future world dominated by exchange, in the sense that an urban hierarchy and a market network were then established. However, the crises of the fourteenth century broke the continuity in the economy. The thirteenth century ended in stagnation. Many of the smaller markets disappeared and some larger towns declined. The aristocracy were shaken by falling incomes, rising costs, war and rebellion. The social structure of village communities was disrupted by the combination of famine, epidemics and migration. Of the groups identified above as showing capitalistic characteristics, the merchants and gentry can be traced back before 1300. There were peasants with large holdings who profited from the expanding market of the thirteenth century, but they were less numerous and their holding generally smaller than those of their fifteenth-century successors. And their accumulations of land were even more fragile. A numerous body of

[45] M.K. McIntosh, *Autonomy and Community: The Royal Manor of Havering, 1200-1500* (Cambridge, 1986), pp. 221-63.

yeomen, farmers and clothiers were produced by the peculiar combination of low population, falling landlord incomes and expanding rural cloth-making that occurred after 1348/9 and especially after 1400. The thirteenth century had been a period of high economic pressure, in which any innovation might have been dangerous. In the fifteenth century there was more opportunity and incentive for lords, tenants and entrepreneurs to experiment. But the disadvantages of the fifteenth-century economy for market production are manifest. It was a hard school, in which profit-making was only possible for those who judged the market carefully, and made the most efficient use of expensive labour.

On the sources of social change, the idea that the growth of commerce would in itself lead to capitalism is not supported by the English experience of the thirteenth century, when serfdom and other seigneurial institutions were strengthened by the rising market. Brenner believes that the key episode in the later Middle Ages was the expropriation of the peasantry to create larger units of production. There is insufficient evidence that this happened on a general scale. Brenner was right to see the formation of larger farms as an important trend, but he misunderstood the cause. Weakened lordship and cheap land provided the environment for the engrossing of holdings. The landlords who expelled tenants in the decades around 1500 were merely tidying up and completing a process that had been begun by the peasants themselves. Brenner underestimated the capacity of peasants to run their own lives, and to take the initiative in reorganising their holdings. Was the birth of capitalism painless, then? Engrossing was easy when peasants voluntarily abandoned their holdings, or when, if they were pushed out, they could obtain land elsewhere; the agony came in future generations when their more numerous sixteenth-century successors found that the old holdings were not available for new tenants, and that the enclosure of common fields and pastures was irreversible.

To sum up, capitalists and potential capitalists lived in fifteenth-century England. The appearance of these people was made possible by the earlier commercial revolution, and the crises of the fourteenth century. Structural change, especially in rural society, preceded the enclosure movement and the voyages of discovery. Early capitalists appeared in a context of struggle and adversity, not because they depended on the expulsion of the weak and poor, but because they had to organise production in the midst of a market recession.

Index

Ewell, John, 215
Exeter, Devon, 263, 267
—, bishopric of, 149
Exmouth, Devon, 300
Exton, Hampshire, 120
Eye, Middlesex, 122
Eylof, John, 9
Eyre family, 126, 269, 270, 271, 276

Fakenham, Norfolk, 299
famuli, *see* servants
farming, *see* agriculture
Faxton, Northamptonshire, 156, 162
Fécamp, abbot of, 243
Feckenham, Worcestershire, 20,107, 296
Feckenham Forest, Worcestershire, 17, 20, 23-5, 56
Feldon (district of Warwickshire), 23-5, 42, 315-16, 318
Felixstowe, Suffolk, 193, 213, 228
—, prior of, 235-6
Fenman, Agnes, 205
fields, 4-5, 11, 15, 18, 22-3, 24, 25, 29, 31, 39, 40-3, 45, 47, 49, 50, 56, 68-9, 74, 75, 86-7, 118, 125, 129, 287, 316, 321
Fillol, John, 213, 215
Fingrith, Essex, 202, 206n., 211, 212
Finham, in Stoneleigh, Warwickshire, 273
fish-ponds, xiv, 101-11
Flixton, Suffolk, 210
Fobbing, Essex, 198
food, *see* diet
Ford, James atte, 198, 213, 214
forests, *see* woodland
Forncett, Norfolk, 74, 151n., 176, 177, 178
Forth, John atte, 6, 232-3
Foscott, Buckinghamshire, 248
Fouke, Richard, 174
Fountains Abbey, Yorkshire, 276
Foxearth, Essex, 196, 197, 205, 213, 216
Framlingham, Suffolk, 230, 265
Frampton, in Toddington, Gloucestershire, 43
Framsden, Suffolk, 216
Fristling, Essex, 201, 202, 206n.
Friston, Suffolk, 239
Frocester, Gloucestershire, 73
Fryerning, Essex, 194, 196, 199
Fulbrook, Warwickshire, 32, 35, 41
Fulham, Middlesex, 21, 121, 122, 246
Fyfield, Essex, 159

Gamen, Katherine, 231, 239
Gardener, Richard, 210
gardens, xii, 21, 90, 113-31, 246, 250-1
Gardiner, Thomas, 213, 214, 225, 230, 236
Gauber High Fell, Ribblehead, Yorkshire, 17
Gawcott, Buckinghamshire, 248, 251
Geffrey, John, 193,198, 213, 277
gentry, 3, 38-9, 62, 80, 98, 170, 200, 222, 224, 225, 269-70, 278, 320, 322-4
Gerard, William, 238
Gere, John, pikemonger, 108
Gerneys, Edmund, 213, 237
—, John, 237
Gernon, John, 226

Gibbes, William, 270, 272, 273
Gibbons, Richard, 318
Giffard family, 269
Gildeborn, William, 197n., 198
Glascote, Warwickshire, 249
Glastonbury Abbey, Somerset, 115, 128
Gloucester, 54, 55, 70, 118, 241, 242, 244, 298, 299
—, earls of, 54
Godhewe, Alice, 237
Godmanchester, Huntingdonshire, 127
Godwyn, Adam, 182
Goldicote in Alderminster, Warwickshire, 33, 40
Goltho, Lincolnshire, 156, 162
Gomeldon, Wiltshire, 155
Gonerby, Lincolnshire, 246
Gosbeck, Suffolk, 229
—, Ralph or Richard de, 229
Gosforth, Cumberland, 7
Gower, John, 203
Grafton, in Bromsgrove, Worcestershire, 139
Grantham, Lincolnshire, 121, 245, 246, 252
Great Barton, Suffolk, 228
Great Bromley, Essex, 193, 195
Great Cressingham, Norfolk, 151n.
Great Leighs, Essex, 210
Grene, Thomas, 41
Grenstein in Tittleshall, Norfolk, 162

Hackney, Middlesex, 319
Hadleigh, Suffolk, 200, 232, 239
Halford, Warwickshire, 298
Hales, John, bishop of Coventry and Lichfield, 104-7,109
—, Robert, 193
Halesowen, Worcestershire, 4, 25, 157, 289, 291
—, abbey, Worcestershire, 105, 266, 267, 268
Hall, John, 273
Hammersmith, Middlesex, 126
Hamond, John, 207, 229, 230
Hampton-in-Arden, Warwickshire, 294
Hampton Lucy, Warwickshire, 140
Hamwih (early medieval Southampton), 255
Hanbury, Worcestershire, 19, 28
Hangleton, Sussex, 155
Hanley Castle, Worcestershire, 70, 263
Haras, John, 237
—, Matthew, 237
Hardwick in Tysoe, Warwickshire, 39
Hardyng, Thomas, 216
Haresfield, Gloucestershire, 61
Harford, in Naunton, Gloucestershire, 30-1
Harkstead, Suffolk, 239
Harlestone, Northamptonshire, 115, 158, 162
Harlow, Essex, 117, 123
Hartlepool, co. Durham, 275
Harwell, Berkshire, 158
Harwich, Essex, 239
Hassop, Derbyshire, 269
Hastings, Sussex, 243, 249, 264
Hastyng, John, 37
Hatton-on-Avon, Hampton Lucy, Warwickshire, 32, 35n.
Havering atte Bower, Essex, 20, 196, 202, 217, 277